First Nations Education in Canada

Edited by Marie Battiste
and Jean Barman

First Nations Education in Canada:
The Circle Unfolds

UBCPress / Vancouver

10   5 4

Printed in Canada on acid-free paper

Library and Archives Canada Cataloguing in Publication

First nations education in Canada

   Includes bibliographical references and index.
   ISBN-13: 978-0-7748-0517-9. ISBN-10: 0-7748-0517-X

   1. Native peoples – Canada – Education.* 2. Education and state – Canada.
I. Battiste, Marie Ann. II. Barman, Jean. 1939-

E96.2.F57 1995   371.97'97071   C95-910104-7

Canadä

UBC Press gratefully acknowledges the financial support for our publishing program of the Government of Canada through the Book Publishing Industry Development Program (BPIDP), and of the Canada Council for the Arts, and the British Columbia Arts Council.

This book has been published with the help of a grant from the Heritage Cultures and Languages Program, Multiculturalism and Citizenship Canada, Department of Canadian Heritage.

The editors wish to thank William Asikinack and Don McCaskill for their assistance in the early stages of the manuscript.

UBC Press
The University of British Columbia
2029 West Mall
Vancouver, BC V6T 1Z2
604-822-5959 / Fax: 604-822-6083
E-mail: info@ubcpress.ca
www.ubcpress.ca

Contents

Western Door: Meeting the Challenge of Incoherence

Northern Door: Transforming First Nations Education

Introduction

Marie Battiste

Every generation of Aboriginal parents has had to reinvent 'education' for its children. Every generation of Aboriginal peoples has had to struggle with the painful contradictions inherent in humankind's earthly situation. Aboriginal peoples have had to learn to be flexible and patient in their approach. In my generation, 'Indian education' has become a particularly adaptable site for confronting the formal contradictions besetting Aboriginal consciousness within Canada.

'Indian education,' although difficult to define, is a significant process to all Aboriginal parents and communities. It firmly raises the issue of humanity: What does it mean to be an Aboriginal person? It addresses the paramount issue of education in a multicultural state: What should education achieve for Aboriginal peoples? The various answers to these questions form the concept and processes of First Nations education. Purpose is the unifying theme of modern education and has always been the starting place for discovering the 'whys,' 'whats,' and 'hows' of educational theory.

Community-based education is more widely accepted than the need for self-government. First Nations communities see community-based education as a fundamental responsibility and requirement. Their demand for educational choice has provided an innovative context for reconciling both historical and modern contradictions. It has also provided a context for cultural and cognitive renewal among the First Nations. The concept of 'Indian education' has required continual refurbishing. Even the terms used to express the concept have shed their colonial cognitive trappings and have embraced a more empowering and reflective concept. The initial goals of federal, provincial, and band-operated schools proved restrictive when matched against the broad goals of tribal consciousness and the emerging knowledge of modern educational purpose and process in a multicultural state.

The year 1969 is viewed by Aboriginal peoples in Canada as a crucial turning point in the transformation of Indian education through Indian control. The federal government's announced new policy, the so-called White Paper Policy, sought to transfer federal responsibility for First Nations education on reserves to the provinces. Various treaties had delegated educational responsibility to the Crown, which transferred administrative authority to the federal government under the Indian Act. Under this act, the federal government assumed total control of First Nations children and their education on all reserves across Canada.

The Department of Indian Affairs and Northern Development (DIAND) thus invaded the Aboriginal home.[1] It inappropriately politicized the educational process. For a century or more, DIAND attempted to destroy the diversity of Aboriginal world-views, cultures, and languages. It defined education as transforming the mind of Aboriginal youth rather than educating it. Through ill-conceived government policies and plans, Aboriginal youths were subjected to a combination of powerful but profoundly distracting forces of cognitive imperialism and colonization. Various boarding schools, industrial schools, day schools, and Eurocentric educational practices ignored or rejected the world-views, languages, and values of Aboriginal parents in the education of their children. The outcome was the gradual loss of these world-views, languages, and cultures and the creation of widespread social and psychological upheaval in Aboriginal communities.

Aboriginal peoples began to see educators, like their missionary predecessors, as nothing more than racists, patriarchs, and oppressors who hid behind fine-sounding words or ideology. Their objectives were viewed as tainted and hypocritical. In effect, education did little except equip Aboriginal youth with resentment and cynicism and erode human consciousness within Aboriginal communities.

In its 1969 policy proposal, the federal government still hoped that all Aboriginal students would be inevitably absorbed into provincial systems and mainstream society. Aboriginal peoples, however, objected to the new policy and issued their own 'Red Paper Policy,' a paper that gave birth to the National Indian Brotherhood's *Indian Control of Indian Education*. In this document, Aboriginal peoples vociferously opposed the government's intent to surrender its administrative responsibility for education to the provinces. In particular, they argued that Aboriginal communities themselves had the right, based on their Aboriginal status and treaties, to administer educational programs for their children. The purpose of Indian education was defined as salvaging Aboriginal languages, cultures, and societies, and of transmitting those cultures, with their unique understanding of North American ecology and their distinctive world-views. Finally, Aboriginal peoples pointed out that the provinces could do no better in educating Aboriginal youth than the federal government had done.

In 1973, the federal government accepted the *Indian Control of Indian Education* policy paper in principle as national policy. Furthermore, it rescinded the proposal to turn over education to the provinces and acknowledged the right of national Aboriginal leaders to assume jurisdictional control and parental responsibility for Indian education. However, it was acknowledged that much work was required to lay this foundation, including research and development in cultural education and studies.

As a first step, the federal government funded regional Indian cultural centres throughout Canada to help in researching and developing cultural studies and to enhance participation by Aboriginal communities in educational institutions. Second, the federal government funded several Indian education training centres at various universities across Canada. The universities' response was either to insist that established methodologies of teacher training would have similar results among Aboriginal and non-Aboriginal students or to advocate multicultural methods of instruction which promoted respect for racial or ethnic cultures within a dominant society. In Saskatchewan, where the population of Aboriginal peoples was growing rapidly, the Indian Teacher Education Program (ITEP), Northern Teacher Education Program (NORTEP), and the Saskatchewan Urban Teacher Education Program (SUNTEP) were developed in response to the need for Aboriginal teachers. They promoted teacher training for Aboriginal teachers outside regular channels of instruction, although they utilized the same courses of instruction and content.

In diverse teacher-training programs, professors thought they could give the benefit of their experience to Aboriginal schools and teachers, although they soon found that their experience was significantly different from what was needed in Aboriginal communities. The lingering questions of who was to define cognitive styles embedded in Aboriginal world-views and the parameters of Indian education remained unresolved. How educators unfamiliar with Aboriginal cultures were to achieve educational reform remained at issue, for one culture's definition of education will not be identical to or may not significantly overlap that of another.

Attempts to define Indian education relied on a complex relationship to traditions, place, and time. The ways in which Aboriginal educators acknowledged and viewed their cultures and languages, as well as their views of the authoritative traditions of provincial education, formed the framework of their understanding of education. Indian education became the subject of ongoing discussion on the meaning of language and traditions and how they ought to be affirmed or challenged. These discussions have given Aboriginal educators a unique place in our history, and in the history of education.

Aboriginal elders and educators have since worked to build a base of information and historical research and to infuse this information into different educational materials. In some areas, this base has promoted effective curriculum revision, while in others the results have been dismal. Debate persists about whether the cultural centres' goals and processes diverged too much from those of schools attended by Aboriginal children and whether the educational institutions needed complete transformation before they could accept these services.

Could it also be that social stress in Aboriginal communities, indicated by high levels of poverty, alcohol and substance abuse, child abuse, and crime, could not be diminished solely by a new educational system? Many problems and issues continued to evolve during the years after the nation had accepted *Indian Control of Indian Education*. Most importantly, how could educators who had been subjected to the oppressive and abusive systems of the past transform the future education of their own children?

Once the federal government had reluctantly allowed Aboriginal communities to develop their own educational models and to gain jurisdiction over their children's education, more communities sought the opportunity to do so. However, the Department of Indian Affairs and Northern Development's reluctance to release its hold on Aboriginal communities discouraged them from establishing or taking control of their own schools. DIAND data indicate that in 1975-6 only fifty-three communities had assumed control of their schools. Low self-esteem coupled with doubts about the government agenda for Indian education restrained many communities from taking the bold initial steps necessary to correct the problems in First Nations education. This bilateral reluctance gradually diminished as various Aboriginal communities began to demonstrate how effective they could be in operating schools, albeit using old models of Eurocentric education. With some training and consultation, they assumed administrative control over their schools and financial accountability with little difficulty. By 1991-2, the number of band-operated schools had increased to 329 (INAC 1992).

Twenty-five years of First Nations control of education in some schools have ushered in a new era in which Aboriginal education has been redefined. First Nations have begun to move from models of colonial domination and assimilation to those that are culturally, linguistically, and philosophically relevant and empowering. The first bold steps by a few communities have led many other First Nations communities to assume jurisdiction over their schools, although initially that control was primarily administrative. Once communities felt secure about handling the school system, they quickly realized that the outcomes of education were inconsistent with their educational hopes and desires.

It was not enough that Aboriginal students should succeed in the school system and receive diplomas or certificates. It was also important that the educational processes of Indian education should strengthen First Nations languages and cultures, build upon the strong foundations of ancestral heritage and culture, and enlist the invaluable advice and assistance of elders. The very tenets of Indian education had to change from accepting acculturation and cognitive assimilation as final ends to revitalizing and renewing language and cultural identity and dignity.

Early questions about jurisdiction, management, control, and evaluation of Indian education were studied extensively as the Assembly of First Nations (formerly the National Indian Brotherhood) prepared its three-year research study on Indian education in 1984. This was the most extensive study to date of First Nations education. The national review's mandate was to examine the impact of the 1973 Indian Control of Indian Education Policy, synthesize available research on the subject since 1972, examine First Nations jurisdiction over First Nations education, and recommend improved education policy and appropriate legislation that would support a government-to-government relationship between the First Nations and the government of Canada.

In *Tradition and Education: Towards a Vision of Our Future. A Declaration of First Nations' Jurisdiction over Education* (1988), the Educational Secretariat of the Assembly of First Nations found that Aboriginal communities had limited jurisdiction over education because the federal government had merely envisioned Indian control as administrative control of programs, not the redefinition or restructuring of Indian education. Furthermore, Aboriginal communities had neither the resources nor the authority to evaluate and implement the necessary services. The federal government was also found to be transferring money to the provinces on behalf of Indian communities while not seeking any accountability from the provinces. In effect, the government of Canada had failed to implement the 1973 policy as it was intended (Assembly of First Nations 1988, 12-14).

These same conclusions were reiterated in the final report of the Assembly of First Nations Language Revitalization Strategy Committee entitled *Towards Linguistic Justice for First Nations* (1990). Their research, completed over two years, sought to develop a long-term plan to revitalize Aboriginal languages. Their general needs assessment chronicled the rapid and continuous loss of Aboriginal languages throughout Canada. The report noted that only 16 per cent or 21 First Nations have flourishing languages; 21 per cent or 28 First Nations have enduring languages; 26 per cent or 35 First Nations have declining languages; 26 per cent or 35 First Nations have endangered languages; and 11 per cent or 15 First Nations have critical languages (AFN 1990, i).

A parlimentary Standing Committee on Aboriginal Affairs in Canada painted a similar picture of the effect of language loss on education and literacy. In their report on the general consultative meetings with national Aboriginal peoples and organizations, the authors found that at least 45 per cent of on-reserve Indians and over 50 per cent of the Inuit were functionally illiterate (Standing Committee on Aboriginal Affairs 1990, 8). Other important factors arose in testimonies regarding education, including the complicating legacy of residential schools, second-language issues, lack of community-based high schools, and lack of culturally relevant curricula. The Standing Committee suggested several ways of reversing language and literacy loss in Aboriginal communities. To date, the federal government has not acted upon these recommendations.

During the course of these studies, several key organizations in Canada sought to bolster Indian education with conferences, think tanks, and networks. The Assembly of First Nations, the national body of chiefs from each province, has taken the lead in bringing Indian education issues to the forefront of Canadian and Aboriginal consciousness. Their community hearings throughout Canada attracted leaders and community educators who spoke of the diversity of educational motives and intentions and the myriad difficulties they had encountered in reversing the dismal historical trends. On every front, historical oppression, insufficient funds, and underdeveloped services led to developmental difficulties.

Other professional organizations laboured to help define and shape the future of Aboriginal education. Indian educators established the Mokakit Education Research Association in 1984 as an educational research forum for Aboriginal researchers and scholars. It was located at the First Nations House of Learning at the University of British Columbia. The association's first conference was held in London, Ontario, and gave rise to a committed following of Native and non-Native professionals interested in the meaning and processes of Indian education, bringing them together under the theme 'Developing Excellence in Indian Education.' This organization has since begun publishing and researching widely in the area of Aboriginal education through the *Mokakit Educational Research Journal*. The journal is a scholarly publication aimed at demystifying research methods among Aboriginal communities, raising awareness among educators of the value of research in establishing and sharing information, and researching essential issues affecting Aboriginal education processes and results.

Short-lived, but nonetheless effective, was the National Indian Education Forum, which was formed in 1988 to develop a national platform to oppose the federal government's cap on post-secondary Indian education. This organization effectively coordinated a national protest in 1988 over the government's policy. The government of Canada had once again decided on action without Aboriginal involvement. The subsequent conference, as well as later national think tank and strategy sessions, brought together key leaders to shape ideas about Indian education. As their discussions evolved, it became clear that the education of First Nations children constituted a national agenda involving Aboriginal communities. Aboriginal peoples' resolve to assume control in every community was strengthened by the need to ensure that students who succeeded in high school could find a place in post-secondary institutions.

However, the national dialogue and the issues surrounding Aboriginal education have not yielded the anticipated increase of funds to support services and development throughout Canada. Rather, as Canada entered deepening recession and economic hardship in the 1990s, it cut funds to all groups, including Aboriginal organizations and communities, while offering some groups only modest additional funds to help continue the dialogue about education or to assume control over community schools and educational programs. Without adequate funds to develop services, programs, and networks, Aboriginal communities have had to develop what they can with what they have.

Schools and students in higher education were hard hit by the recession. In 1970, only 432 Indian students were enrolled in universities and receiving aid from the Department of Indian Affairs and Northern Development. By 1991, the number of Indian students in post-secondary institutions in Canada had risen to 21,442 (INAC 1992). As a result of the increasing aspirations and achievements of Aboriginal students, allocations for their higher education were being overtaxed. Caps on higher education limited the number of students who could take advantage of university or college education and forced bands to adopt new allocation priorities for funds according to federal guidelines that appeared arbitrary or that pitted students against each other.

There were no funds to redefine the parameters of Indian education or to develop new cognitive bases for achieving cultural and linguistic integrity. Nor did anticipated support for Aboriginal languages result from the Heritage Languages Act, which supported the maintenance of ethnic group languages in Canada. There were no 'Institutes for Aboriginal

Languages' and no central institution for supporting the development of curricula. Communities had control of Indian education, but no services, resources, or networks to help achieve their goals and objectives. Hence, the struggle and quest for cultural and linguistic integrity continues.

Clearly, education in Aboriginal communities is as distinctive as are those communities and their languages. With over fifty-two Aboriginal languages in Canada in over 300 Aboriginal reserve communities, and with large numbers of off-reserve Aboriginals in all major cities, the diversity of Aboriginal cultures and communities is immense. Provinces have controlled education and curricula for the last century, and it is difficult, if not impossible, for Aboriginal peoples to achieve complete change in twenty years. The questions about Aboriginal education continue, the debate and doubts linger, and the funds and resources to achieve new ends continue to dwindle.

More importantly, Aboriginal communities that have assumed control of their schools are still plagued by questions of how to implement Indian education in the twenty-first century: What goals and outcomes are important? What processes must accompany cultural and linguistic development and inclusion? What is the meaning of renewal and revision in the contemporary and traditional educational context? How do we represent our cultures in schools? What is appropriate, meaningful, and necessary? Should we teach and evaluate in traditional Aboriginal ways or adopt contemporary Eurocentric models of education to achieve a diversity of goals? How can Aboriginal communities be healed of past tragedies? How can cultural and linguistic integrity be achieved?

At the 1992 Mokakit conference in Vancouver, an elder admonished the audience that we cannot change the past, but we can change tomorrow by what we do today. We all have a responsibility to bring balance and harmony to the children of the earth. Educators and researchers in First Nations education have pressed to bring this balance and harmony through the cultures and languages of the communities. First Nations peoples have begun to shift from control of administration to implementation of a transforming education. However, this paradigmatic shift has caused confusion and incoherence, as is evidenced by several contributions to this book.

But contradiction and incoherence are inevitable in and indispensable to successful transformation. We need to be mindful of this fact, not allowing fear and doubt about confusion and incoherence to lead us to structures and systems that resemble the old assimilationist models. Aboriginal communities cannot rely on old models of Eurocentric education to transform themselves. We must search beyond. We must expect to find incoherence and contradiction on our way towards the transformation and revitalization of Aboriginal languages and cultures.

The writings offered in *First Nations Education in Canada: The Circle Unfolds* continue the quest among both Aboriginal and non-Aboriginal educators to resolve the dilemmas and questions posed elsewhere about First Nations education (Barman, Hébert, and McCaskill 1986, 1987). The essays have been organized around the concept of the Sacred Circle, to emphasize the unity, continuity, and interconnectedness of each issue. The circle opens at the Eastern Door, where light from the dawn and the spring emanates. This door offers new light and new beginnings in reconceptualizing First Nations education.

Eber Hampton's essay 'Towards a Redefinition of Indian Education' opens with a medicine-wheel typology as an organizing tool to discuss principles and boundaries in the redefinition and theory of Indian education. Hampton identifies the strands of unity that embrace Indian education. In defining the central standards of First Nations education, he examines the different transformative paths that schools and communities have taken from assimilation to self-defining and culturally transmitting models that build on the recognition of unique First Nations cultures, communities, and elders. For Hampton, Indian education must enhance Aboriginal consciousness of what it means to be an Indian, thus empowering and enriching individual and collective lives.

Sharilyn Calliou, in 'Peacekeeping Actions at Home: A Medicine Wheel Model for a Peacekeeping Pedagogy,' shares her personal reflections on racism and multiculturalism, while constructing a peacekeeping pedagogy built from within the medicine wheel and the Iroquois Great Law of Peace. The circle typology illustrates the continuum and interconnectedness of the events and conditions that shape racism, multiculturalism, anti-racism, and peacekeeping. Revealing the inherent dilemmas within the denials of racism and the secularized dimension of anti-racist citizenship, Calliou proposes seeking guidance from the Great Law of Peace, guidance that is shaped by unconditional consensus, equality, respect, compassion, participatory democracy, strength, courage, and reverence. Calliou calls for a balance of these dimensions across the curriculum.

The concluding essay in the Eastern Door section, 'Redefining Science Education for Aboriginal Students,' argues that locally developed cultural content need not and should not be confined to social studies and language arts but must be integrated holistically into all areas, including science. Madeleine MacIvor reveals how non-inclusive content in mainstream science education has resulted in low Aboriginal student enrolment and low achievement in science. She offers a more inclusive science education model that is illuminated by Aboriginal education principles and transformed by Aboriginal concepts, knowledge, and skills. As conventional science reveals its inadequacy in confronting the growing global environmental crisis, Aboriginal principles and knowledge may promote awareness of the need to reevaluate relationships with and responsibilities towards the world.

The Southern Door is representative of summer, the emotional realm, where we make connection with our relations through our languages and cultures that are fostered by the ceremonies and rituals of our ancestors. From this perspective we search for ways to continue our relations, to maintain our languages and cultures, to develop our unique Aboriginal ways of relating and knowing, while struggling with the contradictions inherent in the human condition in modern society.

Willie Ermine in 'Aboriginal Epistemology' describes the conflicts between knowledge configurations within Eurocentric and Aboriginal world-views, utilizing the metaphors of outer and inner space. The two different processes in the quest for knowledge inform different ideologies about education and knowing. His perceptive survey of the foundations of Aboriginal epistemology and of the traditional ceremonial path of the Old Ones raises questions about the kind of education and curriculum needed to develop Aboriginal consciousness. These insights establish the need for educational reform that will continue the exploration and growth initiated by our ancestors. The ancient traditions of Aboriginal peoples recognize and affirm teachings that deepen understanding and appreciation of the self's inner walk, which connects us with the vital forces of the universe. As we tap into this inner life force, we develop a greater appreciation of wholeness, connectedness, and relationships, the essence of the spiritual and the educational journey.

Shirley Sterling's 'Quaslametko and Yetko: Two Grandmother Models for Contemporary Native Education Pedagogy' is the powerfully captivating story of Sterling's grandmothers. Their lives yield an understanding of socialization in the traditional family and illustrate the intersection of traditional education with modern youth and the complexities of that union because of loss of language and culture through schooling. Sterling captures the beauty and quiet but restless energy of her grandmothers. These reflections are mixed with sadness and joy as she considers the loss of connectedness with the tribal souls of her grandmothers and the discovery of another realm of consciousness transmitted to her through the great silence.

Most schools that accept language education and cultural relevance for their students must also take some stand on how teachers will teach and the educational implications of their choices. Robert Leavitt's 'Language and Cultural Content in Native Education' describes a fundamental difference in world-view in the Aboriginal and English languages and its implications for teaching styles and methods for Aboriginal children. Central to the exploration of language is the awareness that Aboriginal languages reflect Aboriginal ways of knowing, ways of interacting, and ways of using language. His research underscores the need to understand that Aboriginal education implies the integration of different levels of Native culture and thought in classroom strategies and events with and for Native children, and he offers ways to balance and enrich the knowledge bases and processes.

In a complementary essay, 'Learning Processes and Teaching Roles in Native Education: Cultural Base and Cultural Brokerage,' Arlene Stairs sheds light on two models of Inuit teaching in North Baffin communities. One is based on traditional cultural values and content inherent in the traditional Inuit socialization style, which informs views on how children learn and how teachers teach. The other is based on mainstream educational theories. Stairs highlights the contradictions between these different models, and notes that Native teachers, in their new role as cultural brokers, act as a buffer between these contradictions.

As we turn to the Western Door, we encounter autumn, the dying of the grass, and some of the harsher realities. These include those historical complexities that have rendered Aboriginal education incoherent. The result has been areas of dissidence and disappointment and the frustration of Aboriginal communities' hopes for educational change. These issues move beyond elementary schooling to levels of higher education and teacher development.

Ron Mackay and Lawrence Myles, in 'A Major Challenge for the Education System: Aboriginal Retention and Dropout,' present the findings of their survey into the causes of failure or dropout among Aboriginal youths in Ontario schools and the reasons for success among the same students. The findings represent an important litany of causes of failure in the processes of educating Aboriginal students, and, more importantly, a balance of causes for success as well. Interestingly, these successes occur in institutions where Aboriginal education is related to developing partnerships with, fostering respect for, and encouraging acceptance of Aboriginal communities. Educators in band-operated and provincial schools will find hope in the authors' final assessment of schools which enjoy high success among Indian and Métis and will be guided by their suggested principles for successfully enabling and enhancing Aboriginal education.

Rick Hesch's 'Teacher Education and Aboriginal Opposition' offers an illuminating account of the experience of Aboriginal student interns in the Saskatchewan Urban Native Teacher Education Program (SUNTEP). Focusing on four ideological problems he found in curriculum content and practices, Hesch contributes to the body of research on the teacher-intern-supervisor triangle. Add provincial Department of Education manuals and prescribed curricula, and one has a complex educational situation which pulls the Native student teacher and the Native student in many directions.

Agnes Grant's 'The Challenge for Universities' complements Hesch's essay by discussing yet another aspect of the student teacher in the community. As schools seek to include and legitimize Aboriginal knowledge, they must include elders in the process. Given that not all Native communities and not all Aboriginal and non-Aboriginal teachers are alike, both communities and teachers can learn from Aboriginal elders in their teacher training. The Bear Lake Stevenson Island Project is an example of an innovative project that involves education students in bush life for university credit and in preparation for their work among Cree children. Grant offers a self-initiating and self-analyzing evaluation model which could provide the prescriptive solution to some of the problems discussed by Hesch while continuing to articulate the values and philosophy of Native education in one community.

John Taylor's 'Non-Native Teachers Teaching in Native Communities' is invaluable for non-Native teachers who are considering teaching on rural reserves. Many difficulties confront the new non-Aboriginal teacher who is unaware of social and professional expectations in a reserve community. Taylor's personal experience of reserve schools provides newcomers to reserve life with concrete advice on their role in the community and how they might adapt to the new environment to develop positive experiences for themselves and their students.

Finally, as the Northern Door opens to winter, we are reminded of the Aboriginal peoples' legacy of endurance and survival, and of the painful contradictions in their position in modern society. In Aboriginal education, we must find the strands of power in our ancestors' teachings and resistance which we can use to continue our struggle for cultural and linguistic integrity. We must know our treaties, our ancestral heritage, and build new partnerships to continue our quest. In this section we look anew at the treaties, the contradictions inherent in transformation, new models of inclusive and participatory education, and find solace in the healing circle in community-based Aboriginal education.

Youngblood Henderson's 'Treaties and Indian Education' draws critical attention to the provisions for Aboriginal choice in the Indian treaties with the Crown of Great Britain and how these have been restored as post-colonial constitutional rights in Canada. With the constitutional affirmation of existing Aboriginal and treaty rights in Section 35, the 1982 Constitution Act reaffirms that treaty rights to Indian education are equal to provincial educational rights. Securing these existing obligations is a new educational mandate, as Indian peoples seek to remedy past abuses by the federal government which created the modern crisis in Aboriginal education.

As Aboriginal communities assume control of their institutions or establish new ones, systems will inevitably undergo tremendous stress from which conflicts and collaboration will arise. Celia Haig-Brown's 'Taking Control: Contradiction and First Nations Adult Education' addresses some of these conflicts and struggles, maintaining that they are a necessary developmental process which can be constructively used to deal with transformation. Her research in adult Aboriginal education offers helpful and positive examples of balancing conflict and contradiction.

Jo-ann Archibald's 'Locally Developed Native Studies Curriculum: An Historical and Philosophical Rationale' describes the struggles and process that the Sto:lo Nation in British Columbia has undergone in shifting from assimilationist educational models to integrating Sto:lo cultural content, concepts, and skills in the provincial curriculum and band-operated schools. The need for relevant curricula has shifted the focus from exclusive development structures to inclusive community participation that has reawakened the silenced knowledge of the elders and revitalized education for Sto:lo communities.

Finally, Robert Regnier's 'The Sacred Circle: An Aboriginal Approach to Healing Education at an Urban High School' describes the healing process at the Joe Duquette High School in Saskatoon, Saskatchewan. Through a unique arrangement between the Saskatoon Native Survival Parent Council, the Catholic School Board, and the Saskatchewan Department of Education, the school is a local parent-governed school, an alternative urban school dedicated to nurturing the minds, bodies, and souls of its students. The school draws upon the strength of the Indian world-view and its spiritual philosophy to support the creativity and foster the self-actualization of its students. Regnier's essay illustrates the use of the Sacred Circle to symbolize the teachings of the elders and the processes embedded in the school's rituals and ceremonies as well as to reflect the interconnectedness of human beings and nature, enabling students to construct their ultimate meaning and purpose.

The essays in this volume do not provide easy answers to the complex world of First Nations education in Canada, nor are they intended to do so. The goal is to stimulate discussion in this important area of inquiry and to encourage more Aboriginal and non-Aboriginal people to move forward to meet the challenge of First Nations education in the twenty-first century as the circle unfolds.

Note

1 The name of the federal agency for carrying out the obligations of treaties and lands reserved for Native people was changed from the Department of Indian Affairs and Northern Development (DIAND) to Indian and Northern Affairs Canada (INAC) after 1985. The use of terms in this chapter reflects the context of these times.

References

Assembly of First Nations. 1990. *Towards Linguistic Justice for First Nations.* Ottawa: Assembly of First Nations

–. 1988. *Tradition and Education: Towards a Vision of Our Future. A Declaration of First Nations Jurisdiction Over Education.* Ottawa: Assembly of First Nations

–. 1992. *Towards Rebirth of First Nations' Languages.* Ottawa: Assembly of First Nations

Barman, Jean, Yvonne Hébert, and Don McCaskill, eds. 1986-7. *Indian Education in Canada.* 2 vols. Vancouver: UBC Press

Indian and Northern Affairs Canada (INAC). 1992. *Basic Department Data 1992.* Ottawa: Supply and Services

National Indian Brotherhood. 1972. *Indian Control of Indian Education.* Ottawa: National Indian Brotherhood

Canada. 1990. House of Commons Standing Committee on Aboriginal Affairs. Fourth report. *You Took My Talk.* Ottawa: Queen's Printer

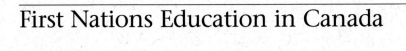

First Nations Education in Canada

Eastern Door: Reconceptualizing First Nations Education

1

Towards a Redefinition
of Indian Education

Eber Hampton

I was born in Talihina, Oklahoma, and am a member of the Chickasaw Nation, as was my father, Eber Hampton, Senior. My mother is white; her maiden name was Evelyn Cowling. I have been educated in two different cultural traditions. My white education was in public elementary and secondary schools, Westmont College, the University of California at Santa Barbara, and the Harvard Graduate School of Education. My Indian education was different from the white education in both structure and content. While some of it was explicitly taught, I mostly felt as though I acquired my own knowledge with the assistance of elders who taught me a little of what they knew of plants, ceremonies, and healing.

This chapter is an analysis of the problematic practice of so-called 'Indian education.' One purpose of the analysis was to clear the underbrush in my own thoughts about Indian education. The interviews I conducted were an attempt to think along with other Indians in the hope of making a reflective contribution to the conversation among Indian educators about defining and implementing an education worthy of our children and our ancestors.

The chapter is written for both Indian and white educators, and I request their patience as I belabour the obvious or drift into esoteric obscurity. I follow my impulse to interlace narrative vernacular with academic discourse. Hugh Brody, in *Maps and Dreams* (1981), dealt with a similar impulse by alternating chapters of social science discourse with chapters of narrative. I use whatever tools I have to understand and communicate. My hope is that the reader will think along with me and will take what is useful and leave the rest.

Even the most basic terms need definition. I was in the mail room at Mankato State University, where I was the only Indian faculty member, when a colleague, in all seriousness, asked if it would be better to say 'Native American Summer' than 'Indian Summer.' I respected his question. The right of a people to define themselves and choose their own name is basic. I face a similar problem in referring to whites, sometimes calling them Anglos as is common in the southwest, non-Natives as is common in Alaska, or Caucasians. No name encompasses a people, and none is truly accurate. Correctness is not nearly so important to me as accuracy in feeling as well as in fact. Similarly, originality is subordinated to accuracy. I name sources when I can. But many of my words and thoughts were first spoken by my many teachers, and I cannot disentangle those that I now hear in my own voice. As I prepared to enter a sweat lodge ceremony in Minnesota, the leader of the sweat said, 'Eber, I know you can't pray in Indian, but pray in Indian in English.' So, as much as I am able, I have written in my vernacular hoping thus to speak person-to-person about what I care so deeply about. I hope you will join the conversation and continue to do what you can to help Indian education.

The structure of the chapter is iterative rather than linear. It progresses in a spiral that adds a little with each thematic repetition rather than building an Aristotelian argument step-by-step. Working with other editors of the *Harvard Educational Review* on a special Third World issue, I became aware of how deeply ingrained this iterative structure is, not only in my own thoughts but in those of Third World writers. Almost all the pieces by Third World authors were criticized by the other editors as repetitious, while I found new meaning in each turn of the spiral. An iterative structure is made explicit in the six-directional patterns of heaven, earth, east, south, west, and north that I use in this chapter. It implies circular movement in both the natural and spiritual worlds. As a twentieth-century Native American, I worship and am comforted by the great mystery. There are many things I do not understand and many gaps that I have not filled. I ask you to read carefully not so much what I write as the way I write it, and especially what I do not write.

The Current State of Indian Education

For most Indian students, now as in the past hundred years, Indian education means the education of Indians by non-Indians using non-Indian methods (Hawthorn 1966-7; Barman, Hébert, and McCaskill 1986; National Education Association 1983). Far too few Indian students have contact with Indian educators who are attuned to their culture and who can serve as models of educational achievement (Edwards and Smith 1981). Native educators are needed both to encourage Native children who want to go to college and to teach them once they get there (Ortiz 1982; Barman, Hébert, and McCaskill 1987).

If Native nations are to have engineers, managers, business people, natural resource specialists, and all the other experts we need to meet non-Indians on equal terms, then we must have educational leadership that makes mathematics, science, and computers accessible to our students. We need to train our educators so that the next generation of students is more comfortable with these tools than the previous generation has been (Cheek 1984).

Most Indian parents want their children to be taught those things needed for success in both the white and the Native worlds (Bradley 1980). We need educational leaders who can confidently deal with all aspects of modern society. Natives are most poorly represented among occupations in the natural sciences, the health sciences, and mathematics. Many Native students report being counselled against mathematics because it has been perceived as too difficult for them or as unnecessary to their future (Green 1978). In this increasingly technological society, mathematics has become the 'critical filter' that often prevents Natives from attaining careers in high-income fields (Sells 1980).

For the vast majority of Indian students, far from being an opportunity, education is a critical filter indeed, filtering out hope and self-esteem. The Native student who sees the 'teacher as an enemy' (Wolcott 1987) may have the more realistic and, in some ways, more hopeful view than the student who fails to see beyond the apparently benign purposes of schooling. The failure of non-Native education of Natives can be read as the success of Native resistance to cultural, spiritual, and psychological genocide. For whatever reason, whoever is to blame, Indian education defined as non-Indian education of Indians has a long and conclusive history of failure. Fortunately, other meanings are possible.

What is Indian Education?

No aspect of a culture is more vital to its integrity than its means of education. As I have been taught, nourished, and sustained by my culture, so it is my duty and privilege to transmit it. I value my Anglo education and respect its necessity and power in this society, but my deepest values and my view of the world were formed within an Indian culture. Consequently, my goal is to contribute to what the former director of the Penn State Indian Leadership Program calls the 'redefinition of Indian education' (Noley 1981).

As a first step towards redefining 'Indian education,' it is necessary to examine various meanings that the term has had. The juxtaposition of the two words 'Indian' and 'education' has almost always been problematic in spite of the agreement by Indian parents and Anglo policymakers on the importance of education for Indians (Bradley 1980). Part of the problem is that Indian education is inherently a bicultural enterprise that has been directed at two sometimes competing and sometimes complementary goals: assimilation and self-determination (Havighurst 1981). The relationship between these goals and the structures of Western education has not been defined. Currently, each Indian-controlled school, project, parent committee, or program adopts, adapts, or invents those methods or techniques that it feels will best serve its children.

I believe that the term 'Indian education' has five different meanings: (1) traditional Indian education, (2) schooling for self-determination, (3) schooling for assimilation, (4) education by Indians, and (5) Indian education *sui generis*. These five meanings are like five currents in a river. It is not always easy to identify the edges of the currents but some currents are stronger than others in a particular time or place.

(1) *Traditional Indian Education.* Both Native and white education have long histories and complex modern realizations. Prior to the influx of Europeans, each Indian nation had its own forms of education. Generally, these traditional Indian forms can be characterized as oral histories, teaching stories, ceremonies, apprenticeships, learning games, formal instruction, tutoring, and tag-along teaching (Buffalohead 1976).

Noley (1981) describes the Choctaw practice of having certain respected elders gather the children together each day for the purpose of teaching, a practice that was common in many tribes. McLean (1981) describes educational methods that centred on the qargi (big house) in Inupiat villages. Oral histories and stories told to children have important moral and factual purposes. They help children learn history and how to be respected persons. They point out difficulties and dangers in both the social and the natural worlds and illustrate various ways of meeting them. For example, Auston Hammond, a contemporary Tlingit elder, speaking of the central character in many Tlingit stories, said, 'Raven makes mistakes so we don't have to.'

All traditional Native methods occurred within cultural settings that were characterized by subsistence economies, in-context learning, personal and kinship relations between teachers and students, and ample opportunities for students to observe adult role models who exemplified the knowledge, skills, and values being taught. In attenuated form, many Indian families and communities continue to use these methods to teach their children content from both Indian and Anglo cultures (Forbes and Adams 1976). Indian methods and content have been largely ignored by the educational establishment, but with the current rapid increase in the number of Native educators (Chavers 1982; Havighurst 1981), there is new interest in both Indian content and method (Noley 1981; NEA 1983).

(2) *Schooling for Self-Determination.* The second phase of Native education was the establishment of schools for Native children. Although schools as institutions were non-Native in origin and character, there have been such vast differences in the goals, methods, and outcomes that it is possible to distinguish two kinds of schooling for Natives: schooling for self-determination and schooling for assimilation. Although neglected in standard histories of Native education, there have been many examples of highly successful Native-oriented schools. For example, schools established and controlled by the Chickasaw, Choctaw, and Cherokee nations, as well as Russian mission schools among the Yup'ik people, were characterized by the use of Native languages, positive attitudes towards Native cultures, good school-community relations, and emphasis on self-determination rather than assimilation. These schools also had high success rates in literacy and educational attainment (Oleksa and Dauenhauer 1982). Unfortunately, they were all closed by the unilateral action of government.

(3) *Schooling for Assimilation.* Historically and in most contemporary situations, the education of Indians is carried out by Anglos using Anglo models to satisfy Anglo purposes (American Indian Policy Review Commission 1976). In contrast to schooling for self-determination, these schools for assimilation have been characterized by high failure rates in literacy and educational attainment, having assimilation rather than self-determination as goals, poor school-community relations, negative attitudes towards Native cultures, and prohibition or non-use of Native languages (Oleksa and Dauenhauer 1982).

(4) *Education by Indians.* Since the passage of the Indian Education Act of 1972 in the United States and of the Canadian government's adoption of the National Indian Brotherhood document *Indian Control of Indian Education* a year later, there has been a rapid development that promises to change the term 'Indian Education' to mean education *by* Indians rather than simply education *of* Indians (Chavers 1982; Havighurst 1981). In this phase, Native people began to take an active role in the schooling of Native children as board members, teachers, administrators, and resource people. Small numbers of Native personnel have been introduced into non-Native structures and some Native content is provided through Native Studies, elders in the school, and other programs. Most schools for Native children retain assimilation goals, lack Native-language instruction, and have high failure rates.

Although this phase of education continues, for most Indian students the increase in the number of Indian educators has prepared the way for a move towards Indian control through the establishment of Native-controlled schools and Native school boards. This is apparently a transitional phase because even with Native control, most of the structures, methods, content, and faculty remain predominantly non-Native. A century or more of cultural conflict, non-Native-oriented schools, and non-Native-trained Native educators has left major obstacles in the way of Native-controlled schools. Native languages have declined, non-Native standards are usually used to evaluate Native schools and Native teachers, the development of Native curricula and Native educational methods is an enormous task, and funding is uncertain and usually controlled by non-Natives.

In spite of these difficulties, there are encouraging trends in Native-controlled schools in both the United States and Canada. The self-determination goals of Native education are being served in Indian-controlled schools and are strongly articulated by Native personnel in other schools; school-community relations have improved; a Native curriculum has and is being developed in most Native communities; the numbers of Native educators have increased dramatically; Native cultural values and languages are being actively promoted; and there is recognition of the need for Native approaches to educational methods and structures. 'What we ultimately need may not be a grafting of Indian content and personnel onto European structures, but a redefinition of education' (Noley 1981, 198). It is the last point that leads towards phase five: the creation of Native education *sui generis*.

(5) *Indian Education Sui Generis.* Indian education *sui generis* is Indian education as 'a thing of its own kind' (National Advisory Council on Indian Education 1983), a self-determined Indian education using models of education structured by Indian cultures. The creation of Native education involves the development of Native methods and Native structures for education as well as Native content and Native personnel. It is the tension felt by Native educators, teachers, administrators, and curriculum developers as they attempt to fit their practice into non-Native structures that generates the creativity necessary for the development of the new Native education.

The recognition of the uniqueness of Indian education and the contribution it has to make to society does not imply a kind of segregation. Most Native cultures have tended towards inclusiveness and have valued diversity (Deloria 1970). Indian parents and educators want Indian children to learn everything that education has to offer, as well as their own cultures (Bradley 1980). The recognition of Indian education as distinctive indicates a legitimate desire of Indian people to be self-defining, to have their ways of life respected, and to teach their children in a manner that enhances consciousness of being an Indian and a fully participating citizen of Canada or the United States.

Methodology

The lack of a theory of Indian education not only hampers research, it also impedes the practice of Indian education. Currently, each Indian-controlled school, project, parent committee, or program adopts, adapts, or invents a model of education as best it can. In many cases, this has led to significant local improvement. The strength of these individual efforts has been their reliance on local communities. Unfortunately, not all Indian education efforts have been so successful. In many instances, Indian education programs have expended human and financial resources with little success.

I believe that the limited success of programs designed to educate Indians, the prevalence of isolated research findings, and the tacit nature of Indian educational practice all point to the need of an articulated approach to Indian education. A theoretical articulation would serve to organize research, guide practice, and serve as an explicit aid to discussion and clarification.

This chapter cannot articulate a comprehensive theory, but I hope to make explicit some of the themes that such a theory should address. The preliminary empirical base of this construction of theory is a series of interviews that I conducted with Native graduate students at the Harvard Graduate School of Education. The exploratory and hypothesis-generating purpose of these interviews led me to conclude that grounded theory (Glaser and Strauss 1967), qualitative analysis (Miles and Huberman 1984), and participant observation would be the most useful methodological approaches. I draw on interview data, the existing literature, and an analysis of my own experience to move towards a theory of Indian education.

According to Pelto and Pelto (1978), 'the method of interviewing key people is used to best advantage when it is closely integrated with participant observation.' When the researcher has observed and participated in the 'event and has command over a considerable portion of the relevant information he or she is in a position to vastly improve the data by systematic checking' with key people. This is, in essence, what I did. By reason of race, culture, profession, and inclination I have been a participant observer in Indian education.

The generality of this study is restricted by the specificity of my own experience and my decision to interview only American Indian Program participants. In the trade-off between depth and range of information, the primacy of personal experience and observation for Indian ways of knowing (Colorado 1985) led me to choose depth. I believe that at this stage I can make the greatest contribution towards a theory of Indian education by careful work with what is close to me rather than by an attempt to gather all disparate tribes and communities into one grand model.

All research participants were Indians. Their tribes are Mi'kmaq, Skatakoke, Chippewa, Oneida, Tlingit, Menomini, Apache, Uchi, and Blackfoot. At the time of the interviews, all participants were enrolled in the Harvard Graduate School of Education.

One of the criteria for admission to the American Indian Program is a demonstrated commitment to Indian education. The interview participants have an average of six years of professional experience in Indian education and variously hold the position of elementary teacher, secondary teacher, program administrator, community college teacher, and administrator. Not only have they worked as Indian educators in a wide variety of settings, but their experience as students covers the range of Indian education: public, private, federal, and Indian-controlled schools.

The interviews were tape-recorded and transcribed, and I made written notes of what I took to be significant points raised in the interviews. I began each interview with a brief statement of the purpose of the research (Brislin, Lonner, and Thorndike 1973). For the first two interviews, I used an interview schedule that I had prepared in advance. The interviewees attempted to answer the questions, but it was very apparent that the interview schedule disrupted the process of learning together that the more open-ended questions seemed to facilitate.

One of the consistent criticisms that Native scholars have made of Indian education research has been that it is most often designed around non-Indian concerns, usually articulated as an academic theory (LaFromboise and Plake 1983; Trimble 1977). The interview schedule had exactly this problem. I was embarrassed to hear myself asking such questions as, 'How do you see the American Indian Program handling issues of change and continuity?' and 'On a scale of 1-7, how characteristic of the American Indian Program is emphasis on performance rather than outcome?' The questions had originally interested me within their theoretical context but in the interview they seemed artificial, abstract, and incomprehensible without inordinate amounts of explanation.

The happy solution was to drop most of the questions from the interview schedule and to encourage the participants to elaborate by my active listening and co-participation (Spradley 1979). My introductory statements about the purpose of the research and the exploratory question, 'What is Indian about Indian education?' seemed well understood by the participants as they talked about their own experiences. I discussed with the participants my interest in the question, and I responded freely to their answers. I then revised the interview process and continued to conduct interviews on the basis of an intuitive, ill-defined feeling of authentic engagement on the part of the participant and myself. Even though I enjoyed and was satisfied with the revised interview format in a way that I had missed in the first two interviews, I was uncomfortable (vulnerable in Katz's [1985] sense) with the lack of explicit structure and my inability to describe the intuitive feeling that these interviews were good. The interviews seemed real in a way that was both exhilarating and frightening in that I felt that powerful learning that I could not describe was happening.

I reviewed my notes after each interview but it was not until the eighth interview that I began to create a verbal understanding of the interview process. This verbal understanding provided a label for the process, 'reflective thinking,' and allowed me to explain my feeling of vulnerability as openness to learning and growth as a participant, as I explored topics that were of central importance. The eighth interview participant contrasted what he called critical thinking with reflective thinking. His concept of reflective thinking described what I saw happening in the interviews. They constituted neither question-and-answer nor a critical discussion but a reflective discussion that enabled the participants, including me, to build our thoughts together in a cumulative or sometimes exponential way. Rather than striving to achieve my original purpose of determining the fit between Indian education and theories derived from other areas, my focus had changed to using interviews for gathering our scattered thoughts and experiences to create a better understanding of Indian education.

The moments of shared insight that several participants and I reached were the most rewarding personal features of the research. In general, the interview process was rewarding, inspiring, intellectually stimulating, and helpful. As humans we always know more than we can say (Polanyi 1964). The interviews helped to make some of this implicit knowledge explicit. Data analysis let me continue moving towards what I see as the explication of implicit consensus.

A concrete example from an interview may best convey the flavour of the process. The following example was chosen haphazardly from an interview that was at the top of the stack that I had shuffled many times. I chose a few exchanges that I found personally interesting and that illustrate the process:

Eber (E): Yeah, that historical responsibility or to generation after generation.

Participant (P): It's really neat to think about. It's really special. I believe that I really understand and appreciate the fact that I'm only here because back when, an ancestor of mine, they decided that ... even though it was going to cause them misery ... they decided to give up fighting and surrender, because if they didn't they would have been wiped out and there would have been no descendants. So, they went ahead and put their lives in such jeopardy and twisted everything around for them, and lived miserably, because they knew that in doing that, maybe ... maybe their children, etc., would have a better life.

E: That's a real nice way to think about it. I never quite thought about it exactly like that, that even in surrendering it was so that their great grandchildren would have a chance.

P: And that's why. That's how I see it. That's why I'm here.

E: That it would have been easier to fight to the death ...

P: And that's the kind of people many of them were, where I came from. It would have been better to fight, rather than to be caged up and taken out of their homes. They had to suffer, but there was a reason for it and that's why I'm able to come to school, why I'm here.

The first step towards generating conceptual categories was coding the interview data. In qualitative data analysis, codes are retrieval and organizing devices that allow the analyst to sort quickly, extract, then cluster all the segments relating to the particular question, hypothesis, concept, or theme (Miles and Huberman 1984). Codes are purposely broad and subsume much detail. I sat down with the transcripts, scissors, and tape. As I read a transcript, I looked for themes that seemed to have some bearing on my central question of 'What is Indian about Indian education?' Each time I encountered such a theme, I coded it with a brief label which was close to the concept. Next, I clipped the coded quotes and stacked them in piles according to the codes.

The second step in my analysis of data was a process of comparing each incident within a coding category to all previous incidents within that category. By using this method, I felt I was beginning to get a sense of how propositions about Indian education could be stated. Very tentatively, I suggested the following propositions as steps towards a theory of Indian education:

• Spiritual concerns are an important part of Indian education.

- There are distinctive Indian styles of thought and communication with educational implications.
- For most Indians, education has the dual purpose of promoting Indian features as well as providing skills and information relevant to non-Indian society.
- Indian education cannot be understood apart from an historical analysis.
- Indian education occurs in a cultural atmosphere that is permeated by both strong group bonds and great individual freedom.
- Indian education is service-oriented.

To recapitulate, my goal was not to describe the views that Indians had about education. Rather I was working with interview data from a small group of highly articulate Indian educators to generate a preliminary theory of Indian education. The opinions of these particular Indians deserve attention for two reasons. First, in striving to identify the common themes within this group I believe I have found themes that are worth discussing across Indian groups. They may not be generally accepted, but they should not be foreign to the discussion. Second, these particular graduate students are likely to be important in Indian education in the near future.

Then I let the data gestate for about nine months. Eventually, under pressure from the calendar, my job, and my conscience, I retrieved the computer disks and the shredded transcripts and began the data analysis anew. This time I started by using the same coding, clipping, and compiling procedure, only instead of paper and scissors I used a computer. The result was that instead of a desk messy with strips of paper, I had a clutter of computer files. I did not refer back to my first coding efforts until I had completed the second coding. This procedure led to somewhat different labels for the codes, collapsing two of the codes into one, and the discovery of some new categories. This second coding step allowed for more diversity in emergent categories and was enhanced by my reflective thinking on the data and by comparison with other writers' ideas.

After gathering all the instances of each category into a separate file, I read through each category and noted in the margins instances of reference to other categories (in addition to the ones I had already double- or triple-coded). I also made notes on other possible themes and began to develop propositions about the way the themes might relate to each other.

This step, where comparisons between incidents change to comparisons between incidents and properties of the category that arise from initial comparison of incidents, is the third step towards discovery of grounded theory. As Glaser and Strauss describe it, 'In the beginning, one's hypotheses may seem unrelated, but as categories and properties emerge, develop in abstraction, and become related, their accumulating interrelations form an integrated central theoretical framework – the core of the emerging theory' (1967, 48).

Following this process, I began a diagram to show the interconnections but quickly saw that everything was connected. So I began to search for a model, a metaphor, or a pattern that would somehow organize the themes and serve both as a mnemonic and a matrix for new ideas and actions.

The Six Directions: A Pattern for Understanding the Data

The first ceremony that I was taught was the pipe ceremony. In it, the pipe is offered to the six directions; first to the one above, then to the east, then to the south, then to the west, then to the north, and then to the earth. The first time I fasted for a vision, I spent four days walking and praying in a pattern that started in the centre facing the sky. Then I walked and prayed facing the east; then back to the centre and out to the north; back to the centre to pray looking to the earth. Each direction reminds me of a complex set of meanings, feelings, relationships, and movements. Even though I initially resisted this way of thinking as too deep, too private, too Indian, I finally could not deny the six directions as I sat with Miles and Huberman's (1984) *Qualitative Data Analysis* and tried to formulate a tactic for generating meaning.

My only remaining qualm is that I will be misunderstood as using the six directions as a model rather than allowing it to direct me. This way of thinking is sacred in the sense that it is bigger than anything I might say. It helps me to understand in that it stimulates my thoughts and feelings rather being contained in my words. It structures some ceremonies and, as Allen Wolfleg (1979) said, 'Ceremonies are something we usually do more than talk about.'

The six directions are not a model but a pattern or an organizing principle (see Figure 1.1). Models connote a small, imperfect copy of something more real. The six directions are a way of thinking about existing in the universe. This pattern organizes and clarifies thoughts. It directs us to think of Indian education as dynamic. There is movement. There is historical development. Each of the participants in these conversations, when asked to define Indian education, gave both an historical and a value-laden definition of Indian education. This is what Indian education was, this is what it is, and this is what it should be.

If we return to the six-directional pattern and place traditional Indian education at the east, with the east reminding us of spring, of green and growing things, of a time when the world was young – and then move to

Figure 1.1

The six directions

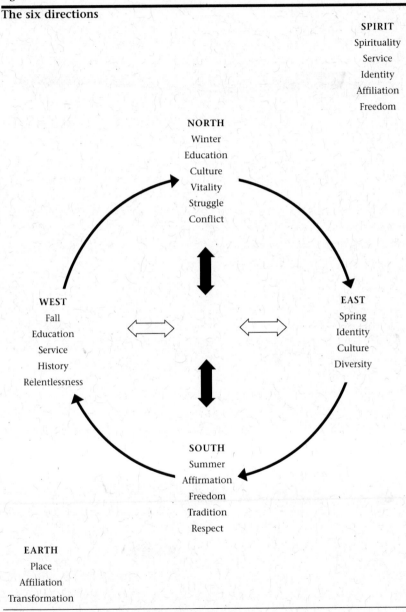

the south, and the full light of traditional education as it developed and
served the tribes of this continent for thousands of years – and then move

to the west, to the western twilight of European conquest – and to the north, the great winter of the reservation period, we see the hardy seeds of traditional cultures ready for rebirth, a new life, a new day in a new world. The pattern suggests hope where few but Indians would find it. In the turning of the seasons and in the natural processes of nature, we see a new spring. The European tendency to see history as a linear progression is different and does not nourish my hope so well.

As I worked on the explication of this six-directional pattern of Indian education, it was encouraging to find other authors who were using organizing principles rooted in tribal or natural sensibilities. As part of an effort 'to minimize academic scaffolding' and 'to root scholarship in living experience and dialogical interaction,' Kenneth Lincoln and Al Slagle (1987) organize their book, *The Good Red Road: Passages into Native America* into four narrative parts: 'Wintering home,' 'Spring tribe,' 'Summer visions,' and 'Fall return.' Their ethnographical narrative is strongly auto-biographical where necessary, and the book is one of a growing body of works that takes the dialogue between cultures seriously.

As humans, we always know far more than we can say (Polanyi 1964). What I can say about the interviews are the simple things that almost every-one agreed on. This agreement makes these simple things worth writing down in the hope that others will test them and see if they also agree. I coded the interview data into eight categories: place, identity, spiri-tual, culture, affiliation, education, freedom, and service. In this section, I organize the eight categories and discuss the interview data in relation to the six-directional pattern, integrating my own experience and other authors' discussions of Indian education. All quotes from the interviews are identified by a two-letter person code. Working from the interview data I suggest twelve standards for Indian education on which I believe Indians will generally agree – standards that should be addressed by any theory of Indian education.

The relationships between the six directions, interview categories (themes), and the standards for Indian education are complex. Generally, I let the directions and the interview data evoke meanings and I then summarized the meanings in standards. Figure 1.1 graphically states the relationships, which should be understood as dynamic and overlapping. The four directions (or winds) are commonly associated with the four sea-sons as well as with dawn, midday, sunset, and night so that seasonal and temporal as well as spatial concepts are evoked. The pattern is further complicated by my historical understanding of east as the time of origin, south as the flowering of traditional culture and methods of education, west as the period of European invasion, and north as the continuing conquest and subjugation of Indian nations. The remaining two directions, heaven (spirit) and earth, evoke meaning associated with the great mystery – the ultimate source – and mother earth, the sustainer and source of rebirth. The cosmology I describe is syncretistic because I have had teachers from different cultures. My understanding of these things is necessarily limited by my own experience and abilities and I ask the reader to be cautious in interpreting this writing, taking only what you can find out for yourself.

Spirit

Starting at the centre of the six directions and looking to the Great Spirit we begin with the issues of identity and spirituality.

> I feel like internal development is part of being Indian and part of being spiritual. That's linked. External development is important but I think that internal development is the more important. I have been raised that internal development is much more important. But, they affect each other and can't be separated. (SW)

> My view of education is that the individual is not only responsible for educating the mind with the facts but also for nurturing the soul. (CM)

The first standard of Indian education is *spirituality*. At its centre is respect for the spiritual relationships that exist between all things. In the six-directional pattern, education starts with prayer, standing in the centre of the world and looking towards the sky. The central prayer is, 'Help me for my people's sake.' Or as Brown (1971) translates it, 'Have mercy on me that my people may live.' Another version that I have often heard is, 'Pity me ... for all my relatives.' The first time I fasted for a vision I remember that prayer working on me, defining me, creating deep within me an identity as an expression of my people. The prayer seemed at the same time to exalt and humble me as an autonomous individual in union with and able to work for my people.

It is through me no less than anyone else that my people live. As one of my teachers told me when I felt conflicts between being Indian and being educated, 'There is not just one way for an Indian to live because you are life.' The prayer is answered with identity, an unalienated self. On the second day of the fast, as I prayed I began to ask myself, 'Who are my people?' Over the following days my identity expanded from my own skin outwards to family, friends, relatives, Indian people, other humans, animals, growing things, to finally reach the earth itself and everything that is. I came away from the fast with a deep awareness of feeling at home, related to all that is.

The vision quest and the prayer for one's self as an expression of the people's life is a crystallization of one of the most powerful forces of Indian cultural identity. And it is expressed in service 'for my people's sake,' 'that my people may live,' and 'for all my relatives.'

[Is it] better to just come to university and just get skills, go for learning skills, or to try to involve your own spiritual background? And we were talking and I said I thought you would be using both no matter what. Just by who you are. Then, on the other hand, the true spirituality is in participating in it, in that life. And, the trouble we have in education is trying to get the two together. We are all God's children. We all have that potential in us, that life. (WM)

Everyone's intent is to go back home. We are doing all this so that we can help our people, a tribe or Indians in general. Most of the students I talk to show concern for being of service in the Indian community, or concern for people, maybe it's general. I didn't hear it typically outside of our group, and I've been with a lot of non-Indians in school. We must get it from home. I get it from home. Like there's a purpose, you know, and [I] talk about it with my mother and my brother, and other people. (SW)

They're all programs that conceivably could make one better able to go back home wherever that is, whether it's a reservation or whatever community that is. And utilize those skills. So they would then be able to make things better for others and would be role models for kids to grow up to be like. And they'd be able to run, conceivably would be able to help run tribal groups or tribal things so that outsiders weren't necessary. I'm not sure it works that way, but that's how I see it ideally working ... I said, have you ever worked with American Indian tribes? He said, no. I said, well, to be honest with you, working with tribal groups is the biggest pain in the ass I've ever experienced in my whole damn life. I think I'd almost rather take a beating with a stick than work with any tribal group on a long-term basis. That doesn't mean I won't go back and work with Indian people. That commitment's there within me. And no matter what I do I always end up working with Indian people ... I'll always do it and I'll always bitch about it, and that's the reality of it. And so until you've worked with them you can't know what it's like. So that's, you know, I don't know how much that answers it, but that for me is it ... (TM)

You get 99 per cent of Indian students who come to school and say that's what I want to do. I want to learn something and go back and see if I can be of some service to my people ... It'll help. It is pretty strong in a lot of people to give the children something, a gift of some sort to them, that they can carry on, the next generation. (WM)

Indian education orients itself around a spiritual centre that defines the individual as the life of the group. The freedom and strength of the individual is the strength of the group. I was struck by the intense feelings of group membership and individual freedom. This wider identity is celebrated and perhaps promoted by rituals (Rappaport 1978). The tension that Levine and White (1986) find between social ligatures and individual options is resolved in Indian cultures by a process of identity recognition. The individual does not form an identity in opposition to the group but recognizes the group as relatives included in his or her own identity.

The second standard of Indian education is *service*. Education is to serve the people. Its purpose is not individual advancement or status. As Levine and White point out, Western society and education too often promote and glorify individual options for achievement at the expense of the social connections that make achievement meaningful. There is an inevitable conflict between Western education and Indian education on this point. The competitive success of the individual is an implicit value of Western schools and, as such, is in direct conflict with the Indian value of group success through individual achievement.

The Indian student enrolled in an Anglo school, which not only exalts Anglo values but sets the individual in opposition to the group, will feel the conflict between being Indian and being educated.

Going to [school], there's a certain amount of alienation from our people inherent in doing that. The people back home kind of admire you but also don't like it. There's a mix, there's ambivalence. (SW)

It is no light matter for an Indian graduate student to articulate a communal purpose in his or her education. Virtually all these students fulfil that purpose, working with and for Indian people. Today's educated Indian is a triumph of Indian people over a school system that in most senses is the enemy (Wolcott 1987). The reasons that Indians have persevered, have not vanished, and are the continuance of hope for Indian education, are rooted in the spiritual values and traditions that make us who we are. These traditions stretch back into the dawn of our existence as Indian peoples, and it is the morning star of the east that reminds us of what is Indian, the origins of our existence.

East

East is the direction of spring. I remember an early spring in Minnesota. The roads were still lined with banks of snow, snow fouled by thousands of cars, grimy and dirty in the bright spring sunlight. Car shit I usually called it as I trudged up the hill to work. But this day was different. The sunlight seemed to meet its own reflection inside me. I had been in a sweat lodge ceremony the day before, and I kicked through the car shit with childish joy. Looking with new eyes, I saw that the particles of dirt and soot had gathered the sun's warmth and melted tiny caverns into the snow bank, tiny jewelled caverns with rainbow colours on their walls.

I began to smile at myself – finding rainbows in the car shit – and then I laughed out loud. There frozen into the snow was a five dollar bill. I chipped it out, folded it into my shirt pocket, and continued up the hill. In the mail room at work I picked up the new issue of *Accession Notes* and noticed an article by Gael High Pine, 'The Great Spirit in the Modern World' (1973). Her first paragraph gripped my heart, 'It is not important to preserve our traditions, it is important to allow our traditions to preserve us.' And then the final paragraph changed my life. On the morning that I found jewelled rainbow caverns in the car shit, I read, 'My children, there is no modern world, there is no Indian world. There is only the Great Spirit's world and the same Creator who made the beautiful forests traces the cracks in the sidewalks and puts rainbows in the oil slicks on city streets.'

Walking the circle of Indian education, facing the east, it is traditional to pray for our children. It is an Indian tradition – it is a deeply human tradition – to pray for future generations. Those traditions – those prayers, hopes, and dreams of our Old Ones – mark us as much as, perhaps more than, their defeats, their fears, and their errors. To educate ourselves and our children, we must start with who we are, with the traditions, the values, and the ways of life that we absorbed as children of the people. An elder told me, 'I am just one day old.' This day connects our past and future, the child within to the elder we hope to become. The identity of Indian people is that which links our history and our future to this day, now.

A history of a people who relived their history for the sheer joy of dancing and storytelling are almost forgotten. These old people were human beings with failings of course. But their way of life, their history, their peoples were so advanced – much older than the people themselves. And these peoples' Chiefs flowed out of – but never away from – their life which was older than themselves. (Toghotthele Corporation 1983, 26)

To answer the questions of Indian education, we must recognize our *identity* – past, present, and future – and confront Ira Hays's question, 'What's an Indian anyway?' (Cash 1962). Finding that the US federal government used over 100 different definitions of 'Indian,' the Department of Education commissioned a report in 1984 on 'The Definition of Indian' and held hearings from Boston to Alaska. The conclusion of the report was that the more precisely Indian was defined, the more unreliable the results were.

So who is an Indian today? The BIA director in Sacramento testified before a 1954 Senate committee:

I just don't think there is any definition that you can give to an Indian. He is an Indian for some purposes and for other purposes he isn't an Indian. I am sorry, I cannot make a definition. We in the Indian Bureau are concerned with it also. We don't know how to define an Indian. (Cited in Lincoln and Slagle 1987, 68)

My first foray into Indian education other than as a student was in Mankato, Minnesota, the site of America's largest mass-hanging. In 1892, thirty-eight Sioux Indians were hanged there. The third year that I was in Mankato, the chamber of commerce asked for a meeting with the Indian students. The chamber wanted to organize an annual historical pageant, a tourist attraction, depicting the hanging. As I listened to the chamber's executive secretary propounding the educational and economic value of the pageant, I saw in the faces of the other Indians my own feelings. One hundred and twenty years were as nothing to the spirits who touched our restless nights with their pain, and I knew that there would be no pageant. Our turn to speak and each student in turn opened his or her talk with a statement.
'I am Lakota ...'
'I am Creek ...'
'I am Ojibway ...'
'I am Chickasaw ...'
'I am Winnebago ...'
'I am Dakota ...'
Bewildered at last, the secretary rightly focused his question on the first statement that he had heard from each of us, 'What is it that all Indians

have in common?' Iris Drew, the Creek, answered for all of us with the true bitter-sweet joke, 'The white man.' As so many Indians have pointed out, Indian identity is essentially tribal. 'Indian' originated as a case of mistaken identity. Columbus persisted in his error throughout his life and went to his grave convinced he had discovered a new route to India. 'Tribalism' is a good word to most Indians.

The people of this continent trace their tribal diversity back to the dawn of time. The east is a direction of beginnings and reminds us that our cultural differences are not a recent development. *Diversity* is the third standard of Indian education. Multiplicity, diversity, tribalism, and community-based education are words that point to the active implementation of diverse cultures. Local control is a defining characteristic of Indian education, not just a philosophical or political good. There can be no true Indian education without Indian control. Anything else is white education applied to Indians. Indian control is dependent on a specific Indian community. The fact that over half the Indian community lives in multi-tribal, multicultural urban areas complicates the issue by requiring that Indians of different tribes cooperate to implement their multitribal definition of Indian education.

> Indian education as it should be would focus on the values of individual tribal groups, the kinds of things that the parents from those groups wanted their kids to learn, specific to their tribe. Something that stresses the language so the kids have the language. So kids understand that while being Indian is different, that there is nothing negative about that. (CM)

The east reminds me that our cultures reach back to the time of beginnings. Each Indian culture is a pattern of relationships and has its own way of thinking and communicating. There are enough general differences between white cultures and Indian cultures to point to some likely sources of misunderstanding, conflicts rooted in our origins, but the lessons of conflict and transformation are for the north and the earth. The lesson of the east is that we exist as distinctive peoples. We have our ways, culture is real.

> [In white universities] you are encouraged to criticize your colleagues or somebody you don't agree with and sometimes, to me, that looks kind of harmful. Sometimes what you are learning is that you have to be critical in order to succeed at what you are learning. That's hard. I understand constructive criticism and not constructive criticism. But, it's just that one of the things they teach is that critical thinking. It has its advantages. But,

the Indian child when he sits, he listens to his grandparents or his parents. He's not going to criticize what they say. And he is listening, taking, trying to do what they say ... respectfully. And even when they're older, like myself, I thank the old people, and they tell me. I don't criticize what they say. I take what they say and I'm glad of it. Especially since nowadays there is so little of that wisdom.

A lot of the kids are growing up to criticize their own ways, their own language, their parents, the teaching, the older people ... criticizing people. It's funny that it took that form. I even heard someone say, 'You don't know what you're talking about.' I've heard them say that. It hurts to hear young people say, 'You don't know what you're talking about.' So, it has its harmful effects: encouragement to use critical skills. I hate to do it. But, at times I do it. Reflective thinking should go along with it. I think reflective thinking would also be something that we try to transmit. (WM)

Reflective thinking suggests a habit of mind that thoughtfully considers a speaker's words and seeks in them for what can be built on. This style of thought may underlie the longer 'wait times' commonly heard among Indian speakers. Carol Barnhardt (1982), in searching for reasons why Native students succeeded in Alaskan schools with more than 50 per cent Native faculty, studied video tapes of Native and non-Native teachers of Native children. On first impression, the teachers seemed similar in their use of a variety of conventional teaching methods, but closer examination of the tapes using a metronome disclosed a phenomenon she called 'tuning in.' Both students and teachers had a rhythm and tempo in both their body movements and in their talk. White teachers set the rhythms in their classrooms, while Indian teachers observed and then matched student rhythms.

It would be misleading to fix on reflective thought, or wait time, or tuning in as characteristics of Indian education. The data are not strong enough yet, and it would be too easy to focus on what may be artifacts or gimmicks. What is essential to recognize is that there are culturally characteristic ways of thought and communication that are of value and interest in themselves and worthy of consideration and study. A teacher with no knowledge or interest in such topics is incompetent in multicultural settings.

These ways of thinking are language-based as well as culture-based. Pinxten, van Dooren, and Harvey (1983), in their brilliant *Anthropology of Space*, show a possible relationship between Navajo language and the teaching of mathematics to Navajo-speaking students. By carefully delineating the spatial concepts embedded in the Navajo language, they were able to specify some important differences between Navajo spatial language and English. In Navajo, for example, it is relatively easier to speak of centres than boundaries. Dynamic shapes are more commonly dealt with than static shapes, and order and position seem more salient than number. From these and other examples, Pinxten argues that concepts such as triangle and square, and operations such as counting, which are elementary for English-speaking students (embedded as they are in the language and culture) are in fact difficult abstracts for Navajo-speaking students.

Pinxten further argues that the concepts of dynamic topology and fuzzy sets, difficult and abstract as they seem for speakers of English, are, in fact, elementary for Navajo speakers. He thus turns mathematics education on its head with the suggestion that Navajo- and English-speaking students require radically different curricula. For Navajo students, dynamic topology and fuzzy sets belong in the primary grades rather than in graduate school. His work also has important implications for the construction of so-called 'culture-fair' tests, suggesting that this effort is doomed to failure at best and is a sham at worst. Pinxten's results may be of crucial importance for Indian education and deserve further study.

Vera John-Steiner and her associates (1975) found a striking difference between forty Pueblo interviewees describing learning by observation and fifty whites giving only one instance of learning by observation. Some teachers have difficulty with the concept of equally valid learning styles. One, unblushingly, described learning by observation as 'lazy learning' and told of chastising Native students for not asking questions and participating. When one of the students attempted to explain to her that they were carefully watching out of respect and would indicate appreciation as soon as they were ready, she argued that other Native students were participating and expelled the observers from class. Later conversations with her led to the realization that she forced herself to participate in spite of her deep feelings of inferiority and incompetence. It seemed to me that she was projecting these feelings onto Native students and angrily demanding that they overcompensate for non-existent feelings of inadequacy rather than realizing their comfort and feeling of competency with a learning style different from her own. The respect for diversity embodied in the third standard of Indian education requires self-knowledge and self-respect, without which respect for others is impossible.

Two of the people I interviewed deserve to be quoted extensively. Both are highly successful Indian educators who are doing excellent graduate work at Harvard. They still struggle with the difference between Anglo and Indian thought and communication styles.

It seems as if in the homes and the upbringing of Anglo children, that they must have talked about things or looked at life a certain way that differed from the way we looked at things at home. I use the word holistic ... I don't know if that really describes what I mean but it's the best word that I can find, of how I view life or think about life, as things being very connected and that you don't separate and look at something just in and of itself. But I went to the same schools. I went to white schools, so I had that white education and I was able to compete pretty successfully and yet I came out still feeling like, as far as logical thinking and analytical thinking, somewhere that was not reinforced either in school or in my home, but I think I had a very similar education to most white people and I wonder why so many of them seem to think so much differently and have that ability to look at things in detail or see the details, whereas I look upon the whole. (LW)

You can follow a paper down and understand what they are saying, but you don't understand why they don't understand what you're saying, because, to you, your logic is there, but it's not recognized as being logical. Another thing is that – is always writing on obvious things, describing obvious things, and I don't know how to do it, I have a hard time doing that. If a white man wanted to describe a can, he could probably take up three pages describing that can! I would probably look at the things that were not obvious about a can, and yet, if you were writing a paper, that's how you would write a paper here, you would say, well, it's so tall, and it's round and all of these things, and yet, you or I would look at it and see that, I mean that would be obvious, so you wouldn't bother with those kind of things. We were talking a lot about that and what is logical to us and what is logical to the instructors here, or what is obvious to us and what is not obvious, I guess. We thought it was funny.

I look at papers ... when I write papers, I want to say things that will create some thought in the person that's reading them, and I find out that that kind of style is not acceptable. You have to state everything obviously ... and not trust in someone else's intellectual ability to draw their own conclusions or make their own inferences. You have to lay that all out for them. It's weird.

I remember being in a class one day, and the instructor wanted to start discussing the readings. So, he asked questions about the readings, 'What was so and so's theory?' and nobody said anything. The whole class was just silent for about a minute, so it was obvious that very few people had done the reading. Well, I had done the reading, but I'm usually quite verbal in this course and I just decided to lay back and not say anything. So, about a minute of silence had gone by, and finally I said, 'Well, Joe, don't you know?!' (laughter). The whole class was cracked up, nobody got serious for the rest of the class. But, I think that exemplifies that we ask students, when we're teachers, we and teachers, you know, other teachers, they ask people the obvious. I've been fighting that traumatically at times. I came away from one class with a paper that I thought was fantastic. I was so proud of it when I handed it in. I just thought it was a great paper, I put a lot of time and effort into it. I put my heart into it, really thinking about things. When I got it back I felt like I was mutilated. I felt like someone just stood there with a knife and just cut me all to shreds. To me there were so many things in it that were obvious. I had my brother read the paper and I had other people read the paper because I was really trying to give a good paper. It was like the person who read the paper was stupid, and she is not a stupid woman; far from it, but the comments she made were that I hadn't explained what I thought were obvious points. It really shook me and made me start thinking about how we think and how we relate this in our papers. There is a big gap there, and I don't know how to close it. I'm trying very hard. (HW)

The fourth standard of Indian education is *culture*. Indian cultures have ways of thought, learning, teaching, and communicating that are different from, but as valid as, those of white cultures. These thought-ways stand at the beginning of Indian time and are the foundations of our children's lives. Their full flower is being one of the people.

South

The south is the direction of summer, the home of the sun, and the time of fullest growth. It is clear that just as the seasons come and go, so too Indian education has its seasons of increase and decline. The summer of Indian education was before the European invasion. Oral histories, the narratives of early European plunderers, and current traditional practices give us a partial understanding of traditional education and how it adapted to the invasion.

It is sort of a clue to what might be a solution to hard work. I used to realize that a lot of what Indian people did was a lot of hard work to make everything so much from scratch. What the sweat taught me was the way spirituality lightens the load. By praying over every step of the process of putting together the sweat lodge, then the impact of that work becomes less because everything has so much meaning. (MW)

In the interviews I asked for a definition of Native education. Most participants gave historically conditioned descriptive and prescriptive definitions. The responses of the participants, what they got 'back home,' are indications of the persistence of traditional educational methods.

Back home character is stressed and that came first [before technique]. Indian education, I mean typical back home or how they used to do it, was that they didn't separate education from living, from everyday living's requirement. (SW)

The fifth standard of Indian education is *tradition*: Indian education maintains a continuity with tradition. Our traditions define and preserve us. It is important to understand that this continuity with tradition is neither a rejection of the artifacts of other cultures nor an attempt to 'turn back the clock.' Asking Natives to eschew automobiles, television, and bank accounts in the name of 'preserving their culture' makes as much sense as asking whites to give up gunpowder because it was invented by the Chinese or the zero because it was invented by Arabs. It is the continuity of a living culture that is important to Indian education, not the preservation of a frozen museum specimen. 'If a snowmobile is perceived to have greater utility than a dog sled, then the ownership of a snowmobile will become one of the criteria defining the traditional hunter' (Kemp 1971).

For most Native groups, summer is a time when people get together. Feasts, potlatches, ceremonies continue to be an important part of Native life. In all of the interviews I asked, 'If you were to pick out a typical AIP [American Indian Program at Harvard] event, situation, or interaction in which you were involved, what would it be?' Most participants had a similar response:

I suppose it's the potluck suppers and those get togethers we have from time to time where everybody brings something and pitches in and helps out and everybody gets together for sitting down and having something to eat. That's been a fairly typical experience among tribes all over. Coming together, sit down and share something to eat, then maybe have something after whatever. But it's that getting together to eat kind of thing which is very typical of Indian get togethers all over, the tribes that I've seen anyway. I sense that Indian people have a preconception for community. I mean the idea of community is important, and I think psychologically that has positive impact. (IM)

In a small way, these potlucks express the gathering of the people, affirming each individual's freedom and the group identity.

The one that I think comes to mind first are the potlucks, the informal gathering, I mean informal but structured. And it's like, come as you are, just bring, come if you can come, if you can't, no hassle about it. Except it's just to bring food. And then you have to do that. But it's a structuring of, here's a time and a place where we as a group are going to get together. And in my mind, I mean, I think that's pretty significant, that we do that. Because I remember it afterwards, I don't always remember especially having a great time or being comfortable, but I always remember being compelled to come and wanting to come, and meeting people and stuff. And the differences, kind of even are set aside for a while. And another facet of it is, I've often thought of bringing non-Indians there and wondered whether I should or not. I mean it doesn't matter one way or the other when other people bring them. I mean I don't care, it doesn't matter, it doesn't change it. But it's an Indian thing, I think. The food is Indian, mostly Indian, the jokes, and the way we interact. (PM)

The comfort whenever we're here together and enjoying another's company, the other people's company, but also not feeling put upon to have to be maybe, I can't be sure, but I think just the ability to say nope. I don't want to do that. And a little bit of pressure but nothing that people are going to say, oh, he's an awful person or she's an awful person, because they're still a part of our group of people. But more than anything I'd say the way that people use humor. Everybody bringing something that they think other people are going to want to eat and they're going to want to eat themselves. And some people getting here early and some people getting here on time and some people getting here late. And everybody being pretty happy about it. Teasing everybody around about this or that, kind of catching up a little bit. Just a chance to get together and share a bit of our lives. I feel good about being a part of a community. (LM)

Those that sit back and probably do nothing, you don't really notice them I guess. Things just sort of get done, everyone contributes, you don't really notice how much any one person is contributing necessarily. (MW)

Europeans summed up their difficulty in understanding and dealing with Native forms of organization by saying 'too many chiefs and not enough Indians.' The individual Indian's sense of personal power and autonomy is a strength that lies behind the apparent weakness of disunity. I believe we would have indeed vanished if we had confronted the European invaders with a unified hierarchical structure. Our survival rests on the fact that *each* Indian is at heart a king or queen who serves the people.

The Indian program makes the student aware that they are Indians and that they are here to help each other to share in the community setting. Rather than bringing each one in as a separate entity and treating each one as a go your own way, do you own thing. It is trying to help each other become aware of each other. (PM)

The quality of the group is dependent on the qualities of the individuals. And the strength of that group and the clarity of that group depends on the strength and clarity of the individuals. And somehow, I don't know how, but being Indian, being Native American, there is an essence to that. You know, that no matter how much we can change on the inessentials, there is a core, an essence of being who we are that makes us who we are. (LM)

The sixth standard is *respect*. Indian education demands relationships of personal respect.

West

The west is the direction of autumn, the end of summer, and the precursor of winter. On the great plains, thunderstorms roll in from the west. In Lakota cosmology, the good red road of life runs north and south and the road of death runs east and west.

The coming of Western civilization (meaning western Europe), with its Western forms of education, to this continent was the autumn of traditional Indian education. In the fall, the wild grass dies. The Europeans took our land, our lives, and our children like the winter snow takes the grass. The loss is painful but the seed lives in spite of the snow. In the fall of the year, the grass dies and drops its seed to lie hidden under the snow. Perhaps the snow thinks the seed has vanished but it lives on hidden, or blowing in the wind, or clinging to the plant's leg of progress.

How does the acorn unfold into an oak? Deep inside itself it knows –

and we are not different. We know deep inside ourselves the pattern of life. The source of our traditions is present.

It is good that the pattern of six directions reminds us of fall and winter, because otherwise we might not speak directly of some of the harsher realities of Indian education. As often as I had been through the interview transcripts, by the time I came to write this section, I still could not recall any instances of conversations dealing directly with the European conquest and subsequent exploitation and domination. Even a thorough search failed to find these themes. Indirectly, the conquest influences almost all the themes. One of the participants in this research gently chided herself along with me for falling into a pattern of we-they thinking and speech. 'Listen to us, "we-they."'

Wolcott (1987) suggests that white teachers of Native students would do less harm if they recognized their status as enemies (not personal, but cultural) of their students.

> I think that I might have been a more effective teacher if I had taken the perspective of regarding the teacher, me, as an enemy. By effective I mean that I would have remained more objective about my lack of success, and I would have been more sensitive to the high cost for each pupil by accepting me or my instructional program. Appropriate to antagonistic acculturation as manifested in school might be an analogy to a prisoner-of-war camp. The purpose of instruction is to recruit new members into their society by encouraging prisoners to defect, and achieving this by giving them the skills so that they can do so effectively. (p. 420)

Certainly, it seems that it is good for those concerned with education to face unflinchingly Native perspectives on the history and politics of education.

Physical, mental, and spiritual – it is all one thing to the Indian. Physical effects of the conquest on Indian education include otitis media, fetal alcohol syndrome, material poverty, poor housing, poor nutrition. Treaty provisions were not met, schools were not built, teachers were not sent. The mental effects include the erosion of our self-concept, denial of worth, the outlawing of languages. The spiritual effects include the outlawing of our worship, the imposition of Christian denominationalism, the destruction of Indian families. Standard seven is *history*. Indian education has a sense of history and does not avoid the hard facts of the conquest of America.

Standard eight is *relentlessness*. Indian education is relentless in its battle for Indian children. We take pride in our warriors, and our teachers are warriors for the life of our children. The war is not between Indian and white but between that which honours life and that which does not. It is fought within ourselves as well as in the world. We are as relentless as seeds breaking through concrete.

North

North is the home of winter. It is the time of night and evokes thoughts and feelings of those times. Both have their positive aspects, but it is their difficulties and their challenge that are in my mind when I think of contemporary Indian education. The north demands that we understand survival; it teaches endurance and wisdom. Its lessons can be hard and it is not enough to be good, or smart. The north demands knowledge.

The current situation in Indian education is cold and dark with just a hint of light that makes it possible to hope for spring. The horrors that Native people are going through are not as bad as the horrors that previous generations faced, and the fact that we have survived and are in some ways stronger bodes well for our future. It is important, therefore, to understand both the statistics of pain and the rays of hope.

The post-invasion story of Native education is almost always told as the story of white education applied to Natives. The other story of individual and tribal educational initiatives is much harder to tell. It is not one story but many individual stories of which we have only scattered and fragmentary knowledge.

I start with the clearest example in print of the way many whites have viewed Native culture. It is commonplace to recognize the tendency to project onto Native people the alienated attributes of European society so that Natives are seen as either noble savages or degenerate races. I have nowhere found the stereotyping so clearly drawn as in the two books by Colin Turnbull, *The Forest People* (1961) and *The Mountain People* (1972). The fact that he is writing about African Natives rather than Native Americans in terms that are completely transposable between continents makes it clear that the books are really about the European mind.

Turnbull describes the Forest People as noble savages: open, loving, creative. Although innocent and childlike, they possess wisdom and are noble in all respects. Even if we make generous allowance for Turnbull's projection of alienated attributes of European society, these people can be seen as relatively free people enjoying a high quality of life by their own admirable standards. By contrast, the Mountain People are a miserable lot. They are hostile, suspicious, torn by crime, and have a full range of problems including devastating generation gaps. Again, we must make allowances for Turnbull's projection, in this case of the undesirable aspects of European society, in order to attain a picture of a people that are relatively oppressed, fearful, with a 'low quality of life,' and over-whelmed by issues of day-to-day survival.

Several things are striking about Turnbull's work. First, there is his per-verse ignorance of the different colonial contexts of these two peoples. He attributes their differences to culture or morality and seems blissfully ignorant of the vast difference in levels of oppression that the two groups endured. Everywhere on the globe at all times, history is unequivocal: col-onization brings misery and societal dysfunction. Although Turnbull might argue the strength of the statement, he can hardly be ignorant of the general relationship. He is, however, quite capable of ignoring the sin-gle greatest determinant of the Mountain People's pain.

Second, it is instructive to read his descriptions of the two groups for par-allels with Western society. Clearly, the Mountain People with their crime, suicide, and competition between generations are strikingly similar to Western societies. Nevertheless, he strongly, even desperately, argues that the Mountain People's children should be taken from them and raised by Europeans. He completely neglects the fact that European society is suffer-ing from the same ills which he criticizes in the Mountain People, that the ills were inflicted on the Mountain People by the Europeans, and that his suggestion would see the children suffer even more than the parents.

Turnbull argues that the Natives' children should be taken from them for their own good. So must I lay aside my incredulity and patiently tutor him with the examples of Indian Affairs boarding schools? No, that would be misdirected and fruitless. The delusion is self-sustaining. What then shall we do to protect ourselves from those millions of whites, high and low, who believe that all others are deluded and that they know what is best for the Indian? I have heard countless white educators passionately, even desperately, argue for their vision of Native education. Their despera-tion to save the Indian on white terms makes me believe that it is their own world-view that the existence of Indians threatens. We are victims of the best intentions of white educators.

I believe it is clear that white educational systems and procedures are not competent to educate Indian peoples. This is not simply an inability to admit failure. I believe that Indian children struggle against a patholog-ical complex endemic to North American society. The pathology is made up of the largely unconscious processes of: (1) a perverse ignorance of the facts of racism and oppression; (2) delusions of superiority, motivated by fear of inadequacy; (3) a vicious spiral of self-justifying action, as the blame is shifted to the victims who must be 'helped,' that is, controlled for their own good; and (4) denial that the oppressor profits from the oppression materially, as well as by casting themselves as superior, powerful, and altruistic persons. Indian children face a daily struggle against attacks on their identity, their intelligence, their way of life, their essential worth. They must continually struggle to find self-worth, dignity, and freedom in being who they are. I know that I participate in my own oppression. I did not make the winter wind but I have sometimes carried it to my children. I could not always shelter them but I am relentless in my effort.

All Native communities suffer from these forms of oppression. It is a mark of human strength and resilience that Indians continue to survive and individual Indians manage to make productive lives despite the extremes of the oppression that they face. The problem is how to paint a picture of the horrors that is not overwhelming and that does full justice to the strengths and resilience of Native people. We have been through the fiery furnace of war for a continent, and we have been quenched in the icy waters of indifference. We lost the continent, and for five generations we have been told that we are a 'vanishing race.'

Standard nine is *vitality*. Indian education recognizes and nourishes the powerful pattern of life that lies hidden within personal and tribal suffering and oppression. Suffering begets strength. We have not vanished.

Statistics show the inroads of winter. Just as counting the dead plants is an inadequate measure of the life of the seeds, so counting the deaths, the alcoholism rates, the suicides, the murders, and the dropouts is inadequate to measure the vitality of Native life. The horrors and indescribable pain of Native existence after the European conquest cannot be minimized. Neither can the vitality of Native resistance and resurgence.

Native education cannot be understood without the concepts of oppression and resistance (Iverson 1978; Churchill 1982; Jennings 1975; Deloria 1982). Cultural genocide is the open but unacknowledged policy of every white educator who says, 'These people must learn what we have to teach.' Wolcott (1987) has offered a provocative analysis of *the teacher as an enemy*. He shows how the resistance and hostility of Native students is an assertion of Indian integrity. If educators realize that they are agents of cultural brainwashing rather than altruistic helpers, much that is otherwise incomprehensible becomes self-evident.

Standard ten is *conflict*. Indian education recognizes the conflict, tensions, and struggle between itself and white education as well as with education generally. Western education is in content and structure hostile to Native people. It must be straightforwardly realized that education, as currently practised, is cultural genocide. It seeks to brainwash the Native child, substituting non-Native for Native knowledge, values, and identity. The individual teacher, administrator, or counsellor may, indeed should, attempt to mitigate or subvert the purpose of Western education but in so doing assumes a difficult and ambiguous position. I may seem to be over-stating the case, so it is worthwhile considering carefully the inherent contradictions between Western education and Native cultures, as well as the plight of the well-intentioned educator.

Let us start with the concept of perverse ignorance. By perverse igno-rance, I mean motivated apparent ignorance about issues of culture or race. I have heard otherwise intelligent educators make statements such as: 'Indians don't take to education any better than they do to farming.' 'Culture doesn't matter. I read about seals and polar bears when I was growing up in Iowa, and that's the same as these Inupiat kids reading about trees.' These statements are logical only if the speaker is truly igno-rant of facts that they clearly know. The first statement was made by a dis-tinguished professor of educational sociology, who in other contexts knew that many Indian groups were excellent farmers; that several Indian tribes had implemented exemplary schools; and that, in fact, the type of schooling and farming that Indians have rejected is schooling and farm-ing that was chosen, designed, and administered by non-Indians. The sec-ond statement was made by a highly regarded teacher with many years of experience teaching for the North Slope School District of Alaska. His statement rests on apparent ignorance of the fact that he read about seals in the language of his home community while Inupiat children read about trees in an alien language; the fact that the books about seals assumed that he knew little if anything about seals while the books the Inupiat children read about trees assume that everyone has seen a tree; and that trees, books, teachers, and schools are all common to his culture but alien to Inupiat culture.

The educator who sees education as culturally neutral is similar to the spouse of an alcoholic who denies the alcoholism. There are implications for practice, self-concept, and feelings that both are unable to face. Perverse ignorance is a particular form of the defence mechanism of denial. As such, it is an unconscious process that is 'compelled, negating, rigid, distorting of intersubjective reality and logic, allows covert impulse expression, and embodies the expectancy that anxiety can be relieved without directly addressing the problem' (Haan 1977, 34). It is under-standable that the educator with a self-concept tied to the ideal of helping children, with preparation that does not include multicultural compe-tence, with a curriculum that ignores or systematically distorts the culture of his or her students, and with unresolved personal issues of racism and ethnocentrism could not recognize the extent to which education is both culturally bound and actively hostile to Native culture.

Perhaps the most common statement I hear from white educators in varying forms is, 'These kids have got to learn this stuff for their own good.' Of course, that is the refrain from most of us when teaching subjects that do not appeal to our students, but it takes on another dimension in the cross-cultural situation. In the mono-cultural case, the subject content and structure are part of the student's own culture and, as such, are not subversive or hostile to the student. In the cross-cultural (and to a large extent in the subculture/dominant culture) case, the 'stuff' subverts the student's self-concept and cultural values. The educator who consciously recognizes this is free to develop mechanisms to cope with the real problem while the educator who allays anxiety by unconscious defence mechanisms is caught in a vicious spiral. The more the problems are denied, the less effective the teaching becomes and the more there is to be defended.

Western education is hostile in its structure, its curriculum, its context, and its personnel. First, the context of Western education is cultural. Whether we trace the beginning of schools to Greece or to the Roman attempt to standardize orthography throughout the empire, schools have been central in perpetuating Western civilization. The contemporary North American school is a political, social, and cultural institution that embodies and transmits the values, knowledge, and behaviours of white culture. The call for higher standards in education is invariably a call for the standard of the whites. It is never a call for a more adequate presentation of the knowledge of devalued minorities, creative thinking about pressing social problems, higher standards of equity and respect, or recognition of institutional racism. The idea that different cultures and different races may have equally worthy standards seems never to have crossed the minds of the proponents of 'higher standards.' Rather, they assume that they possess the one true yardstick and that any consideration of Blacks, Indians, Asians, or Chicanos would simply lower standards. The challenge is not higher standards on the yardstick that has give us a world in chaos but the negotiation of multicultural yardsticks. We live in a world of many cultures, all of which have different standards. It is not necessary to devalue the standards of Western society, except insofar as they claim to be the only worthwhile standards.

The structure of North American schools is hostile to Native cultures in ways that seem unavoidable to white educators. Age-segregated classrooms; Natives as janitors and teacher aides; role authority rather than kin and personal authority; learning by telling and questioning instead of observation and example; clock time instead of personal, social, and natural time; rules exalted above people and feelings; monolingual teachers;

alien standards; educated ignorance of cultural meanings and non-verbal messages; individual more than group tasks; convergent thinking; all these and more are structural features that undermine the Native child's culture. I do not argue that the child cannot learn another culture or even that there is not great value in knowing another's world, only that the structure is alien and hostile, not in intent, but in its assumption that it is the only way things should be (Schaef 1987). To use one example, to the extent that the school socializes the child to work individually, it subverts his or her cultural knowledge that while individual work is necessary and good, so is group work, especially group problem-solving.

As director of the Center School in Minneapolis, I was free to hire certified or non-certified faculty. After three years, I found that it took six months of hard work with good certified teachers to teach them to teach Native children and that even then they did not teach as well as uncertified non-white teachers. I found a negative correlation between certification and accreditation and the ability to educate Native children. The structures of school accreditation and teacher certification are hostile. They perpetuate schools that don't educate Indian children. The failure of schools to educate Indian students proves the incompetence of white educators to accredit schools and certify teachers for Native children.

The structure of North American education is hostile in its institutional racism. The standardized tests that are used to evaluate schools and students are the products of a white establishment that hires no Indian question writers, that uses test norms that are far from the reserve, and that assumes its own knowledge of both the relevant questions and the correct answers. The children of the elite grow up in homes that use a particular dialect of English and use it incessantly. Children are told what moves to make, then have their actions described to them as they perform them, and then are questioned about their actions.

In Barrow, Alaska, my friend's children will not do well on multiple-choice tests. Riding in a truck in companionable silence, all I could see was flat snow to the horizon when suddenly my friend's five-year old pointed. His father stopped the truck and got the binoculars out. He used them to look in the direction his son had pointed and nodded as he handed them to me. After some searching, I found five little dots in the snow. One moved. 'What are they?' I asked. 'Tutu' (caribou). 'Are you going to shoot them?' his son asked? 'No son, we have enough.' And to me, 'He has good eyes.'

Earth

The earth is our home. Our bodies come from and return to the earth.

The earth is stable through all our changes, we travel to the four directions and celebrate the passing seasons and still it is the earth we rest on. The earth sustains and comforts us as we are her children. We do not own this place – we belong to the land. It is an intensely personal relationship. My son, wiggling his toes in the mud, reminds me of eternity and time. Eternity, because I know the feel of it in the mud between my toes. Time, because the child I once was I still am – taught by the elder I may be. Humans do belong. The out-of-place feeling is just forgetting our place. We have a place, it is here. Generations of children our mother earth has borne. Her well-being is our grandchildren's future.

The earth reminds me of the importance of a sense of place. That theme was clearly linked to education in the interviews. Participants referred to 'back home,' 'on the res [reservation],' and 'the people at home' often and in varied contexts.

> It is a place to see other students about school work. It just kind of seems that most of the students taking course work in particular come in and out a lot in the AIP office. Sort of a stopping point ... oasis. Someone used that last year and I thought that that was a nice term. Learn a lot about the ed. school. So I guess basically I think territory is very important. (MW)

> Running into AIP students downstairs in the conference room is typical, you know. You just kind of greet each other or talk a few minutes about papers or what we're doing, just kind of chat a little bit. So that would be the typical interaction. (HW)

Territory is important. The American Indian Program at Harvard has been located in the Read House for the past fifteen years. Six years ago, when the program was temporarily without funds, the administration attempted to use that space for other purposes and give the students a meeting room in another building. Native students argued strongly and successfully the importance of continuity and tradition in location. Indian people feel the pain of being a minority in our own land. A sense of turf, a place that is Indian, a place where one is free to relax from the conventions of white society and be one's Native self is essential to well-being. In other institutions without an Indian program office or meeting place, I have seen Native students appropriate a Native faculty member's office for their turf.

Native community demands a place. The AIP lounge at Harvard is easily the grubbiest, most poorly maintained and furnished meeting area on campus. The linoleum is worn. The furniture is uncomfortable, worn out cast-offs from other Harvard offices, and the small room is cluttered with books and papers belonging to the fifteen students who use it. In spite of its drab and dingy appearance, the air seems a little freer there, laughter comes more easily, and Native people can feel at home with each other.

It serves as a home base away from home. It allows Indians to communicate with each other relatively free from interruption, from the Anglo world. Sort of a place of nurturing. (MW)

The nurturing effect of a place for Natives is not an isolating or segregating process, instead it frees people to be themselves and to make their contribution to non-Native society.

Even though we spend an awful lot of time together in here, I think in reality it decreases our isolation from the rest of the university for a number of reasons. One is the geographical, physical location. We come here a lot, which is easier to go to and from the library. To and from Longfellow [building], to and from classes. To and from anything. It's very difficult if you don't have a home base, and this is like a home base. Second, it helps us be visible as students, working with each other. For our per cent of numbers, a good many of us are very involved in the other HGSE [Harvard Graduate School of Education] community organizations. If you really look at us by numbers, I think that we're very active. We're very involved, and I think that if the AIP program wasn't here, where we all get together, encourage each other, let each other know what's going on, that we would be more isolated, we would tend to stay more in our rooms or our apartments and go to and from classes. And I don't think we would be as involved in the community, the HGSE community as a whole. But if you really look at it, I think that we're very involved.

Standard eleven is *place*. Indian education recognizes the importance of an Indian sense of place, land, and territory. From this point of view, it is clear that a uniquely Indian place promotes involvement rather than isolation or segregation. It is best to admit that in general Indians and whites have not worked well together. Certainly there have been many occasions of goodwill, but despite the friendliness and good intentions on both sides we have not done very well in most of the everyday business of life for most of our people. Part of the problem may be that there are some things that can only be said from an Indian place. The depth and breadth of misunderstandings and differences in perspective between Native and white is little understood. The differences are on at least three levels: personal, historical, and cultural. The transformation of personal, cultural, and historical misunderstanding into understanding demands that both Native and non-Native have a place to stand, that both accept the other's right to be, and that the fact of misunderstanding is recognized.

At the cultural level, Native and non-Native conceive of their meeting in different terms and do not understand the other's actions, thoughts, or purpose. Their sense of time, of space, of energy, of humanity, are all different. Truth, beauty, and justice are all marked and evaluated differently. Epistemology, ontology, and cosmology are all different. The European segments his or her thoughts, stories, and speeches in three and the Native in four. The list goes on and there is at once the richness of opportunity and the difficulty of communication.

At the historical level, Native and non-Native look at the world from opposed positions. Not only must they contend with personal differences in viewpoint, language, and experiences; not only must they contend with cultural differences in value, understandings of human relationships, and modes of communication; but they must contend with the world-shattering difference between the conquered and the conqueror, the exploited and the exploiter, the racist and the victim of racism. It is this historical difference of perspective that demands more than 'learning about each other's cultures.' It demands that we change the world. The graduates of our schools must not only be able to survive in a white-dominated society, they must contribute to the change of that society. Standard twelve is *transformation*. Indian education recognizes the need for transformation in relations between Indian and white as well as in the individual and society.

In Mankato, Minnesota, I walked down the stairs to a little convenience store, I stood in the aisle hesitating over the choice of soups when an old white man confronted me, 'Do you have a little time?'

I looked at him, shaking where he stood, bright eyes, open but complex face. I expected he wanted me to carry something and felt good to be chosen. I had the spacious time of youth and in his eyes I liked myself; strong, young, and respectful. 'Yes, I have time.'

'Wait here,' he said and walked away with the slow, small steps of a well-balanced old man. I stood with a slightly top-heavy feeling of youth's incipient motion until he slowly returned. He came up the aisle with a large cardboard box. It seemed empty and I was puzzled until he thrust it forward, holding it in front of my face. My centre of gravity dropped and I felt the earth's strength through my body. Relaxed and ready I waited for his move as I had learned to wait in the dojo, in alleys behind bars, in classrooms, and in sacred ceremonies. His question came from behind the box. 'How many sides do you see?'

'One,' I said.

He pulled the box towards his chest and turned it so one corner faced me. 'Now how many do you see?'

'Now I see three sides.'

He stepped back and extended the box, one corner towards him and one towards me. 'You and I together can see six sides of this box,' he told me. Standing on the earth with an old white man I began to understand. I had thought he wanted me to carry his groceries but instead he gave me something that carries me, protects me, and comforts me.

You can see that in writing about Indian education I am often so close that I can only see one side. Rarely am I able to step back and see one or two other sides but it takes many of us to see more than that. As in all conversations, it is the difference in our knowledge and language that makes the conversation difficult and worthwhile. It is this common earth that we stand on that makes communication possible. Standing on the earth with the smell of spring in the air, may we accept each other's right to live, to define, to think, and to speak.

Note

Another version of this chapter, entitled 'Toward a Redefinition of American Indian/Alaska Native Education,' appeared in *Canadian Journal of Native Education* 20, 2 (1993):261-309. The chapter originated as an Ed.D. dissertation at Harvard University, 1988.

References

American Indian Policy Review Commission. 1976. *Report on Indian education – Task force five: Indian education.* Washington, DC: Congress of the US

Barman, Jean, Yvonne Hébert, and Don McCaskill, eds. 1986. *Indian education in Canada.* Vol. 1, *The legacy.* Vancouver: UBC Press

–. 1987. *Indian education in Canada.* Vol. 2, *The challenge.* Vancouver: UBC Press

Barnhardt, C. 1982. Tuning-in: Athabaskan teachers and Athabaskan students. In R. Barnhardt, ed., *Cross-cultural issues in Alaskan education.* Vol. 2. Fairbanks: University of Alaska Center for Cross-Cultural Studies

Barnhardt, R. 1973. Being Native and becoming a teacher in the Alaska rural teacher training corps. In F. Berry, ed., *The collected papers of the northern cross-cultural education symposium.* Fairbanks: University of Alaska

–. 1985. *Maori makes a difference: Human resources for Maori development.* Waikato, New Zealand: University of Waikato

Barsh, R., and J. Henderson. 1980. *The road.* Berkeley: University of California Press

Berkhofer, R., Jr. 1978. *The white man's Indian: Images of the American Indian from Columbus to the present.* New York: Knopf

Bogdan, R., and S.K. Biklen. 1982. *Qualitative research for education.* Boston, MA: Allyn and Bacon

Brislin, R.W., W.J. Lonner, and R.M. Thorndike. 1973. *Cross-cultural research methods.* New York: Wiley

Brod, R.L., and J.M. McQuiston. 1983. American Indian adult education and literacy: The first national survey. *Journal of American Indian Education* 22:1-16

Brody, H. 1981. *Maps and dreams.* New York: Pantheon

Brown, J. 1971. *The sacred pipe: The seven rituals of the Oqalala Sioux.* Baltimore, MD: Penguin

Buffalohead, R. 1976. *Higher education of Indian students: 200 years of Indian education.* Tempe: Arizona State University Center for Indian Education

Carnoy, M. 1974. *Education as cultural imperialism.* New York: Longman

Cash, J. 1962. The ballad of Ira Hays. *Indian Drums.* Columbia Records. Album

Chavers, D. 1980. Isolation and drainoff: The case of the American Indian educational researcher. *Educational Researcher* 9:12-16

–. 1982. False promises: Barriers in American Indian education. *Integrateducation* 19:13-17

Cheek, H. 1984. A suggested research map for Native American mathematics education. *Journal of American Indian Education* 23:1-9

Churchill, W. 1982. White studies: The intellectual imperialism of contemporary US education. *Integrateducation* 19:51-7

Clignet, R. 1971. Damned if you do, damned if you don't: The dilemmas of colonizer-colonized relations. *Comparative Education Review* 15 (3):296-312

Coladarci, T. 1983. High school drop-out among Native Americans. *Journal of American Indian Education* 23 (1):15-22

Colorado, P. 1985. The concept of Native American alcoholism. Ph.D. dissertation, Brandeis University

Deloria, V. 1970. *We talk you listen.* New York: Macmillan

–. 1973. *God is red.* New York: Rosset and Dunlap

–. 1982. Education and imperialism. *Integrateducation* 19:58-63

Edwards, E., and L. Smith. 1981. Higher education and the American Indian student. *Journal of Humanics* 72-85

Equal Opportunity Commission. 1979. *Higher education staff information report: EEO-6.* Equal Opportunity Commission

Falk, D., and L. Aitken. 1984. Promoting retention among American Indian college students. *Journal of American Indian Education* 32 (2):24-31

Fanon, F. 1963. *The wretched of the earth.* New York: Grove

Ferguson, M., and D. Fleming. 1984. Native Americans in elementary school social studies textbooks. *Journal of American Indian Education* 23:10-15

Forbes, J., and H. Adams. 1976. *A model of grass-roots community development: The University Native American language education project.* Davis: University of California Native American Studies

Geertz, C. 1975. *The interpretation of cultures*. New York: Basic Books

Glaser, B., and A. Strauss. 1967. *The discovery of grounded theory: Strategies for qualitative research*. Hawthorne, NY: Aldine

Green, R. 1978. Math avoidance: A barrier to American Indian science education and science careers. *Bureau of Indian Affairs Education Research Bulletin* 6 (3):1-8

Haan, N. 1977. *Coping and defending: Process of self-environment organization*. New York: Academic Press

Halpern, M. 1977. Toward a transforming analysis of social classes. In C.A.O. van Nieuwenhuijzer, ed., *Commoners, climbers and notables*. Leiden: Brill

Havighurst, R. 1981. Indian education: Accomplishments of the last decade. *Phi Delta Kappan* 62:329-31

Hawthorn, Henry, ed. 1966-7. *A survey of the contemporary Indians of Canada*. Ottawa: Indian Affairs

Herzberg, H. 1971. *The search for an American Indian identity*. Syracuse: Syracuse University Press

High Pine, G. 1973. The non-progressive Great Spirit: Traditionalism in the modern world. *Akwasasne Notes* 5 (6):38-9

Iverson, K. 1978. Civilization and assimilation in the colonized schooling of Native Americans. In P. Altbach and G. Relly, eds., *Education and colonialism*. New York: Longman

James, M.A. 1981. Higher educational needs of Indian students. *Integrateducation* 19 (8):7-12

Jennings, F. 1975. *The invasion of America: Indians, colonialism, and the cant of conquest*. Chapel Hill: University of North Carolina Press

John-Steiner, V. 1975. *Learning styles among Pueblo children: Final report*. Washington, DC: National Institute of Education

Katz, R. 1981. Education as transformation: Becoming a healer among the Kung and the Fijians. *Harvard Educational Review* 51:57-78

–. 1985. Hearing healers: The contribution of vulnerability to field work. In A. Schenk and H. Kalweit, eds., *The scientist and the shaman: The interplay of rational thought and spiritual feeling*. Munich: Dianus-Trikont Verlag

Kemp, W. 1971. The flow of energy in a hunting society. *Scientific American* 224 (3):104-15

LaFramboise, T. and B. Plake. 1983. Toward meeting the research needs of American Indians. *Harvard Educational Review* 55:45-51

Levine, R., and M. White. 1986. *Human conditions: The cultural basis of educational developments*. New York: Routledge and Kegan Paul

Lincoln, R., and A. Slagle. 1987. *The good red road: Passages into Native America*. San Francisco: Harper and Row

Maynard, E. 1974. The growing negative image of the anthropologist among American Indians. *Human Organizations* 33:402-3

McLean, E.A. 1981. *Teaching traditional Inupiat skills in a traditional setting*. Fairbanks: University of Alaska, Alaska Native Language Center

Memmi, A. 1965. *The colonizer and the colonized*. Boston: Beacon Press

Miles, M., and A. Huberman. 1984. *Qualitative data analysis*. Beverly Hills, CA: Sage

Naroll, R., and R. Cohen. 1970. *A handbook of method in cultural anthropology.*
New York: Natural History Press

National Advisory Council on Indian Education. 1983. *Indian education sui
generis.* Washington, DC: US Government Printing Office

National Education Association. 1983. *American Indian/Alaskan Native
education: Quality in the classroom.* Washington, DC: National Education
Association

Noley, G. 1981. Review of the schooling of Native America. *Harvard
Educational Review* 51:197-9

Novack, G. 1979. History of Choctaw education. Ph.D. dissertation,
Pennsylvania State University

–. 1979. *Genocide against the Indians.* New York: Pathfinder Press

Oleksa, M., and R. Dauenhauer. 1982. Education in Russian America. In G.
Stein, ed., *Education in Alaska's past.* Anchorage: Alaska Historical Society

Ortiz, R. 1982. Developing Indian academic professionals. *Integrateducation*
19:38-41

Pearce, H.R. 1953. *Savagism and civilization: A study of the Indian and the
American mind.* Baltimore: Johns Hopkins University Press

Pelto, P., and G. Pelto. 1978. *Anthropological research: The structure of inquiry.*
Cambridge: Cambridge University Press

Philips, S. 1983. *The invisible culture: Communication in classroom and
community on the Warm Springs Indian Reservation.* New York: Longman

Pinxten, R., I. van Dooren, and F. Harvey. 1983. *The anthropology of space:
Explorations into the natural philosophy and semantics of the Navajo.*
Philadelphia: University of Pennsylvania Press

Polanyi, M. 1964. *The tacit dimension.* San Francisco: Harper and Row

Prucha, F. 1985. *The Indians in American society: From the revolutionary war to
the present.* Berkeley: University of California Press

Rappaport, R. 1978. Adaptation and the structure of ritual. In E. Blurton-Jones
and V. Reynolds, eds., *Human Behaviour and Adaptation.* London: Taylor
Francis

Reinharz, S. 1984. *On becoming a social scientist.* New Brunswick, NJ: Transaction

Ryan, F. 1982. The federal role in American Indian education. *Harvard
Educational Review* 52:423-30

Schaef, A. 1987. *When society becomes an addict.* San Francisco: Harper and Row

Sells, L. 1980. The mathematics filter and the education of women and
minorities. In L. Fox, L. Brody, and D. Tobin, eds., *Women and the mathematical mystique.* Baltimore, MD: Johns Hopkins University Press

Spradley, J. 1979. *The ethnographic interview.* New York: Holt, Rinehart, and
Winston

Task Force Five on Indian Education. 1976. *Final report to the American Indian
Policy Review Commission.* Washington, DC: US Government Printing Office

Thornton, R. 1982. *The urbanization of American Indians.* Bloomington, IN:
Indiana University Press and Chicago: Newberry Library Center for the
History of the American Indian

Toghotthele Corporation. 1983. *Nenana Denayee.* Nenana, AK: Toghotthele
Corporation

Trimble, J. 1977. The sojourner in the American Indian community: Methodological issues and concerns. *Journal of Social Issues* 33:159-74

–, A. Goddard, and N. Dinges. 1977. *Review of the literature on educational needs and problems of American Indians: 1971-1976.* Seattle, WA: Battelle Human Affairs Research Center

Turnbull, C. 1961. *Forest people.* New York: Touchstone Books

–. 1972. *Mountain people.* New York: Touchstone Books

Turner, A. 1984. *Utah Paiute tribal restoration.* Pocatello, ID: Idaho State University

Weyler, R. 1984. *The blood of the land.* New York: Vintage Books

Wilcox, P. 1970. Social policy and white racism. *Social Policy* (May/June):41-5

Wolcott, H. 1987. The teacher as an enemy. In G. Spindler, ed., *Education and cultural process: Anthropological approaches.* Prospect Heights, IL: Waveland Press

Wolfleg, A. 1979. Blackfoot seminar. In E. Waugh and K. Prithipual, eds., *Native religious traditions.* Waterloo, ON: Wilfrid Laurier University Press

2

Peacekeeping Actions at Home: A Medicine Wheel Model for a Peacekeeping Pedagogy

Sharilyn Calliou

Introduction

A multicultural Canada requires more than the celebration of secular and sacred events unique to particular cultural communities, the constitutional recognition of diverse cultures and languages, the ad hoc study of curricular experiences about cultures other than our own, or the development of lesson plans or kits which highlight fragments of the multicultural national fabric. Racially motivated incidents demean, denigrate, and debilitate (physically, emotionally, psychologically, spiritually) both perpetrator and victim. Whether these daily occurrences in Canada are micro- or macro-acts of aggression, they undermine the 'goodness' of multicultural intent. Such incidents indicate that Canada is multicultural in name only and has a multi-ethnic problematique that challenges First Nations and non-First Nations classroom teachers alike.

Multiculturalists require special courage to acknowledge the inadequacies of a policy that may only create 'good-old-boy' tolerance and mask systemic inequities and that views racism as a separate issue not to be discussed openly at food fairs, intercultural dances, and other publicly funded celebrations. The word tolerance indicates to me the limited hopes of multiculturalism, for it suggests no more than the strength of will needed to visit the dentist or discharge an unavoidable social obligation. Tolerance more often implies differences than similarities, and naming differences begins the dance of 'otherness' that obscures the shared humanity of classroom communities – communities which are themselves sites of the dialectical tensions of power, privilege, and state policy.

The individuation inherent in naming 'otherness' seems to legitimate boundaries and other such nonsense which can justify inequitable, even violent, treatment of diverse individuals or groups. The Canadian policy of multiculturalism is founded on difference and may only reproduce the anthropologized exoticism of lifestyle differences. Food fairs may have

widened the diet of Canada's fabled four food groups. Multi-ethnic sharing will stimulate community education on the need for inclusiveness
only if discussion of underlying issues is as freely accessible as bannock
and chapatis.

Food fairs and summer holidays, indicative of Canadian 'non-conflictual'
consciousness, have not proved adequate to the pressures of an increasingly
multi-ethnic nation. A multicultural pedagogy which promotes quaint
studies of food, traditional dress, and famous people who have contributed
to Canada's recent history may only provide what Eisner called a null curriculum (1979), leaving fundamental issues of humanity to fester like
untreated wounds.

Multiculturalism must be linked to other philosophical ideals of
Canadian identity. A cornerstone ideal of this uneasily shared territory, a
gift of the Creator, is peacekeeping. This ideal is exemplified in our
international reputation as truce-keepers and in the nations within, in
First Nations philosophies like the Great Law of Peace of the Iroquois confederacy. If multicultural events or attitudes are presented without a
simultaneous effort to identify, name, and cripple systemic, institutionalized, and individual racism, then educators deny the incompatibility
between racism and our nation's peacekeeping potential. If we cannot be
peacekeepers at home, the lessons we teach here and abroad are both
fraudulent and self-destructive.

As a member of the Michel Band (Alberta), once deemed extinct by the
Canadian federal government, I have grown up with the everyday facts of
external and internal racism. As a teacher for ten years in an inner-city
community school, I have witnessed acts of racial hatred among newcomers and old-timers in classrooms and the larger community. I have also
witnessed the ease with which some children accept each other, seemingly oblivious to the construct and problematique of *race*. As the sole
First Nations staff member for ten years, I knew that sense of drowning or
suffocation as colleagues reinforced racially disempowering attitudes or
dismissed unresolved tensions of racial and other issues. I have also experienced the support of colleagues as they attempted to deflect blows
aimed at me or First Nations generally. I have been confronted with ignorance and wounded by statements like: 'The Native students seem to be
a problem this year' or 'I didn't know Indians could get a university
degree.' I have confronted the anger of my own racism, too, which some
days leaves me feeling that white people cannot possibly be good two-
leggeds.

As a university instructor for courses about First Nations issues, I have
heard First Nations students describe Euro-Canadian or Western racist

incidents within a highly integrated setting, while they attempt to acquire a post-secondary education with the hope of returning to communities recovering from the near-fatal legacy of colonization. One student brought me an educational psychology text, an offering resembling a repeatedly run-over dead cat, to show me the inaccurate descriptions and conclusions about 'Native' language learners. As a graduate student, I, too, grapple with personal dilemmas based on irrational racism and compassionate anti-racism. I heard one of my thesis committee members insist I possessed a tradition of orality even though I can barely tell a joke and my thesis topic had nothing to do with storytelling or orality. All First Nations students, including myself, have heard the resentful accusation that our education is paid for at public expense (i.e., their pocketbook); the accuser is seemingly oblivious to the fiduciary responsibilities of treaties and agreements between the nations within and the colonial government of the 'settler nations' (Young-Ing 1988, 24).

And, as a Canadian citizen, I have been schooled about Canada's reputation for United Nations peacekeeping in nations like Kashmir (1949), Palestine (1954), Egypt (1956-7), West New Guinea (1962-3), Cyprus (1964), and so on to Bosnia-Hercegovina (1992-). In April 1993, approximately 4,500 Canadian peacekeeping troops were stationed abroad. The global capacity for violence seems as perverse as our capacity for compassion.

This strong image of Canadians as peacekeepers that brings pride to many Canadians is a troublesome contradiction for me as a teacher. For I know that raising issues of land claims, economic marginalization, and colonizing policies can release hidden, and not so hidden, tensions of racial backlash. The image of international peacekeeper was cruelly stripped away for me when the federal government sent 3,300 Canadian infantry, artillery, engineers, military police, medical corps, air force pilots, and sailors to Kanesatake and Kahnawake with three high-tech, German-built Leopard tanks, twenty Huey Kiowa troop-carrying helicopters, and two CF-5 Freedom Fighters (Maclaine and Baxendale 1990, 52-3) to 'subdue' elders, men, women, and children who had exhausted their legal options to defend Onen'to:kon – a sacred burial ground and ceremonial place. Ironically, a team of twenty-four observers from the Paris-based International Federation of Human Rights was assembled to monitor Canada's historic battle to maintain cultural hegemony and deny the existence/ resistance of the Mohawk Nation. Federation president Jean-Claude Fouque made an eight-day tour of the two Mohawk settlements and found over fifty violations of basic human rights by and against all parties concerned (Maclaine and Baxendale 1990, 41). The media docudrama from 11 March to 26 September 1990 brought sharply into question, for me, the hopes for peaceful multicultural coexistence in a democratic country. This display of military hardware left me wondering why Canada's peacekeeping troops were not involved before the military.

School-based programs to reinforce social skills and campaigns to 'Catch Students Being Good' appear absurd in light of televised broadcasts of a domestic, uncivil war. Pedagogy in an increasingly multi-ethnic community needs to consider creating right relations (that is, balanced, harmonious, unconditionally respectful relations) which engender peacekeeping rather than merely promoting multi-ethnic awareness and tolerance or curbing racism. Peacekeeping implies that conflicts must be self-mediated and -resolved, and conflict mediation and resolution imply that the source of these conflicts (race, power, gender, economic disparity, sexuality, etc.) must be openly discussed. The multicultural classroom teacher is expected to be a sort of minicultural expert – a piñata here, an obi there, and a totem pole elsewhere.

A peacekeeping classroom teacher who ventures beyond food, glue, and fabric requires the skill to raise difficult, complex, and interconnected issues which will challenge the power and privilege of some individuals in Canadian society. Such dialogue necessitates levels of trust and intimacy in the classroom similar to those in a good marriage. Classroom teachers cannot perform this liberatory function alone: the schools concerned must revisit their educational mission statements to establish where, when, and how decolonization can become the educational project.

Objectives

This chapter attempts to fulfil two objectives. First, I share some of the daily events relevant to these issues in diary-style entries at the beginning of each mini-section. Second, I make a proposal for a peacekeeping pedagogy which explores the interconnectedness of four major constructs – racism, multiculturalism, anti-racism, and peacekeeping.

The Medicine Wheel

Each of these four constructs can be visualized as a medicine wheel continuum to show the interconnectedness and simultaneousness of events and conditions. Frank Black Elk (1982), in his discussion of Marxism and Lakota traditions, described interconnectedness as an encompassing relatedness between everything – stars, two-leggeds, bears, cougars, rivers, flowers, planets. He stated that 'everything in the universe is related within the tradition of Lakota spirituality; everything is relational, and can only be understood in that way' (p. 148). I needed a method to help me visualize how these four constructs could illustrate the way in which our lives are lived relationally, 'as a relation among relations, *not* at the expense of our relations' [original emphasis] (p. 148). The medicine wheel provided me with this beginning.

Medicine wheels can be pedagogical tools for teaching, learning, contemplating, and understanding our human journeys at individual, band/community, nation, global, and even cosmic levels. However, one should keep in mind Black Elk's caution that the 'relationality of the universe is a spiritual proposition, a force so complex and so powerful that it creates a sense of wonder and impotence in any sane human who truly considers it' (Black Elk 1982, 148). Sun Bear, Wind, and Mulligan (1991) state that medicine wheels are found from Europe to India and that their configuration reminds us of our past 'when the world was guided by the law of right relationship, and humans respected themselves and all their relations – mineral, plant, animal, spirit – on the Mother Earth' (p. 2). Pepper and Henry (1991) characterize the wheel as 'a circle of harmony and courage' which symbolizes the integration of physical, mental, spiritual, and cultural aspects of living (p. 146).

I am no medicine wheel expert, but more and more I appreciate its internal wisdom and its ability to explain relationships. Not all First Nations used this instructional device and there is no one absolute version of the wheel.

This type of holistic examination is presented in classes when we try to show our students some understanding of water, air, plant, or other cycles, although our focus on these units of analysis can obscure the relation of events to conditions of which humans are only a part. This is the beginning of many years of study to understand the complex, seemingly chaotic organization of relationality observed by Black Elk, and to witness if we can live our lives in a harmonious way that always 'respects the sacred circle and all other beings in it, [so that] every step [we] take can be a ceremony that celebrates [our] connection with the Creator' (Sun Bear, Wind, and Mulligan 1991, 9).

The Circle and the Four Directions

A wheel drawing simply begins by making a circle. The circle symbolizes the continuity and connectedness of events with the added dynamism of movement. Superimposed on the circle are four equidistant points. These points symbolically identify the power/medicine of the four directions: east, south, west, north. Various cultural communities associate different aspects of their humanness, seasons, colours, animals, plants, minerals, etc., with each of the four directions. The final drawing resembles a compass for human understanding. A basic medicine wheel is illustrated in

Figure 2.1. It is a pedagogical device designed to assist contemplation of the continuity and interconnectedness of events and conditions of all beings.

Figure 2.1

The medicine wheel

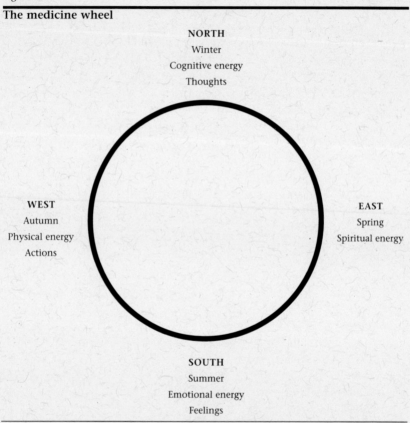

NORTH
Winter
Cognitive energy
Thoughts

WEST
Autumn
Physical energy
Actions

EAST
Spring
Spiritual energy

SOUTH
Summer
Emotional energy
Feelings

The number four is considered significant among First Nations peoples, but with some differences. In undoing the misrepresented politics of identity, the learner must guard against a pervasive reductionism that posits an inflexible and inaccurate Pan-Indianism. For example, Eber Hampton (1988) used six directions in his medicine wheel to develop a foundation model for First Nations education across North America. The additional two directions in his model are above and below to symbolize Sky Father and Earth Mother.

East is associated in this discussion with the sun – dawn – and symbolically refers to spring, light, beginnings, fire, and enlightenment (illumination) which brings transformation. South is associated with water and symbolically refers to summer. West is here associated with earth and symbolizes the value of introspection and insight. The west could relate to grounded experience where introspection and insight arise out of our being bound to the earth. North is associated with air and winter. In some traditions, I have seen north associated with earth and west associated with fire.

Each direction generally corresponds to a phase of human evolution from north (newborn or elder) to east (child) to south (adolescent) to west (adult). Each direction also corresponds to an aspect of humanness: north with the mental realm (cognitive, intellectual), east with the spiritual, south with the emotional (psychological), and west with the physical. However, these aspects of humanness are not discrete elements of being. The wheel connects these and this holistic sensibility exemplifies the Cree sense that heart, spirit, mind, and body are integrated without disconnection. Humans are not vertical beings with four separate, pull-out drawers in which to store emotions, thoughts, physical sensations, or spiritual enlightenment. The production of knowledge is a holistic, self-constructed process.

A Peacekeeping Pedagogy Model

In Figure 2.2, I have placed each of the four constructs (racism, multiculturalism, anti-racism, and peacekeeping) on a wheel. As a teacher, I can see that lessons developed in this fashion enlarge the scope of the lesson beyond a myopic focus on a construct, even if lesson plans may take longer to prepare and think through in terms of placement.

I placed our denial or awareness of racism at the south to represent the emotional realm and psychological responses to constructed 'otherness.' Racism enables and sustains great powers to erect or resurrect institutional, social, or other barriers against some members of society based on feeling rather than reasoned argument. Racism, therefore, creates imbalance, disharmony, and harmful relations among all beings. This can undermine the community-building at classroom level which teachers may struggle to articulate in the Canadian context of denying and obscuring violations against human rights. Steward (1976) ironically described the reticence of some Canadians to admit or even examine aspects of racism thus:

> Well, I admit it, I am slow; when I look back along the corridors of
> Canadian history, I see a series of vignettes, all of them open to misunder-

Figure 2.2

A medicine wheel illustrating a peacekeeping pedagogy

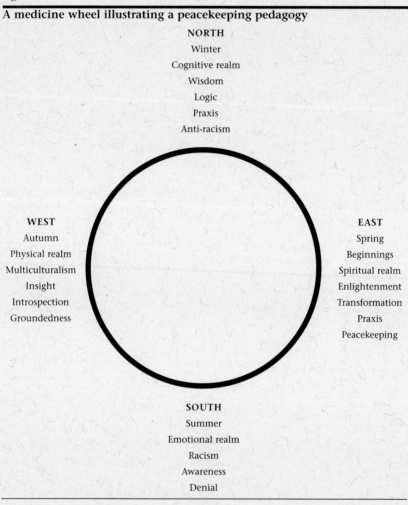

NORTH
Winter
Cognitive realm
Wisdom
Logic
Praxis
Anti-racism

WEST
Autumn
Physical realm
Multiculturalism
Insight
Introspection
Groundedness

EAST
Spring
Beginnings
Spiritual realm
Enlightenment
Transformation
Praxis
Peacekeeping

SOUTH
Summer
Emotional realm
Racism
Awareness
Denial

standings; the wanton slaughter of the Beothuck Indians of Newfoundland; the brisk slave trade in the colonies; the destruction of the Indians, always for their own good ... the exploitation and humiliation, and slaughter of Orientals brought in to work on the [Canadian Pacific Railway], the incarceration of the Japanese – but not German-Canadians during World War II, and so on. To an uncritical mind like mine, a mind incapable of fine distinctions, it looks as if there is, after all, a hint of racism in our make-up. (pp. 205-6)

Teachers of all nations will have to struggle with this Canadian denial embedded in our consciousness, fuelled by a history of schooling which propounded a lopsided Grand Narrative of things as they were and ought to be.

I placed multiculturalism at the west to represent the actions to promote ethnic awareness. Anti-racism is to the north to represent the wisdom of reasoned argument, reason which is both highly intellectual and compassionate. Elder Louis Sunchild urges humans to try and 'understand the compassionate mind,' for 'mind is life' and the two-leggeds need to understand that the 'we have opportunity to be in a mental state, and to use words in such a way that others have *life*' [original emphasis] (Sunchild in Lightning 1992, 238). However, north is not isolated. The cognitive energy there includes the experiences and actions of the west and the emotional energy of the south. I have placed the goal of peacekeeping to the east to include the ideal that teaching is an act of love and healing whose purpose is to promote understanding of and respect for that highly spiritual proposition set out by Black Elk and others.

The totality of the wheel illustrates that the tensions and balances between the four constructs do not exist as singular entities. Balance refers to honest, open interactions which emphasize the need to humanize members of the same species and the shared nature of our journey. Lightning, in examining the teachings of Sunchild, noted the interconnectedness of all beings and explained that 'when one person violates that potential [of respecting and giving life], or abuses self or others, or denies himself or herself the possession and practice of the compassionate mind, all suffer the consequences' (Lightning 1992, 239).

I believe these four constructs, or interconnected tensions, are evident in all beings, events, and conditions simultaneously. Racism, anti-racism, multiculturalism are all anthropocentric constructs and are not manufactured and peddled as ideological differences by the other beings. I am not wise, as some plants and beings are. In a day, in a moment, I can be peacemaker, anti-racist, racist, and multiculturalist. I have struggled with my will to be a pacifist, especially in light of continuing acts of oppression like those at Oka. I strive for the perfection of *spiritus* through peacemaking, but, oh, I am human and I forget.

My yearning for peace has a philosophical history in both First Nations and non-First Nations traditions in Canada, which incorporate the conditions of racism, multiculturalism, and anti-racism. Lester B. Pearson's Nobel Peace Prize lecture, delivered on 11 December 1957 in Oslo, underscores the necessity to choose peace, for it 'is as clear for nations as it was once for the individual: peace or extinction' (p. 177). Treaties, signed and unsigned, were made between the settler nations and First Nations with peacekeeping objectives. Erasmus noted that, before contact, agreements made between different groups of two-leggeds were 'always extremely sacred,' with spiritual leaders guiding the shaping and unfolding of arrangements (Erasmus in Cassidy 1991, 23). He also noted that agreements were made after contact which respectfully acknowledged that the newcomers could 'live amongst us [but that] they would not have to live under the institutions of the indigenous nations' (p. 22). In 1986, John Mohawk, Iroquois, discussed the compassionate rationale behind the philosophy and praxis of the Great Law of Peace as being to enable peacemaking, because a 'people living in fear cannot apply their potential best thinking to solving their problems' (p. 20). Indigenous and newcomer traditions speak about peace, yet, as a teacher, I am saddened at the turbulent conflicts which do not teach our children the ways of peace.

South: Racism

Wed., 7 April 1993: A student announces in an anti-racist pedagogy course that, generally, racism does not happen at her school. I nearly bite through my lower jaw but resist the urge to ask which suburb of Utopia she teaches in. It's the end of term, final class, and I don't particularly want to 'get into it.' I'm tired. Undaunted, another student tacks and sets sail by attacking the seeming invincibility of denial which condones systemic racism. I learn while I listen and understand that before multicultural, multicultural-anti-racist or racist-desist or peacekeeping pedagogies can begin, the bedrock of denial must be dynamited. I envy her ability to bring this issue out in this manner. The racist-aholic is like the alcoholic who cannot admit to addiction and thus allows the sickness to continue. Denial is a nice place to be because the emotions don't come spilling in, or is it? Emotional energy must be consumed to create such hatred, fear and violence.

Thurs., 8 April 1993: I am answering the phones. I receive two calls. One is a young man digging about, personal excavation work, to understand the subtle micro-aggressions occurring in his graduate work. No one has been obvious, you know, like calling him Boy or Red Man or making war whoops during his orals. However, he is feeling the pressures of that omnipresent force of irrationality. I scarcely place the phone down when the brave-hearted woman from the previous evening calls. She has sat through a lunch listening, observing, and experiencing the pain of a speaker, a Woman of Colour, discuss the dehumanizing events of her efforts to survive in a mainstream post-secondary institution. The caller's voice quakes with the centuries of tears which commemorate this needless and uncivilized war-making amongst ourselves. I want to hold her but can only send her a phone hug. She must get back to work. I hang up and tell my cousin that we need to set up a Racist Crisis Line. I feel emotionally wiped. Lived experience brings empathy; and there is an emotional price to pay; then again, ignorance is not bliss ... it is just ignorance.

Racism begins in denial, denial that we are, quite simply, one species. Racism is physically, emotionally, psychologically, and spiritually draining to both sender and receiver. Racism can be defined as belief in the superiority of some members over others of the same species, or the justification for antagonism or violence towards other members of the same species. Racism legitimates military, political, social, legislative, individual, or other acts of dehumanization. And denial enshrines racism as acceptable when we cannot name it in our classrooms or textbooks honestly. If education is to achieve the Socratic maxim to 'know thyself' as educated citizens, then teachers and learners cannot gloss over these deeper issues. This does not have to mean confrontation, although some individuals may feel challenged – even hostile – for always there is Sunchild's reminder (in Lightning 1992) to know and attempt the ways of the compassionate mind.

A peacekeeping pedagogy cannot survive on the multicultural prattle that assumes, as Gill, Singh, and Vance (1987) have ironically noted, 'that if pupils learn to appreciate each other's culture, then all will be well' (p. 126). To begin the journey on this wheel, teachers and learners need to confront unspoken feelings of internal or external racism, need to confront denial. Multiculturalism, a glamorous *National Geographic* voyeurism, can become meaningless if racism is not named as the impetus behind the need for racial harmony.

One text which might begin the dialogue is Howard Adams's (1975) *Prison of Grass*. Adams, who grew up in a Métis colony in Saskatchewan, links racism to Euro-imperialism and economic factors where 'Indian stereotypes created by the exploiters had reduced native people in the eyes of the public to animal-like creatures' (p. 13). In order to remove himself from his 'Indian' roots, Adams 'made a complete break with' his parents, home, and community because he perceived his identity as 'ugly and shameful' (p. 15). He understood that in a 'white-supremacist society, more opportunities and privileges exist for Indian and halfbreeds who can pass' (p. 15). However, he came to realize how badly he needed his cultural heritage, but not before he began to internalize feelings that he was 'a stupid, dirty breed, drunken, and irresponsible' which 'stripped [him] of all humanity and decency' (p. 16). Adams attended formal classrooms and the larger classrooms of interconnected communities. What is our responsibility to such learners who feel demoralized and 'stripped of all humanity and decency'?

The brutality of Adams's tale may offend those still in denial. Yet this text may be as appropriate to Canadian high school English curricula as the fictional account of a troubled Danish youth's entanglement with incest and greed. Adams's self-revelation can begin to deflate the smug false consciousness of denial.

South, the emotional realm, provides the groundwork where learners can begin to sense joy or pain, denial or awareness, justice or injustice. Racism is an emotional roller coaster. Adams's self-portrait is a reflection of that, and his experience of conflicting internal and external pressures happens daily in Canadian multicultural communities. Fear or denial of confronting racism, however, can be just as emotionally crippling. Feelings of anger and hate stew, or feelings of helplessness and grievance brew. 'To hold in feelings of hurt or anger without being able get rid of them can be very damaging to our physical, emotional, mental, and spiritual well-being' (Bopp 1988, 53).

Thus, racism cannot be dealt with as only a cognitive curricular experience with 'safe' (that is, not self-revealing) exchanges of experiences conveniently placed on the timetable, or as 'southern [US] politeness: interchange without dialogue' (Roman 1993, 197). Racism must be named, and teachers must know that in so doing emotion will emerge from the underground of denial within individuals, lunch rooms, classrooms, textbooks, media, or schoolgrounds. These events can provide the occasion for lessons to unlock the cycle of denial and begin the dialogue to generate awareness. The emotional content enables both parties to link experience to the theoretical knowledge of racism's poor science, overt consequences, and continuing denial of full citizenship to some members of society. Racism cannot be unlearned like mistaken geographical knowledge can be unlearned. Instead, emotional life history needs to be relived and re-examined and emotional impacts felt in the presence of compassionate teachers and learners who wish to understand and confront what happens when denial stops.

D'Oyley and Stanley (1990) state that racism abounds in Canada and that classrooms cannot be public, affirmative spaces unless teachers demonstrate and model 'the right of all those present to be there and to

participate' in curricular experiences which do not victimize, delegiti-
mate, or denigrate some members with words and images (pp. 30, 27). Yet
teachers are often 'sublimely ignorant of these [racial] tensions, and sometimes choose to remain so even after organized violence erupts' (p. 30).
Denial affronts open, equal legitimation of everyone's voice, what
Mohanty (1989-90) describes as 'authorization' of marginal experiences
which creates an inclusive, 'crucial form of empowerment for students – a
way for them to enter the classroom as speaking subjects' (p. 193). Thus,
teachers will need to understand even more the emotional content of
learning – something textbooks or self-directed software will never convey
– since racist and anti-racist events involve interactions based on the
mistaken racial identity of two-leggeds.

Making public space *truly* public will introduce feelings into curricular
experiences which Tatum (1992), an anti-racist pedagogue, discusses as
'quite predictable and related to their own racial identity development'
(p. 19). She affirms that educators must be aware of the cognitive and
affective potential within a community of learners which begins to examine its knowledge about racial identity. Thus, the emotional realm is a
sensing system which identifies the extent and presence of denial or
awareness about the nature and consequences of racism. Teachers, in their
lesson plans and classroom management, need to focus on this emotional
realm which removes the safety of lectures, reading, and critique divorced
from the everyday realities faced by many 'Canadians.'

West: Multiculturalism

January 1990, Ed. Fdns. 495-B1, My Response Journal: One day as I watched
the children on the playground, my foot pawing at the snow like a deer
looking for twigs, I noticed something curious. All about me the voices of
the children rose and fell like the song of waves coming ashore. The children engaged in an activity they need no schooling for: play. I felt as if I
was looking at the school playground through new eyes. The Oriental
children, newcomers from lands where a terrible war of mistakes had
been fought, played with their own kind. The Occidental children
skipped and sang only with those who looked familiar. A few children
[cross-pollinated] ... I felt like I was looking at a picture of an English
Garden where the Dahlias bloomed colourfully in a grouping; where the
Roses smelled sweetly amongst themselves; where the Morning Glories
twined and climbed alongside the wall alone; and, where the Lupines
stood separately tall and proud ... In my mind I observed and wondered

why the playground was not a mosaic of individuals merrily mixed like a scatter of wildflower seeds. Instead, I saw pockets of children living separately side by side in a land, Canada, rapidly becoming a home for newcomers ... I felt a chill of puzzlement. I did not like this image of children in these [ethnic enclaves]. I wondered what direction aims of education could give to promote an integrated peaceful coexistence. I did not [like] this ghettoization of the playground [in a multicultural Canada].

Multiculturalism is another helping from the Utopian smorgasbord. Multiculturalism was born of the womb of a Canadian tradition, the Royal Commission. This one was related to issues of biculturalism and bilingualism among French and English Canadians who were 'condemned to live together' for economic and nationalist reasons (Boyer 1972, 194). When in doubt, Canadians set up Royal Commissions. The prodigious outpourings of Royal Commissions have Whole Language potential for teachers and constitute a suitable detention resource (say, copying fifty pages of any one related to the student offence), and ex-Royal Commission personnel can always be asked to address local career fairs. However, this particular Royal Commission elicited such an emotional outpouring that it urged the adoption of broad actions on a multidimensional front.

On 8 October 1971, a policy labelled 'Multiculturalism within a Bilingual Framework' was announced in parliament. This was the unplanned offspring of the 1963 Royal Commission on Bilingualism and Biculturalism in Canada. Multiculturalism was proposed as a policy to support programs aimed at retaining, developing, and sharing cultural pluralism on a larger scale. In 1972, the position of minister of state responsible for multiculturalism was created. Multicultural heritage, equality, and recognition was enshrined in Section 27 of the Canadian Constitution (1982). French and First Nations believed that the Multiculturalism Act was a means of dilution and submergence rather than a means of maintaining distinct peoples, self-determination, and self-government. The glamour of Canadian pluralism, healthy multi-ethnicism, is lessened when the obvious discussions about power, power relations, balances of power, and resultant inequity are neglected.

Hazel Carby, who describes herself as a black intellectual, argues in her article 'The Multicultural Wars,' that multiculturalism 'is one of the current code words for *race* ... that is just as effective in creating a commonsense awareness that race is, indeed, the subject that is being evoked' (1992, p. 9). She argues that cultural, political, or social politics segregate when emphasis is placed on difference: the 'theoretical paradigm of

difference is obsessed with the construction of identities rather than relations of power and domination, and in practice, concentrates on the
effect of this difference on a (white) norm' (p. 12). The concept of race
becomes marginalized when concern about the 'right' to individual identity is emphasized rather than genuine concern about 'structures of
inequality and exploitation' (pp. 12-13). First Nations and non-First
Nations teachers alike need to practise (re)education projects in home/
band or mainstream Canadian classrooms. We must learn to speak about
those events, conditions, and policies which demeaned the autochthonous citizens of Turtle Island and not just about cultural identity.

Bullivant (1986) criticized the masked classism and racism of Canada's
multicultural policy, which seemed 'to guarantee that we can each do our
little dance and flash our pretty, lacy petticoats while we drink our ethnic
drinks and admire each other's handicrafts as long as we realize that in
reality the mosaic is vertically organized' (p. 12). Some Canadians obviously expected much more than multi-ethnic celebrations. Multicultural
flavours of the month without classroom discussion of multi-ethnic conflicts (race, class, power, etc.) do not prepare students for future cooperative living or survival in a larger context of intensified economic, spiritual, political, and environmental distress.

Thus, to the west, the physical realm of the senses (sight, touch, taste,
smell, hearing) has yielded the action of multiculturalism which is
directly related to the emotional realm (the south) of conflict, tension,
tolerance, and love. The west is also associated with the earth, with introspection and insight. We are grounded and potentially grounded on
earth, and the lived experience of multiculturalism's weaknesses, built
onto awareness of racism and ethnicity, can assist Canadians to develop a
wiser, more rational peacekeeping pedagogy. Combining emotions with
thought can help us see the shortcomings of our actions. However, the
language of critique without strong emotions is dead rationality.
Emotions have been given to us as a gift for a reason: these humanized,
life-embracing emotions can ground reason to demonstrate our shared
humanity. Some voices have denounced multiculturalism's myopia, and it
is time we teachers and learners travelled north.

North: Anti-Racist Pedagogy

Tues., 6 April 1993: I called my cousin tonight. She was away ill and I was
worried about her. We catch up on things. She tells me about her day and
then asks her son if she has his permission to talk about his day. He
agrees. I am considered a distant Aunty to this family. He has encountered

and handled a racist incident. While in class, working away at some curricular experience, he asks some other students what they are listening to on their walkman. They tell him he won't like it. He insists on hearing the tape anyway. He listens. He identifies the home-made tape as racist in content. Some students are offended by the behaviour of a First Nations student. Rather than attacking his violence, they attack his race. All the clichés are on the tape. Outraged, morally righteous and indignant, my cousin's son goes to the principal's office to protest and demand anti-racist action. He is told to take a number (3) and wait. He storms out to find his counsellor. He's out. He is moving down the hallway like a misplaced Alberta tornado. A teacher he feels OK with meets him and they talk. He demands that something be done. He wants the incident out in the open. The principal is alerted. The issue is discussed. My cousin's son is given the comment that he 'was told he wouldn't like the tape.' I almost swallow my cigarette at the principal's crass victimization of his bravery. Later, the mother of one of the homemade rappers calls my cousin. They talk. I am in awe of my cousin's son's bravery, courage, awareness (not denial), willingness to confront. In the discussion, they recognize that the 'victim' really is guilty of jerky behaviour, but this is not because of his race. I am proud of my cousin. Her son has a home, he can go home to talk these things through. His emotions brought him to reasoned action. He knew what he wanted. He wanted the racism stopped, not a food fair.

Sat., 2 April 1993: I am in a bookstore in Victoria. I am reading through a book about American 'Indian' history considering the gleeful contradiction I have found where the author states in one mouthful that aboriginal people had control of their reserves but, adds, a few sentences later, that 'Indians' need an Act of Congress to sell their land. I am angry, irritated, annoyed at this legalistic oppression. I am trying to imagine what letter I will send this Bozo. My book-hunting partner begins to tell me the old paternalistic mumbo-jumbo that this is for the protection of ... I do not hit him with the volume written by one of his own. Angrier, I retort, 'Oh, come on, what if you had to get an Act of Congress passed every time you wanted to sell your land.' He capitulates quickly. I see a flash of public education bull's eye. No doubt he considered the acreage he wants to unload in Ontario. I fume, but recover temporarily when I find another Vine Deloria classic, a hard cover edition, to add to my Library. How many times have I had to speak up and out? Sometimes, I tell my partner, 'I want a day off,' and, for me, that would mean 'I don't want to be Indian today.'

Thoughtful actions, perhaps even wisdom, do not begin or end with thinking. These two diary-style entries illustrate how the emotional realm can provoke thoughtful anti-racist responses. Descartes's belief that truth is primarily clarity of thought with distinct ideas renders truth-making a clever abstraction. The continuum of the wheel illustrates that the processes of the emotional, physical, intellectual, and spiritual are connected and that we should not be easily seduced into believing that living occurs from the neck up. Instead classrooms also need to nurture Sunchild's compassionate mind because right relations include knowing how to act with a connected heart-mind, which is more than a display of rationality. Racism hurts; anti-racism is not just about changing disliking into liking through cultural exposure. Anti-racism involves the application of compassionate insights to begin healing among ourselves. Anti-racism has been characterized by Gill et al. (1987) as more than 'just about helping individuals to like each other' (p. 124). Anti-racism is the willingness to confront the pain of self and others, to challenge the denial from self or others, and to create change for self and with others.

However, before I could consider the dimensions of an anti-racist pedagogy, I needed to understood what race, racism, and hence anti-racism meant and mean to me. First, race is a concept or construct I do not believe in, nor have I been provided with evidence to prove its existence. I have been socialized to believe that all humans are members of the same species – the two-leggeds – and my acceptance of this has never been difficult. However, I am aware of those who have been socialized or schooled differently and who believe that there are distinctions among groups of this species that can legitimate particular, dehumanizing behaviour or attitudes. Like Freire (1989), I believe that as 'the oppressors dehumanize others and violate their rights, they themselves also become dehumanized' (p. 42).

I do believe that individuals are members of distinct cultural communities based on ethnicity or regionalism in Canada (for example, Québécois, Vietnamese, Japanese, Newfoundlanders, Cape Bretoners, Swampy Cree, Mohawk, Michel Band Mohawk-Cree, etc.). I understand that all members of all cultural communities possess a melange of life-enhancing or life-degrading emotional responses and actions, and can be equally guilty of logical/illogical and rational/irrational behaviour. I also believe that cultural community membership does not predispose one to violence or compassion, war-making or peacekeeping.

For me, racism is a confounding construct. With Montagu, in his *The Concept of Race* (1964), I agree that 'it would be better if the term "race" were altogether abandoned' (p. 12) and 'dethroned from the vocabulary' for 'the meaning of a word is the action it produces' (p. 27). This is not to say I blame language, for language is only use. Montagu is a forerunner of those who question the short-sightedness of and barriers to a particular discourse. He states that race 'is a word so familiar that in using it the uncritical thinker is likely to take his own private meaning for it completely for granted, never thinking at any time to question so basic an instrument of the language' (p. 26).

I acknowledge and have witnessed actions which are racially based. Most notable have been military, political, and legislative means to 'disappear' the autochthonous citizens of North America. Stiffarm and Lane (1992) deconstruct the racial extinction attempted by some Euro-North American anthropologists, statisticians, and others to diminish the size of the First Nations population at contact. They concluded that these are attempts to minimize the scale of genocide, rights to land, and claims to recourse, while providing an effective public relations gloss about the vanishing 'Indians' (Stiffarm and Lane 1992, 23-8). The superiority complex which fuelled invasion and attempted conquest was based on this construct of 'otherness' – race – which continues to haunt some classrooms and curricula.

For me, racism is not as elaborate as Tatum suggests (1992). She defines race as a systemic advantage based on race in order to distinguish it from prejudice, which she characterizes as preconceptions and judgments about individuals which are 'often based on limited information' (p. 3). Prejudice, I assume, can be positive or negative; for example: 'Those white people sure are good with technology,' or 'Those First Nations people sure know how to be ecologically sensitive.'

Advantage has been buttressed in various shaky and interlocking ways, including gender, territory, wealth, class, ideology, religion, and such. One of the advantages is the way the irrationality of racial dislike and hatred enables individuals to assume positions of self-privilege and self-justified violence, which can be spiritual, emotional, physical, and intellectual in its form. I think Freire's (1989) description of oppression could be applied to my sensibility about racism:

> One of the basic elements of the relationship between oppressor [racist] and oppressed [receiver] is *prescription*. Every [racially] prescribed prescription represents the imposition of one's choice upon another, transforming the consciousness of the one prescribed to into one that conforms with the prescriber's consciousness. Thus, the behaviour of the oppressed is a prescribed behaviour, following as it does the guidelines of the oppressor. (p. 31)

Thus, I see racism as a continuum spreading from racial dislike or hatred (which may motivate and legitimate termination) to self-justified advantage or superiority (which enmeshes all parties to no one's benefit). Therefore, an anti-racist pedagogy is not just anti-Western or anti-Euro or anti-White, but more an attack on racially based actions and attitudes which extend from misinformed or misshapen acts of prejudice, to systemically institutionalized or socially sanctioned policies of unequal power, to violent events deliberately intended to harm or extinguish a collective.

Canada has numerous examples of internal unpeacemaking. One obvious example is the strained, violent, misunderstood relations between English and French Canadians/Canadiens. Quebec was founded as la Nouvelle France, on appropriated territory of the resident Iroquois, in 1534 when Jacques Cartier 'claimed' the 'vast land in the name of the greatest power in Europe.' Québécois have been engaged in a simultaneous struggle to maintain the integrity of their cultural community as a legitimate entity while attempting to suppress that right for First Nations communities (Ah, what a trangled web we weave). The struggle has impressed Canadian history dramatically, including the first invocation of the War Measures Act (1970) to suppress Québécois nationalism during the FLQ crisis. This revolutionary nationalism eventually spawned a Québécois power structure to oppress Anglo-Quebeckers through economic, language, and educational sanctions. This is clearly not a case of race versus race, but illustrates how cultural-communities from the same 'race' can struggle to remove oppression and gain an 'advantage' in order to oppress others.

An anti-racist pedagogy is, therefore, not just a question of cultural community advantage over others, broadly based on racial constructs (cognitions, beliefs, irrationalities, fears, prejudices). It is an historical, economic, social, political, religious relationality which speaks of imbalance (lack of peacekeeping relations) among species members. Like Gill et al., I agree that a holistic contextualization of interpersonal or organized racism is required in order to 'analyze the ways in which oppressive ideologies are mutually reinforcing' (1987, 125). I also agree with their conclusion that this will be 'by no means a simple task' (p. 125).

To the north, the cognitive realm, is the expressed need to integrate emotions and actions with rationalism. Rational thought is not viewed as a separate and better human faculty but as part of an integrated construct. Mere instruction of students in problem-solving, logical thinking, synthesis, or factual memorization about racism/multiculturalism/anti-racism will be dead rationality if it is not complemented by compassion. Critical compassionate thinking skills are necessary if the oppressed are to avoid becoming dehumanizers as well. This is the failure of taxonomies like Bloom's (1956) hierarchy of educational objectives, which stresses the cognitive domain as disconnected from three other vital parts of our humanness. For classroom teachers of all nations, a critique limited to the construct of race, without examining issues of power and advantage and the reasons for such hierarchies, cannot be enough. Again, the need to consider living interconnectedness and purpose, that is, to respect life and the unfolding story, means that students must be provided with methods to examine their personal and global position in contexts of oppressor-oppressed or respectful-disrespectful. Thus, to the north the symbolic journey progresses towards the light, towards spring, towards an affirmation of our *spiritus*.

East: Peacemaking

Fri., 16 April 1993: I have come through a long struggle to find these words, and passed, with ease, through many walls I thought were solid. I had to begin with the four directions and peacemaking. I talk here of what might be considered simple things, but a pedagogy of peacemaking is what I contemplate. When I think too much on this, the invasion of the immigrants of the settler nations, I can get angry or I can, at times, find forgiveness, or, lapse into the release or the weapon of humour. I can, at times, be irrational, without emotion, and hate White people and all they symbolize; I can do this while understanding my reductionism. I am at times shaken and I retreat. I get tired. But inside, I always hear the voice for peace. The Cedar trees do not make war on us or each other. The buttercups do not do violence to the lilies. There is a symbiosis understood there among the other spiritual beings that we humans can intellectualize as mutual interdependence, sustainable development or an eco-social contract. I do not know the answer for everyone but myself. It is a choice. It is a choice I am often confronted with; sometimes I react rather than act. I want to travel the way of the peacemaker. Would that our classrooms teach all children the emotional, physical, intellectual, spiritual skills to set up peace camps. I weep when I see our children being violent. I cry when I see them treated violently. Yet, I know violence can bequeath both violence and compassion/forgiveness.

Lord, make me an instrument of Your Peace. Where there is hatred, let me sow love. Where there is injury, pardon. Where there is doubt, faith. Where there is despair, hope. Where there is darkness, light. Where there is sadness, joy. Oh, Great Spirit, grant that I may seek not so much to be consoled as to console; to be understood as to understand; to be loved as to love; for it is in giving that we receive; it is in pardoning that we are pardoned. St. Francis of Assisi and Paulo Freire and John Lennon and Mother Theresa and Lester B. Pearson and Chief and Elder Chief Louis Sunchild. These are the models and heroes I want to study, I want to contemplate and bring to classrooms.

In the text *Black Elk Speaks* (Neilhardt 1961), there is a passage where the author recalls that all is sacred and holy: our hands, our eyes, our ears, our mouth, our being. In a secular world, 'concepts' or 'constructs' which discuss holiness or living in a 'state of grace' become marginalized as separate faculties and facilities. I have been told that these are the preserve of theology or philosophy departments. Yet in First Nations cultures, there is an omnipresent emphasis that all is spiritual, that integration of the four worlds/directions/states of being is necessary, and that neglect of any of these aspects leads to disintegration. This fourth component of all beings is still recognized. Thus, I have placed peacemaking at this spiritual place on the wheel. I believe that peacemaking embodies two components – unconditional respect and compassion.

The east is, through its association with the sunrise, a place of beginnings and enlightenment, and a place where new knowledge can be created or received to bring about harmony or right relations. For me, the construct of right relations refers to those interactions with all beings which derive from our understanding of the wisdom of treating each other with unconditional respect. Respect is most closely related to the concept of unconditional love. Respecting someone or loving someone is not conditional upon an appropriate response, failing which love or respect may be withdrawn. I did not see this connection until a student, Sandra Johnson, made me conscious of this insight in a class discussion about respect. Sometimes in Canadian society respect is to be earned, like payment or wages in capitalist consciousness.

A premise of the First Nations world is that we unconditionally respect all beings because we all begin as seeds from the same materials of this Mother Earth. In the circle, no one individual being (two-legged, four-legged, mineral, plant, etc.) is deemed 'more than' or 'less than' another, so that treatment which elevates or denigrates one or the other is ruled out. The intent is to honour the similarities of the being in an egalitarian contract based on dignity, integrity, and respect. Differences are accepted as the gifts of diversity from the Mother Earth and the Creator. This view coincides with Western systems theory, which acknowledges the need for species diversity.

This is the idealization of respect, the respectfulness to strive for when each moment is an act, a prayer of respect. This is not to stereotype First

Nations people as faultless. There is an understanding that we are weak and can behave pitifully. However, a basis of existence is the striving for this unconditional respectfulness. Therefore, a pedagogy of peacemaking would have at its heart this sensibility about respect.

Racism is not an act of respect. Racism is a complex set of feelings, behaviours, and rationalizations that deny the wisdom of this sensibility of respectfulness. Racism is not concerned with the promotion of right relations or harmony but becomes an instrument to justify disrespectful, harmful, and oppressive actions rendered by force or by more gentle methods like legislation. The emotionalism of racism and its inherent oppression fixes beings in a polarized non-egalitarianism as *oppressor* and *oppressed*, where, in essence, no such distinction exists. Racism's emotional denial of the humanity of others breaks the circle, and in a First Nations world the circle must never be broken; collective cohesiveness must be maintained. A peacemaking pedagogy would, therefore, not condone acts of racism. In a peacemaking pedagogy, racism, and all the other 'isms,' are acknowledged as threats to the power of the circle and to our need as two-leggeds to protect the life force of all beings. To harm one, harms all. To honour one, honours all..

A second related characteristic of a peacemaking pedagogy is compassion. Matthew Fox, a Dominican scholar, wrote in his book *Original Blessings* (1983) that compassion 'is not only about waking up to a consciousness of the action born of the truth of cosmic interdependence. And, those actions fall into two basic kinds: celebration and justice-making' (p. 281). I believe that Fox's description of compassion captures the actions of multiculturalism as multi-ethnic celebration and of anti-racist pedagogy as justice-making. Both respect and compassion are, for me, gifts of wisdom attained when one truly begins to recognize and understand the wastefulness and harmfulness of violating the autonomy (that is, the right to be) of any other being. These effects can be rationally considered when one is conscious (that is, not in denial) of the potential of one's actions, and even thoughts are actions. Teachers and learners, roles we play through all ages of life, need to be taught to identify harmful thoughts and feelings and then to put them aside. If we do not put illusions of separateness aside, violence becomes a self-justifying and self-fulfilling prophecy.

A peacekeeping pedagogy is evident in the teachings of the Gayaneshakgowa, the Great Law of Peace, which is the constitution of the Iroquois Confederacy, where peace is considered to be more than the absence of conflict in that events must proceed to resolution, reconciliation, balance. Praxis is required to negate oppression. Thus, peacemaking is not a Utopian ideology wherein planetary inequity is levelled. Instead, there is recognition that laws and principles are needed to guide right relations, for we are too human and have a great capacity to harm and to heal. The Great Law of Peace was a gift of words from Daganawida, the Peacemaker, who met with the League of Nations to plant Tsioneratsekow, the Great White Pine. This set of principles was not considered exclusive to the Iroquois. In Article 2, any individual or nation is invited to obey the Law, for if 'their minds are clean and if they are obedient and promise to obey the wishes of the League, they shall be welcomed to shelter beneath' the Great Tree of Peace (The Great Law of Peace, c. 1539, in Maclaine and Baxendale 1990, 100).

For teachers of all nations working in secular classrooms, opening discussion to spiritual matters may prove troublesome. But to focus on the potential conflicts is again to further fragmentation based on differences, with possibly little more than legalistic solutions. Classroom discussions need to identify common ground, for are there any genuine religious or spiritual teachings which truly teach disrespect and sanction violence?

Ah, yes, John, I imagine all the people ...

Conclusion

The circularity of the wheel's continuum illustrates that we do not reach a Utopian, nirvana-like state where living is free from 'isms,' and emphasizes the need to be relentlessly vigilant about states which create and conflict with peacemaking. The recognition of the need for peacekeeping is shared by both First Nations and non-First Nations peoples. This chapter has laid out an initial proposal for and model of a peacemaking pedagogy which integrates elements of racism's denial/awareness, multiculturalism, and anti-racist ideologies. The medicine wheel assisted me to examine the interconnectedness of these elements while considering the emotional, physical, cognitive, and spiritual realms of peacekeeping at micro- and macro-levels. I have found that the circle assisted me to fuse understandings rather than to deconstruct realizations without hope of glimpsing the totality of the relationality of which Frank Black Elk spoke. Lessons can too easily become disconnected reductionisms.

Racism is a form of denial: of self, of relatedness, of voice, of rights, of emotions. Racism is founded on a transparent concept of 'race' which has much emotive power but little substance. Racism can bring shame and self-loathing to both sender and receiver, whether or not they acknowledge its presence.

Multiculturalism reaffirms the strength of system diversity and can dispel ignorance of racism or the impotence of merely being aware of racism. Multiculturalism allows us to see ourselves as citizens of one world although cultural variations occur. However, too much focus on separateness and uniqueness perpetuates the discourse of differentiation whereby 'I-thou' or 'subject-object' or 'oppressor-oppressed' or 'centre-periphery' are reinforced and the outcome is toleration of difference rather than respectful and unconditional appreciation of diversity and the recognition that all is truly related. Multiculturalist pleas for tolerance and understanding have been judged as facile by some. However, efforts are made to mingle the cultures and present each as a unique part of a common human inheritance. Canada needs more than multiculturalism, however, and peacekeeping ideals provide a foundation for discussions about this multi-ethnic policy.

Anti-racism is a cognitive act in that reason and rationality are applied to deconstruct and understand the complex nature and purpose of events and conditions which create and reinforce racism at all levels. Anti-racist theorists have also discussed the need for a holistic approach, although the holism is defined along Western lines of social, political, economic, and material conditions and overlooks the spirituality of humanness. At one time I thought that multiculturalism and anti-racism were synonymous. My use of the wheel leads me to believe that these constructs are interrelated and not separate. However, for me, anti-racism is not enough. The spiritual aspects, and the potential for enlightenment, continue to highlight secular traditions which are not of my world or my understanding of my humanness. 'Good' anti-racist citizenship, no matter how cogently argued, is a puzzle to me if the *spiritus* is excluded. We more readily trade discussions and debate about 'isms' than spirituality because secular rationality excludes this aspect of who we are.

A peacekeeping pedagogy, therefore, is one where the integration is complete. It has an emotional realm where racism's harm is felt intuitively or as fully kinaesthetic experience, and the facts of racism are not denied. It has a physical realm where actions to celebrate the multicultural/multi-ethnic nature of humanity are evident. It has a cognitive realm with reasoned arguments to deconstruct the flimsiness of separation justified by racist ideology. However, anti-racism contents itself with the absence of conflict and hierarchy rather than with the active courage of peacemaking. A peacemaking pedagogy invites each of us to become peacemakers in our own hearts, in our own communities, and in our shared world, where unconditional respect, compassion, participatory democracy, strength, courage, and reverence are daily lived ideals.

For me, the time has come to begin to discuss and envision peace-making-across-the-curriculum. Our teachings, learnings, curricula, texts, audio-visual and other support materials, lessons, instructional methods, and devices must become those which promote our understanding of a shared his/herstory of violence and peacemaking and which foster a multi-ethnic perspective and honesty. Curricula and instruction must consider the sensibility of unconditional love/respect and compassion required for sustainable peacemaking for ourselves and our children in classrooms and other communities. For it is our children who will inherit the future we teach. These are my thoughts and feelings.

References

Adams, H. 1975. *Prison of grass, Canada from a Native point of view.* Saskatchewan: Fifth House

Black Elk, F. 1982. Observations on Marxism and Lakota tradition. In W. Churchill, ed., *Marxism and Native America.* Boston: South End Press

Bloom, B. 1956. *Taxonomy of educational objectives.* Handbook 1, *Cognitive domain.* New York: McKay

Bopp, J. et al. 1988. *The sacred tree.* Lethbridge, AB: Four Worlds Development Poject

Boyer, A. 1972. Condemned to live together. *Le Soleil*, 19 June 1972. Reprinted in B. Hodgins, R.E. Bowles, J. Henley, and R. Rawlyk, eds., *Canadiens, Canadians and Québécois.* Scarborough, ON: Prentice-Hall

Bullivant, B. 1986. Multiculturalism – pluralist orthodoxy or ethnic hegemony? *Canadian Ethnic Studies* 18 (2):2-12

Carby, H. 1992. The multicultural wars. *Radical History Review* 54:7-18

Cassidy, F., ed. 1991. *Aboriginal self-determination. Proceedings of a conference held 30 September-3 October 1990.* BC and NS: Oolichan Books and Institute for Research on Public Policy

D'Oyley, V., and T. Stanley. 1990. Locating the multicultural classroom: Wrestling with the impact of public policy. In V. D'Oyley and S. Shapson, eds., *Innovative multicultural teaching*, 17-35. Toronto: Kagan and Woo

Eisner, Elliot. 1979. *The educational imagination.* New York: Macmillan

Fox, M. 1983. Theme no. 24, Compassion: Interdependence, celebration, and the recovery of eros. In M. Fox, *Original blessings*, 277-85. Santa Fe: Bear and Company

Freire, P. 1989. *Pedagogy of the oppressed.* Translated by M. Ramos. New York: Continuum

Gill, D., E. Singh, and M. Vance. 1987. Multicultural versus anti-racist science: Biology. In D. Gill and L. Levidow, eds., *Anti-racist science teaching*, 124-35. London: Free Association Books

Hampton, E. 1988. *Toward a redefinition of American Indian/Alaska Native education.* Unpublished Ed.D. dissertation, Harvard Graduate School of Education

Lennon, J. 1988. Imagine (Side 1:2:59). *Imagine.* Producers: John Lennon, Yoko Ono, Phil Spector. Apple Records. Record no. SW-3379. Distributed in Canada by Capitol Records

Lightning, W. 1992. Compassionate mind: Implications of a text written by Elder Louis Sunchild. *Canadian Journal of Native Education* 18 (2):215-53

Maclaine, C., and M. Baxendale. 1990. *This land is our land: The Mohawk revolt at Oka*. Toronto: Optimum

Mohanty, C. 1989-90. On race and voices: Challenges for liberal education in the 1990s. *Cultural Critique* 179-208

Mohawk, J. 1986. The Origins of Iroquois Political Thought. *Northeast Indian Quarterly* 16-18

Montagu, A. [1953] 1964. *The concept of race*. New York: Free Press

Neihardt, J. [1932] 1961. *Black Elk speaks, being the life story of a Holy Man of the Oglala Sioux as told to John G. Neihardt Flaming Rainbow*. Lincoln, NB: University of Nebraska Press

Pearson, L.B. 1957. Reading no. 25, Hon. L.B. Pearson's Nobel Peace Prize lecture, 11 December 1957. *New York Times*, 12 December 1957. Reprinted in D.C. Masters, ed., *A short history of Canada*, 177-84. Toronto: Van Nostrand

Pepper, F., and S. Henry. 1991. An Indian perspective of self-esteem. *Canadian Journal of Native Education* 18 (2):145-60

Roman, L. 1993. 'On the ground' with antiracist pedagogy and Raymond Williams's unfinished project to articulate a socially transformative critical realism. In D. Dworkin and L. Roman, eds., *Views beyond the border country: Raymond Williams and cultural politics*, 158-221. New York: Routledge

Steward, W. 1976. We love our niggers. In W. Steward, ed., *But not in Canada*, 204-25. Toronto: Macmillan

Sun Bear, W. Wind, and C. Mulligan. 1991. *Dancing with the wheel, the medicine wheel workbook*. New York: Simon and Schuster

Stiffarm, L., and P. Lane, Jr. 1992. The demography of Native North America, a question of American Indian survival. In M.A. Jaimes, ed., *The state of Native America, genocide, colonization and resistance*, 23-53. Boston: South End Press

Tatum, B. 1992. Talking about race, learning about racism: The application of racial identity development theory in the classroom. *Harvard Educational Review* 62 (1):1-25

Young-Ing, G. 1988. A comparison between administration of First Nations education in Canada and Peru: Divestment, losses and lacks. *Canadian Journal of Native Education* 15 (3):24-38

3
Redefining Science Education for Aboriginal Students
Madeleine MacIvor

In 1972 the National Indian Brotherhood (NIB) issued the historic policy paper *Indian Control of Indian Education*. This was based on principles of parental responsibility for and local control of an education system in which traditional and contemporary values could intertwine and provide quality education for Aboriginal students. In spite of the federal government's reluctance to grant the power, funding, and legal authority for our peoples to control our educational future, many improvements have been made to our children's education since the inception of 'Indian Control.' Numerous bands are operating their own schools; language and cultural programs have been implemented; retention, attendance, graduation, and post-secondary attendance rates have increased; adult education programs have been initiated; and a number of Aboriginal controlled post-secondary institutions have been established.[1]

Despite these changes, much remains to be done. At the elementary and secondary levels, attendance and retention, motivation and attitude towards school, and the integration of school and Aboriginal cultures continue to be problematic.[2] The rate of functional illiteracy among on-reserve peoples is twice as high as that for other Canadians. Only 25 per cent of the on-reserve population earn high school diplomas (or equivalent), while among other Canadians, over 50 per cent of the population attain similar levels of education. In terms of university participation, only 6.2 per cent of registered peoples attend university, compared to 18.5 per cent of other Canadians. Only 1.3 per cent of registered Indians receive university degrees as compared to 9.6 per cent of the non-Aboriginal population.[3]

Information regarding the state of science education for our peoples suggests that little is being done. While some schools incorporate Aboriginal content and even Aboriginal languages in the science curriculum, this is atypical. At the secondary level, science education is characterized by low enrolment and achievement levels among our students. This limits the number of our young people who can gain entry into post-secondary science, technology, and health-related programs. Not surprisingly, Aboriginal people are very under-represented in science, technology, and health-related programs and professions.[4]

Ironically, it is also clear that a very real need exists for our peoples to gain expertise in the sciences. Science education has been promoted by the Science Council of Canada (SCC) as a critical aspect of every student's education. It contributes to intellectual growth, facilitates informed decision-making, provides a foundation for further scientific and technological learning, and prepares students for employment in an increasingly technological world.[5] Aboriginal students share these needs for understanding science.

But there are additional reasons which make scientific and technical education even more necessary for Aboriginal students. Land claims settlements in the north, which have been driven in part by the desire to exploit energy resources, have resulted in increased Aboriginal control over the management, development, use, and conservation of lands and resources.[6] Future settlements will have a huge economic, political, and environmental impact on Canada's resource sector. Resolution of these claims will result in our peoples taking a much more direct and active part in the governance, management, development, protection, and enhancement of natural resources and non-renewable resources.[7] Consequently, the need for the development of scientific and technical skills among our peoples is pressing. Similarly, reasserting authority in areas of economic development and health care requires community expertise in science and technology.

Because of the under-representation of our peoples in the sciences, and the great need for scientific and technological skills within our communities, efforts to encourage Aboriginal participation in school science are crucial. However, those of us committed to Aboriginal education must remember the questions posed by Vine Deloria: 'How does what we receive in our educational experience impact the preservation and sensible use of our lands and how does it affect the continuing existence of our tribes?'[8]

Given that Western education of Aboriginal peoples, whether by missionaries or by federal or provincial governments, has aimed at cultural domination and has complemented government initiatives for land expropriation and resource exploitation, this question suggests that a radically different approach should be taken to the science education needs of our students. This chapter will address this issue.

Redefining Science Education

What should we consider in constructing the science curriculum for Aboriginal students? First we must confront the much more basic question, What is Aboriginal education? This brought me back to Eber Hampton's work, 'Toward a redefinition of American Indian/Alaska Native education.' Hampton's work provides a comprehensive and holistic framework for envisioning and organizing thoughts on curricular change.

Hampton identifies twelve standards of education for consideration: spirituality, service, diversity, culture, tradition, respect, history, relentlessness, vitality, conflict, place, and transformation.[9] Each of these standards enables reflection on science education.

Spirituality

> The first standard of Indian education is spirituality, at its center is respect for the spiritual relationships that exist between all things.[10]

Aboriginal and non-Aboriginal scholars have noted the essentially spiritual view of the natural world embodied in traditional science.[11] Aboriginal peoples' knowledge of the natural world and their religious traditions are so closely interwoven that Vine Deloria suggests we speak of metaphysics rather than of science or religion. Aboriginal metaphysics, according to Deloria, refer to 'the realization that the world, and all its possible experiences, constitutes a social reality, a fabric of life in which everything had the possibility of intimate knowing relationships because, ultimately, everything was related. This world was a unified world, a far cry from the disjointed and sterile world painted by western science.'[12]

The centrality of the sacred in traditional science suggests that the standard of spirituality is particularly appropriate to science education. However, such content must be incorporated into the classroom with care since traditional perspectives need to be treated respectfully, and a complete understanding of Aboriginal cultures is beyond the grasp of non-Aboriginal peoples.[13] Community members may hold strong feelings about the appropriateness of various topics in school curricula, and such feelings will vary on individual, community, and tribal levels. Content which deals with spiritual knowledge is particularly problematic.[14]

Many Aboriginal communities may see non-Aboriginal teachers of traditional science as inappropriate. In this case, non-Aboriginal educators can serve their students by facilitating the participation of parents and other community members in the teaching of tribal-specific information. In any event, working closely with the community is essential for successfully developing and implementing a culturally appropriate curriculum.[15] As Green and Brown state:

> Where traditional modes of Indian scientific inquiry are still functional and operative and where native specialists (herbalists, astronomers, healers, diagnosticians, etc.) can take part in the sharing of knowledge with children, this approach should work well. Programs should draw heavily on the knowledge of members of the community when their knowledge can be shared (for example, when it is not specialized knowledge meant only for clan initiates or healers-in-training).[16]

While incorporating spirituality into the curriculum requires care, it is of cardinal importance. As Jerry Mander points out in his criticism of Western technology, it is the absence of spirituality which has allowed the growth of technology to the detriment of the planet and her inhabitants. To paraphrase Mander, in the absence of the sacred, nothing is sacred.[17]

Service

> The individual does not form an identity in opposition to the group but recognizes the group as relatives (included in his or her own identity). The second standard of Indian education is service. Education is to serve the people. Its purpose is not individual advancement or status.[18]

This notion of service is central to contemporary perspectives on Indian education. Moreover, the need for Aboriginal scientists and technologists who can work with the community to address community concerns has been frequently articulated.[19] But how can the science curriculum respond to this need for service?

Much of what is learned in contemporary science classrooms is seen as divorced from community concerns. This is particularly true in the case of Aboriginal communities, where the national or provincial curricula present science in unfamiliar contexts. Nan Armour, education consultant for the Labrador Inuit Association, states that 'one of the main problems with science education was that it had always been presented in "white" terms and that examples of science in action were often chosen from the white world. Thus science is considered to be a largely foreign subject by the local population.'[20]

In an attempt to make the high school science curriculum more relevant to the community in Nain, Labrador, educators are incorporating local terms and examples, and offering an environmental studies course which focuses on local issues.[21] Such an approach may help students see scientific and technical knowledge and skills as important to future community development, and as important to their future roles as community decisionmakers. Outreach components can be included to involve the community, particularly in issues which will have an impact on it.[22]

At a more direct level, the standard of service can be taught by actively involving students in science and technology activities which contribute to community life. Rather than creating artificial, decontextualized learning experiences (e.g., growing seeds in glass jars), students could raise a garden for elders or other community members; use their knowledge of food gathering, preparation, and preservation to help prepare a community feast; or perpetuate sustenance activities through involvement in salmon enhancement programs.

However, if service is to be a standard in science education, and Aboriginal scientists and technologists are to return to their communities, employment opportunities must be created. Educational change cannot occur in a vacuum but must be coordinated with economic, social, and resource developments to ensure that students can apply their new skills within their local communities.

Diversity

> The respect for diversity embodied in the third standard of Indian education requires self-knowledge and self-respect without which respect for others is impossible.[23]

As Hampton points out, the standard of diversity necessitates recognition of and respect for cultural diversity among our peoples. This diversity is captured, in part, by our linguistic complexity. Within Canada, our peoples continue to speak fifty-three different languages belonging to eleven different language families.[24] Our linguistic and cultural diversity is further complicated by post-contact categories such as Métis, status and non-status, treaty and non-treaty, on- and off-reserve, urban and rural, and most recently, Bill C-31. The generic term 'Indian' applied to us by outsiders has little meaning in our own lives.

The historic policy paper written by the NIB (now the Assembly of First Nations or AFN), *Indian Control of Indian Education*, recognizes the importance of diversity in its demand for local control of and parental responsibility for our children's education.[25] This position is reasserted in the AFN's 1988 report, *Tradition and Education: Towards a Vision of Our Future*.[26] The principal of local control applies to the science curriculum like any other curriculum; it must be based on community input and community approval. This need for local control of science education is clearly recognized and supported by the 1992 Science Council of Canada (SCC) report, *Northern Science for Northern Society: Building Economic Self-Reliance*:

> The Science Council supports the long-term goal that the science education and technical training programs be located in the North and designed and delivered by Northerners. For the immediate future, the Council calls for Northerners to assume increasing control over the design and delivery of local programs. The Council also encourages northern school boards and colleges to base their courses and programs on the northern environment and local cultures.[27]

Culture

> The fourth standard of Indian education is culture. Indian cultures have ways of thought, learning, teaching, and communicating that are different than but of equal validity to those of White cultures. These thought-ways stand at the beginning of Indian time and are the foundations of our children's lives. Their full flower is in what it means to be one of the people.[28]

The most obvious culturally specific form of communication is language, and lack of competency in English is frequently cited as a barrier to success in school science for Aboriginal and other minority students.[29] Furthermore, specialized science vocabulary may create further barriers for some students and its impersonal and passive style can be alienating.[30] In communities where students speak Aboriginal languages, it is suggested that a bilingual approach to science education be used, particularly at the elementary level.[31] Educators may also want to explore alternative ways of communicating (e.g., drawing and painting, making models, graphs, and displays, and audio and video recordings) which are not so heavily dependent upon language skills.[32]

The use of Aboriginal languages in the science classroom may boost achievement and may increase the use of traditional science.[33] However, success in Western school science requires understanding and manipulating scientific vocabulary. The science teacher can help students gradually enlarge their own language base to incorporate the language of science.[34] This may best be accomplished by allowing children to express themselves in their own languages first, and then gradually developing conventional scientific language competencies.[35] Language acquisition could be assisted by identifying difficulties which may be specific to certain language groups.[36] In collaboration with ESL teachers, strategies could be developed to help students learn the necessary language skills.[37] Comprehending textbook reading assignments could be facilitated by pre-reading activities which have explicit reading objectives, introduce new vocabulary, and provide links with previous experiences or knowledge.[38]

A variety of other cultural factors may affect classroom communication. For example, some of our students' conversations may have a longer 'wait time' between responses. Learning may be enhanced by teachers 'tuning in' to the students' rhythms of conversation and movement. Aboriginal students may tend to utilize certain learning styles.[39] It is important to point out, however, that there is no generic 'Indian' learning style. While some research may identify patterns of learning among some groups of Aboriginal peoples, there are significant variations between tribes and individuals. Uncritical application of learning style theory is potentially racist.[40] Educators must guard against stereotypical views gleaned from representations of a culture in the literature which ignore the dynamic lived realities of the people. While such literature is a first step, it must be supplemented with real interaction with students, parents, and the community.[41]

Attention to the standard of culture also means that the science curriculum should incorporate culturally appropriate teaching methodology. Traditional cultures had richly diverse approaches to educating their young, and as Deloria bluntly states, 'there is no excuse for avoiding traditional ways of teaching in favor of non-Indian techniques which have proven themselves failures.'[42] The adaptation of traditional teaching methodologies such as experiential learning, storytelling, observation, supervised and unsupervised participation, inter-generational teaching, apprenticeship, dreaming and imagination, and ritual and ceremony, can provide powerful educational tools for Aboriginal (and other) students.[43]

The hands-on approach to science education is thought by some to be particularly effective with Aboriginal students, and several authors have suggested its use.[44] However, such an approach may, at times, be problematic as traditions among some tribes or clans may be violated by the killing, collecting, dissecting, handling, or even viewing of animals and plants. Burgoyne suggests that educators speak to Aboriginal students, parents, and spiritual leaders so that school expectations can be clarified, areas of concern identified, and possible solutions or alternatives explored.[45]

The use of traditional stories as a vehicle for science education is gaining popularity.[46] Through traditional stories, 'generations of understanding' about the natural world, and the philosophy and values which guided the

Aboriginal people's interaction with it, are kept alive. As Cajete points out, 'because many Native American myths relate the learner to paradigms of proper relationships to plants, animals, and all of nature, as well as to the consequences of mis-relationship to nature, they provide an important place to begin a greatly humanized discussion of the general areas and underlying assumptions of modern science.'[47]

However, educators must be cautious about incorporating traditional stories into the curriculum. Traditional stories are not just teaching aides, they have power and integrity of their own.[48] This integrity can be destroyed by poor translations, omissions, and elaborations.[49] As Walter Lightning points out, certain stories

> can only be told by persons who have the authority to do so, during the proper season, and under the proper conditions ... Keeping constraints on the telling of these stories is for a purpose. It may be said that all of the stories form a huge and complex fabric. The stories cannot be understood unless they are told by persons who know (1) how to put the specific narrative within the context of all the other possible narratives in that complex fabric; (2) how to fit the way the story is told to the specific audience at the specific time; (3) the system of metaphor that is used or adapted in the story; (4) the authority under which the story is told.[50]

These issues underscore the need to pay attention to the standard of diversity in developing culturally appropriate curricula.

Educators must realize that some of the skills valued in Western education may be seen to undermine traditional values and behaviour. For example, critical thinking and questioning may be viewed as challenging the traditional etiquette of respectful listening and competitiveness and individualism may be an affront to cooperation and social cohesion.[51] If these skills are to be encouraged in the school room, teachers and students may first find it useful to spend time discussing context-specific behaviour.

Tradition

> The fifth standard of Indian education is tradition: Indian education maintains a continuity with tradition. Our traditions define and preserve us. It is important to understand that this continuity with tradition is neither a rejection of the artifacts of other cultures nor an attempt to 'turn back the clock' ... It is the continuity of a living culture that is important to Indian education, not the preservation of a frozen museum specimen.[52]

One way of incorporating traditional content into the curriculum is exploring the way in which different cultures have incorporated science and technology into their lives historically.[53] Unfortunately, such information about our peoples seldom finds its way into the science curriculum, and students, both Aboriginal and non-Aboriginal, often remain unaware of our historical contribution in these areas.

Incorporating Aboriginal historical contributions into the science curriculum may give students insight into the wealth of knowledge and understanding inherent in traditional cultures. In addition, students will be able to explore the cultural contexts in which Aboriginal scientists and technologists historically lived and worked. This approach will contribute significantly to the presentation of a more authentic view of science in an historical, social, cultural, and Canadian context, as recommended by the SCC.[54]

However, educators should avoid portraying our peoples in historical contexts alone and thereby contributing to a frozen, static picture of our cultures. While traditional knowledge is that which has accumulated over time and is transmitted across generations from elders to young people, it is far from static.

> The term 'traditional knowledge' should not, however, be understood in a static sense, thereby implying that it represents a finite body of information, an unchanging legacy from the past. Traditional knowledge is really part of the evolving culture of a community. It includes all the current intellectual, social and material elements of that community's life; it provides the context by which people in that community interact with the world.[55]

Utilizing Aboriginal resource people, including traditional and conventional scientists and technologists, will do much to show science as a relevant and vital part of the Aboriginal and wider communities.

Respect

> The individual Indian's sense of personal power and autonomy is a strength that lies behind the apparent weakness of disunity ... Standard Six: Respect, Indian education demands relationships of personal respect.[56]

Traditional child-rearing practices respected the autonomy of the individual. Independent exploration was encouraged and parenting was often characterized by non-interference:

Children are expected to constantly observe the world around them and learn from it. From this it can be seen that one does not 'teach' a child to learn. This amount of intervention in the child's autonomy would risk forever destroying the child's ability to observe and learn from his [sic] own motives. The child is encouraged only to seek out knowledge of human experience and skills by being present in [the] practice of their telling.[57]

One way to respect this personal power and autonomy is to recognize and honour the knowledge and skills children bring with them into the classroom. Aboriginal students bring rich and varied experiences with them, and educators have been recommended to use this experience as a basis for their science instruction.[58] However, despite research findings which highlight the importance of building on such previous knowledge, science teachers apparently ignore the cultural influences on students' knowledge and experience. Hodson suggests that students' knowledge and experience may be more important than the teacher's own cultural knowledge as it validates the expertise of *all* students and reverses the teacher's usual position as the authority, thereby promoting a more demo-cratic learning environment.[59]

A more democratic learning environment is important for respecting individual autonomy. Power and authority now reside almost totally with administrators, curriculum experts, and teachers who may ignore the wishes of elders, parents, and students. Students are expected to master the same curriculum, at the same rate, at the same age, and demonstrate their mastery by the same means. A more democratic system might give students greater choice in what is learned, when it is learned, how it is learned, and how learning is assessed. It could also end the isolation of the student from the community in age and ability groupings by embrac-ing multi-age, -grade, and -generation learning environments.[60]

History

Standard seven: History, Indian education has a sense of history and does not avoid the hard facts of the conquest of America.[61]

The history of the colonization of the Americas has an important role in the science education of our children. Scientific and technological devel-opments have served to benefit the few at the expense of many. Science education, through its avoidance of the social, political, and economic contexts in which science and technology are developed and applied, and through its promotion of the scientific and technological fix, sustains these inequities. Educators should question assumptions about who benefits and who suffers from scientific and technological development.[62]

Conventional biology, with its theories of evolution and natural selection and survival of the fittest, may lead students to internalize a hierarchical view of human evolution, with Westerners at the apex and tribal peoples at the bottom.[63] Studies of the concept of race, of its use in perpetuating individual and institutional racism, and of how scientific racism was used to justify the colonization and oppression of our peoples would be appropriate.[64]

Of course, racist and ethnocentric materials have no place in the school room, and curriculum materials need to be reviewed. The involvement of students in reviews will alert them to issues of invisibility, bias, stereotyping, and racism while providing them with the skills to evaluate information in other contexts.[65]

The social, political, and economic influences on and of science and technology may be explored by having students delve into the way in which science and technology have affected their own history and environment.[66] It was, and continues to be, the desire for economic gain which fuelled the exploration and colonization of our lands. The desire to exploit resources resulted in the usurpation of our lands, the displacement of our peoples, the undermining of our economic independence, the annihilation of plant and animal life, and the contamination of our air, water, and food sources. Science educators could, for example, inform their students of how corporate water development in Canada has flooded our people's traplines, hunting grounds, and burial grounds; contaminated fish which traditionally formed a major part of many peoples' diets; and displaced peoples from their traditional territories.[67]

Such examination can be expanded to the international application of science and technology.[68] It becomes very apparent that it is often the colonized peoples who pay the price for development. As Eduardo Galeano states in *Open Veins of Latin America*, 'Our defeat was always implicit in the history of others; our wealth has always generated our poverty by nourishing the prosperity of others, the empires and their native overseers ... In the colonial and neocolonial alchemy, gold changes to scrap metal and food into poison ... [We] have become painfully aware of the mortality of wealth which nature bestows and imperialism appropriates.'[69]

Throughout the world, indigenous peoples suffer the consequences of colonization and development. In Oceania and Micronesia nuclear testing has destroyed the land, uprooted the peoples, increased radiation-related illnesses, and undermined indigenous economies and political structures. The Ainu of Japan and the Sami of northern Scandinavia are both fighting water-development projects which threaten to flood their lands and radically alter their environment and their lives. The lives and cultures of the peoples of Southern Africa, the Amazon basin of Brazil, Peru, and Ecuador are threatened by deforestation and agribusiness.[70] Such studies clearly fall within the realm of an anti-racist science education which calls attention to attitudes and practices which discriminate against certain groups and foster inequality.[71]

Relentlessness

> Standard eight: Relentlessness, Indian education is relentless in its battle for Indian children. We take pride in our warriors and our teachers are warriors for the life of our children.[72]

In our role as warriors for the science education of Aboriginal children, we must, of course, be committed to teaching science. Such a statement may seem obvious, but according to the SCC there is inadequate science instruction in schools, particularly at the elementary level.[73] On rural reserves in the United States, science instruction seldom begins before grade six, and the inadequacy of pre-college science tuition is one of the reasons for Aboriginal under-representation in science studies.[74] The same dynamics are probably present in Canada.

Furthermore, as Aboriginal students are often in compensatory programs where 'basics' are stressed, science instruction is often limited. Small high schools may offer a limited number of science courses, and as a result students begin university with a deficit.[75] Schools, particularly in remote areas, may lack adequate facilities, equipment, and materials. Moreover, parents apparently hold conflicting attitudes towards institutionalized education, seeing it as beneficial to their children's future but threatening to their culture. Hence, support for science education in the home may be limited.[76] These factors suggest that teachers will have to be particularly relentless in science education.

While many students need better counselling on career opportunities in the sciences, various authors have stressed the need for better counselling services for Aboriginal students specifically.[77] The lack of science role models for Aboriginal students has been particularly acute. In the USA, tribal colleges and schools are creating opportunities for college and high school students to serve as role models for younger students in science-related activities. Science fairs, community workshops, field trips, summer science programs, visiting scientists, and establishment of chapters of the American Indian Science and Engineering Society or the Canadian Aboriginal Science and Technology Society are all ways in which our young people can be exposed to role models.[78]

The lack of basic academic skills is also a barrier to continued studies in the sciences, and mathematics has been identified as a primary obstacle.[79] Science education cannot, therefore, be divorced from other educational studies. As Ovando states, 'a science curriculum which has been carefully adapted to reflect culturally-compatible classroom practices and home experiences may not be effective unless teachers are deeply committed to the academic and personal growth of their students.'[80]

Haig-Brown reminds science educators that social 'passes' cannot be justified. She points to Kleinfeld's work, which shows that the teachers who are most effective with Aboriginal students are those who are able to demonstrate both personal warmth and high expectations.[81]

The need to create and implement unique approaches to science education for Aboriginal students suggests a concomitant need to address teacher education. Here universities, particularly those which have teacher education programs for our people, have a role to play. The Division of Native Education at the Northern Arizona University is taking the lead by developing a curriculum which challenges the stereotype of our peoples as non-scientific, promotes traditional contributions to science, and provides alternatives to classroom activities which may conflict with traditional values. The curriculum also incorporates traditional teaching approaches, provides a holistic approach to science education, and incorporates traditional values and ethics.[82]

Another model of professional development is the Lakota Outdoor Summer Science Camp. This provides an opportunity for teachers to develop their science teaching skills while working with students and promotes a hands-on, cooperative approach to science education.[83] The Kativik School Board in northern Quebec is using a community-based model which includes teacher education in subject content, collaboration with elders to identify concept and content areas relevant to Inuit language and culture, and the development of detailed, activity-centred programs.

Vitality

Standard nine: Vitality, Indian education recognizes and nourishes the powerful pattern of life that lies hidden within personal and tribal suffering and oppression. Suffering begets strength. We have not vanished.[84]

Our peoples have not vanished, nor has our traditional knowledge. Despite the fact that our understanding of the world has been 'denied or denigrated, rather than respected and utilized,'[85] traditional knowledge continues to exist in the living memories of elders. However, the passing away of the old necessitates efforts to gather and preserve their knowledge in a form that can be transmitted to subsequent generations.[86]

Colorado points out that we cannot just 'go learn from the Natives.'[87] Working with elders requires an understanding of protocol and the establishment and maintenance of relationships between elder and apprentice. We must demonstrate our worthiness to receive teachings, and we must relearn how to make meaning through reflection and prayer. Furthermore, work in this area requires new approaches to research which allow intellectual exchange while honouring both the knowledge and the people as partners in the research. Aboriginal people, trained in Western science, may have a special role in ensuring the preservation and revitalization of traditional science.[88]

Colorado suggests that participatory research may be a useful and appropriate method of investigating traditional science. However, Aboriginal research organizations, such as the Kuujjuaq Research Centre in northern Quebec, can provide for greater Aboriginal control and responsibility for research while ensuring that research meets the needs of the people themselves. The Kuujjuaq Research Centre plays a crucial role in facilitating Inuit control of scientific research and in investigating traditional science, and provides valuable information for the science curriculum. The development of more organizations like this has been recommended by the SCC.[89]

Conflict

Standard ten: Conflict, Indian education recognizes the conflict, tensions, and struggle between itself and white education as well as with education generally. Western education is in content and structure hostile to Native people. It must be straightforwardly realized that education, as currently practiced, is cultural genocide.[90]

Students from diverse backgrounds commonly envision science as a Western activity, and Aboriginal students are said to share this view.[91] Rayna Green states that 'contrary to the general insistence of Western scientists that science is not culture bound and that it produces good, many native people feel that science and scientists are thoroughly Western, rather than universal, and that science is negative.'[92]

The alienation that many Aboriginal students feel towards science may be due to the apparent conflict between traditional and conventional science: 'The sources of knowledge of nature and the explanations of natural phenomena within a traditional Native American context are often at odds with what is learned within "school science" and proposed by Western scientific philosophy.'[93]

Educators may dismiss traditional perspectives as unscientific and attempt to replace them with ideas from conventional science. This approach may result in conflict between Aboriginal students, families, communities, and the school. As a result, students may feel anger and frustration and may not grasp, may misinterpret, or may reject conflicting scientific concepts.[94] To counter these feelings, more emphasis is being placed on developing culturally relevant curricula.

Some authors advocate the use of exemplars from Aboriginal tradition to illustrate conventional scientific concepts in order to increase students' academic achievement and self-concept. Such an approach is important because it may allow students to succeed with school science, and provide a foundation for future work or study in science-related areas.[95] However, educators must realize that this approach is not science education from an Aboriginal perspective, but rather involves the appropriation of Aboriginal content to further the goals of Western school science. Educators need to question the ethics of this and to teach students that Western science is one way, not *the* way, to perceive the world.[96]

Another way of incorporating cultural content into the curriculum is to highlight the complementary nature of some traditional teachings and conventional science. This may be valuable in teaching and reinforcing Aboriginal perspectives, but educators should guard against inadvertently telling students that only the perspectives affirmed by conventional science are valuable. Traditional perspectives stand on their own without verification from conventional science.[97] As has been said about oral traditions and teachings such as the Navajo Blessing Way, 'Navajo people have never had to assert [that they] were true or self-evident, because they form the ground for asserting anything; they generate meaningfulness itself; they give cohesion to a whole people and restore cohesion to disturbed minds and bodies; they guarantee belongingness in the universe.'[98]

A more radical curriculum might select certain aspects of conventional science which complement and are validated by traditional perspectives. This is under consideration at the Navajo Community College.[99] While this approach may be of questionable validity in the public education system, it may be appropriate in educational institutions controlled by Aboriginal communities.

Cajete's suggestion that the science curriculum combine both traditional and conventional science seems like a reasonable compromise. In creating a science curriculum for Aboriginal students, conventional science has a place. Not only is a background in conventional science essential for finding employment and providing services to our communities, but, as Deloria reminds us, we need to understand how the Western view of the natural world affects our land and her inhabitants. But conventional science must be presented as a way, not *the* way, of contemplating the universe.

Hence, conventional science needs to be presented in a more realistic way than it has been historically in school science. Scientific and technical knowledge are social constructs and reflect the values of the cultures from which they emerge. This realization challenges assumptions about the universality, rationality, and objectivity of Western science, and opens the mind to other ways of perceiving the natural world.[100]

In addition to reconsidering conventional science, traditional science (also referred to as ethnoscience) must become an integral part of the curriculum. Cajete defines ethnoscience as 'the methods, thought processes, mindsets, values, concepts and experiences by which Native American groups [and other aboriginal peoples] understand, reflect and obtain empirical knowledge about the natural world.'[101] This perspective acknowledges science as a universal activity while recognizing that methods, concepts, and experiences used to gain knowledge of the natural world, and ways in which that knowledge is interpreted, applied, and exploited vary across cultures.[102] All science, including conventional science, can be seen as ethnoscience.

Nor do students need to limit their scientific study to conventional Western science and traditional Aboriginal science. Throughout the world, different cultures have evolved unique ways of perceiving and interacting with the natural world. Islamic science is guided by humility, respect, and recognition of the limits of science; respect and spirituality are key to Maori science; harmony with the natural world is central to many African cultures; and a love of nature is inherent in traditional Japanese science.[103] An international study of indigenous science will help students understand that the Western scientific perspective is a minority view that has been applied aggressively throughout the world – Westerners are anomalous in not perceiving the world as living and female.[104]

Place

Standard eleven: Place, Indian education recognizes the importance of an Indian sense of place, land, and territory.[105]

In his work, Hampton points out that the creation of a sense of place for Aboriginal students at educational institutions can nurture them and contribute to their involvement in the wider educational environment. While creating a meeting place for our students is one way to incorporate a sense of place within a school, changes within the science classroom and curriculum can also lead to an increased sense of place for Aboriginal students.

A sense of place for Aboriginal students in science classrooms may be enhanced by posters of Aboriginal peoples in science-related activities, displays of traditional technology, and labels on materials and equipment in Aboriginal languages. A more significant change would involve hiring Aboriginal science teachers, who could serve as role models and give the classroom a uniquely Aboriginal atmosphere.[106] But there is no reason why the classroom must be contained within the school structure. By expanding the walls of the school into the community, the 'Indian sense of place' is seemingly greatly expanded, as is the involvement of the community in the students' science education.

Hampton also connects a sense of place with our peoples' relationship with the earth. Our identities as Aboriginal peoples have always been based on our connection to the land and all her inhabitants. As Knudtson and Suzuki remark, indigenous peoples 'have a profound and deeply rooted sense of place and relationship with the entirety of the natural world.'[107] Land-based identities cannot be nurtured and perpetuated through classroom activities alone, but require sustained contact with the natural environment. Hence, outdoor education could form a vital part of science education. Fishing camps and traplines could provide wonderful settings for such outdoor experiences.[108]

Nor can our traditional relationship with the land and our knowledge, which is an expression of that relationship, be nurtured in a political vacuum: 'Respect for Native spirituality and the nature-wisdom embedded within it is inseparable from respect for the dignity, human rights, and legitimate land claims of all Native peoples.'[109]

The survival and continued development of traditional science depends upon our continued relationship with the land, a relationship which cannot persist if we remain alienated from our territories. Ruby Dunstan, former chief of the Lytton Band, notes that while ensuring planetary survival is our first priority, 'the second role of indigenous peoples is to protect what is left of the natural world within their traditional homeland with every ounce of their strength and every resource at their disposal.'[110]

Science education can play a role in protecting traditional territories by involving students in activities that contribute to the struggle. Students can, for example, be involved in activities to map out traditional territories, to document resource use and traditional sustainable methods, and to challenge the ideology of development. Continuation of a 'sense of place' requires that attention be paid to the standard of history.

The significance of a sense of place within the natural world is important to non-Aboriginal people as well. Recently, scientists from the Western world have voiced concerns which resonate with traditional wisdom, and called for a change in how conventional scientists view their relationship with and responsibility for the natural world. As Suzuki states, the solution to the environmental crisis lies beyond scientific knowledge or technical know-how. Rather 'we must create for ourselves a sense of place within the biosphere that is steeped in humility and reverence for all other life.'[111] This is a radical departure from conventional science, and calls for both personal and global transformation in conventional views of and relationships to the natural world.

Transformation

The graduates of our schools must not only be able to survive in a White dominated society, they must contribute to the change of that society. Standard twelve: Transformation, Indian education recognizes the need for transformation in the relation between Indian and White as well as in the individual and society.[112]

By incorporating the standards of spirituality, service, diversity, culture, tradition, respect, history, relentlessness, vitality, conflict, and place, we transform the science curriculum from one which is essentially assimilationist to one which honours, respects, and nurtures our traditional beliefs and life-ways, and which presents science and technology in a more authentic way. Such a curriculum transformation could greatly benefit our students.

It may transform the Aboriginal students' experiences in school because the inclusion of traditional science reportedly enhances self-image and improves student behaviour and attitudes towards science; leads to improvement in basic science skills and retention of concepts; motivates students to use communication and mathematical skills in learning activities; and contributes to the recognition, preservation, and development of traditional science. And because researching traditional science necessitates communication with elders and other community members, it may lead to improved relationships between students and the guardians of cultural knowledge.[113]

This recreation of science curricula would also benefit non-Aboriginal students. An understanding of traditional science may result in increased respect for Aboriginal people and their experience, knowledge, and values. And an understanding of traditional values about the natural world can benefit all people.[114] Furthermore, as Snively states, the inclusion of both traditional and conventional science 'provide[s] a broader perspective on the natural environment than can either by itself. It is possible and even desirable to explore the different perspectives each tradition generates during instruction.'[115]

Transforming the school experience of our young people could lead to a transformation of our communities. The development of Aboriginal scientists and technologists will enable more of our people to obtain profitable employment. More importantly, their professional expertise can help guide community decision-making in a variety of areas, including economic, resource, and social development.

Ultimately the transformation of school science may lead to a transformation of science itself as Aboriginal students obtain 'the armour they need to maintain a sense of difference' while undertaking further studies in science.[116] A sense of difference in traditional perspectives on the natural world may provide the foundation upon which Aboriginal scientists can work synergistically with Western scientists to develop a relationship between traditional and conventional science for the benefit of all.[117]

Given the inadequacy of conventional science in dealing with the growing environmental crisis, the need to reevaluate relationships with and responsibilities towards the natural world is urgent. Many look to traditional science to address this need. As Tom Henley states, 'Native pathways (lifestyles, value systems, and traditions) are as likely to hold a key to human survival as the trend toward western culture. As in the biological world, cultural diversity may be more than the "spice of life"; it may prove the secret to our survival.'[118]

Conclusion
The standards proposed by Hampton can be a powerful framework for reconsidering science education for Aboriginal students. Some of the standards, such as spirituality, conflict, vitality, and transformation, ask us to reconceptualize science. Others, such as service, tradition, history, and place, ask that we recontextualize our teaching. The standards of culture and respect challenge us to reconsider our teaching practices. The standard of diversity requires that our peoples reassert our authority over their children's education. And the standard of relentlessness demands that we remain dedicated, determined, and ceaseless in the struggle for their education. The thoughtful reconsideration of science education, based on

these standards, may also help us develop a curriculum which promotes 'the preservation and sensible use of our lands' and ensures 'the continuing existence of our tribes.'[119]

Notes

1 National Indian Brotherhood 1972; Barman, Hébert, and McCaskill 1986, 15-17; Kirkness 1986, 74-9; Kirkness 1992, 27-55.
2 Kirkness and Bowman 1992, 27-55.
3 Armstrong, Kennedy, and Oberle 1990, 6-12.
4 Assembly of First Nations 1988, 107; Kirkness and Bowman 1992, 39; Science Council of Canada 1991, 25; Urban Native Indian Education Society 1987, 11-21.
5 Science Council of Canada 1984, 13-18.
6 Science Council of Canada 1991, 14-22.
7 Cassidy and Dale 1988.
8 Deloria 1991, 50.
9 Hampton 1988.
10 Ibid., 42.
11 Following Killackey 1988, 6, the term traditional science is used to discuss the science of Aboriginal origin, while conventional science applies to that of Western origin.
12 Deloria 1991, 10.
13 Snow 1977b, 28.
14 Killackey 1988, 22; MacIvor 1990, 92.
15 Killackey 1988, 20-3.
16 Green and Brown 1976, 7.
17 Mander 1991.
18 Hampton 1988, 45.
19 Green and Brown 1976, 5; Deloria 1991, 49; Boult, Pokiak, and Weihs 1991, 31.
20 Boult, Pokiak, and Weihs 1991, 36.
21 Ibid.
22 Green and Brown 1976, 5.
23 Hampton 1988, 57.
24 Kirkness 1989, 26.
25 National Indian Brotherhood 1972.
26 Assembly of First Nations 1986.
27 Science Council of Canada 1991, 9. While the quote is phrased in terms of 'Northerners' rather than Aboriginal peoples, the SCC makes it clear that Aboriginal peoples form a significant percentage of that population.
28 Hampton 1988, 59.
29 Boult, Pokiak, and Weihs 1991, 27, 36, 59, 94; Hodson 1992, 17-18; Green and Brown 1976, 7; Hoyle 1987, 30; Smith 1982, 14; Ovando 1987, 165-7; Science Council of Canada 1991, 24.
30 Chamberlain 1987, 8; Hodson 1992, 18; Hoyle 1987, 28.

31 Green and Brown 1976, 7; Ovando 1987, 165-7; Science Council of Canada 1991, 32.
32 Hodson 1992, 17; Smith 1982, 14.
33 Ovando 1987, 65; Swift 1992, 16.
34 Hodson 1992, 18.
35 Ibid.
36 Ibid., 17.
37 Hoyle 1987, 30.
38 Ovando 1987, 167-8.
39 Hampton 1988, 53-7.
40 More 1987, 27; Hodson 1992, 20.
41 Haig-Brown 1990, 93; Cajete 1986, 199.
42 Deloria 1991, 64.
43 Cajete 1986, 151-67; More 1987, 22-4.
44 Boult, Pokiak, and Weihs 1991, 36; Lawrenz 1988, 681; Smith 1982, 13; Green and Brown 1976, 6; Science Council of Canada 1991, 35.
45 Burgoyne 1988, 315.
46 See for example Skinner 1976; Caduto and Bruchac 1989.
47 Cajete 1986, 233.
48 Hampton, personal communication, November 1992.
49 Knudtson and Suzuki 1992, xv-xviii, discuss how Chief Seattle's famous speech has been reinterpreted by others to such an extent that it cannot be said to represent an Aboriginal voice. They point out the need to ensure the authenticity of text.
50 Lightning 1992, 3.
51 Hampton 1988, 53; Hodson 1992, 19-20. Hodson's discussion pertains to multicultural science education, but it is important in the context of Aboriginal education as well.
52 Hampton 1988, 60-1.
53 Bentley and Ditchfield 1987, 12-13; Hodson 1992, 23-4.
54 Bentley and Ditchfield 1987, 12-13; Hodson 1992, 23-4; Snively 1990, 56; Science Council of Canada 1984, 37-8.
55 Boult, Pokiak, and Weihs 1991, 88.
56 Hampton 1988, 63.
57 Scollon and Scollon cited in More 1987, 23.
58 Green and Brown 1976, 6; Snively 1990, 57; Science Council of Canada 1991, 33.
59 Hodson 1992, 19.
60 Ibid., 21-2; Campbell 1992, 100-9.
61 Hampton 1988, 65-6.
62 Hodson 1992, 24; Chamberlain 1987, 8.
63 Chamberlain 1987, 7.
64 Hodson 1992, 22.
65 Ibid., 20-1.
66 Bentley and Ditchfield 1987, 13.
67 Quinn 1991, 137-54.

68 Hodson 1992, 24-5.
69 Cited in Churchill and LaDuke 1992, 241.
70 For an overview of indigenous struggle against Western-style development see Mander 1991, 263-376.
71 Ditchfield 1987, 39.
72 Hampton 1988, 66.
73 Science Council of Canada 1984, 25.
74 Hill 1991, 24.
75 Ovando 1987, 167; Leonard, Freim, and Fein 1975, 10-11. While these works refer to Native American education, it is likely the same dynamics are at work in Canada.
76 Science Council of Canada 1991, 25; Boult, Pokiak, and Weihs 1991, 59, 86.
77 Science Council of Canada 1984, 36; Green and Brown 1976, 6-8; Hill 1991, 25; Urban Native Indian Education Society 1987, 21; Science Council of Canada 1991, 24.
78 Boult, Pokiak, and Weihs 1991, 37, 60; Science Council of Canada 1991, 24; Indians in science: Tribal colleges take the lead 1992, 88-93. The Canadian Aboriginal Science and Technology Society (CASTS) is currently located at the Treaty 7 Tribal Council, Suite 525, 10333 Southport Road SW, Calgary, AB T2W 3X6.
79 Boult, Pokiak, and Weihs 1991, 38, 57; Science Council of Canada 1991, 25; Hill 1991, 26; Green and Brown 1976, 7.
80 Ovando 1987, 163.
81 Haig-Brown 1987, 18-19; Kleinfeld 1972, 18-44.
82 Greer 1992, 12-18.
83 Hamilton 1992, 74-9.
84 Hampton 1988, 71.
85 Science Council of Canada 1991, 23.
86 Deloria 1991, 18.
87 Colorado 1988,62.
88 Deloria 1991, 18.
89 Colorado 1988, 62-4; Science Council of Canada 1991, 34, 37.
90 Hampton 1988, 72.
91 Bentley and Ditchfield 1987, 11; Boult, Pokiak, and Weihs 1991, 16, 36, 93-4; Science Council of Canada 1991, 25.
92 Cited in Cajete 1986, 16.
93 Cajete 1986, 188.
94 Ibid., 189; Snively 1990, 54.
95 Snow, 1977a, 55-7; 1977b, 30; Cajete 1986, 37; Snively 1990, 54-5.
96 Snively 1990, 54-5.
97 Knudtson and Suzuki 1992, 86.
98 Navajo Community College 1989, 2.
99 Ibid., 44.
100 Hodson 1992, 25-6.
101 Cajete 1986, 123.
102 Ibid., 123-4.

103 Hodson 1992, 25; Ogawa 1989, 248. For an overview of traditional perspectives of the natural world held by indigenous peoples see Knudtson and Suzuki, 1992.
104 Mander 1991, 212.
105 Hampton 1988, 81.
106 See for example Lipka 1990, 18-32.
107 Knudtson and Suzuki 1992, 7-8.
108 Kawagley 1990, 15.
109 Knudtson and Suzuki 1992, 18.
110 Cited in ibid., 189.
111 Knudtson and Suzuki 1992, xxiv.
112 Hampton 1988, 82-3.
113 Cajete 1986, 39; Killackey 1988, 16-20.
114 Green and Brown 1976, 7; Killackey 1988, 21.
115 Snively 1990, 56.
116 Haig-Brown 1990, 103.
117 Boult, Pokiak, and Weihs 1991, 88.
118 Henley 1989, 26.
119 Deloria 1991, 50.

References

Armstrong, R., J. Kennedy, and P. Oberle. 1990. *University education and economic well-being*. Ottawa: Indian and Northern Affairs Canada

Assembly of First Nations. 1988. *Tradition and education*. Vol. 1, *Towards a vision of our future*. Ottawa: Assembly of First Nations

Barman, J., Y. Hébert, and D. McCaskill. 1986. The legacy of the past. In *Indian education in Canada*. Vol. 1, *The legacy*, ed. J. Barman, Y. Hébert, and D. McCaskill, 1-22. Vancouver: University of British Columbia Press

Bentley, D., and C. Ditchfield. 1987. The contributions of the SSCR groups to the development of science education in a multicultural society. In *Better science*, comp. C. Ditchfield, 11-15. London: Heinemann

Berg, D.L., and D. MacKeracher. 1985. Science Education. In *Science education in Canada*. Vol. 1, *Policies, practices, and perceptions*, ed. F.M. Connelly, R.K. Crocker, and H. Kass, 59-81. Toronto: Ontario Institute for Studies in Education

Boult, D., R. Pokiak, and F.H. Weihs. 1991. Science and technology in the development of northern communities. Manuscript. Science Council of Canada

Burgoyne, P. 1988. Native American problems in biology classes. *The American Biology Teacher* 50 (5):315

Caduto, M.J., and J. Bruchac. 1989. *Keepers of the earth*. Saskatoon: Fifth House Publishers

Cajete, G.A. 1986. Science: A Native American perspective. Ph.D. dissertation, International College, Los Angeles, California

Campbell, A. 1992. Are traditional and modern education incompatible?

Winds of Change 6, 4 (Autumn):100-9

Cassidy, F., and N. Dale. 1988. *After Native claims?* Lantzville, BC: Oolichan Books and Halifax, NS: Institute for Research on Public Policy

Chamberlain, P.J. 1987. Science teaching in multicultural Britain and the SSCR. In *Better Science*, comp. C. Ditchfield, 6-10. London: Heinemann

Churchill, W., and W. LaDuke. 1992. Native North America. In *The state of Native America*, ed. M.A. Jaimes, 241-66. Boston: South End Press

Colorado, P. 1988. Bridging Native and Western science. *Convergence* 21 (2/3):49-68

Cove, J. 1987. *Shattered images*. Ottawa: Carleton University Press

Deloria, V. Jr. 1991. *Indian education in America*. Boulder: American Indian Science and Engineering Society

Ditchfield, C, comp. 1987. *Better Science*. London: Heinemann

Green, R. 1976. *The barriers obstructing the entry of Native Americans into the natural sciences*. Washington: American Association for the Advancement of Science

Green, R., and J. Brown. 1976. *Recommendations for the improvement of science and mathematics education for American Indians*. Washington: American Association for the Advancement of Science

Greer, S. 1992. Science: It's not just a white man's thing. *Winds of Change* 7, 2 (Spring):12-18

Haig-Brown, C. 1987. *Bridging the gap*. Vancouver: Urban Native Indian Education Society

–. 1990. Science teaching. In *Innovative multicultural teaching*, ed. V. D'Oyley and S. Shapson, 92-105. Toronto: Kagan and Woo

Hamilton, C. 1992. Science education on Pine Ridge. *Winds of Change* 7, 4 (Autumn):74-9

Hampton, E. 1988. Toward a redefinition of American Indian/Alaska Native education. Ed.D. dissertation, Harvard Graduate School of Education

Henley, T. 1989. *Rediscovery ancient pathways – new directions*. Vancouver: Western Canada Wilderness Committee

Hill, N. 1991. AISES: A college intervention program that works. *Change* 23 (2):24-6

Hodson, D. 1992. Towards a framework for multicultural science education. *Curriculum* 13 (1):15-28

Hoyle, P. 1987. Science education in and for a multicultural society. In *Better science*, comp. C. Ditchfield, 28-32. London: Heinemann

Indians in science: Tribal colleges take the lead. 1992. *Winds of Change* 6, 4 (Autumn):88-93

Kawagley, O. 1990. Yup'ik ways of knowing. *Canadian Journal of Native Education* 17 (2):5-17

Killackey, A. 1988. *The outdoor world science and mathematics project, life sciences teacher's guide*. Flagstaff, AZ: Northern Arizona University

Kirkness, V. 1986. Indian control of Indian education: Over a decade later. In *Selected papers from the first Mokakit Conference July 25-27, 1984*, ed. H.A. McCue, 74-9. Vancouver: Mokakit Indian Education Research Association

–. 1989. Aboriginal languages foundation: A mechanism for language renewal. *Canadian Journal of Native Education* 16 (2):25-41

Kirkness, V., and S. Bowman. 1992. *First Nations and schools*. Toronto: Canadian Education Association

Kleinfeld, J. 1972. *Effective teachers of Indian and Eskimo high school students*. Fairbanks, AL: Centre for Northern Educational Research

Knudtson, P., and D. Suzuki. 1992. *Wisdom of the elders*. Toronto: Stoddart

Lawrenz, F. 1988. Native American school environmments. *School Science and Mathematics* 88 (8):676-81

Leonard, L., J. Freim, and J. Fein. 1975. Introducing engineering to the American Indian. *Journal of American Indian Education* 14 (2):6-11

Lightning, W. 1992. Compassionate mind: Implications of a text written by Elder Louis Sunchild. M.A. thesis, University of Alberta, Edmonton

Lipka, J. 1990. Integrating cultural form and content in one Yup'ik Eskimo classroom. *Canadian Journal of Native Education* 17 (2):18-32

MacIvor, M. 1990. Research into traditional First Nations healing practices. *Canadian Journal of Native Education* 17 (2):89-95

Mander, J. 1991. *In the absence of the sacred*. San Francisco: Sierra Club Books

More, A. 1987. Native Indian learning styles. *Journal of American Indian Education* 27, 2 (October):17-29

National Indian Brotherhood. 1972. *Indian control of Indian education*. Ottawa: National Indian Brotherhood

Navajo Community College. 1989. Dene philosophy of learning: Faculty implementation handbook. Draft. Navajo Community College

Ogawa, M. 1989. Beyond the tacit framework of 'science' and 'science educa-tion' among science educators. *International Journal of Science Education* 11 (3):247-50

Ovando, C. 1987. Teaching science to the Native American student. In *Teaching the Indian child*, ed. J. Reyhner, 159-77. Billings: Eastern Montana College

Quinn, F. 1991. As long as the rivers run. *Canadian Journal of Native Studies* 11 (1):137-54

Science Council of Canada. 1984. *Science for every student*. Ottawa: Science Council of Canada

–. 1991. *Northern science for northern society*. Ottawa: Supply and Services Canada

Skinner, L. 1976. *Star Stories*. Washington DC: Native American Science Education Association

Smith, M. 1982. Science for the Native oriented classroom. *Journal of American Indian Education* 21 (3):13-17

–. 1984. Astronomy in the Native oriented classroom. *Journal of American Indian Education* 23 (2):16-23

Snively, G. 1990. Traditional Native Indian beliefs, cultural values, and science instruction. *Canadian Journal of Native Education* 17 (1):44-59

Snow, A. 1977a. Ethno-science and the gifted in American Indian education. *The Gifted Child Quarterly* 21 (1):53-7

–. 1977b. Ethno-science and the gifted. *Journal of American Indian Education* 16 (2):27-30

Swift, D. 1992. Indigenous knowledge in the service of science and technology in developing countries. *Studies in Science Education* 20:1-28

Urban Native Indian Education Society. 1987. *A research report on Indian and Inuit health careers in British Columbia.* Vancouver: Urban Native Indian Education Society

Southern Door:
Connecting with and Maintaining
Our Relations

4
Aboriginal Epistemology
Willie Ermine

When I heard the learn'd astronomer,
When the proofs, the figures, were ranged in columns
before me,
When I was shown the charts and diagrams, to add,
divide, and measure them,
When I sitting heard the astronomer where he
lectured with much applause in the lecture room,
How soon unaccountable I became tired and sick,
Till rising and gliding out I wander'd off by myself,
In the mystical moist night air, and from time to time,
Look'd up in perfect silence at the stars.
                                    – Walt Whitman

The year 1492 marked the first meeting of two disparate world-views, each on its own uncharted course of exploration and discovery for purposeful knowledge. The encounter featured two diametric trajectories into the realm of knowledge. One was bound for an uncharted destination in outer space, the physical, and the other was on a delicate path into inner space, the metaphysical.

The Aboriginal world has since felt the repercussions of that encounter of world-views. The relentless subjugation of Aboriginal people and the discounting of their ideas have hurt those aboard the Aboriginal voyage of discovery into the inner space. The tribal crews, along with their knowledge and secrets, came precariously close to aborting their inward missions. Meanwhile, the Western world-view and the concomitant exploration of the outer space continued unabated for the next five centuries. Acquired knowledge and information were disseminated as if Western voyages and discoveries were the only valid sources to knowing. The alternative expeditions and discoveries in subjective inner space by Aboriginal people wait to be told.

This chapter aims, first, to discuss ideology in relation to the Aboriginal world-view. The ideology that directs information- and knowledge-gathering determines the purpose and method of knowing. Second, the chapter examines the premise that Aboriginal people were on a valid search for subjective inner knowledge in order to arrive at insights into existence. What Aboriginals found in the exploration of the self became the basis of continued personal development and of Aboriginal epistemology. This chapter's basic assumption is that individuals and society can be transformed by identifying and reaffirming learning processes based on subjective experiences and introspection. For Aboriginal people, first languages and culture are crucial components in the transformative learning process. The three specific orientations of the transformation are: skills that promote personal and social transformation; a vision of social change that leads to harmony with rather than control over the environment; and the attribution of a spiritual dimension to the environment (Miller, Cassie, and Drake 1990, 4).

Ideology is one determinant of the quality of research on epistemology. Early ideas such as Destutt de Tracy's (1801) definition of ideology as the science of ideas used to distinguish science from the metaphysical suggest the Western world's direction and purpose in seeking the nature and origin of knowledge. Subsequent categorization and selective validation of knowledge by Western science has inevitably influenced Western ideology as the driving force behind knowing. Engels's later definition of ideology as the 'attitudes and ideas concealing the real nature of social relations to justify and perpetuate social dominance' (1893) also illustrates the Western world's degenerate outlook on knowledge. For Engels, Western attitudes and ideas were such that knowledge was being used for dominance and in effect produced a state of 'false consciousness.' The implication of this 'false consciousness' is that the Western world is guided by invalid criteria in its synthesis of total human knowledge. In short, the Western world has capitulated to a dogmatic fixation on power and control at the expense of authentic insights into the nature and origin of knowledge as truth.

The greater menace to Aboriginal thinking are the assumptions that drive the search for knowledge in the Western world. One assumption is that the universe can be understood and controlled through atomism. The intellectual tendency in Western science is the acquisition and synthesis of total human knowledge within a world-view that seeks to understand the outer space objectively. In the process, Western science, the flagship of the Western world, sought answers to the greatest questions concerning our existence and our place in the universe by keeping everything separate from ourselves. In viewing the world objectively, Western science has habitually fragmented and measured the external space in an attempt to understand it in all its complexity. Fragmentation of the universe has led to what Bohm (1980) calls a 'fragmentary self-world view.'

The fragmentation of the constituents of existence has invariably led to a vicious circle of atomistic thinking that restricts the capacity for holism. Western science's division of the universe into neatly packaged concepts has permeated Western understanding of the world. We see the wretchedness and world despair that Western science has produced based on this fragmentary self-world view, in Purpel's words a 'moral and spiritual crisis' (1989, 28). Fragmentation has become embedded in the Western worldview and is the cornerstone of Western ideology. Aboriginal people should be wary of Western conventions that deny the practice of inwardness and fortitude to achieve transformative holism.

Those people who seek knowledge on the physical plane objectively find their answers through exploration of the outer space, solely on the corporeal level. Those who seek to understand the reality of existence and harmony with the environment by turning inward have a different, incorporeal knowledge paradigm that might be termed Aboriginal epistemology. Aboriginal people have the responsibility and the birthright to take and develop an epistemology congruent with holism and the beneficial transformation of total human knowledge. The way to this affirmation is through our own Aboriginal sources.

As with many other cultures around the world, the holy people and philosophers among Aboriginal people have explored and analyzed the process of self-actualization. The being in relation to the cosmos possessed intriguing and mysterious qualities that provided insights into existence. In their quest to find meaning in the outer space, Aboriginal people turned to the inner space. This inner space is that universe of being within each person that is synonymous with the soul, the spirit, the self, or the being. The priceless core within each of us and the process of touching that essence is what Kierkegaard called 'inwardness' ([1846] 1965, 24). Aboriginal people found a wholeness that permeated inwardness and that also extended into the outer space. Their fundamental insight was that all existence was connected and that the whole enmeshed the being in its inclusiveness. In the Aboriginal mind, therefore, an immanence is present that gives meaning to existence and forms the starting point for Aboriginal epistemology. It is a mysterious force that connects the totality of existence – the forms, energies, or concepts that constitute the outer and inner worlds. Bohm has written that this way of looking at the totality can best be called 'undivided wholeness in flowing movement' (1980, 11). Couture has described this immanence as 'the pervasive, encompassing reality of the life force, manifest in laws – the laws of nature, the laws of energy, or the laws of light' (1991a, 208). To the Cree people it is *muntou*, the mystery. For our Aboriginal scientists, the potential and implications of such insight were gripping. With this 'force,' knowing becomes possible. The Old Ones focused on this area for guidance and as the foundation of all Aboriginal epistemology.

The idea of our progenitors was to try to gain understanding of many of the greatest mysteries of the universe. They sought to do this by exploring existence subjectively; that is, by placing themselves in the stream of consciousness. Our Aboriginal languages and culture contain the accumulated knowledge of our ancestors, and it is critical that we examine the inherent concepts in our lexicons to develop understandings of the self in relation to existence. The Cree word *mamatowisowin*, for example, describes the capability of tapping into the 'life force' as a means of procreation. This Cree concept describes a capacity to be or do anything, to be creative. Couture (1991a, 208) has said that 'elders are familiar with Energy on a vast scale, in multiple modes, e.g., energy as healing, creative, life-giving, sustaining.' *Mamatowisowin* is a capacity to tap the creative force of the inner space by the use of all the faculties that constitute our being – it is to exercise inwardness. Bohm (1980) has discussed Aristotle's notion of causality. His life force or 'energy on the vast scale' is the 'formative cause' that creates *mamatowisowin*. This energy manifests itself in all existence because all of life is connected, and all of life is primarily connected with and accessed through the life force. Huston Smith has said, 'there is, first, a reality that is everywhere and always the same; and second, that human beings always and everywhere have access to it' (1953, 276). To Smith, this is the 'primordial experience.' The Cree concept goes further than Smith, however. For the Cree, the phenomenon of *mamatowan* refers not just to the self but to the being in connection with happenings. It also recognizes that other life forms manifest the creative force in the context of the knower. It is an experience in context, a subjective experience that, for the knower, becomes knowledge in itself. The experience is knowledge.

Indication that Aboriginal people were attaining knowledge of a very different nature and purpose from Western peoples is evident in Aboriginal language and culture. Ancestral explorers of the inner space encoded their findings in community praxis as a way of synthesizing knowledge derived from introspection. The Old Ones had experienced totality, a wholeness, in inwardness, and effectively created a physical manifestation of the life force by creating community. In doing so, they empowered the people to become the 'culture' of accumulated knowledge. The community became paramount by virtue of its role as repository and incubator of total tribal knowledge in the form of custom and culture. Each part of the community became an integral part of the whole flowing movement and was modelled on the inward wholeness and harmony.

The various Aboriginal cultural structures that have survived attest to the conviction of our progenitors and to the depth of their explorations and understanding of the cosmology of the inner world. The deliberate probing of the incorporeal by tribal groups reveals similar experiences and themes in the inner space. Each successive generation of Aboriginal people inherited the fascination with inwardness and has continued the quest for enlightenment in existence. The value of the ancient 'cultures' and of the education system through time is borne out by the persistence of the promise of introspection in constructing meaning for contemporary Aboriginals.

Inquisitiveness about mystery and continued exploration of the inner space is a legacy we must promote in our own time. The accumulation and synthesis of insights and tribal understandings acquired through inwardness, and the juxtaposition of knowledge on the physical plane as culture and community, is the task for contemporary Aboriginal education. The necessary capacity and willingness to be creative by developing *mamatowisowin* is achievable through Aboriginal systems of education.

We have within our tribal communities and cultures vestiges of extraordinary journeys into the unknown by our people. For example, we have from the mists of unremembered time a character in our traditional oral narratives who speaks to us about how we may travel the path into knowing the unknown. The trickster-transformer continues to guide our experiences into the deep reaches of the psyche and the unfathomable mystery of being. The Old Ones knew of this character who directs us around the inner space and saw in him the potential for much deeper exploration into and knowledge from the very self. For this reason, our people's education systems esteemed the Old Ones highly. It was the Old Ones, from their position in the community, who guided young people into various realms of knowledge by using the trickster. The Old Ones, above all, knew the character of the trickster and his capacity to assist with self-actualization. The fact that this trickster-transformer continues to intrigue us speaks of our unfinished exploration of the inner space.

The rituals and ceremonial observances still practised by our Old Ones in our tribal communities compel us to make more inward journeys. Tribal rituals are the calculated trajectories to the world within and any such journeys can only be propelled by the collective energy of a people ordained to explore that domain. The tribal ceremonies display with vivid multidimensional clarity the entries and pathways into this inner world of exciting mystery that has been touched by only the few who have become explorers of sacred knowing. Rituals and ceremonies are corporeal sacred acts that give rise to holy manifestations in the metaphysical world. Conversely, it is the metaphysical that constructs meaning in the corporeal. Continuation of rituals and ceremonies will enable the children of those early spiritual explorers to advance the synthesized understanding of inner space.

We have, as well, the physical clues of valuable conceptualizations. The outcrops of stone and rock known as medicine wheels survive from a time when our people were actively exploring the inner space. These wheels convey concepts derived from introspection and illustrate the pathways to self-discovery, the first door to mystery. They speak, in the silence of the unknown, about the progressive growth of self through a cyclical journey of repetition, experience, and construction of meaning. The wheels mirror the cosmology of the inner space. *The Sacred Tree* states the following:

> The medicine wheel can be used as a mirror by any sincere person. The medicine wheel not only shows us who we are now, it can also show what we could be if we developed the gifts the Creator has placed in us ... Many of these hidden gifts might never be developed if we do not somehow discover and nurture them. The great spiritual teachers have taught that all the gifts a person has are like the fruits hidden within a tree. (Bopp et al. 1988, 35)

These stone circles and the indestructible fragments constituting the whole wheel infuse us with thoughts of a universe depicting the wholeness found in the inner space. The stones reveal our subjection to the metaphysics of the inner space. They give us insight into our common humanity and our connectedness. The ancient ones recorded their findings in the inner space in simple stone, and it is only by analyzing and synthesizing the truths of inner space that we can fully decipher the messages of the wheels.

There are also the people of the animal and plant world who steward certain doors to knowledge of the inner space. The Old Ones and the keepers of the earth among our people tell of the rich information about the inner space contained in these life forms. When Old Ones speak of the 'great Peace, the still, electrifying awareness one experiences in the deep woods,' (Colorado 1988) or of the mesmerizing effect of the total interaction in nature, one understands that these are subjective accounts of those who know what it is to tune into the inner world. Deloria has said:

Here, power and place are dominant concepts – power being the living energy that inhibits and/or composes the universe, and place being the relationship of things to each other ... put into a simple equation: power and place produce personality. This equation simply means that the universe is alive, but it also contains within it the very important suggestions that the universe is personal and, therefore, must be approached in a personal manner. The personal nature of the universe demands that each and every entity in it seek and sustain personal relationships. (Deloria 1991, 4)

It is for this reason that the Old Ones, the guides of our communities, have instilled in the young a sense of wonder and have sought to encourage young minds to recognize and affirm mystery aesthetically and spiritually. Thomas similarly stresses the value of searching for knowledge at the conjunction of physical and metaphysical realities:

Teach on the outset, before any of the fundamentals, the still imponderable puzzles of cosmology. Let it be known, as clearly as possible, by the young minds, that there are some things going on in the universe that lie beyond comprehension, and make it plain how little is known ... Teach ecology later on. Let it be understood that the earth's life is a system of interlinking, interdependent creatures, and that we do not understand at all how it works ... teach that. (Thomas 1983, 213)

The guides knew what they were doing and what they were talking about. Much like Thomas, the Old Ones talked about the inner cosmology. The plants and animals were a vital nexus in comprehending the sophisticated directional maps into the metaphysical. Only by understanding the physical world can we understand the intricacies of the inner space. Conversely, it is only through journeys into the metaphysical that we can fully understand the natural world. Those Old Ones who made countless journeys into the inner space have embedded these principles in Aboriginal education systems so that future generations can continue the research.

The language of the people provides another valuable indication of an inner space. The word for 'mystery' usually refers to a higher power and also connotes our own deeper selves as a humble connection with the higher mystery. In conceptualizing this existence of 'ponderable' mysteries, our languages reveal a very high level of rationality that can only come from an earlier insight into power. Our languages suggest inwardness, where real power lies. It is this space within the individual that, for the Aboriginal, has become the last great frontier and the most challenging one of all.

Yet, within the Aboriginal community a paradox seemingly exists. In no other place did the individual have more integrity or recieve more honour than in the Aboriginal community. The individual's ability as a unique entity in the group to become what she or he is ultimately meant to be, was explicitly recognized. There was explicit recognition of the individual's right in the collective to experience his or her own life. No one could dictate the path that must be followed. There was the recognition that every individual had the capacity to make headway into knowledge through the inner world. Ultimately, the knowledge that comes from the inner space in the individual gives rise to a subjective world-view out onto the external world.

Aboriginal epistemology is grounded in the self, the spirit, the unknown. Understanding of the universe must be grounded in the spirit. Knowledge must be sought through the stream of the inner space in unison with all instruments of knowing and conditions that make individuals receptive to knowing. Ultimately it was in the self that Aboriginal people discovered great resources for coming to grips with life's mysteries. It was in the self that the richest source of information could be found by delving into the metaphysical and the nature and origin of knowledge. Aboriginal epistemology speaks of pondering great mysteries that lie no further than the self.

The spirit is the haven of dreams, those peculiar images that flash symbolic messages to the knower. Dreams are the link to the spiritual world from whence our spirit comes, and they are linked with 'undivided wholeness in flowing movement' (Bohm 1980). Our progenitors knew and believed in the power of dreams; it is only through dreams that sacred undertakings are attempted. Dreams are the guiding principles for constructing the corporeal. Dreams, the voice of the inner space, give rise to the holy and prescribe all ceremonies on the physical level. Conversely, the physical ceremony, as an enactment of the holy, nourishes the spirit and the energy of the 'vast scale' (Couture 1991a, 208). The Old Ones, and the culture they developed, understood that dreams were invaluable in understanding self and sought to manipulate the external so that dreams might happen. It is through dreams that the gifted in our Aboriginal communities 'create' experience for the benefit of the community through the capacity inherent in *mamatowisowin*. We have the shaking tent rituals and other 'channelling' capabilities that are great avenues for out-of-body knowledge. Blessings and other assorted gifts that permeate Aboriginal thought all stem from dreams. The fruit of this cyclical process involving dreams is the invaluable experience that we call knowledge. Experience is knowledge.

Visions also derive from the inner space. Aboriginal people greatly valued the quest for visions as one of the primary sources of knowing. Many tribal cultures insist on having and fulfilling visions as part of their grand design and purpose. According to Johnston:

> It is said and believed, 'that no man begins to be, until he has seen his vision.' Before this event, life is without purpose; life is shallow and empty; actions have no purpose, have no meaning ... What makes the search difficult is that the vision is not to be sought outside of oneself: nor is it to be found outside of one's being. Rather it must be sought within one's inner substance and found therein. Since it will be found within a person's inner self, the search must be conducted alone. (Johnston 1976, 114)

The Old Ones promoted the significance of visions and constructed the community to accommodate their fulfilment. In turn, visions received by individuals allowed people to understand and provided the necessary meaning for the continuity of the community. This is reciprocity between the physical and the metaphysical, the wholeness.

Prayer is another significant aspect of the inner space. Colorado states:

> Prayer as a Medicine – Gii Laii is the quiet, still place (a round hole in the bed of a stream or lake of water and the quiet, still place of balance within ourselves). Prayer is a medicine where all life begins, exists within, without and between us and our relationships. It is an actual place and state of being that marks the endpoint/beginning of our science. (Colorado 1988, 54)

In Aboriginal epistemology, prayer extracts relevant guidance and knowledge from the inner-space consciousness. It is the optimal metaphysical idiom that is recognized in corporeal form as chants, dances, language, and meditation. The Old Ones know the intricate and tedious task of fusing the energy that emits from the place of prayer within. Prayer becomes power and by its very nature becomes another instrument in Aboriginal ways of knowing.

In summary, Aboriginal people have inherited from earlier ages a mission to explore and seek metaphysical knowledge. We know that this quest for knowledge took place along various avenues. Mythology, ritual, and ceremonies, the medicine wheel, nature, and language all reveal vestiges of grand discoveries and communion with the universe within. However, the greatest legacy of our ancestors is in what they discovered within individuals of tribal communities. *Mamatowisowin* is the capacity to connect to the life force that makes anything and everything possible. The recording of ancestral pioneering expeditions and associated community structures helped individuals hone their self-development by developing *mamatowisowin* through dreams, visions, and prayer. The culture of the Aboriginal recognized and affirmed the spiritual through practical application of inner-space discoveries.

Aboriginal education has a responsibility to uphold a world-view based on recognizing and affirming wholeness and to disseminate the benefits to all humanity. Our ancestors have done their part in blazing the initial trail into the inner space. Our task is to continue the exploration and ensure that successive generations persist. In *The Sacred Ways of Knowledge, Sources of Life*, Beck and Walters state:

> Native American sacred ways insist on learning, or education, as an essential foundation for personal awareness. A knowledgeable human being was one who was sensitive to his/her surroundings. This sensitivity opened him/her to the Grand mysteries and to the possibility of mystical experiences, which was considered the only way to grasp certain intangible laws of the universe. (Beck and Walters 1977, 164)

The 'fragmentary self-world view' that permeates the Western world is detrimental to Aboriginal epistemology. The Western education systems that our children are subjected to promote the dogma of fragmentation and indelibly harm the capacity for holism. The mind-set created by fragmentation impedes the progress towards inwardness that our ancestors undertook. Only through subjectivity may we continue to gain authentic insights into truth. We need to experience the life force from which creativity flows, and our Aboriginal resources such as language and culture are our touchstones for achieving this. It is imperative that our children take up the cause of our languages and cultures because therein lies Aboriginal epistemology, which speaks of holism. With holism, an environmental ethic is possible.

The last word should come from Cecil King (1989), an Aboriginal educator who, after presenting a paper at the 88th Annual Meeting of the American Anthropological Association in 1989, concluded with this story:

I had a dream that all the people of the world were together in one place. The place was cold. Everyone was shivering. I looked for a fire to warm myself. None was to be found. Then someone said that in the middle of the gathering of Indians, what was left of the fire had been found. It was a very, very small flame. All the Indians were alerted that the slightest rush of air or the smallest movement could put the fire out and the fire would be lost to humankind. All the Indians banded together to protect the flame. They were working to build the fragile feeble flame. They added minuscule shavings from toothpicks to feed it.

Suddenly, throughout the other peoples, the whisper was heard. 'The Indians have a fire.' There was a crush of bodies stampeding to the place where the flame was held. I pushed to the edge of the Indian circle to stop those coming to the flame so that it would not be smothered. The other people became hostile saying they were cold too and it was our responsibility to share the flame with them. I replied, 'It is our responsibility to preserve the flame for humanity and at the moment it is too weak to be shared but if we all are still and respect the flame it will grow and thrive in the caring hands of those who hold it. In time we can all warm at the fire. But now we have to nurture the flame or we will all lose the gift.'

Note
This chapter originated as a graduate paper for a course entitled 'First Nations Curriculum: Theory and Practice' at the University of Saskatchewan and received the Alumni Association Award.

References
Beck, Peggy, and Anna Walters. 1977. *The sacred ways of knowledge, sources of life*. Arizona: Navajo Community College Press
Bohm, David. 1980. *Wholeness and the implicate order*. London: Routledge and Kegan Paul
Bopp, J. et al. 1988. *The sacred tree*. Lethbridge: Four Worlds Development Project
Colorado, Pam. 1988. Bridging native and western science. *Convergence* 21 (2/3):49-68
Couture, Joseph E. 1991a. The role of Native elders: Emergent issues. In John W. Friesen, ed., *The cultural maze*. Calgary: Detselig Enterprises
–. 1991b. Explorations in Native knowing. In John W. Friesen, ed., *The cultural maze*. Calgary: Detselig Enterprises
Deloria, Vine. 1991. Power and place: Equal personality. In Vine Deloria, ed.

Indian education in America. Boulder, Co: American Indian Science and Engineering Society

Johnston, Basil. 1976. *Ojibway heritage*. Toronto: McClelland and Stewart

Kierkegaard, Søren. [1846] 1965. Truth is subjectivity. In H.J. Blackham, ed., *Reality, man and existence: Essential works of existentialism*. Revised. London, ON: Bantam

King, Cecil. 1989. Here come the anthros. Paper presented at the 88th Annual Meeting of the American Anthropological Association, Washington, DC

Miller, John P. 1988. *The holistic curriculum*. Toronto: OISE Press

Miller, John R., J.R. Bruce Cassie, and Susan M. Drake. 1990. *Holistic learning*. Toronto: OISE Press

Purpel, David E. 1989. *The moral and spiritual crisis in education*. New York: Bergin and Garvey

Reading the World and Reading the Word: An Interview with Paulo Freire. 1985. *Language Arts* 62 (1)

Solecki, Sam. 1993. Ideology. In *Encyclopedia of contemporary literary theory*. Toronto: University of Toronto Press

Smith, Huston. 1953. Philosophy, theology, and primordial claim. *Crosscurrents* 28(3):276-88

Thomas, Lewis. 1983. *Late night thoughts on listening to Mahler's Ninth Symphony*. New York: Viking

Whitman, Walt. 1948. *The complete poetry of Walt Witman*. Garden City, NY: Garden City Books

5
Quaslametko and Yetko: Two Grandmother Models for Contemporary Native Education Pedagogy
Shirley Sterling

Introduction

My real name is Seepeetza. I was born to the late Albert Sterling and Sophie Voght Sterling from the Joeyaska Indian Reserve No. 2 which belongs to the Lower Nicola Band near Merritt, BC. I have two brothers, Fred and Austin, and three sisters, Sarah Steward, Deanna Sterling, and Mary Jane Joe. I have three grown children, Bobby, Eric and, Haike.

My maternal grandparents were William Voght Jr. and Shannie Antoine Voght. William Voght's parents were William Voght Sr., originally from Holstein, Germany, and Theresa Klama Voght, a Native girl from Boston Bar, BC. Shannie's parents were Chief Yepskin Antoine and Quaslametko.

We are Nlakapamux, or Thompson speakers, part of the Interior Salish Nation from southern British Columbia.

I am in the process of completing a doctorate in curriculum and instruction as a Ts' 'kel student at the University of British Columbia, in Vancouver, BC. As a student in the Native Indian Teacher Education Program, and a former board member of a band school, I became interested in looking at more relevant pedagogies and curricula for Native students, particularly within band schools. Like many Native educators, I was concerned that the present school system was not a positive, successful experience for many Native students and I wanted to find out why and what to do about it. Pedagogies particularly interested me because I had noticed while doing classroom teaching that children respond differently to different teachers and teaching styles. The connection with Quaslametko and Yetko arose one day when I was telling my mother about how children in a classroom seem to learn more when the teacher likes them. My mother told me about her two grandmothers and I decided to use the models in a paper for my summer course in education administration, taught by Jo-ann Archibald.

I have consulted my mother, Sophie Sterling, on Nlakapamux issues since January 1987 when she helped me make a Salish fishtrap, although she has shared stories and information with me all my life. She told me the one legend of my grandmother Shannie while we were picking saskatoon berries on a hillside at Coldwater one summer. Scribblings on used envelopes have become treasures to me. Now, I always keep a notebook when I visit my mother because I never know when she is going to tell me something relevant or teach me Nlakapamux phrases or vocabulary. My mother's recall is best when she is allowed to speak uninterruptedly on whatever topic comes to mind. She becomes flustered when I question her, so I find it best to ask just one question and let her reminisce without my stopping her to check the information.

I realize that my mother is the most valuable resource that I know and I am very concerned to learn as much as I can from her. Her stories and information have provided me with so many missing links in my cultural past: missing because of the years I was away at residential school where Nlakapamux culture was neither known, acknowledged, nor taught. Recently I asked my niece's husband, Don Collins, to videotape our interviews, and I have a small tape recorder which I also use sometimes.

This chapter on Quaslametko and Yetko is one in a series of pedagogical submissions dealing with Native education which together will form my doctoral thesis. Other submissions include 'The First Nations Learner' published by Amnesty International in the 1992 Spring Issue of *The Fourth R*, which includes the story of my mother, Yetko, and the fishtrap. One paper defined in more depth the attitude of respect as portrayed and defined by the behaviour of the grandmothers. My children's novel *My Name is Seepeetza* (published by Groundwood Press of Vancouver in 1992) deals with my own personal experiences at a residential school in the interior of British Columbia. Interviews will be undertaken with my siblings, children, and various members of my extended family about the continuity of the grandmother models.

Traditional Lifestyle Memories

When she was a little girl, my mother, Sophie Sterling, spent time with two grandmothers, Quaslametko and Yetko. Quaslametko was my mother's maternal grandmother; she had three sons and only one daughter, who was my mother's mother. Yetko was my mother's grand-aunt, sister-in-law to Quaslametko. Yetko had given birth to two sets of twins who died at birth (Field notes, 1987).

Quaslametko was a master basket maker and craftswoman. She made beautiful cedar-root baskets. But she did not want my mother and my mother's siblings to touch the baskets, the cedar roots, or her tools. She scolded the children if they came near her baskets. Upset by her daughter's sometimes poor health and the burden of raising twelve children, Quaslametko told the children they were 'too many.' She ordered them outside to pack water and wood for the household, and to cook, wash dishes, and clean house.

> Before we were finished eating she said, 'In tsow zoo zah.' Wash the dishes. She said it in such a mean way. She carried a willow switch too. She never hit us but if we didn't move fast enough she'd slam it down on the table beside us. She didn't like us because we were too many, and we made her daughter sick. (Field notes, 1992)

When my grandfather moved the family from a ranch at Kane Valley to a house in Merritt, Quaslametko told my mother's parents not to send their children to school.

> Quaslametko said 'Chook-oosh ha-ah school. Chook-oosh ex dik shamah school he-ah sk'an-a'sh.' Don't let them go to school. Don't let them go to the White school. They won't like you. She thought we would become like *shamahs* [white people] and forget how to hunt and fish and get food from the hills. She thought we'd never stay with our people. (Field notes, 1992)

Yetko was a herbalist, a gatherer of medicine tea and medicine food. A gentle, kind-hearted woman who laughed a lot, she packed food and camping gear and took my mother, and sometimes my mother's sister, Theresa, into the mountains or down to the Coldwater River on horseback.

> The pony she [Yetko] rode was called Nkwa-lep-eesht. It was a chocolate brown colour and its mane grew so long it almost touched the ground. She used to say to me and Theresa, 'Whee-ken min deep.' Come with us. She adopted Moria, that's Maggie Kilroy's daughter, so she always wanted company for her when she went into the hills. Yetko had no fear of animals. She tells us when we have a set of twins, bears never bother us. (Field notes, 1992)

There they gathered plants and picked berries. Once, they made a small red willow fishtrap (small so the fish warden wouldn't find them and destroy them) and caught fresh trout. They never took weapons because Yetko, having borne twins, was considered a bear person, not needing protection (See Teit 1900, 311-12).

Yetko explained things to the girls as they went along; what the deer root looks like when it's ready to pick; why trout like to rest in fishtraps; which medicine plants to use for headache, for woman trouble, for fever, for rashes, wounds, bee sting, for birth control. Yetko used various plants for manufacture.

She makes her own string. They tear the back off certain plants. She puts them together then twirls them on her leg, about a foot at a time. Pretty soon she has a big bundle. Then she'll use that when she makes something called 'spetzin.' She used red willow to make the [fish]trap. In later years the Fisheries started checking on the rivers. They broke them [fishtraps] and came up to her house and told her not to make them anymore. (Field notes, 1992)

Yetko was also a storyteller.

After dark she would gather all the kids around her and call, 'Choot-ka hap.' The kids would have to say, 'hap.' That meant they were going to be quiet, to listen to the story. If they didn't want to listen they would have to go outside. They could play all they want and make noise out there. But nobody did. We all wanted to hear the stories she told. (Field notes, 1991)

Yetko told stories about the elements spring wind and ice, who had a giant battle once. They were arguing about who was the strongest. Ice said he was more powerful as he was hard like rock. Spring wind claimed he was the strongest because he melted all the snow and ice. Then sun, the sky dweller, came closer to find out what all the commotion was about, and his closeness began to melt ice, which resolved the issue. The children listened and were amazed.

Yetko told of heartless eagle, the hunter, who stalked the little grouse, and of grouse's plight as she dodged and scrambled and hid trembling behind small saskatoon bushes from her formidable foe. The children cried when eagle swooped down and wounded grouse, and they determined in their hearts never to be so cruel. The stories went on and on every night like a serial. And every night the children couldn't wait to hear the next episode in the lives of their favourite characters.

Now my mother is in her seventies. She is a herbalist, a gatherer of medicine tea and medicine food. A gentle, kind-hearted woman who laughs a lot, she loves to go into the mountains with her children and grandchildren to gather plants and pick berries. She knows which plants are good for headaches, for woman trouble, for rashes, wounds, for birth control. She is always teaching these skills to her children and grandchildren, and is one of my son Eric's mentors.

My mother likes to tell stories when we are picking berries, travelling by car somewhere, when we are cleaning and canning salmon, when we are waiting at a funeral or in a doctor's office. She tells bear stories, camping disaster stories, stories about old-timers, and she recalls word for word the many relevant pieces of information about her life, her family, her world.

My mother has never made a basket. Neither have any of her brothers and sisters, their children, grandchildren, or great grandchildren. The exquisite Nlakapamux art of basket making has been lost in our family.

The Two Grandmother Models and Current Pedagogies

In looking for ways and means of effectively teaching Native children in contemporary enculturation settings, whether they be public schools, band schools, or other settings, we can consider the two grandmother models of Quaslametko and Yetko. They were sisters-in-law. So, the two pedagogies they represent, although different, can also be seen as being related by marriage, perhaps complementary, sometimes coexisting, sometimes in conflict, and certainly both of value.

Quaslametko seemed most effective in getting many children to achieve short-term goals such as packing water and filling the woodbox. Her communication with the children became authoritarian and accusatory when she ordered them to do their chores. They were obedient because they were afraid and because they wanted to compensate for causing their mother to be overworked and sick. Quaslametko can be viewed as conservative in nature as she resisted change that might arise from the formal education of her grandchildren.

Yetko spent more time engaging in plant-gathering with one or two individuals. The result of this was the long-term acquisition of skills and knowledge and enjoyment not only for my mother, but also for following generations. For instance, my mother made her second fishtrap in 1987, over sixty-five years after she and Yetko had made her first one near the Coldwater River. Yetko's communication with children was that of storyteller, and she entertained, taught, and controlled them not through fear or guilt, but through interest.

Quaslametko, as an authoritarian figure, may be linked to a hierarchical model symbolized by a triangle. The hierarchical system is evident in the public school system and inherent in North American society. For instance, the organizational structure of a typical school has a principal at the top with several teachers in the middle and many students at the bottom. The communication or 'chain of command' (Hampton 1986, 325) is one way from top to bottom; from the principal, to the teachers, to the students. Other pervasive hierarchies with lasting influence on society were the British class system, and the Roman Catholic Church with its infallible pope at the top, cardinals below the pope, then the archbishops, the bishops, the priests, and lay people at the bottom of the chain of command.

In looking at the history of mainstream pedagogical practice that 'set forth the generalized models of practice-centered thought' we find in the 1790s the Bell Lancaster Monitorial Program, or Monitorial Method (Brauner 1964, 238). This hierarchical system, which met the 'need for economy and control,' used students as tutors and disciplinarians, and 'learning was defined in terms of whatever training would result in the acceptable mastery. Instruction held first place, with consideration for the individual left far behind' (Brauner 1964, 239). The philosophy underlying the Monitorial Method, the present public school system, and in some ways Quaslametko's attitude about training her grandchildren was as follows:

Individual. A child is naturally disruptive and thus must be controlled first to be trained later. Group discipline maintained through obedience of each member allowed efficient organization for drill and memorization. The child was seen as a small beast.

Instructional. Drill, memorization, and perfect recitation led to mechanical techniques of instruction. With attention given to individual units of instruction being mastered by each group, subjects remained discrete and separate. There were fixed standards.

Institutional. The school developed as a military-type hierarchy in which obedience to authority and responsibility within the chain of command were paramount. (Brauner 1964, 244).

In the Intra/Individual approach the child has to be 'controlled first, to be trained later.' The Intra/Institutional approach describes the school as a 'military-type hierarchy in which obedience to authority and responsibility within the chain of command were paramount.' These descriptions stress obedience, control, and authority in the same way that the modern schools tend to, and in the way that Quaslametko did with her grandchildren.

There are many variables to consider in assessing Quaslametko as a representative of hierarchies. Given the number of grandchildren Quaslametko had to care for in the absence of her sick daughter, it is understandable that she chose an authoritarian manner which would get the household jobs done quickly and efficiently. Given the numbers of students that teachers have per classroom, about thirty-two, it is not surprising that some of the points in the Monitorial Method have persisted. However, as the long-term ideal in Native education, authoritarianism and the Monitorial Method are highly questionable, at least in relation to my family's experience. As my mother says of Quaslametko's methods, 'To this day I don't like doing dishes, or housework. We [as children] didn't do a good job because she talked to us so mean' (Field notes, 1992).

Two factors may have had a bearing on Quaslametko's attitudes and behaviour (which do not seem typical of the Nlakapamux). In 1918, when my mother was three years old and the Spanish Influenza epidemic killed a large number of Native people in the Nicola Valley, Quaslametko may have been moved to practise stringent hygiene in the home so as to prevent death by flu. Perhaps she was angry at the whites for bringing the disease. Also, Quaslametko and her husband, Chief Yepskin, had embraced Catholicism and were probably strongly influenced by the teachings of the priest on child discipline. An interesting insight into Quaslametko came from a recent conversation with my mother, who said:

> I finally remembered why Quaslametko was the way she was. The teacher at [Kamloops Indian Residential] School told me to help this girl called Melina. She was from Coldwater too. Anyway she got mad because I got her to fill up the page with numbers. I couldn't help it. That's the way I was taught so I had to do it that way. She thought I was being mean to her so she said, 'Your grandmother wanted your mother to marry a chief's son.' I guess it was true too because my mother was a chief's daughter. Quaslametko was married to Chief Yepskin. William Voght Sr. talked to Yepskin and they arranged the marriage between my mother and my father. My father [William Voght Jr.] was a half-breed and Quaslametko didn't like White People (Sterling 1992).

The reason why Quaslametko may have been so against the marriage was because another white settler in the valley had kept a Nlakapamux woman but later had asked her to leave when he arranged for a white bride from England. The Nlakapamux woman's family had all died in the flu epidemic and, being all alone in the world, she committed suicide by hanging herself from a tree (Field notes, 1992). Quaslametko may have been afraid the same fate would befall her daughter. These explanations are not complete. My mother also said that Quaslametko was so cranky that one by one her three young sons moved out of the house (Field notes, 1992).

There are positive aspects of Quaslametko's methods too. My mother said Quaslametko was always busy working. 'Well, I guess it's a good thing

[Quaslametko] was kind of mean. It helped us not to be lazy. She worked from morning to night herself so we did the same' (Sterling 1987-92). So, in the First Nations tradition of teaching by example, Quaslametko lived her teaching role by keeping busy every day, all day.

Yetko's friendly, respectful manner towards the children and her way of working together with them reflect a more egalitarian style of interaction which can be symbolized by a circle. The circle is often representative of Native societies and philosophies. In *The Sacred Tree*, Phil Lane says, 'the Medicine Wheel is an ancient powerful symbol of the universe. It is a silent teacher of the realities of things. It shows the many different ways in which all things are interconnected' (Bopp et al. 1988, 32).

James Teit, in his discussion of the social organization of the Thompson Indians, points to its egalitarian nature when he says, 'At these councils such subjects as ... matters of public interest were discussed, each man having a voice in the matter' (Teit 1900, 289). In 'Our World According to Ossenontion and Shonaganleh:ra' Shonaganleh:ra says, 'the Elders and Traditional People ... talk about how everyone had her/his own medicine wheel. In that medicine wheel irrespective of colour, was everything that s/he needed ... the values and beliefs, and social mores, about how we were to get along' (1989, 8). The circle provides a contrast to hierarchies, generally symbolizes Native philosophy, and represents egalitarianism.

A modern pedagogical discipline which resembles Yetko's interaction with her grandchildren is the humanistic view of learning. In *Educational Psychology in the Canadian Classroom*, Winzer and Grigg state that the 'humanistic educator acts as a facilitator, concerned with creating an open climate of trust and acceptance in which children are free to experiment and learn' (1992, 300).

According to humanistic educators, good teachers have 'three attitudinal qualities that enhance their ability to work effectively with students':
(1) realness or genuineness; they must be capable of accurately and openly communicating their feelings to their students; they are being themselves (Winzer and Grigg 1992, 400-1)
(2) respect; humanists believe that the second most important characteristic of effective teachers is a profound and deeply felt respect for each student; each is seen as a unique human being who has worth in her or his own right; this respect is unconditional (Winzer and Grigg 1992, 401)
(3) empathetic understanding; the ability to understand student reactions from the inside ... the teacher must be able to view the world through the student's eyes in order to understand his or her feelings and perceptions without analyzing or judging (Winzer and Grigg 1992, 401-2).

Yetko showed herself to be real and genuine when she communicated so effectively with the children that they remembered her teachings over sixty years later. She showed profound respect for them when she took the time to explain the deeper meanings of things such as fish psychology. She showed empathy by speaking to them as fellow human beings with dignity. She explained rather than ordered. She went with the children and showed them how to do things. She participated in every activity. She like them. 'She was my friend,' said my mother (Sterling 1987).

The question is, do these teacher qualities improve student development and learning? One study showed that

[students of] highly facilitating teachers missed fewer days, had increased self-concept, made greater academic gains, presented fewer discipline problems, committed less vandalism, increased scores on IQ tests, made gains in creativity scores, were more spontaneous, and used higher levels of thinking. (Winzer and Grigg 1992, 402)

In the case of Yetko and my mother the outstanding gains were my mother's positive feelings about her traditions and culture, her retention of knowledge over sixty years, her positive self-concept, her enjoyment of learning, and her ability to pass on to future generations her love of plant gathering and storytelling.

The Grandmothers' Influence Continues

In reviewing the two different philosophies of teaching Native children, I admit to a bias in favour of Yetko's methods of teaching, her careful sharing of knowledge with the little girls, her taking them into the mountains to learn by practical experience, her laughter, her spontaneity, her storytelling. She may not have had much choice about the politics in the changing world of her day, or in the structure of the formal educational system, but she had the power to choose what type of person she would be. As Shonaganleh:ra said, 'I understand the code, the law, that I am to follow. I understand that I have the strength of my relationships to honour the smallest plant and the smallest child and the most sacred of ceremonies. In the context of all that I don't need to change myself. I don't need a big stick, a loud voice, a women's group to represent me' (Ossenontian and Shonaganleh:ra 1989, 11).

This is perhaps the legacy we as Native people have received from our people and our past: the philosophy of the circle; a recognition not of rights, 'only responsibilities' (p. 11); a perception of strength not as force but as 'internal'; a process of going back 'to pick up those things that were left behind' (p. 17). As educators we may not have the option to overhaul the educational system, or to change society's philosophy of self-concept, but we can, like Yetko, choose a teaching style which is genuine, respectful, and empathetic.

On a more personal level, I can see both Quaslametko and Yetko in myself. I was Yetko when I told stories and sang songs to my children, when I made them puppets and taught them to see the relationship between the sun, the rain, and the branches on trees. I was Quaslametko when as a single working parent of three teenagers I had to establish and insist on a strict, disciplined schedule of household jobs. I was Yetko when I asked my children which school they wanted to attend and Quaslametko when I said, no, they could not go to the local high-school dance.

When he was sixteen, my son Eric wrote a poem which speaks of his grandmother Sophie and the mountains where they had gone many times to gather medicine plants and pick berries. It portrays in imagery the continuity of the learning process and the sharing of information and storytelling passed on from generation to generation, from Yetko to my mother, and from my mother to me and my son.

Up in the Hills

Up in the hills and far away,
My grandmother goes on a summer day.
She tells us stories of long ago,
Where animals water and wildflowers grow,
Stories of people who lived here before
Animals and ancestors who live here no more.

Up in the hills where the air is clean,
The water is sweet and the grass is green,
There's a song and a legend for each time we go,
To the hills far away where wildflowers grow.
(Muller, oral presentation, 1985)

My daughter Haike, now a university student, speaks of her childhood with her grandmother, Sophie. After school every day, Haike stopped off at her grandmother's house to have tea, usually medicine tea, and a treat. During tea they would discuss for hours the symptoms of rare and fatal diseases Haike thought she might have or might get one day. Haike says:

She waited for me to ask questions. When I really wanted to know something, that's when she'd tell me. But she waited for me to take the initiative. She was always the person to consult if I thought I had a fatal disease or strange symptoms. From itchy feet to brain tumour she had an answer. It was not so much what she said but how she said it. She took me seriously. She treated me like an equal. I'd bring some hints of my own from books and things, so it was a sharing. (Muller 1992)

In the spirit of returning the gift, I look forward to taking the many gifts of the grandmothers and passing them on to the next set of grandchildren – through literature.

Note

This chapter was previously published in 'Giving Voice to Our Ancestors,' *Canadian Journal of Native Education* 19, 2 (1992). Permission to reprint has been granted by the editors.

References

Bopp, J. et al. 1988. *The sacred tree*. Lethbridge: Four Worlds Development Project

Brauner, Charles J. 1964. *General methods from six practical traditions, from American educational theory*. Atlanta: Prentice-Hall

Hampton, David R. 1986. *Management*. New York: McGraw-Hill

Muller, Eric. 1985. Speech Arts Festival, poetry section, free verse (oral presentation), Merritt, BC

Muller, Haike Ann. 1992. Personal interview, October, Vancouver, BC

Ossenontian and Shonaganleh:ra. 1989. Our world according to Ossenontian and Shonaganleh:ra. *Canadian Woman Studies* 10 (2/3):11-17

Sterling, Sophie. 1987-92. Personal interview, Merritt, BC

Teit, James A. 1900. *The Jesup North Pacific expedition*. Vol. 1, Part 4, *The Thompson Indians of British Columbia*. Franz Boas, ed. Memoir of the American Museum of Natural History. New York: American Museum of Natural History

Winzer, Margret, and Nancy Grigg. 1992. *Educational Psychology in the Canadian Classroom*. Scarborough, ON: Prentice-Hall

6
Language and Cultural Content in Native Education
Robert Leavitt

In the summers of 1987 and 1988, a course on the cultural implications of teaching English and Native languages to Native Indian and Inuit children was offered at Concordia University in Montreal.[1] Experienced teachers and teachers-in-training (both referred to below as 'teachers') enrolled in the course, each group including both Natives and non-Natives. Only one of the non-Native teachers had previous experience of teaching Native children. A few others intended to work in Native education, but most were planning careers in teaching English as a second language to other linguistic groups. Originally the course was intended simply to help teachers explore methods of teaching Native languages and English, and to offer non-Native teachers insights into the problems encountered by Native children in learning English as a second language. It became apparent during the first summer, however, that the course was accomplishing more than this. Both Native and non-Native teachers were beginning to see the significance of language and culture in children's schooling. Working closely with their classmates of the 'other culture,' they found themselves reevaluating and reshaping their own roles as educators. This and the following chapter, by Arlene Stairs, will explore the outcome of that experience.

The instructors conducted the class as a model of traditional Native educational practices at work.[2] They were able to demonstrate the effectiveness of an approach based upon active participation, student-initiated exploration of selected materials, and planned student-instructor collaboration. In addition, they arranged for participants to hear of first-hand experiences with Native education from Mohawk, Inuit, and Ojibway guest speakers, as well as from Indian classmates.[3] Lectures were kept to a minimum, in favour of small-group and whole-class discussions, presentations, and workshops; course grades were based equally upon individual and group achievement. To clarify the purpose of their approach, the instructors frequently took the opportunity to step back from the experiences in class and to analyze what the teachers themselves were doing.

The written evaluations at the end of the course confirmed that something important had taken place. Participants emphasized the value of their involvement in discussions of cultural identity and relationships. 'The input for me came mainly from my Native classmates, both professionally and personally,' commented one teacher. Another wrote that the course opened up 'social, political, and cultural discussion of what maternal languages mean, in ways the regular TESL [Teaching English as a Second Language] courses do not.'

Their discussions, the presentations they heard, and their research and writing helped teachers discover how traditional Native education relies upon ways of knowing, ways of interacting, and ways of using language which are not normally exploited in formal school. Examples included conceiving of time as sequence rather than duration, collaboration between children and adults, storytelling and oral history. The teachers saw not only that these 'ways' are the basis of culturally appropriate education for Native children, but also that they offer unique alternatives for meeting the needs of non-Native children. How the language and content of traditional Native education might find a place in the classroom is the subject of this chapter.

Native teachers began to articulate the dilemma they face in 'trying to regain both knowledge and understanding of our language and culture' within a European model of education. As they explored ways in which Native language and content might be used in the classroom, they initially thought it feasible only to alternate Native and non-Native approaches during the school day. Not until later did they consider ways of melding the two. One Native-language teacher commented on the need to try 'to sort out differences in value systems and religious beliefs that have been tying us to different worlds without completely letting us into either one.' How, for instance, might myths and legends be used as lesson content, respecting their sacredness and honouring their fundamental truth, while simultaneously helping children to analyze them critically to discover Native knowledge and values? One Native teacher related how she had been told a set of stories as a gift from an elder so that she might share them with her students; the students in turn learned not only of the content of the stories but also of their place in the linguistic culture of their community.

Non-Native teachers, in working with their Native colleagues, discovered how much Native languages, value systems, and traditional educational practices contrasted with their own. They realized that they would have to learn about the first language and culture of *any* child they taught – and would have to take account of these in their teaching. One teacher wrote that she had become aware of her responsibility to 'look at how a Native child develops in her own culture. The child will carry with her the theory of teaching and learning embedded in the Native culture. She is trained for autonomy and self-reliance and to have many and varied relationship with peers and adults.' Another teacher warned that by trying to reshape Native customs and beliefs to fit into a dominant cultural mould, 'educators are changing the whole idea or definition of the term "Natives" or "original peoples of Canada."' He recognized the power of education to create new perceptions and a new culture, and the responsibility teachers assume for shaping students' identities.

Culture-Based Education in the Classroom

The course approached the methodology of teaching Native students as a search for the ideal balance between maintaining a Native way of life and achieving economic and political independence. These goals, which have been set by Indian and Inuit peoples themselves (e.g., Charleston 1988, 71), are not mutually exclusive, as might at first appear. Teachers can address them jointly, however, only by taking account of the continuous development of Native culture from the past to the present and by considering all aspects of the culture that exists today in Indian and Inuit communities:

- *Material culture* is ordinarily the sum total of 'Native content' found in school programs. It includes the objects and skills pertinent to a people's ecology and economy.
- *Social culture* has implications for classroom interactions: How do teachers' roles fit into the patterns of personal interaction, communication, kinship organization, and other relationships within the community?
- *Cognitive culture* has implications for the organization of program content: What are the characteristics of individual and collective worldviews, value systems, spiritual understanding, and practical knowledge?
- *Linguistic culture* consists of the role of language in the community. It includes how language is used (stories, gossip, conversation, negotiation, etc.) and how language maintains individual and group identity and transmits material, social, and cognitive culture from one generation to the next.

To account for all four aspects of culture, the instructors emphasized the need to base education *in* Native culture, rather than simply including components of material culture as content (Stairs, this volume). Few teachers have had the opportunity to address more than the material level of Native culture (or the culture of any English-second-language pupils).

Even where curriculum pays heed to social, cognitive, and linguistic culture, it is almost always from a material point of view. Spiritual beliefs and legends, for instance, are treated as artifacts, and these, together with descriptions of kinship patterns, transportation and hunting techniques, and the names of languages, tools, and food plants, make up a static set of data about Indian and Inuit peoples. With few exceptions, the educational principles and practices of Native cultures are not applied in the classroom, even for Native students.

But classroom teachers can use the social, cognitive, and linguistic aspects of Native culture. Rather than simply presenting material culture under the title of 'Native studies' or an 'Indian unit,' teachers in a culture-based program will look at their own interactions with children to see where and how they might modify their formal teaching. In particular, how might English and the Native language be used in the classroom? What content will be appropriate in a culture-based curriculum and how might it be organized most effectively?[4]

Language in Native Education

For teachers, the most significant differences between English and the Indian and Inuit languages are to be found in their ways of conceptualizing, preserving, and transmitting knowledge. Until very recently, the Native languages developed entirely in the oral mode. Speakers hold in their individual and collective memories everything that they know and believe about the world and their experiences in it. Always accessible, either in speakers' own minds or through direct conversation with others, knowledge and beliefs have an immediacy not readily apparent to speakers of written languages, who use writing and reading to store and transmit much of what they know (Gill 1982).

Literacy, which puts some distance between spoken words and the reader or writer, makes possible – indeed encourages – the extensive analysis and reworking, sorting, and classifying of ideas, including those gleaned from the writings of others. Writing creates distinctions between facts and beliefs, between ideas and feelings – distinctions which are significant to scholars in general, as well as to those who work in fields such as jurisprudence, applied sciences, or documentary history. For example, the present chapter, which attempts to derive generalized principles about Native education by analyzing a set of events and other writings, together with the language emerging from them (e.g., cited quotations), would not be 'told' in an oral tradition. Rather, the discussion might take the form of a multifaceted conversation and narration about the teaching of Native children, giving accounts of many experiences and resulting in a conceptualization of increasing completeness, with a stated conclusion. Neither approach is superior to the other, but each has its advantages in given situations.

Therefore, it is possible to embrace literacy as a creative, rather than destructive, adjunct to the oral tradition. Teachers can facilitate this helpful blend, however, only by acknowledging the value of both components.

In the actual case, the ascendancy of spoken English and English literacy in Native communities in Canada has threatened not only the oral tradition but also the survival of Native languages themselves (Burnaby 1986; Foster 1984) – people's ways of thinking, communicating, and establishing identity. In some cases, the intruding language has undermined oral tradition by imposing a new reliance on writing for the authentication of knowledge and ideas. In Native communities, however, the transmission of a distinctive culture still depends upon the maintenance of Native languages in their oral mode. Myths and legends, for example, are seldom, if ever, told in English, and the lessons they contain about history, human relationships, proper behaviour, and universal truths are thus lost on younger generations. To overcome this loss, one teacher in the Maine-Maritime region engaged her students in a bilingual study of the contrasts between their grandparents' childhoods in the 1920s and their own in the 1980s. She compiled transcriptions of stories told by elders into a book (Socobasin 1979) and told stories herself as a way of presenting the lessons to students. At the same time, she showed the children how the contrasts they were discovering related to broader changes in the region – as found in written histories and diaries, census data, church records, and other archival documents, including maps and photographs. The teacher, her students, and the adults in the community gained a clearer understanding of the continuing role of the oral tradition in their lives.

Literacy in the Native language holds the promise of providing a bridge between the oral tradition and English literacy. Until recently, however, written Native language has been used mostly in the non-Native fields of journalism, formal education, and religion – in transcriptions of news and history, myths and legends, songs and liturgy – and only tentatively in the creation of a distinctive literature per se. There are, however, exceptional circumstances which suggest the potential of such a literature. As it develops, it encourages writers to take their language in new directions. Young Inuit, for instance, become literate in Inuktitut not only through classroom instruction but also by reading and writing with their parents and grandparents, who use syllabics in personal correspondence. Inuit elders discussing education have added another use for writing to the

Native-language repertoire, saying that traditional knowledge and skills 'should be recognized in paper.'[5] Several published biographies are now being used widely in Inuktitut education, demonstrating to students the vitality and cultural appropriateness of many types of literacy.

A series of Micmac writers' workshops held recently in New Brunswick and Nova Scotia resulted in three volumes of stories for readers of all ages (Metallic and Metallic 1985; Milliea 1985; Leavitt, Francis, and Paul 1986). The contents ranged from traditional tales and classical mythology to fantasy and personal reminiscences. Each submission was carefully scrutinized by Native editors, who took pains to ensure that it met standards of good oral expression, but who at the same time wished to encourage innovation. They accepted poetry and play scripts, neither one a traditional form, but each true to Micmac culture in its style, wording, and point of view – and thus a 'logical' modern extension of the oral tradition.

Defining the roles of oral and written language in children's education should help teachers determine the best use of the language in classroom interactions. In Micmac community schools in the Maritime provinces, for example, Micmac teachers have been using the Native language regularly and comfortably, but for the most part only on the periphery of educational activities – in giving directions, maintaining order, chatting informally with children between classes, and occasionally in clarifying ideas the children find difficult in English. How else might it serve the goals of formal education? One teacher in Cape Breton has had her students tell stories in Micmac as a way of practising the language and learning appropriate forms of communication. Their stories become the basis of writing and reading activities in follow-up lessons, and of planned interviews with adults. Because the teacher herself also tells stories and writes and conducts interviews in the community, the children are naturally steeped in real-life language use. Speaking Micmac in specific contexts has become for these children a productive way of learning to communicate.

The teacher who uses the Native language in instruction will learn how it differs from English. This kind of meta-linguistic perspective helps her to understand the Native language as a valuable complement – not a hindrance – to the students' English. Her knowledge of the Native language tells her, for example, that while children may be able to use shapes and understand them in relation to particular objects, they may not be able to talk about them as abstractions.

In Native languages, such basic notions as the shape of concrete objects may be expressed in ways unfamiliar to speakers of English, allowing a more effective view of the world for certain purposes. In English, for example, speakers consider the shape of a basket or a tree-limb (e.g., square or cylindrical) separately from the object itself; that is, the designation of shape is based on arbitrary or idealized forms rather than on the properties of certain objects. Speakers of English imagine a square without picturing a particular square object. Even with non-geometrical 'shapes' such as lump, it is possible to picture a lump not made of any particular substance. In contrast, in languages like Maliseet, a close relative of Micmac spoken in New Brunswick and Maine, speakers perceive shape as a property of the object in question; it is expressed only as part of the noun or verb denoting or referring to the object. No shape-names are whole words, and Maliseet-speakers do not ordinarily talk about shapes in isolation from the natural and manufactured objects around them. These different ways of thinking – Maliseet and English – are indicated not only in the lexicons, but also in the perceptions which form the basis of description. The single word *etutapskonuwat* ('he/she has very chubby cheeks') is a verb which describes someone's face by synthesizing the abstract concepts of 'degree,' 'shape' (*-apsk-*), 'body part,' and 'state of being.' In contrast, the English equivalent analyzes the face, expressing each idea – person, possession, degree, shape, body part – in a separate word.

The Maliseet approach to shape is similar to that of the other North American Native languages. At one level, it would appear, the child accustomed to a Native system may have no use for simple geometric shapes. At another level, however, like Jennifer MacPherson's Inuk student Norman, who created a perfectly scaled miniature dogsled, he may be capable of astounding feats of applied geometry. 'Norman showed an extraordinary ability to deal with shape, with space, and with size, which seemed inconsistent with his general disinterest in the number-based mathematics we offered in school' (1987, 25). Encouraged to develop the Inuktitut thought-patterns his work reveals, a student like Norman can approach everyday math problems with confidence. He can then use English to tell, for example, how he made his model, or how he will use it, and from there learn to analyze the model in abstract terms.

Shapes and other properties of material objects seem self-evident to native speakers of any language, who do not question their inherent usefulness or their universality. Similarly, relationships among events are understandable only in terms of one's own way of verifying the truth. For example, in teaching natural sciences, the English-speaking teacher will begin with the assumption that the moon and the wind are 'things' which move, and whose appearance or strength changes with time. In contrast, Maliseet-speakers do not know the wind and the moon as things. There is no Maliseet noun 'wind,' but only a verb, which means 'blow' or 'be windy.' The wind is not a thing, but an action. It can be named only by expressing this action – as when it is performed by a character in a story. Thus Wocawson is the name of the great bird who flaps his wings to make the wind. But he is not 'the Wind.' His name means 'It Is Windy.' When he blows too hard, and people can't go about their daily business, Koluskap, the culture hero, ties down one of his wings, weakening the action but not the bird himself (Wabnaki Bilingual Education Program 1976). The Indo-European perception is exemplified by Aesop, who presents the wind as a person striving to make a traveller remove his cloak.

The moon is also named by a Maliseet verb – *nipawset*, 'walks at night.' A multitude of other English nouns are expressed as verbs in Maliseet, including weather conditions, tides, land forms, and time. Thinking of these phenomena as actions helps students see their connection with other actions, including the students' own.

These ideas about shapes and natural phenomena illustrate only a few of the fundamental differences in the thinking of people who speak different languages. They point to deeper differences in the nature of knowledge itself, in approaches to reasoning, and in the creation of new ideas. Speakers of North American Native languages do not necessarily organize reasoning according to a linear sequence of cause-and-effect, or axioms-theorems-corollaries, as do speakers of European languages. Instead they may keep a number of related ideas in mind, without assigning them an order or hierarchy. To linear thinkers, this approach may seem scattered and unfocused. Native-language thinkers, on the other hand, may find logical sequences rigid and narrow, because they themselves commonly approach an idea or a topic from many different directions. Norman's teacher would have approached model-making step by step, measuring distances and angles separately, then calculating the correct proportions to achieve an accurate representation of the original dogsled. Norman integrated all these features without making any of them explicit to himself or to his teacher (MacPherson 1987).

Distance, angle, and proportion, treated as self-contained ideas, are abstract concepts derived from logical analysis of the physical world. In Native languages, these attributes are specified only in respect to actual objects and relationships; the abstractions do not occur as words, as subjects for discussion, or as explicit considerations in perception. Similarly, there are no words meaning size or colour. Geography, mathematics, and fine arts are practised – but not discussed as areas of study; the same is true of traditional Native 'disciplines' such as music, spirituality, and history. Yet Native people become well versed in these fields and may even specialize in one of them. They attain the particular skills without having them isolated by teachers for practice and perfection. This approach to learning persists even among children whose first language is English, but whose parents' maternal language was Indian or Inuit.

In Native communities, parents and elders maintain the integration of knowledge as they teach younger people by sharing experiences with them, by not isolating the knowledge and skills required by certain disciplines. Each skill has a social, economic, spiritual, and historical context. Children participate in the daily activities of adults, instead of practising in an artificial setting like a classroom. Knowledge about 'fish spawning,' for example, is acquired not by taking biology or zoology, but through participating in what English-speakers might call travel, fishing, aquaculture, storytelling, economic development, history, art, environmental studies, law, and so on. From each repeated experience, the student learns more about fish spawning, its relations to other natural processes, and its 'place' in society and in the ecosystem. There is, in effect, only one, all-encompassing subject and one, lifelong lesson.

Rather than organizing vocabulary or the social studies curriculum by noun-centred topics, teachers need to look at each area of study in the context of the children's daily lives. Inuit children, for example, do not spontaneously sort rocks by size, colour, shape, or mineral composition. They begin by considering which would be good for holding down tents, or for using as sinkers or projectiles (Stairs, personal communication). Children learn skills through experience with adults, not by having adults tell them what to do in recipe-book or instruction-manual fashion:

> You just had to watch your grandparents or your parents to learn [to knit Cowichan sweaters]. No one taught me; I picked it up on my own. That was sort of a traditional way, for grandparents to let you learn on your own. They were just there to answer questions ... You show it to them and ask if there's any faults. I guess that's where we spoil our children. We try to show them and now they're not interested. (Irene Cooper, quoted in Meikle 1987, 13)

The implications for teaching are clear. Whether conducted in the Native language or in English, whether they address manual dexterity, general knowledge, or skills like writing and mathematics, classroom activities will be most effective when centred on real-life tasks, with children involved as apprentices. Children will also benefit from participating in meaningful projects outside the classroom. School becomes a place where in daily life they become better and better at all the skills required by their community – in the present and in the future. The teacher will think, for example, of the many contexts in which students can learn the history and geography of their community – hikes and canoe trips, map study, readings, oral history, road-building, religious and legal history, archaeology, mythology, hunting and fishing activities, agriculture.

Teachers of Native students will want to inquire about the best situations for conversation, the most natural methods of description and classification, and the real functions of language in their students' lives. They will want to let students integrate their experiences, spiritual beliefs, and social values with what they read and hear. Using this approach to language, teachers will be able to help Native students find their way into the continuum of interconnections between the generations, between people and the world about them, between the knowledge of individuals and that of the community. The dominance of verbs in Native languages may be thought to exemplify awareness of happening, eventuating, change, flow, interrelationship. Literacy is making it possible to discover parts and distinctions, to distil and classify, to apply Native language to non-Native ideas in areas such as science, law, government, and economic development.[6]

English literacy is also having an impact on the social culture of Native communities. Learning by reading (teaching with texts) removes education from the realm of personal interaction and breaks the link between knowledge and the value system (see Stairs, this volume). Teachers in the Concordia course became aware of their responsibility to maintain the kind of interpersonal communication – conversation, storytelling, talking-while-doing – which they find in their students' communities. Even where students work entirely in English, their personal relationships often retain features of the oral tradition, such as extensive, egalitarian peer integration and collaboration. Like the Cowichan knitters, teachers cannot afford to be 'showing' their students. They must let the students show them. Then English language and literacy, with its analytical approach, will help both the individual and the community. Culture and identity change with the introduction of English, but the changes can be positive.

The Cultural Component of Programs

In comparing English-second-language and Native-second-language curricula, the teachers observed that both have cultural contents; that is, students learn about the culture of people who speak English or a given Native language. In the case of programs for Native students, this usually means the inclusion of information in both languages about Native material culture – artifacts, traditional skills, and related knowledge and beliefs – which is seen as essential to understanding the Native way of life. Typically, this kind of content is presented as lessons in social studies, but perhaps also in art (Native crafts and design), history (events and personalities), music (songs and dances), geography (territories and resources), language arts (legends and oral history), and in other disciplines, such as religious or governmental studies. Including such content in areas of the school curriculum would seem to validate the culture Native students bring with them into the classroom. This approach, however, segments Native life in a non-Native way, by viewing it in English terms as a composite of specializations. This may happen even when the medium of instruction is a Native language.

When instructing Native children in English, teachers often strive to create a cultural curriculum, one which takes into account both the mainstream culture and that of the community. The purposes of the bicultural curriculum are to help students feel that the school program is a natural part of their lives and to help them move smoothly back and forth between one culture and the other. First attempts often focus on the attributes that Native and non-Native cultures have in common, recognizing that Native communities share many experiences with their neighbours. Much has been written and taught about the similarities and contrasts between Native and non-Native governments, clothing, religion, and decorative arts.

To make further progress towards appropriate Native education, teachers must choose whether programs will simply include Native culture as content, or whether they will be based on Native culture through the adaptation of traditional educational practices. Only the latter approach takes advantage of what both cultures have to offer and helps students move confidently – using familiar processes – from what they know into the discovery of what is new and useful in English (Leavitt 1987).

The educational vocabulary of the Maliseet language is indicative of the greater Native concern with process than with outcome.[7] While modern English also treats education as a process (except for 'pupil,' the words in Table 6.1 are verbs), it makes a clear dichotomy between the role of teacher and the role of learner. In Maliseet, however, there is only one verb root – *kehk* – common to all the words listed. This root means 'know,' and it is combined with other roots[8] and inflections to produce the words listed in Table 6.1.

In practice, a Maliseet subject or lesson has no existence apart from the teaching of it. Children do not learn 'something'; they teach themselves how to do it by watching, imitating, and participating. The Cowichan knitter quoted above saw herself not as having been taught, in the English sense, but as having 'picked it up' (i.e., having taught herself). Her grandparents customarily let children teach themselves. For many Native

Table 6.1

Maliseet education vocabulary

English word	Maliseet word	Literal translation
teach	ntokehkikem	I teach
teach something	ntokehkikemin (eli ...)	I teach (how to ...)
teach someone	ntokehkima	I teach her/him
teacher	nutokehkikemit	one who teaches
learn, study	ntokehkims	I teach myself
learn, study something	ntokehkimsin (eli ...)	I teach myself (how to ...)
learner, student, pupil	nutokehkimut or etolokehkimut	one who is taught or one who is being taught
my pupil	etolokehkimuk	one who I am teaching
school (education)	kehkitin	there is teaching
school (a building)	ihtolokehkitimok	where there is teaching
subject	ekehkitasik	what is taught
lesson	kehkitasu	it is being taught

children, school instruction, with its assumption that children will 'learn,' has resulted in failure. In order to help their Native students succeed, teachers must become models, not simply instructors.

An additional point of view on the differences between European and Native pedagogies is expressed by a teacher from Kahnawake, Quebec, who contrasts the English maxim, 'If at first you don't succeed, try, try again,' with the Mohawk version, 'Watch and listen and do it right, watch and listen and do it right.'[9] In the one culture, all attention is on the goal; the assumption is that it will be difficult to attain, but that the obstacles are worth overcoming. In the other culture, eyes and ears attend to what is happening now; this is the desirable strategy, successful in and of itself. These two maxims exemplify the contrast between education as the imparting of skills, knowledge, and content which will be useful in future activities and education as the achievement of significant participation in continuing adult work, where the content is the real-life task at hand. Teachers must distinguish between what is creative and helps students inquire into and build upon their own experience and what is assimilative and consequently destructive. They must consider whether they are encouraging students to take English and use it appropriately within their own culture. Only as they develop an understanding of students' needs and knowledge of students' communities will teachers be able to find this ideal cultural balance in their work. English offers new speakers a chance to see, as it were, new content in everyday experiences. Native students can learn that systems of distinct disciplines (law, spirituality, geography, history, economics) and the notion of 'forces' or 'elements' (historical continuity, the Crown, land use, economic influence) can be useful tools in managing experience, setting goals, becoming proactive, and negotiating (e.g., defining and defending land claims and hunting and fishing rights). The teacher's task is to help students discover the information and 'ways of knowing' accessible to them through English, as well as to recognize the insights their mother tongue has given them.

Notes

This chapter was previously published in the *Canadian Modern Language Review/La Revue canadienne des langues vivantes* 47, 2 (January 1991):266-79. Permission to reprint has been granted by the editors.

1 TESL 398A: Language and Culture in Native Education, taught by Arlene Stairs and Robert Leavitt. This and the following chapter in this volume are based on the authors' findings in developing and implementing the course. Quoted comments are taken from students' written evaluations.
2 For discussion of aspects of Native pedagogy, see for example Briggs 1983; Cronin 1982; Erickson and Mohatt 1982; Macias 1987; and Modiano 1975.
3 Guest speakers were Annette Jacobs (Kahnawake Mohawk School Board), Peesee Pitseolak (Baffin Divisional School Board), and Shirley Williams (Trent University).
4 See Stairs 1988 for a description of an Inuktitut-language teacher education program which addresses these questions, as well as teaching processes and educator roles. There remains, however, an urgent need for non-Native teachers to be trained in cross-cultural pedagogy.
5 Elders' discussion in Philosophy of Education workshop, Symposium '85 on Inuit Education, Kuujjuaq, Quebec, November 1985.
6 Interesting work in these areas is being done by Emmanuel Metallic of Restigouche, Quebec, and Bernie Francis of the Micmac Language Institute, Sydney, Nova Scotia, among others.
7 For an Inuit example of this focus on process rather than product, see Carpenter et al. 1959.
8 For example, *-im-* ('to effect by speaking'), as in *ntokehkima*, 'I teach her/him.' This way of teaching appears to be the Maliseet equivalent of Inuit *ilisayuq*. See Chapter 7.
9 B. Brisebois, in a presentation at the Atlantic Native Teacher Education Conference, Eskasoni, Nova Scotia, 1986.

References

Briggs, J. 1983. Le modèle traditionnel de l'éducation chez les Inuit. *Recherches Amérindiennes au Québec* 13 (1):13-25

Burnaby, B. 1986. *The use of Aboriginal languages in Canada: An analysis of the 1981 census data.* Ottawa: Department of the Secretary of State

Carpenter, E., F. Varley, and R. Flaherty. 1959. *Eskimo.* Toronto: University of Toronto Press

Charleston, G., ed. 1988. *Tradition and education: Towards a vision of our future.* Vol. 1. Summerstown, ON: Assembly of First Nations

Cowan, W., ed. 1987. *Papers of the eighteenth Algonquian conference.* Ottawa: Carleton University

Cronin, Mary. 1982. Cree children's knowledge of story structure: Some guidelines for the classroom. *Canadian Journal of Native Education* 9 (4):12-14

Cummins, J., and T. Skutnabb-Kangas, eds. 1988. *Minority education.* Clevedon, UK: Multilingual Matters

Erickson, F., and G. Mohatt. 1982. Cultural organization of participation structures in two classrooms of Indian students. In G. Spindler, ed., *Doing the ethnography of schooling: Educational anthropology in action*, 132-74. New York: Holt, Rinehart, Winston

Foster, M.K. 1984. Canada's first languages. *Language and Society* 9:7-16

Gill, S.D. 1982. *Beyond the primitive: The religions of non-literate peoples.* Englewood Cliffs, NJ: Prentice-Hall

Leavitt, R. 1987. Fluency is not enough: Reassessing the goals of Native language instruction.' In W. Cowan, ed., *Papers of the Eighteenth Algonquian Conference*, 165-72. Ottawa: Carleton University

Leavitt, R., B. Francis, and E. Paul, eds. 1986. *A'tukwaqnn: Micmac stories.* Fredericton, NB: Micmac-Maliseet Institute

Macias, J. 1987. The hidden curriculum of Papago teachers: American Indian strategies for mitigating cultural discontinuity in early schooling. In G. Spindler and L. Spindler, eds. *Interpretive Ethnography of Education at Home and Abroad*, 363-80. Hillsdale, NJ: Erlbaum

MacPherson, J. 1987. Norman. *For the Learning of Mathematics* 7 (2):24-7

Meikle, M. 1987. *Cowichan Indian knitting.* Museum Note 21. Vancouver: UBC Museum of Anthropology

Metallic, E., and A. Metallic, eds. 1985. *Atugwagnn: Micmac stories.* Fredericton, NB: Micmac-Maliseet Institute

Modiano, N. 1975. Using Native instructional patterns for teacher training: A Chiapas experiment.' In R. Troike and N. Modiano, eds., *Proceedings of the First Inter-American Conference on Bilingual Education* (Mexico City, 1974-5), 349-55. Mexico City

Socobasin, M.E. 1979. *Maliyan: Mary Ann.* Indian Township, ME: Wabnaki Bilingual Education Program

Spindler, G. 1982. *Doing the ethnography of schooling: Educational anthropology in action.* New York: Holt, Rinehart, Winston

Spindler, G., and L. Spindler, eds. 1987. *Interpretive ethnography of education:*

At home and abroad. Hillsdale, NJ: Erlbaum

Stairs, A. 1988. Beyond cultural inclusion: An Inuit example of indigenous educational development. In J. Cummins and T. Skutnabb-Kangas, eds., *Minority Education*, 308-27. Clevedon UK: Multilingual Matters

Troike, R., and N. Modiano, eds. 1975. *Proceedings of the First Inter-American Conference on Bilingual Education* (Mexico City, 1974-5). Mexico City

Wabnaki Bilingual Education Program. 1976. *Koluskap naka 'Siwiyi, Oqim, Wocawson: Koluskap and his relative, Loon, Wind*. Indian Township, ME: Wabnaki Bilingual Education Program

7
Learning Processes and Teaching Roles in Native Education: Cultural Base and Cultural Brokerage
Arlene Stairs

Introduction

Reflecting the historical foundation of all formal schooling, language has been our primary focus in developing Native and minority education in Canada (Burnaby 1982; Cummins 1983). Early initiatives in Native education focused on teaching the dominant language (usually English) to Native children. As the philosophy and policy of multiculturalism took hold over the last decade, our focus expanded to bring Native languages into the formal school setting. Native languages were first taught as cultural inclusion programs – limited components appended to the mainstream curriculum – and remain as distinct Native language courses in many parts of the country. These programs gradually moved beyond language to include elements of Native cultural content, and in certain regions Native language spread into lower levels of the standard primary curriculum. With rare exceptions, however, the learning-teaching processes in the education of Native children have been unaffected by this inclusion of Native language and content. In Canada, as in the American Native schools studied by Susan Philips, 'surprisingly little attention has been given to the teaching methods used in teaching ethnic minority children in this country, particularly when the notion of culturally relevant curriculum materials has been around as long as it has. It is as if we have been able to recognize that there are cultural differences in *what* people learn, but not in *how* they learn' [italics added] (Philips 1983, 133). My first purpose in this chapter is to explore what we are beginning to discover (or rediscover) about the 'how' of Native learning – about traditional Native processes of education. I seek to show that the linguistic and curricular content of Native education can be adequately pursued only when embedded in traditional cultural values concerning ways of using language, of interacting, and of knowing. Second, I examine how brokerage between Native (traditional) and school (formal) learning processes is being concentrated in the new cultural role of 'Native educator.' I try to face and make objective the strong subjective feelings and conflicts arising when process and role are added to language and content issues in Native education. In conclusion, I try to map out a path, should we choose to follow it, from language and cultural inclusion to a broad cultural base in Native Canadian education.

Native Learning-Teaching Processes

North Baffin Inuit recognize two radically different concepts of education (Wenzel 1987). We will borrow the Inuit concept labels to help our discussion of Native learning and teaching processes, acknowledging that our grasp of the full implications of these two different approaches to knowledge is far from complete.

Isumaqsayuq is the way of passing along knowledge through the observation and imitation embedded in daily family and community activities, integration into the immediate shared social structure being the principal goal. The focus is on values and identity, developed through the learner's relationship to other persons and to the environment. In contrast, *ilisayuq* is teaching which involves a high level of abstract verbal mediation in a setting removed from daily life, the skills for a future specialized occupation being the principal goal. While conventional formal schooling reflects many *ilisayuq* features, certainly some features of *isumaqsayuq* are paralleled in such current non-Native educational movements as experiential education and whole-language approaches. However, we are just beginning to comprehend Native learning models in terms of their rich, historical integrations of ecological, social, and cognitive cultural systems (Stairs 1988b).

Ecological Culture

Isumaqsayuq is perhaps most obviously distinguished from formal schooling or *ilisayuq* by its adaptive fit into Native ecology and economy; that is, into the traditional material culture. Mistakes are more critical in real settings than in protected learning situations, thus extended observation before first attempts is more functional in traditional life than is the trial-and-error learning encouraged in modern formal education. Because the use of acquired skills in very particular community tasks is the goal of traditional learning, education in real-world settings, 'in context,' makes sense. Inuit and other Native children are often taught through a process of 'backwards chaining' in which final steps of essential adult tasks are progressively left undone for children to complete, thus giving them an immediate and important role in community work. A young girl may first complete the final trim on her father's new pair of *kamiks* (skin boots), then the next year sew together several of the cut pieces as well as trimming. She would do the initial skin preparation and cutting only when older, not as isolated early steps in the learning process.

Native learners typically develop concepts and skills by repeating tasks in many different situations, such as hunting under varying conditions of weather and animal movement and with various types of equipment. They do not traditionally make explicit verbal formulations of basic ideas or rules for success, but rather recount what they have experienced and listen to stories which present concepts and principles implicitly. Formulation of the big ideas is left to the minds of the individual participants or listeners according to their own experience levels and perspectives. Clues for appropriate uses of language in formal Native education might be found in this contextualized verbal aspect of *isumaqsayuq* (cf., Scollon and Scollon 1981).

Teachers unfamiliar with the type of contextualized education exemplified by *isumaqsayuq* often worry that students do not 'know' a particular topic or concept when they cannot verbalize the knowledge; they assume that verbal abstraction is a necessary mediating step in high-level understanding. Teachers may also conclude that Native students are not involved in their learning when they reject early attempts at a new skill, or that they are lost and unable to learn a skill when they fail at preliminary isolated steps. In fact, in a situation such as an introductory computer programming class, a non-participating Native student may be watching the process until she or he feels ready for a proficient first try or until a real-world practical application, such as preparing graphics for a community newspaper, arises and contextualizes the skill being learned.

Many steps in school learning, as in the mathematics requirements for technical and scientific careers, are even further removed (often by years) than this computing example from target skills practised by competent adults. Native teachers and parents sometimes worry that a great deal of such decontextualized *ilisayuq* education may be damaging to children in pushing them beyond relevant experiences and outside ecological harmony. Traditionally, children's learning is monitored by their direct testing of social and environmental reactions. New skills, such as adjusting a ski-doo starter or organizing a toss game, either work in the real world or they do not; there is no need for mediation by a specialized teaching authority who passes or fails the new learning. The praise and punishment so central to the 'push' of *ilisayuq* are in *isumaqsayuq* either the positive inclusion of the child in community activity or the negative nonresponse – and sometimes teasing – of the group (cf., Briggs 1979). In its potential for overloading students with content disconnected from lived experience, *ilisayuq* can conflict with the Native view of children as complete beings who are in charge of their own development and not to be directly formed by adult manipulation.

Social Culture

It must already be clear that *isumaqsayuq* not only integrates teaching and learning into traditional material culture but also transmits Inuit social culture. *Isumaqsayuq* is characterized by the ultimate value placed on group cohesion. Awareness of interpersonal relationships and one's role in the social network is what constitutes maturity; this social competence has priority over individual excellence and productivity. In small communities, where interdependence is necessary for survival and where there is little choice in companions or co-workers, the goal of education is the well-being of the group rather than personal self-sufficiency. Cohesion is supported through extensive interactions among learners and between learners and teachers. Roles of learners and teachers continually shift, and the learning of skills and knowledge from a wide range of teachers is embedded in and subordinate to the learning of multiple kinship and social roles. Knowledge is a shared resource acquired cooperatively. This 'circle of learning' (Harrison 1982) is demonstrated as older siblings teach newly acquired skills to younger ones, and it is evident even in formal higher education when, for instance, adults returning from courses or conferences immediately present new information to their communities.

Perhaps paradoxically on the surface, Native social cohesion is seen to rest on individualism. The community respects individual differences within the bounds of cultural norms and takes advantage of the various talents among its members: a leader's political skill, a hunter's knowledge of animals, a storyteller's way with words, a business person's financial ability. Young learners, too, are accepted as individuals and are not expected to progress all in the same direction at the same time or to meet set standards of achievement. They are expected to attend to adult activities around them according to their own motivation, or to approach teachers and elders themselves, before direct instruction is given. The cultural resilience of learner-initiated education and the focus on social cohesion is revealed in recent reversals of expected teaching and learning roles. An Inuk elder, speaking at a circumpolar symposium on the future of Native education, and a Shuswap leader, in a video documenting community recovery from alcoholism and economic failure (both in 1985), advised others not to reject but to respect, approach, and learn from their formally educated children.

The social structure of *isumaqsayuq* is easily and often misunderstood in *ilisayuq* classrooms. In formal schools, where maturity is equated with the achievement of autonomy and individual success, observation and cooperation may be interpreted as inattention or even 'cheating.' Personal relationships between teachers and learners are discouraged as distracting students from achievement and generating teacher favouritism. Teachers keep a social distance in the classroom in order to evaluate and rank students by periodically assessing independent products. This kind of final evaluation differs sharply from evaluation in traditional learning where mastery is 'kept open' (Annahatak 1985) and refined through continual social and environmental feedback.

The possibility of such 'open' learning in school settings was demonstrated in an upper primary class making beginning reading booklets for younger children. Students worked in groups with no clear leaders, variously contributing artwork, writing, or technical skills according to their abilities and interests, helping and correcting each other, and responding to the reactions of their young readers. The teacher was essentially a team member and a resource in this learning activity, providing students with requested information and skills (such as spelling or a binding technique) rather than judging and grading their individual contributions. Evaluation of the booklets was largely qualitative and was conducted on a group rather than an individual basis. The work was highly contextualized, both materially and socially, and much of the evaluation came continually and directly to the students from their work environment. Native educators attempting to introduce the *isumaqsayuq* social structure into schools may find that the usual competition inherent in formal teaching and evaluation, particularly the recognition of individual star learners or the identification of failures, is inimical to their primary purpose, successful group cohesion in learning.

In general, teachers from either a formal or a traditional background observe in students of the 'other school' what they see as that system's shortcomings. Native teachers find that many non-Native children are unaware of the network of social roles, the orienting social context surrounding the skills and information they are acquiring. They do not internalize what they learn and 'do not know what they know' until it is confirmed by a teacher. One can observe, for example, a junior high school boy learning metalworking as an industrial arts subject, with his productions judged only by a professional teacher in a classroom setting – a skill for which he has neither the need, social structure, nor equipment to apply for himself or others at home. In contrast, one can observe a Native child learning to hunt ptarmigan with his older brothers, using tools he is also learning to construct – he is acquiring skills which will contribute food to and help define his social role in his family and his community.

Teachers in formal settings find equally disturbing shortcomings in traditional Native education. They see self-initiated learning as incompatible with the modern world – too accepting of deviance and learning weaknesses, too inefficient for use with large numbers of students, too random and too parochial in the face of the vast range and complexity of contemporary knowledge. From both formal and traditional educational perspectives, a key to dealing with the perceived shortcomings and incompatibilities of the other perspective may be recognition of the social nature of these differences. Interesting and unanswered questions concern the extent to which students can learn non-Native information and concepts through *isumaqsayuq* interactive processes and the extent to which relatively decontextualized learning processes characteristic of *ilisayuq* can be used to acquire Native knowledge and skills.

Cognitive Culture

At the cognitive level, *isumaqsayuq* and *ilisayuq* are comprehensive systems which guide the life and learning of individuals within their cultural contexts. As described by a Native educator (Annahatak 1985), cognitive culture underlies a people's outward material and social culture and integrates the affective ('what they feel ... and value') and perceptual ('what their minds make them see') with the intellectual ('the way they imagine and design ... their way of thinking and language [*sic*]'). A people's cognitive model of the world is evident in the ways they organize knowledge (see examples in Chapter 6). In studying Native learning and teaching processes, culturally different ways of knowing are not to be compared according to some assumed acultural criterion of pedagogical effectiveness. Rather these differences in cognitive culture are to be seen as people's collectively preferred ways of thinking about the world, each way offering insights not available to others.

Isumaqsayuq validates knowledge on the basis of life experience and community consensus. This knowledge is conveyed holistically and thematically. From the panoply of her own and her people's relationships with dogs, for example, Mitiarjuk Nappaaluk, an Inuk elder, has provided material for *Qimminuulignajut Ilumiutartangit [The Dog Book]* (c. 1985) which synthesizes knowledge categorized by non-Natives as biology; skills and economics of hunting, transportation, food, and clothing; art forms; animal behaviour and training; history; human/animal/environment cosmology; myths and tales, feats, disasters, and social roles of dogs. Recognizing that children do not learn 'one thing at a time' (Wolcott

1982), Native teachers typically provide meaning in this way; that is, by relating a theme as a number of real-life experiences and feelings.

Ilisayuq validates knowledge on the basis of objective proof and expert opinion. It conveys knowledge in abstract universal categories (for instance, insects, fish, mammals, or science, philosophy, art) rather than situational specifics, and it organizes these categories into hierarchies rather than treating each in its own right. Learners are isolated from one another and from their teachers and are generally removed from the social context of their learning. They find themselves required to learn in unfamiliar ways, especially having to make distinctions between thinking and feeling, lest one interfere with the other. These deep contrasts of formal thinking with traditional cognitive culture have largely unexplored implications for all aspects of Native education, from teaching practices to research. Some contemporary Native educators are demonstrating possible cognitive meetings between formal and traditional learning processes. The younger, formally educated Inuk who prepared *The Dog Book* for classroom use cut Mitiarjuk Nappaaluk's material into strips which were then arranged by educational topic. These topics, however, such as 'What young dogs do' and 'How dogs are pregnant,' were still more contextual than textual, and the richness of social, perceptual, and affective elements was preserved.

Cultural Conflict or Cultural Brokerage?

At a major education conference in the Northwest Territories – Canada's region with the highest proportion of Native population – participants rejected the potential political and personal conflicts of officially discussing the process issues of Native education. Planned sessions on culture-based education were cancelled shortly after they began. Also in 1987-8, both Native and non-Native students in a Concordia University Native education course (see Chapter 6) were uncomfortable with the necessity, as they initially understood it from the viewpoint of formal education, to oppose and choose between *isumaqsayuq* and *ilisayuq*. At least some moved towards accepting the juxtaposition of the two models of learning and teaching processes without, for the present, attempting to reconcile them. Most responded both to the excitement of expanding their teaching repertoires by using the two approaches and to the difficulties generated in school settings by the meeting of these two profoundly different systems of human learning. 'One-headed' and 'two-headed' possibilities in the meeting of *isumaqsayuq* and *ilisayuq* were discussed: either the eventual integration of the two models into a new cultural pattern of learning and teaching, or the continuing existence of two distinct models used according to situation and to complement each other. As we now examine, these possibilities become manifest largely through the roles of educators, particularly of Native teachers, as culture brokers in the meeting of *isumaqsayuq* and *ilisayuq*.

Native Educator Roles

In 1982, in her study of learning in a Native Alaskan village, Barbara Harrison observed that 'orientation for new (non-Native) teachers often consisted of nothing more than instruction in how to do the paperwork ... It was the Yup'ik children,' she concluded, 'who were left to resolve the conflicting expectations between the way they were expected to learn in informal settings and the way they were expected to learn in school' (1982, 108, 192). Certainly in some multicultural settings both Native and non-Native educators have become more effective in recent years. However, it has been curriculum more often than teachers themselves that has changed. Certain changes in non-Native teacher roles which are directly implied by recent curriculum developments in Native education have occurred – changes such as teaching second language primarily through the conversation, storytelling, and talking-while-doing typical of students' linguistic communities. Here we will examine the changes and the new roles which formal education is demanding of Native teachers, and the insights which this Native experience can offer all educators.

The culture-based approach to Native education recognizes teachers as the immediate agents of contact – and therefore of conflict or reconciliation – between diverse cultural learning-models. Teachers bring with them not only their fund of knowledge but also their culturally patterned ways of organizing and passing on that knowledge. Even more fundamentally, they bring the value systems of their communities concerning what is important to learn and how most appropriately to learn it. Unlike the paper-managers observed by Harrison, teachers in a culture-based program have as their first priority to establish classroom processes of learning and teaching which connect with the patterns of adult-child and child-child relationship expected by their students and the community. It is significant for the validity of this culturally based approach to educator roles that in many Native traditions teachers are considered an integral part of the knowledge they possess, and their ways of teaching are as important as the knowledge itself (Cooley and Ballenger 1982, 97-9).

The dual role of teachers, as sociocultural agents and as technical educators (Piddington 1951), is evident at several levels in culture-based Native education programs. The teacher is first of all a culture broker between Native and non-Native, selecting and transmitting to students her or his personal synthesis of knowledge, values, and human relationships gleaned from cultures in contact. At a practical level, this brokerage involves the dual role of looking to students for clues about the best ways to help them learn within the formal education system while simultaneously searching the system itself for modifications to allow more appropriate responses to the needs of Native students. Most Native teachers are also faced with the input task of collecting and structuring bicultural information and methods – from such diverse sources as elders, linguistic specialists, media, politicians, assorted consultants, and their own students – as well as with the output task of conventional teaching. Native teachers must be jacks of all educational trades. Lack of existing programs for many Native situations and rapid cultural change make this input-output duality a constant feature of Native educators' roles.

Native educators additionally function as brokers within their own communities, seeking to find the best balance between the divergent goals of education for economic advancement and education for cultural maintenance (cf., Bullivant 1984). In doing so, they serve the community as cultural translators between Native and non-Native life- and learning-styles. In traditional communities, the teacher is often chosen by the population and feels her or his job to be a 'calling' comparable to that of a priest. In addition to requiring professional competence, this calling demands that Native teachers live in the awareness that they are cultural role models for students and others. They must integrate their professional teaching with the daily informal learning-teaching interactions of the villagers – interactions which consistently place skill and knowledge acquisition within the context of local social values (e.g., Briggs 1983). A Native professor of languages and education insists that teachers in a Native village 'must be products of that community in order for the children to learn the value system of the community' (MacLean, in Curwin 1986, 21).

Clearly the roles of a Native and a non-Native educator in ostensibly the same position, even in the same school, differ in multiple ways which are rarely recognized in formal job descriptions. Most basically, non-Native teachers identify primarily with the formal education system and strive to bring the community into the school, while Native teachers identify with their communities and strive to make the school a significant part of the students' community life. Many Inuit teachers in the eastern Arctic remain grounded in their community culture by alternating over the years between professional education and non-professional family roles. While it is a promising creative response to culture contact, such cycling does not solve all the problems of life as both an intimate member of a Native community network and a formally trained teaching professional. Teachers are expected, for example, to deal in the same way with all students and with all colleagues. When the group of students is made up of children in differing kinship and social relationships to the teacher, and when professional colleagues are sometimes family authority figures or proteges, the conflicts between traditional and formal roles can be intense. The quest for *isumaqsayuq/ilisayuq* brokerage is as critical for Native educators as it is for Native students.

Both the cultural conflicts and the creative reconciliations in Native educators' roles are perhaps best illustrated by current developments in Native teacher education (e.g., Stairs 1988a). Native educators have been seen to progress through three stages (extended from Beebe, in Modiano 1974-5):

(a) a 'chaotic' stage of mismatch between traditional informal teaching and the formal education structure, as when a community elder, asked into the school to 'teach' carving, works quietly in the corner of the room while a group of teenagers, used to imposed direction in the classroom, drifts into disruptive activity;

(b) a 'cookbook' stage, in which Native teachers adopt the formal methods demonstrated to them, even to the point, in a typical instance, of having students number the lines in their written work, thereby religiously following a methodological quirk of a favoured non-Native teacher education instructor; and

(c) a 'reconstruction' stage, in which Native teachers integrate at least some aspects of schooling back into their culturally valued processes of learning, as exemplified by an Inuk teacher who takes his class out into the community to help elders with repairs and getting water in exchange for legends and stories, old words no longer in common use, and demonstrations of sled-making and string games.

Until recently, Native teachers only rarely reached the reconstruction stage. Where this third stage of teacher development has been reached, it has generally involved exceptional individuals who were able to maintain their cultural grounding despite long periods of training time away from their roles and identity base in the Native community. Certain genuinely culture-based approaches to Native teacher education are beginning to overcome this professional development barrier, and may be generally easing the cultural conflicts facing contemporary Native educators. In particular, a field-based apprenticeship approach meets the need, expressed urgently by Native teachers, to be providing immediate effective teaching to their children rather than leaving their communities for continued professional development. Successful application of the apprenticeship approach builds on the preferred *isumaqsayuq* learning mode of Native educators, including 'circle of learning' processes through which more advanced educators continually pass on their experience and training by working with newer teachers. In at least one instance, these knowledge-sharing cycles of instruction have made possible a complete first-language, first-culture teacher education program, to full certification and degree level, carried out entirely in Canada's most isolated communities (Stairs 1988a).

To what extent is it possible, and desirable, for Native educators to synthesize traditional and formal teaching? Many Native elders fear that traditional skills and approaches to knowledge will be trivialized or perverted by formal educators, that the informal teaching role of the community will be destroyed, and that the overriding educational goal of social cohesion will be abandoned. Despite deep concern about seeing their children drift away from community tasks and into escapism as they progress through school (e.g., Sindell 1987), parents also fear that children taught Native ways in school will not acquire mainstream ways and so will not be able to cope in either world. Linguists, mindful of historical examples, worry that Native languages will become assimilated through formal teaching or lost in universal bilingualism. Educators and social scientists worry about the panorama of culture-contact problems, but also look optimistically towards new, richer ways of learning being developed by Native educators.

We close this exploration of Native educator roles with one such optimistic example of a setting in which both community elders and professional teachers are finding complementary new educational roles involving the language, content, and learning-teaching processes of the two cultures making up their children's lives. In this setting, the 1983 resolution (83-18) of the Inuit Circumpolar Conference General Assembly – 'that our educational systems are to prepare our children for life based on values and skills from the Inuit culture and the western culture' – is put into action. In northern Alaska, the Inupiaq *qargi* – the community house where youth traditionally went to listen to and learn from elders – is being reestablished on a trial basis as a parallel to the modern formal school. This is a response to almost fifty years of assimilationist education which has resulted in a generation of children who are virtual strangers to the Native culture. In the new *qargi*, in Native language, a young professionally trained

Native teacher 'would work side by side with the elders of each community, thereby allowing the teacher to absorb both the knowledge possessed
by the elder(s), and the manner in which the children were taught ...
Skills learned in school, such as mathematics, could be applied in the
qargi, where children are building sleds or boats, for example' (MacLean,
in Curwin 1986, 21). Here, as *isumaqsayuq* and *ilisayuq* meet, Native educators are in fact creating new cultural roles for themselves.

Conclusion

Optimism for the future of Native education in Canada is difficult in light
of overwhelming failures for which the evidence is all too familiar (e.g.,
high rates of school dropout, language loss, political confrontation, drug
abuse, crime, and suicide). Perhaps we can take some hope from growing
attention over recent years to the idea and dynamics of Native-non-
Native cultural brokerage (Brody 1975; Paine 1971 and 1977; Simard
1983; Williamson 1974; Wyatt 1978-9), and from at least a few successful
educational examples (e.g., Jobidon 1984; Kleinfeld 1979; Macias 1987;
Stairs 1988a; Wyatt-Benyon 1986).

The first feature of these successes is some movement from cultural
inclusion to cultural base in the conceptualization and implementation of
Native education. As illustrated in Figure 7.1, this movement rests on the
progressive incorporation of schools into the Native cultural context –
from the language and content aspects discussed by Leavitt in Chapter 6
to the process aspects (ecological, social, and cognitive) explored in this
chapter. Some next steps in Native educational research and development
might focus on the most apparent correlates of this progress:

- emerging oral and written linguistic forms, in both Native languages
  and English (Burnaby 1985; Leavitt, Chapter 6; Shearwood 1987; Stairs
  1985), as cultural bridges
- developing Native educator roles (see above) as culture brokers between
  Native and Euro-Canadian ways of knowing.

The second feature of success in Native education may be the converse
side of cultural brokerage – attention to and incorporation of certain
Native ways of learning into mainstream formal education. There has
been malaise over the decontextualized nature of much North American
schooling (e.g., Cole 1988; Resnick 1987), and a search for more socially
functional models of learning (e.g., Bruner 1986; Lave 1988; Rogoff 1982).
The Native traditions of contextualized and shared learning may offer
clues for schooling directed towards more effective living in our environment and with each other (Stairs 1988c). Canadian education has much
to gain as well as to give in brokerage with Native cultures. I suggest in

Figure 7.1

The cultural basis of learning and teaching in Native education

Limited cultural inclusion	Cultural inclusion	Narrow cultural base	Expanding cultural base	Broad cultural base
				cognitive process
			social process	social process
		ecological context	ecological context	ecological context
	content material	content material	content material	content material
Native language	Native language +	Native language ++	Native language +++	Native language ++++

Native cultural inclusion → Native cultural base

(Native language inclusion → Native language base)

closing that genuine two-way brokerage between Native culture and formal schooling validates Native ways of learning, responds to urgent mainstream needs, and is our collective path to success in Native education.

Note

This chapter was previously published in the *Canadian Modern Language Review/La Revue canadienne des langues vivantes* 47, 2 (January 1991):280-94. Permission to reprint has been granted by the editors. I thank the Inuit and other Native people with whom I have worked for involving me in the instructive cultural brokerage on which this chapter is based. Preparation of the chapter was stimulated by TESL students in Native language and education courses at Concordia University during the summers of 1987 and 1988.

References

Annahatak, B. 1985. Philosophy of Inuit education. Paper prepared for Symposium '85 on Inuit Education, Kuujjuaq, PQ: Kativik School Board

Briggs, J.L. 1979. *Aspects of Inuit value socialization.* Ottawa: National Museum of Man Mercury Series

–. 1983. Le modèle traditional l'éducation chez les Inuit. *Recherches Amérindiennes au Québec* 13 (1):13-25

Brody, H. 1975. *The people's land.* Middlesex: Penguin

Bruner, J. 1986. *Actual minds, possible worlds.* Cambridge, MA: Harvard

University Press

Bullivant, B.M. 1984. *Pluralism: Cultural maintenance and evolution*. Clevedon, UK: Multilingual Matters

Burnaby, B. 1982. *Languages and their roles in Native education*. Toronto: Ontario Institute for Studies in Education

–, ed. 1985. *Promoting Native writing systems in Canada*. Toronto: Ontario Institute for Studies in Education Press

Cole, M. 1988. A cultural theory of learning and development: Implications for educational research and practice. Paper presented to the American Educational Research Association, New Orleans, LA

Cooley, R.E., and Ballenger, R. 1982. Culture retention programs and their impact on Native American cultures. In R.N. St. Clair and W.L. Leap, eds., *Language renewal among American Indian tribes: Issues, problems and prospects*. Arlington, VA: National Clearing House for Bilingual Education

Cummins, J. 1983. *Heritage language education*. Toronto: Ministry of Education

Curwin, K. 1986. Edna Maclean of the Alaska Native Language Centre: Traditional qargi can link old ways to western school system. *Inuit (I.C.C.)*. Pamphlet. 20-1

Harrison, B.G. 1982. Informal learning among Yup'ik Eskimos: An ethnographic study of one Alaskan village. Ph.D. dissertation, University of Oregon

Jobidon, O., ed. 1984. *Successes in Indian education: A sharing*. A conference to assess the state of the art. Vancouver, BC: British Columbia Ministry of Education

Kleinfeld, J. 1979. *Eskimo school on the Andreafsky: A study of effective bicultural education*. New York: Praeger

Lave, J. 1988. *Cognition in practice*. New York: Cambridge University Press

Macias, J. 1987. The hidden curriculum of Papago teachers: American Indian strategies for mitigation cultural discontinuity in early schooling. In G. Spindler and L. Spindler, eds., *Interpretive ethnography of education*. Hillsdale, NJ: Erlbaum

Modiano, N. 1974-5. Using native instructional patterns for teacher training: A Chiapas experiment. In R. Troike and N. Modiano, eds., *Proceedings of the First Inter-American Conference on Bilingual Education* Mexico City

Nappaaluk, M. ca. 1985. *Qimminuulignajut ilumiutartangit (The dog book)*. Dorval, PQ: Kativik School Board

Paine, R., ed. 1971. *Patrons and brokers in the east arctic*. St John's: Memorial University, Institute of Social and Economic Research

–, ed. 1977. *The white arctic: Anthropological essays on tutelage and ethnicity*. St John's: Memorial University of Newfoundland

Philips, S.U. 1983. *The invisible culture: Communication in classroom and community on the Warm Springs Indian Reserve*. New York: Longman

Piddington, R. 1951. An anthropologist's viewpoint. In J.A. Lauwarys and N. Hans, eds., *The yearbook of education*. London: Evans

Resnick, L.B. 1987. Learning in school and out. *Educational Researcher* 16 (9):13-20

Rogoff, B. 1982. Integrating context and cognitive development. In M.E. Lamb and A.L. Brown, eds., *Advances in development psychology.* 2 vols. Hillsdale, NJ: Erlbaum

Scollon, R., and S.K. Scollon. 1981. *Narrative, literacy, and face in interethnic communication.* Norwood, NJ: Ablex

Shearwood, P. 1987. Literacy among the aboriginal peoples of the Northwest Territories. *Canadian Modern Language Review* 43 (4):630-42

Simard, J.J. 1983. Par-delà entre le blanc et le mal: Repports identitaires et colonialisme au pays des Inuit. *Sociologie et Sociétés* 15 (2):55-71

Sindell, P. 1987. Some discontinuities in the enculturation of Mistassini Cree children. In G.D. Spindler, ed., *Education and cultural process: Anthropological approaches.* Prospect Heights, IL: Waveland

Stairs, A. 1985. La viabilité des langues autochtones et le rôle de l'écrit: l'expérience de l'inuktitut au Nouveau Québec. (Native language viability and the role of literacy: The experience of Inuktitut in Arctic Quebec.) *Recherches Amérindiennes au Québec* 15 (3)

–. 1988a. Beyond cultural inclusion: An Inuit example of indigenou educational development. In T. Skutnabb-Kangas and J. Cummins, eds., *Minority education.* Clevedon, UK: Multilingual Matters

–. 1988b. Native models for learning (A reply to Lauren Resnick). *Educational Researcher* 17 (6)

–. 1988c. The professional development of Native educators: Context, culture and language. *TESL Canada Journal* 5 (2)

Wenzel, G. 1987. I was once independent. *Anthropologica*

Williamson, R.G. 1974. *Eskimos underground.* Uppsala: Uppsala University Press

Wolcott, H. 1982. The anthropology of learning. *Anthropology and Education Quarterly* 13 (2):83-108

Wyatt, J. 1978-9. Native involvement in curriculum development: The native teacher as culture broker. *Interchange* 8 (1):17-28

Wyatt-Benyon, J. 1986. The Mt. Currie Indian community school: Innovation and endurance. In H. McCue, ed., *Selected papers from the First Mokakit Conference.* Vancouver: University of British Columbia

Western Door:
Meeting the Challenge of
Incoherence

8

A Major Challenge for the Education System: Aboriginal Retention and Dropout

Ron Mackay and Lawrence Myles

The Canadian model of education is largely based on the expectation that all students will graduate from high school. After graduation, students will then separate into two streams – those destined directly for the work force and those destined for post-secondary education (college or university). For those who enter the work force directly, further training is often available on a part-time or release basis, and those who continue into college or university may do so part-time or full-time. Without a high school graduation diploma, school leavers are largely denied the opportunity for further training, promotion, and indeed access to a general 'career structure.' The importance of the graduation diploma cannot be overestimated in Canada.

Those who obtain the graduation diploma have many doors open to them – to further study, training, and diverse employment opportunities. Those without the graduation diploma are more likely to encounter difficulty in entering and progressing in the work force, and to end up in seasonal work, unskilled work, or be underemployed, unemployed, and dependent upon welfare.

It is the importance attached to the benefits of completing high school that underlie Canadian society's concern with 'dropouts.' Educators and parents, as well as legislators, planners, and politicians, desire to increase the proportion of Canadian youth who graduate from high school. As a result of this concern, high school retention rates within the publicly supported education systems of all Canadian provinces have increased in this century (Zsigmond and Wenaas 1980).

Information on Native Student Retention
While it is unwise to use graduation rates as the sole measure of the intellectual vitality of Canada's Aboriginal youth, or the ability of provincial secondary schools to educate them, graduation is important since it is

the principal gateway to further education, university degrees, and the professions. However, it is surprisingly difficult to obtain accurate statistics on Aboriginal students in Canada who abandon school before obtaining the graduation diploma. There are no provincial or federal databases specifically designed to provide information of this type for the purpose of monitoring student progress, evaluating Aboriginal student support programs, or undertaking empirical research. Indian and Northern Affairs Canada (INAC) maintains the nominal roll, a record of school registration for registered Indian students resident on reserve, principally for accounting purposes arising from the federal responsibility to pay for their education.

The departments of education of the Northwest Territories and the Yukon, because of the political importance of the various ethnic groups within their populations, keep high school enrolment and graduation figures for students, broken down into Métis, Inuit, Dene, and non-Native groups. Similarly, the Kativik School Board of Arctic Quebec keeps records on its almost entirely Inuit student population and has recently reported that 'most of the youth of Nunavik (Arctic Quebec) drop out of school' (Makivik Corporation 1992).

In Ontario, schools provide Native education counsellors with registration and attendance records of registered Indian students primarily so that accurate invoices for contracted education services can be submitted to INAC. Some, but not all, First Nations use these records to inform parents about the progress of their children in provincial secondary schools. Few, if any, First Nations maintain accurate and up-to-date student information systems to monitor student progress and identify poor attenders or de facto dropouts needing support and counselling.

In other words, the primary purpose of educational records on Aboriginal students outside Arctic Quebec, the Yukon, and the Northwest Territories is to support the management of their education and the disbursement of public funds. However, the nominal roll and the school records are an inadequate research base for monitoring either the educational progress of individual cohorts of students or the educational system that serves them. The potential for individual First Nations to adapt the school records with which they are provided to systematically monitor the progress of their students remains largely unexploited.

It is impossible to obtain statistical information for Métis students outside the Territories or for Indians resident off reserve. For virtually all educational purposes, they are seen as part of the general population and no educational records which identify them as Native are kept by the federal or provincial governments, school boards, or schools.

Trends in Native Student Retention in Ontario

During the 1970s and 1980s, the number of registered Indian students attending Ontario provincial secondary schools has risen by approximately 60 per cent from about 2,000 to 3,200. During the 1988 school year, approximately 3,220 registered Indian students attended over 200 of the 780 Ontario provincial secondary schools. Some 80 of these schools had 5 or more Indian students enrolled, 65 schools had more than 20, 30 schools had more than 50, and 15 schools had more than 100 registered Indian students enrolled in secondary grades.

Table 8.1 shows the increasing trend in retention rates between 1974-5 and 1985-6. However, the Indian students recorded in the nominal roll as being registered in Grade 12 may simply be in their fourth year of secondary school rather than within eight credits of the graduation diploma, which is the definition of a Grade 12 student in the Ontario Ministry of Education's directives. Many principals do not follow these directives to the letter and permit students to remain with their home-room class for registration purposes so as to improve their self-esteem. Since for most purposes students will be in subjects and levels appropriate to their career choices, there can be no educational harm in this practice.

Hence, while a large proportion of those registered Indian students who enrol in Grade 9 in Ontario provincial schools do not earn sufficient credits to obtain a graduation diploma, the majority are remaining in school until Grade 12 (four years of secondary education). Many Native and non-Native educators view the increasing retention rates positively. They believe that they reflect the persistent hard work of Native education counsellors over the years, their increasing professionalism in dealing with both schools and students, and their effective grasp of the underlying principles of band participation in day-to-day monitoring and management of the education of Native students, even when this is off reserve in provincial schools.

Educators point out that the upward retention trend reflects increased satisfaction by Native students with provincial schools, the development by such students of better habits of regular attendance, punctuality, and persistence, and the recording of credits on their transcripts which may give them better employment opportunities even without the graduation diploma. Increased retention rates are thus seen as a slow but sure indication that registered Indians perceive education in provincial secondary schools as an instrument to promote their own development in ways which they themselves can determine. These trends towards increased retention and graduation are supported by the research of the Assembly of First Nations: 'Greater numbers of First Nation students are graduating

Table 8.1

Progress of registered Indians through Ontario provincial schools, 1974-86

School year	Grade 9 students (provincial students only)	Grade 12 students as % of Grade 9 students three years earlier (all schools)
1974-5	723	36
1975-6	556	52
1976-7	579	54
1977-8	671	51
1978-9	711	52
1979-80	687	60
1980-1	647	90
1981-2	656	80
1982-3	585	91
1983-4	894	63
1984-5	933	65
1985-6	912	67

Source: Mackay and Myles (1989, 13)

from high school and obtaining training at post-secondary and vocational institutions' (Assembly of First Nations 1988, 77).

Patterns of Aboriginal Student Retention
The retention rate is not uniform across Ontario or across any other province or territory in Canada. According to the nominal roll figures for the 1980s, in Ontario retention between Grades 9 and 12 varies from an annual average of more than 90 per cent for registered Indian students attending provincial secondary schools in the Peterborough and Brantford districts to a low of about 11 per cent for provincial secondary schools in the Nakina district and 9 per cent in James Bay district.

This lack of consistency underlines the danger of making generalizations about Aboriginal education based on aggregate statistics. For example, aggregated statistics for Ontario suggest that in the 1980s between one-third and just over half of registered Indian students who entered Grade 9 in provincial secondary schools would graduate three years later.

Such generalizations disguise the very significant variations in school retention and graduation rates between Native communities and within the contexts in which they receive their education across the province. They also tend to obscure the fact that appropriate solutions to dropping out must be sensitive to particular contexts. Successful intervention for the students of one First Nation may be very distinct from successful intervention for the students of another First Nation. Native education counsellors are rightly distrustful of information aggregated across communities and shorn of the particulars which make each community situation interpretable and understandable.

Understanding Aboriginal Student Dropout

Retention statistics may give a general picture of the proportions of students dropping out, remaining in secondary school till Grade 12, or even obtaining high school graduation diplomas. However, statistics alone provide no insight into why students stop attending school or what can be done to influence their behaviour.

Based on a review of the literature on Native and non-Native dropouts and on information obtained from dropouts, students, teachers, parents, counsellors, and key informants in the Native education community, Mackay and Myles (1989) drew up an inventory of forty-two factors believed to be closely associated with or to contribute to dropping out. These factors are shown in the appendix at the end of this chapter. Using a questionnaire with these forty-two factors built into a Likert Scale as a way of framing open-ended, in-depth interviews, Mackay and Myles obtained information from 310 informants (see Table 8.2), including key persons from both Native and non-Native communities in Ontario.

Dropout Survey Results

Earlier research on dropouts, based mainly on statistical correlations, located the main 'cause' in socioeconomic factors such as family background (parents' occupation, income, educational background, ethnicity, family size, etc.), which lay largely beyond the control of the school system. More recent research has begun to focus on school culture or climate (Anderson 1982), posing the very pertinent question 'How much do schools contribute to the problem?' (Wehlage and Rutter 1986).

The results below do not attempt to establish causal links between dropping out and factors in the home, the community, or the school. Instead they explore the often conflicting perspectives on, or constructions of, the problem held by parents, Native and non-Native educators, and the young people themselves.

Table 8.2

Number, location in Ontario, and percentage of informants in six categories from whom interviews were obtained

Informants	North and South		North		South	
	n	*%*	*n*	*%*	*n*	*%*
Educators – non-Native	84	27	39	25	45	29
Educators – Native	38	12	17	11	21	14
Dropouts – on-reserve	91	29	41	26	50	33
Dropouts – off-reserve	41	13	29	19	12	08
Parents – on-reserve	28	09	15	10	13	09
Parents – off-reserve	28	09	16	10	12	08
Total surveyed	310	100	157	100	153	100

Source: Mackay and Myles (1989)

Informants indicated the extent to which they agreed that a particular factor contributed to the student's decision to drop out. These responses, which were based on the informant's particular experiences as a student, parent, or educator, were then used to focus an open-ended interview. Informants were asked to expand on how statements with which they agreed contributed to dropping out.

Although there was often consensus among stakeholders on key contributory factors in Native student dropouts, the salient factors were almost invariably intertwined with other factors. It was therefore impossible to identify a particular factor or cluster of factors and recommend appropriate remedial steps in the school, home, or community that might directly increase Native student retention. More importantly, the interpretation of these factors, their relative weight, their provenance, and the steps necessary to deal with them varied considerably among stakeholder groups and also among regions. In order to get at the problem, the first step is to make available to all parties the opposing constructions held by stakeholder groups. In this section we examine the stakeholder constructions of three of the issues identified by most informants: language skills, parental support, and home-school communication.

Language Skills
One questionnaire item dealt with the extent to which principal stakeholders perceived difficulty with English language skills by Native students as contributing to their dropping out. The relevant Likert item was phrased for dropouts as 'I had difficulty with English language skills (reading, writing, listening, and speaking) in class.'

There is considerable agreement among Native and non-Native educators that inadequate English language skills contribute to a Native youth's dropping out. The interview data reveal three areas of concern. Educators throughout the province of Ontario cited weaknesses in basic English literacy skills as characteristic of dropouts, irrespective of their ethnicity. With respect to Native students, educators held that in some cases these language problems were the result of inadequate instruction in elementary school, but most linked the difficulties to socioeconomic factors: parents' lack of education, a dearth of reading activity and materials at home, lack of encouragement to read at home, the dominance of television for recreation, and inadequate or non-existent library facilities on some reserves. Native students from such backgrounds are likely to experience difficulty with the reading and writing requirements of secondary school. While educators believe that lack of support for and reinforcement of literacy in the home exacerbates poor language skills, parents are more likely to feel that the educational system bears full responsibility. 'The three Rs are not what they should be in school today – they're not what they were years ago' (Parent, Métis).

A second area of concern cited by Native and non-Native educators was some students' use out of school of non-standard English. The sociolinguistic background to this is complex, but the fact is that many Ontario Native children come to school with little previous exposure to the academic English commonly used in textbooks and classrooms. Insensitivity by the school community to the students' variety of English and their need for time, possibly unacknowledged by some teachers, to master the new idiom may further undermine these Native students' already fragile sense of identity and self-esteem. Any obstacle to students' mastery of the language and literacy skills required for acceptable school performance will tend to deflect them away from success.

Third, some students, especially those from isolated northern Ontario communities where a Native language is normally spoken, can experience difficulty because English is their second, weaker language. Not only do these students share the same weaknesses in basic literacy skills observed in many dropouts for whom English is the mother tongue, they also have difficulty in understanding what is said and in participating in class. While some schools with a high proportion of Native students from the north do offer English language transition programs, the feeling is that the 'southern English-as-a-Second Language (ESL) establishment' has focused its professional attention on recent immigrants and has neglected the particular needs of Canada's Native people.

Although fewer dropouts and on-reserve parents linked language difficulties directly to early school leaving, they confirmed the educators' perceptions that language problems did negatively effect the academic and, to a lesser extent, the social life of many dropouts from provincial secondary schools. Educators suggested that discomfort with English leads to avoidance behaviour. Students with weak language skills may remain silent in class and this may be interpreted by teachers as unwillingness to participate or even to pay attention in class. Some dropouts confirmed that when they did not completely understand what was being said, they felt unable to participate fully in class and were more inclined to daydream. When students with weak English language skills do not comprehend the task that is being asked of them, they may be too shy to ask for clarification.

Deficiencies in reading and writing skills have additional repercussions. Students may avoid submitting homework for fear that it will be graded poorly or even rejected outright. Several educators made a further link between this language-related behaviour and poor attendance. They suggest that if assignments and homework are not completed, students may skip that class in order to avoid trouble with the teacher. By missing classes, they fall further behind until they have no idea what is required of them or how to complete further homework assignments. They find themselves sucked into a vortex from which the only escape is opting out.

The discrepancy between the proportion of educators (both Native and non-Native) and the dropouts (resident both on and off reserve) who believe that poor language skills contribute to dropping out appears to have a simple explanation. Teachers may soon discover that students exhibit weaknesses in language skills such as writing or presenting extensive, well-reasoned, and well-organized oral responses to complex questions. Teachers in Ontario secondary schools are subject specialists. They may deplore the students' deficiencies in language skills and may ascribe them to inadequate instruction in primary school. At the same time, as subject specialists they believe that they are not responsible for either helping students overcome these deficiencies or for extending the students' linguistic repertoire in their specialist subject. Their solution to this dilemma is simply not to ask students to perform tasks that they have difficulty in performing. Hence, instead of requiring long, complex written and oral discussions, the teacher will provide multiple-choice questions, dictated notes, and fill-in-the-blank exercises which require no active production, only recognition, from the students. This solution allows instruction to continue without interruption due to faltering oral responses or embarrassing written language (Mackay 1990, 1992).

However, this solution has several disadvantages. Neither the students nor their parents may become aware of their inadequate language skills. They may be equally unaware that multiple-choice questions, dictated notes, and fill-in-the-slot exercises are considered by the teacher as poor substitutes for preferred tasks which make more complex linguistic demands on the students. Neither the students nor the parents realize that the process of education is being simplified for them. Nor are they aware of the latent resentment harboured by teachers who adopt a subterfuge which they believe falls below the appropriate level for that grade (Mackay 1990).

Parental Support
Two items dealt with the extent to which parental interest and encouragement contributed to the Native student's decision to remain in or abandon school. The Likert items containing this factor were phrased for dropouts as 'My parents didn't have much interest in how well or badly I did at school' and 'My parents didn't encourage me to stay on at school.'

On the whole, non-Native educators were either uncertain or thought that parents of dropouts did lack interest in their children's education and failed to engender in them an appreciation of its value. In very few cases were the judgments based on direct conversation between educators and Aboriginal parents. Indeed, the vast majority of teachers and non-Native education counsellors had never visited the reserves, and few had had personal conversations with the parents of their Aboriginal students.

One indicator that educators use to judge parental interest is the extent to which parents participate in parent/teacher nights organized by the school. By and large, it was reported that Native parents do not attend these meetings. Both Native and non-Native educators recognized that many parents are uncomfortable coming to school. They cited a number of reasons for this: (1) some parents are unfamiliar with and are intimidated by the educational system; (2) they may view the school as an alien world in which they play no part, considering that the formal education of their children is exclusively in the hands of professionally trained educators; (3) their lack of participation reflects a deeply rooted ambivalence towards the purposes of school education as an institution; and (4) the principal and the almost exclusively non-Native teaching staff may implicitly discourage parents from participating as complementary partners in education. This alienation may be further exacerbated by the parents' own negative experiences of school. Educators reported virtually no contact at all with the natural parents of student boarders from the north, and most were therefore uncertain about the degree of parental support enjoyed by this group of students. However, they pointed out that given the physical separation, opportunities for direct support were nil.

Both Native and non-Native educators recognized that certain Native dropouts lacked parental support because of the many social problems that affected their families. Educators thought that problems facing single parents (family breakdown, alcoholism, finances) were so pressing that such parents had little time for the educational needs of their children. All the educators thought that parental support was a critical variable affecting students' school performance and their decision to stay in school. Many educators used the presence or absence of parental support to explain a student's decision to remain at or drop out of school. 'In homes where graduation and education is stressed and valued by parents, kids graduate; otherwise they rarely do.' Such an apparently cogent explanation can enormously comfort educators because it places responsibility for a student's behaviour firmly with the parents and releases the school system from both blame and remedial action.

Native and non-Native educators suggested that the parents of many dropouts lack the 'know how' to motivate their children. They also suggested that some parents believe that the decision to stay at school should be the child's exclusively. Again, educators return to the ambivalence towards provincial education exhibited by some Native groups. 'How,' they ask, 'can parents effectively encourage their children to achieve educational goals that they themselves view with mixed feelings?' Some Native educators reported that the educational success of the children may pose a threat. Parents may fear that they will 'lose' their children both metaphorically and literally; education will result in a severing of emotional and cultural ties and may eventually lead children to leave the reserve or community for attractive employment elsewhere. These fears are perceived to be greatest in the isolated northerly communities where there are fewer links between white and Native society.

Finally, more than twice as many Métis and off-reserve dropouts as on-reserve Natives considered parental support to be lacking. A far greater percentage of Métis and off-reserve parents agreed that their children received inadequate parental support. This finding adds weight to the view that Métis/off-reserve students are much more at risk due to family problems than are on-reserve students.

Home-School Communication

Two items on the questionnaire dealt with the extent to which there was a close or distant relationship between the Native community and the school. The Likert items containing this factor were phrased for educators as 'The parents and the teachers of Native students didn't talk to each other enough' and 'There was too little communication between the school and their home communities.'

The majority of all respondents – Native and non-Native educators, dropouts, and parents both on and off reserve – believed that home-school communication was lacking in both quantity and quality. In addition to the cultural and psychological barriers discussed above, Native and non-Native educators perceived physical barriers. The problem of geographic distance not only exists for parents from isolated northern Ontario communities, but is also very real for Native parents without their own transport who live in communities that are some distance from towns. For the school, day-to-day communication is further limited because many Native homes do not have telephones. Parents also reported that their children did not always deliver memos and notes and other written communications. Some parents reported that even when these communications were brought home they couldn't always read or understand them.

There is also the issue of the 'psychic distance' of the reserve from many if not most non-Native educators. They may have dealt with Native students for many years without ever visiting the reserve from which they come. For non-Native educators, the reserve, its history, dimensions, reasons for existing, pattern of social life, internal structure, and its relationship to Canadian society at large is virtually unknown. Some non-Native educators were also puzzled about which authoritative figure to contact on a reserve, how that contact might be made, and with what expectation of success.

Native educators observe that such parent-school staff communication that does occur is usually unsatisfactory because it is often initiated by the school and almost invariably involves problems and difficulties. Parents are summoned and the interaction tends to be one-directional: the school tells the parent what is wrong and what must be done to correct the situation. Parents understandably tend to avoid such situations or approach them in a confrontational manner. They complain that they never hear from the school when their child is doing well. Thus, there is often little basis for mutual trust, respect, and understanding in parent-teacher communication. Negative encounters between parents and school staff tend only to reinforce negative mutual opinions.

Poor school-community communication is reported as contributing to high dropout rates. Most educators, Native and non-Native, talked of this factor in conjunction with Indian bands rather than Métis/off-reserve Natives. One reason is that most bands have reserves and a central administration whereas the 'community' for Métis/off-reserve Natives is more elusive and usually lacks a formal administrative structure which the school can use as a channel of communication. In some Ontario communities, the education worker in the Native Friendship Centre and the social/education counsellor in the Youth Employment Training (YET) Centre (or its local variant) serve as a link between Métis, off-reserve Natives, and the school. However, this role tends to be sporadic and dependent upon the individuals concerned rather than being a reliable channel upon which all parties can count.

Native and non-Native educators frequently expressed limited satisfaction or open dissatisfaction with school-band communication. Some Native educators felt enormously burdened because the school assumed that they alone were the natural channel for communication with on-reserve students and the reserve in general. Schools did not fully appreciate educators' problems – the difficulty in contacting some parents and the problem of being an effective intermediary between schools and various reserve committees and decision-making bodies which they could not influence or from which they might receive no assistance.

Clear channels for successful school-community communication are reported by Native and non-Native educators as forming the basis for positive parent-teacher communication. Poor home-school communication is seen as arising from a lack of will on the part of one or both parties. Without goodwill and genuine commitment on both sides, such contacts will not result in closer collaboration and cooperation.

Ontario Métis and Off-Reserve Registered Indian Students

As part of the larger study, the dropout risk factors for registered Indian students residing on reserve and for Aboriginal students (Métis and registered Indians) residing off reserve were compared. Students were assessed in Grade 9 in two large provincial schools, one located in northern Ontario and the other in southern Ontario. The predictive instrument consisted of thirty-six multiple-choice questions about family environment, personal traits, educational plans, school achievement, teacher-student relationships, and motivations for schooling (Quirouette 1987). Students who answered the survey were asked to identify themselves as on-reserve Native residents, off-reserve Natives, and non-Natives.

Of the 206 students surveyed who identified themselves as Aboriginal, 115 (56 per cent) were shown to be at risk of dropping out. This proportion is considerably higher than that in the general population except in a few vocational secondary schools in southern Ontario. As was expected on the basis of nominal roll statistics, northern Aboriginal students are generally at greater risk of dropping out than their southern counterparts. Somewhat surprisingly, a substantially higher percentage (65 per cent versus 45 per cent) of Métis and registered off-reserve Indian students than registered on-reserve Indians were identified as potential dropouts. And a higher percentage of Métis and off-reserve girls (70 per cent) was identified as 'at risk' than boys (61 per cent). Paradoxically, fewer support programs are available for Métis and off-reserve Indians than for Indian students resident on reserve.

Native Students from Isolated Communities

Students from many isolated northern Ontario communities must leave home after primary school and attend high school in unfamiliar towns and cities many miles from home. Despite the sincere efforts of advocacy and support groups on behalf of these students, many find difficulty in coping with an alien environment. In addition to the general linguistic, academic, and cultural problems, students from 'fly-in' communities face a host of other difficulties that are directly connected to the boarding home situation and that decrease their chances of completing secondary school.

The Ontario Native and non-Native educators who were interviewed reported that the greatest factor affecting student boarders who drop out is simple homesickness. Not only do they pine for family and friends, they also long for their accustomed food and lifestyle. Most educators talked of the serious risks associated with requiring young adolescents to leave the comparative security of their small homogeneous communities to undertake secondary education in an alien environment far from the support of their families.

At this age, many of these students are not ready emotionally to be away from family and friends. Native educators report that these students are most frequently in danger of dropping out in Grade 9 or 10 although many will make another attempt at resuming their schooling when they are a year or two older. Students who had previously dropped out from boarding homes and who subsequently resumed study in community schools, which had been extended to Grade 10, expressed great satisfaction with the new arrangement and felt they would be better prepared to complete their senior years in the city.

Although many boarding parents do their best to care for their northern charges, some take on boarders for purely economic reasons. Educators reported that some Native students are fed a poor diet of pasta, hot dogs, and indifference. Native boarding parents, who might be more knowledgeable and sympathetic, are reportedly difficult to find. Although some dropouts said that their boarding parents offered them support and encouragement, others reported that they received inadequate physical and emotional nourishment and little academic and social supervision.

Both educators and dropouts referred to unmediated culture shock as contributing to the dropping out of these students. Northern Ontario students encounter an overwhelming variety of new experiences which may sometimes frighten, distract, or attract them. Educators reported that many student boarders found it extremely difficult to adapt to the new environment and at the same time to respond to the increased academic demands of secondary school. These adolescents were also experiencing puberty with all its accompanying difficulties.

Dropouts in boarding homes reported a number of social problems. Many were shy and found it difficult to get to know local students. In some cases, they only had contact with students from their home communities. Educators reported that this situation often had a 'domino effect' in that the decision of one student to return home precipitated a mass departure. Additionally, student boarders were, in some cases, mistreated by local Native students who often taunted them with being backward 'bush Indians.' In their efforts to be accepted by local students, some boarders developed such behaviour as skipping school, hanging out at amusement centres, drinking, drug-taking, and staying out late at night.

Educators reported that student boarders suffered financially because many parents were unable to supplement their $10.00 per month allowance and most lacked the skills or confidence to seek part-time work. These students sometimes engaged in petty theft to obtain goods or cash that they saw as necessary.

While many Ontario bands and secondary schools have special programs to supervise and assist boarding students socially and academically, others do not, and the maintenance of such programs is not guaranteed. Educators praised the efforts of the friendship centres and local First Nations, who in many areas voluntarily offer counselling services and other concrete support to student boarders. While some northern Ontario bands have organized group homes or have a full-time educational counsellor working with their children, others do not. Métis and off-reserve students who often come from similar situations receive whatever support their home school boards and the host board offer.

Faced with loneliness, homesickness, and an alien environment, these students often abandon an education which they feel will be of little use to them in their home communities. One educator commented: 'I understand why they leave; the better question is, why do some of them stay?'

In the Northwest Territories and northern Quebec, every community, no matter how small, offers at least the first two years of high school, and the last years of high school are offered in their students' regions. This means that students are more mature when they leave their communities and that they attend senior high school alongside Native peers in a largely Native community. Native students who have to leave their parents, families, peer groups, and communities in exchange for alien boarding houses in cities where the schools are frequently larger than their home communities are not well served by the educational system.

Native Student Success in Provincial Secondary Schools
The overall trend towards higher provincial secondary school retention among Native students resident on reserve is no accident, but reflects the individual and collective efforts of the key players in improving educational conditions for Native students. Because First Nations communities across Canada are unique, with different social and cultural values, levels of economic development, and internal administrative structures, it is difficult, if not impossible, to apply a universal blueprint for success. For example, an English second language initiative developed jointly by a Native community and school board where the first language is an

Aboriginal one is unlikely to be of use to a Native community whose first language is English.

The situation is even more problematic in communities with a high proportion of Métis and off-reserve Natives. These communities not only lack a geographic locus, they may also lack representatives who are recognized within the Native community and the community at large as able to voice Native concerns on education. Our study of factors contributing to Native student success in Ontario secondary schools indicates that establishing and maintaining effective structures and mechanisms for community-school communication are superordinate. The need for a coherent, legitimate, and empowered voice from the Métis/off-reserve community is crucial.

The following sections report our findings on the factors that principal Ontario Native and non-Native stakeholders believed contributed to higher rates of graduation. These conditions are examined as they pertain to the First Nation, the school board, and the school itself.

The First Nation

Bands whose children enjoy a high graduation rate appear to be those whose chiefs and councils rank the education of their children as a top priority. They not only regard education and graduation from secondary school as desirable but see it as an important contribution to the band's strategic development plan. These views are communicated clearly both internally to band members and externally to school officials.

The band administration has many of the following leadership and organizational qualities:

- They have gained the confidence and support of the vast majority of band members.
- They have a sound understanding of the politico-educational system at federal, provincial, and school board levels and are capable of using that knowledge to the advantage of the band.
- They have negotiated a comprehensive tuition agreement with the school board that includes provisions related to curriculum, Native counsellor services, and representation on the board of trustees.

Because of the band's concern for education, some or all of the following educational roles have been created:

- The *Native Trustee* is a person capable of representing the band on the school board and communicating the board's deliberations to the band through the council or the education committee. The trustee, who attends all board meetings, is fully informed about the band's agenda and is able to represent the views of the band authoritatively and accurately.

- The *Band Education Committee* meets regularly to deal with educational issues. It has formulated clear and explicit educational objectives for the band and through its open meetings, which are attended by parents, these objectives are understood and widely supported by band members. It closely monitors the educational progress of the band's children, keeping accurate records of dropouts and graduates. The committee keeps abreast of school board policy and communicates the band's concerns via the Native trustee. It has a set of procedures for dealing with conflicts or problems involving parents, students, and school personnel or policy.
- The *Band Educational Counsellor* has formal training in educational counselling, and his or her intimacy with and understanding of both school and Native culture engenders confidence in parents that they and their children have sound specialist advice and mediation in dealings with the school. Within the school, the counsellor's role is well understood by staff, and he or she attends staff meetings and professional development days.

The education counsellor, along with the education committee, has initiated some or all of the following:
- establishing a widely attended, high-profile promotion ceremony on reserve
- establishing an attendance policy which may include incentives
- identifying an elder who is willing and able to assist local schools that wish to include a Native perspective in the curriculum
- raising the level of educational expectations of and from band children
- providing not only encouragement, direction, and support for students at risk of dropping out but also recognition and praise for those who are performing well
- providing guidance to parents on how they can best reinforce their children's efforts to perform to the best of their ability in school.

The School Board
Boards of schools with high Native graduation rates recognize Native students both on and off reserve as legitimate clients whose particular needs and characteristics they are willing to address. In an increasingly multicultural society, the school board is sensitive to all minority students and actively promotes multicultural and anti-racist education. However, the school board acknowledges a special obligation to promoting the success of Native students, who for historical reasons can be considered an 'involuntary minority' (House 1992). It does this in several ways:
- It ensures that the First Nation exercises its right to appoint a Native

trustee to the board and that the trustee is inducted into the workings, policies, and procedures of the board.

- It ensures that the particular requirements of Native students are addressed in Aboriginal language courses, Native studies courses, and, particularly, language development across the curriculum.
- It monitors how well its Native student population is being served by the board's educational system, policies, and procedures with a view to improving these services.
- It opens and maintains a channel of direct communication between senior executives of the board (director, superintendents) and the chief and band council (and/or those delegated with responsibility for education).
- Boards with a large population of Métis/off-reserve students take the initiative in establishing communication channels with local Native social organizations and leaders and, where numbers warrant, in appointing a Native education counsellor.
- It arranges, through tuition agreements with the band and INAC, to hire a Native education counsellor or to work closely with a band-employed education counsellor.
- It appoints principals capable of sympathetically implementing board policy on Native students.

The School

Schools in which Native students enjoy a high rate of success are those with principals who actively promote strategies for maximizing the academic success of all their students and are capable of engaging their teaching and support staff in the same mission. The principal not only poses the question 'What can be done for Native students in this school?' but also 'What can Native students contribute to this school?'

The principals of such schools have taken some or all of the following steps:

- encouraged the establishment of an active Native student council which, like other student groups, organizes meetings and public events in which its interests and accomplishments are shared by the school community
- successfully recruited Native teachers and/or assistants
- established a good working relationship with the chief, education committee, and Native counsellor or with Native support agencies for the Métis/off-reserve constituency
- attended social events on the reserve as well as meetings of the education committee

- established an active strategy with elementary feeder schools, the education committee, and parents to ensure that Native students study subjects at levels which are most appropriate to their capabilities and future plans
- encouraged members of the Native community to participate in school events.

Meeting the Challenge

We have presented the constructions of parents, dropouts, and Native and non-Native educators on just three of the many issues connected with dropping out of school. We have also synthesized the constructions of stakeholders on what conditions contribute to Native students' success in provincial schools. This chapter is yet another construction, albeit one informed by considerable thought and experience. While information on the problem of Native dropouts and frameworks for promoting student retention may be useful, the impetus for meeting the challenge can only come from individuals and groups in a particular setting, with a particular set of problems and concerns.

We have implied throughout that effective solutions and plans of action are the result of negotiation in which 'each stakeholder group comes to understand its own construction better' and 'comes to understand the constructions of other groups better' (Guba and Lincoln 1989, 56). The principles and process guidelines suggested below are aimed at creating a forum in which all parties are simultaneously educated and empowered.

Principles

- commitment from all groups to work from a position of integrity
- competence of all groups to communicate
- willingness by all groups to share power
- willingness by all parties to reconsider their value positions
- willingness by all groups to change their constructions if they find the constructions of others persuasive
- willingness by all parties to make the necessary commitment of time and energy (Guba and Lincoln 1989)

Processes

- identifying all persons or groups who have a stake in Native education
- eliciting from each stakeholder group its construction of the issue and the range of problems and solutions it wishes to raise
- agreeing on procedures by which different constructions, problems, and

solutions can be understood, critiqued, and taken into account (Birchenough et al. 1989)
- following these procedures within each stakeholder group so that a group construction can emerge and a decision can be made about which problems and solutions should be pursued
- cross-fertilizing each group with the constructions of other groups
- working towards consensus on as many constructions, claims, and concerns as desirable
- preparing an agenda for negotiation on items about which there is no, or incomplete, consensus
- collecting information required by the agenda and providing it to all participants
- establishing a forum in which negotiations can take place and from which a plan of action can be developed (Guba and Lincoln 1989)

For First Nations bands which continue to purchase secondary school services from the provinces, for Métis and off-reserve Natives who attend provincial secondary schools as part of the general population, and for Canadian society at large, the costs of dropping out as well as the benefits of graduation will increase from year to year. Successful initiatives to increase graduation rates and reduce dropout rates must be joint efforts involving both the Native and the educational communities.

Appendix

Factors Contributing to Dropping Out
- Difficulty with English language skills
- Getting poor grades on school exams and tests
- Being kept back one or more grades
- Failing one or more courses in school
- Falling behind with homework
- Not paying attention in class
- Unable to do the work required by the teachers
- Getting into trouble with the teachers/principal
- Teachers fail to understand students
- Teachers do not encourage them
- Teachers seldom praise them
- Teachers pick on them unjustly
- Parents have little interest in how well or badly they perform in school
- Parents do not encourage them to remain in school
- Parents and teachers do not talk to each other enough

- Too little communication between school and home communities
- Many friends have already dropped out
- They have few or no friends at school
- They do not expect to finish high school
- They do not care whether they finish high school or not
- Lack clear plans about what they will do after leaving school
- Most school subjects do not interest them
- Feel that school is of little importance to their lives
- Seldom took part in sports or after-school activities
- School seemed to be too big and impersonal
- They had to bus for quite a long time to and from school
- They had to live away from home
- Many teachers could not engage their interest and participation
- Too many pointless school rules
- No professional guidance counsellor with whom they could feel really comfortable
- No professional guidance counsellor, just a regular teacher who did some counselling
- Insufficient career counselling at school
- The school did not really care about Native students
- Much classwork was pointless
- They had to study courses that had little to do with their lives outside school
- No courses of specific cultural relevance to them as Native people
- Non-Native students made them feel unwelcome
- They were discriminated against by others in school
- They skipped school and classes quite a lot
- They left school to get married and/or have a baby
- They left school because of financial problems at home
- They left school to go on welfare

Note

The research project upon which this chapter is based was funded under contract by the Ministry of Education, Ontario. It reflects the views of the authors and not necessarily those of the Ministry. The authors would like to acknowledge the assistance of Keith Lickers, Education Officer, Ministry of Education, Ontario, in carrying out this research.

References
Anderson, C.S. 1982. The search for school climate: A review of the research.

Review of Educational Research 52 (3):368-420

Assembly of First Nations. 1988. *Tradition and education: Towards a vision of our future*. Ottawa: National Indian Brotherhood

Birchenough, A. et. al. 1989. *Reviewing school departments*. London: Sage

Guba, E., and Y. Lincoln. 1989. *Fourth generation evaluation*. Newbury Park, CA: Sage

House, E.R., 1992. Multicultural evaluation in Canada and the United States. *Canadian Journal of Program Evaluation* 1:133-56

Mackay, R. 1992. Embarrassment in the classroom. In A. Van Essen and E.I. Burkart, eds., *Essays in English as a foreign or second language*. Berlin and New York: Foris Publications

–. 1990. Bridging the gap between practice and research: Inuit students and English instruction. *Bulletin of the Canadian Association of Applied Linguistics* 1:9-21

–, and L. Myles. 1989. *Native student dropouts in Ontario schools*. Toronto: Queen's Printer

Makivik Corporation. 1992. *The pathway to wisdom: Final report of the Nunavik education task force*. Montreal: Nunavik Educational Task Force

Quirouette, P. 1987. *L'école et moi*. Ottawa: OISE

Wehlage, G., and R. Rutter. 1986. Dropping out: How much do schools contribute to the problem? *Teachers College Record* 87:374-92

Zsigmond, Z.E., and C.J. Wenaas. 1980. *Enrollment in educational institutions by province, 1951-2 – 1980-1*. Ottawa: Queen's Printer

9

Teacher Education and Aboriginal Opposition

Rick Hesch

> Curriculum ... is not a concept; it is a cultural construction. That is, it is not an abstract concept which has some existence outside and prior to human experience. Rather, it is a way of organizing a set of human educational practices. (Grundy 1987, 5)

Daniel Liston[1] (1988) argues that to understand adequately and theorize about the ways in which formal education functions as a reproducer of social and cultural inequalities, schooling must be seen as an institution of the state. Furthermore, it is inadequate simply to make the claim; rather, the mechanism for this reproductive achievement must be clearly set out. As College of Education graduates at the University of Saskatchewan prepare to enter the labour market as certified teachers, one mechanism for the provincial state in Saskatchewan to assess their competence as acceptable teachers in schools is the internship, or extended practicum. For Aboriginal preservice teachers formerly victimized by the processes of state schooling and now expected to embrace those processes, the experience can be traumatizing. Traumatization is only one response by interns to a hegemonic Eurocentric state enterprise. Another is resistance.

This case study of the experience of a group of Aboriginal interns illustrates the ways in which a state strategy intended to accommodate preservice teachers to schooling as usual – a schooling which systematically excludes many Aboriginal students – is resisted by at least some of the interns. The study illuminates the sources of the stresses and contradictions experienced by the interns and documents the ways in which the internship attempts to homogenize the process of becoming a teacher in Saskatchewan. The study also elaborates on some of the sources of resistance mounted by students to conventional schooling practices and, in particular, the administration and content of the internship. Resistance is facilitated, in part, because interns pass from educational sites where the progressive principles of democracy, child-centred education, critique, contextualized social analysis, and cooperative work are encouraged for ideological reasons to sites where work is essentially undemocratic, the value of student agency is diminished or unrecognized, social and political dimensions of schooling are hidden by positivist and functionalist discourse, and possessive individualism is taken as common sense for ideological, if less explicit, reasons.

The Structural Framework

Students engaged in this study were enrolled in the Saskatchewan Urban Native Teacher Education Program (SUNTEP). SUNTEP is an affirmative action teacher education program for Aboriginal people established in 1980 by the provincial NDP government to prepare Métis teachers to work in urban centres. Both this chapter and the larger study from which it is drawn (Hesch 1992b) focus upon experiences of students in two of SUNTEP's three geographical locations, Forestland and Berryville. At the heart of in this study were six fourth-year SUNTEP students, five of whom were females. This ratio is roughly equivalent to that found in most years in both centres. Structurally, SUNTEP's education program is very similar to that of the university from which it contracts services, in this case the University of Saskatchewan.

The internship is a four-month practicum in which College of Education students, now called interns, work under the supervision of regular classroom teachers in an assumed mentor-student relationship. An intern will usually be assigned to a classroom with one teacher. Classroom teachers become supervising teachers (formerly 'cooperating teachers') by volunteering, with more or less encouragement from their employers. There is no remuneration for the work. In 1989-90, responsibility at the University of Saskatchewan for developing and administering the internship curriculum rested with the Field Experience Office (FEO). When students enter their internship in their fourth year, they do so in the same way, with the same privileges and responsibilities, as all other College of Education students. Their classroom supervisors are selected in the same way, and they are subject to the curriculum and evaluation of FEO. Basically, connections between SUNTEP students and the SUNTEP program end when students enter their internship.

The coordinator of FEO claims that 'by far the great majority [of interns] feel that [the internship] was [a] very exciting and worthwhile experience' (personal communication, 30 April 1990). This is not the experience of most SUNTEP interns 'policed' through the internship (S. Delorme, personal communication, 14 August 1990). For at least eight of thirteen fourth-year students who had entered the internship and were interviewed during this study, the experience ranged from potentially career-ending to utterly miserable to merely dissatisfying. Sharon Delorme questions whether she 'could bear it again' (personal communication, 26 April 1990). Garry Valier had recurring states of depression throughout the university term following his extended practicum which he attributes to the intense hardship of internship. Only one of the interns would have classified the experience as 'very ... worthwhile.'

Tape-recorded, semi-structured intensive interviews were conducted with eight students (two were one-time-only interviews) from the fourth year of the program in both centres in mid-October 1989. Five semi-structured interviews were held with supervising teachers of interns and one with the coordinator of the Field Experience Office at the College of Education, University of Saskatchewan. Two classrooms in which cooperating fourth-year students were interning were observed, as were three internship seminars. Between twelve and fifteen hours were spent in the field each week. The 'text' of the University of Saskatchewan Field Experience Office and the Gabriel Dumont Institute[2] annual report was read and analyzed. As well, implicitly ideological and public materials (such as field experience evaluation instruments), and non-public primary source materials (such as student records of courses taken over time and intern observation forms used by cooperating teachers and field experience supervisors), were analyzed.

Background to Internship
The experience of the SUNTEP students in their internship can only fully be understood against its historical, ideological, and institutional background. This in turn requires some consideration of the ideological precepts underpinning curriculum practice in Western schools. In addition to the exclusionary power of racism, four other concepts or ideologies are significant in the way schooling operates to exclude Aboriginal and working-class children on an everyday basis. These are the ideologies of 'possessive individualism' and meritocracy, and the concepts of the 'Tyler rationale' and the canonical curriculum. They are briefly outlined here by reference to life-history interviews with nine first-year SUNTEP students who were asked what compelled them to leave school (see Hesch 1992b).

(1) *Possessive individualism.* This view forms the foundation for unquestioned assumptions about the worth and priority of individualized instruction. Critics of this hegemonic prescription ask if we are educating children to think of themselves only as individuals, as consumers without any necessary relation to neighbours and extended families (Apple 1989;

Giroux 1988). For students with strong connections to their neighbour-hood, community, or family, learning to work as an individual in school in order to succeed can be personally and culturally disruptive (Connell et al. 1982). One specific problem identified by SUNTEP students in the larger study is that of *negative identification*. Teachers who are taught to focus on students individually can single out students in ways which they find very uncomfortable. Expressed in the lives of SUNTEP students, for example, it means that a young man might be repelled from learning because he 'wasn't into this competition of who could get the highest mark.'

(2) *The Tyler rationale*. The 'Tyler rationale' underlies the basic organiza-tion and procedure for most classrooms. For students training to be ele-mentary school teachers at the University of Saskatchewan, it means 'if a teacher desires to have a strong program in the basic skills, the ... program [must be] structured, systematic, and sequential' (Jarolimek and Foster 1989, 231). Classrooms organized according to the Tyler rationale are well suited to individualized instruction:

> The classroom scenario that fosters ... individualism is a familiar one. Students traditionally sit in rows staring at the back of each others' heads and at the teacher who faces them in symbolic, authoritarian fashion ... Events in the classroom are governed by a rigid time schedule imposed by a system of bells and reinforced by cues from teachers while the class is in session. Instruction and, hopefully, some formal learning usually begin and end because it is the correct predetermined time, not because a cogni-tive process has been stimulated into action. (Giroux 1988, 37)

As a young boy, one first-year SUNTEP student had learned that teach-ers' work produced classroom conditions characterized by 'the limited freedom ... the prison-like atmosphere' of school. He was repelled by 'the routine.' A young SUNTEP woman critiqued her schooling as 'always the same old routine ... a repetitious, repetitious type of day.' Another woman found school 'so confining' with 'so many rules and regulations.' She found that 'everything was so in order ... You do this at that time. At that time you do this.'

(3) *The canonical curriculum*. This concept refers to the historical prac-tice by governments of excluding people's lived cultures from school cur-ricula. Where elements of student culture have been introduced into schools, it has been as 'a motivational ploy that might enhance student interest in a particular lesson or subject' (Giroux and Simon 1989, 225). The *canon* refers to those 'Great Books' by authors such as Shakespeare,

Chaucer, and so on, or the histories of wars, kings, and queens, which are deemed to be worthwhile and safe curriculum content. The curriculum outlined and followed according to this ideology has been called the 'hegemonic curriculum,' that is, 'hierarchically-organized bodies of academic knowledge appropriated in individual competition ... [which have] the effect of marginalizing other kinds of knowledge' (Connell et al. 1982, 120). In the lives of first-year SUNTEP students, the canon meant 'important things were always left out, or things that you're good at are left out ... It was straight whatever the subject was.' These are not school subjects constructed in a social vacuum, but are 'organized and operated by the dominant "race,"' another first-year student argued.

(4) *Meritocracy*. Briefly, the ideology of meritocracy argues that the rewards of schooling and in society go to the 'best and the brightest.' Rich and successful people get their powerful positions in society because they have worked harder and are smarter than most people. The primary requirements for success are individual effort and intelligence. The purpose of schools is to distribute knowledge to those who are able to use it most effectively so that they can contribute to society. If there is an unequal distribution of rewards in school, it is because some people are more 'stupid' or 'dumb' than others. Meritocracy contributed to a number of first-year students' leaving school early. In the case of one who had spent a large part of her time on the streets and was thereafter assigned to a different classroom, 'I knew it was a Special [Education classroom, because] our number was 101S. I always figured, "Well, I'm dumb. They've stuck me in the 'dumb' class. So here I am, dumb."' Fed up with school, and battling with her mother over her school attendance, she and a friend stole money from her mother's house and left for Berryville to seek work.

There is usually considerable correlation between these curricular ideologies at any given time in most schools. These dominant concepts and ideologies are *Eurocentric* to the extent that they (1) utilize curriculum design principles and general schooling practices which privilege individualism and disorganize collectivist Aboriginal cultural forms; (2) construct Aboriginal subjectivities which accept their exit/exclusion from schools as justified by a legitimated meritocracy; (3) homogenize lived cultural difference in schools; (4) select only the traditions of Western culture or reified Aboriginal culture for curriculum content and exclude or disorganize different Aboriginal forms of knowledge and experience; and (5) unproblematically accept or institutionalize racist expressions and practices.

The life-history interviews (Hesch 1992a) indicate that most students who enter SUNTEP do so, in part, with a vision of teaching which is in direct opposition to the schooling they earlier experienced. Students who entered SUNTEP came to know a different approach to living, working, and thinking within educational contexts. Working and learning conditions in SUNTEP were marked, in part, by the collegial dependence of SUNTEP students on each other and by a relatively egalitarian relationship with SUNTEP staff. The sense of collegiality or 'sharing' may to some extent be rooted in Métis cultural forms which were intact at least into the early twentieth century. In an oral history interview conducted for the larger study, Métis elder Bill Favel observed that, 'We shared, we always shared what we had. We shared with the White man too that came over here, too. But then they didn't share back with us. That was the difference [laughs]' (personal communication, 25 May 1991).

The 'sharing' culture was partially reproduced in the everyday life and planned institutional culture of SUNTEP. The cooperation between staff and students in organizing events such as banquets, concerts, and informal sporting activities and parties contributed to a SUNTEP culture where, in the words of one interning student, 'we stuck together. Whenever problems came along there was always somebody to talk to – somebody always had an answer, some way to solve a problem. Without that, I don't think I would have survived' (Jolibois, Larocque, Lepine, Marion, Ross, and Tremaudan, personal communication, 9 January 1990).

The sharing culture was utilized to construct reflective learning conditions by progressive SUNTEP staff as well. For example, key informant and intern Carole Trottier relates how, after students had spent time gaining field experience during their second and third years:

> We'd come back and we'd sit in a circle and we'd share our experience in the classroom ... We'd talk about why certain things happened or how we felt when certain things happened ... what should have happened differently, what could have happened differently ... A lot of the beginning work was just our building our philosophy sort of, asking us continuously ... 'What do you think it should be like?' ... And as we got access to more and more material ... then we could start bringing that material into what we thought. And pretty soon ... we could back up what we thought. (Personal communication, 21 August 1990)

Relations between staff and students were often marked by relative egalitarianism. A first-year student, Walton, summarizes the ambience, which impresses both first-year students and the occasional visitor most clearly:

> There's a good communication between the staff and the students ... I think the way it happens is because the staff are willing to sit down and

listen to you and listen to your problems and are willing to compromise on things ... They're just part of ... the culture ... the little culture that we have there, the little society that we have at SUNTEP ... They're always sitting down with the students chatting ... I think that's what I like about SUNTEP. The staff is willing to talk to you. Either with your problems or just ... for the conversation. I like that. (Personal communication, 7 December 1989)

The implicit and explicit pedagogy of SUNTEP, however, went beyond reconstructing the sharing culture and egalitarian relations with students. In sum, SUNTEP was a teacher education program where, according to intern Carole Trottier, 'the basic assumption [was] that kids are human beings and are to be respected, which was an opinion that everyone, all the faculty and the teaching staff ... had, give or take a couple from the university ... And that education is very important politically. And that things are not right in the schools and they can't be ... or the Native students wouldn't be dropping out like they do' (personal communication, 21 August 1990).

SUNTEP, then, provided the opportunity for Aboriginal preservice teachers to begin to construct alternative views of what schooling, teaching, and learning might be.

Social Relations of Internship

Teachers' work, for example in developing strategies for discipline, is never determined in isolation from the practices of other teachers and school administrators. On the other hand, relative to the work *most* working people do, teachers operate in comparative autonomy within the physical limits of the classroom (Connell 1985). Similarly, preservice teachers entering internship exist within a set of social relations primarily constituted by the children as students, the classroom supervising teacher, the College of Education internship supervisor, and themselves. The intensity of four months of daily contact provides a powerful means for determining both the intern's working conditions and her or his conceptions of teachers' work.

In the internship, the sharing culture and relatively egalitarian social relations of SUNTEP were replaced by an unequal binary relationship between intern and supervising teacher. This transformation could produce considerable tension for interns. In cases where social relations between the intern and supervising teacher were reduced to expressions of power and resistance to it, the potential for developing a different teaching practice atrophied. The result was that the intern could become an embodiment of repressive teaching practices. Marjorie Ross's experience was not unrepresentative:

> My class was Grade 1. [The supervising teacher] had all these rules. The kids had to sit up straight in their desks, their hands on their desks every period, and that was the way they were supposed to stay all the time ... Every time she would catch somebody out, she would say, [snapping fingers] 'O.K. Everyone! Hands on your desks! Feet on the floor!' It was just like a little routine and the kids would say it with her. She expected me to do that all the time too. I thought that as long as I had their attention (you could tell with eye contact ... if they're listening) ... I had a hard time being as strict as her or as mean as her. Like she would just scream at those kids if they did something wrong. And I had a hard time doing that, because I didn't think it was right. She just harped on me all the time to do that: 'I want to see you get mad. I want to see you scream.' That's what she would always say to me every day. I wouldn't do it. I didn't want to ... [But] in the end that's what I would do ... There's a lot quieter people [teaching]. If I would have had somebody like that I would have been able to do what *they* did, and I would have had an easier time controlling kids. (Personal communication, 9 January 1990)[3]

Ross withdrew from her internship early, after being encouraged to do so by her supervising teacher and FEO supervisor. Ross had been trained according to a SUNTEP ideology which did not favour or aim to reproduce her supervising teacher's 'little routine.' Not only was Marjorie Ross ill-equipped by her training to incorporate her supervising teacher's strategy, but she found it difficult to learn it and reproduce it on site because 'she didn't think it was right.' What Ross thought 'was right' was probably constructed from both her own biographical experience as a young school student and from her work and learning in SUNTEP. Ross was not only resisting the practices of her supervising teacher but also an historically constituted set of state practices which have served to exclude Aboriginal students from schools.

In contrast to the autocratic strategy of teacher supervision, the relationship between interns and supervisors could be based on the genuine mutual respect of co-learners, interviews with one team member revealed. This sort of relationship encouraged an intern's willing acceptance of the supervisor's teaching ideology and presumed insight. This might include the following advice and guidance, offered by classroom supervisor Bonnie Nelson:

[The intern] would approach me and ask why a particular student gave that kind of an answer. In several cases it was because of the student's background ... It's all fine and dandy if you're working with a group of enriched students ... students of high academic and achievement level. [But] how do you teach the same concept to a student from a deprived background ... a student who is not academically talented? These are the things that she used me for. How do I modify my materials ... to best meet the individual needs in this class? (Personal communication, 25 April 1990)

With her own training in analyzing classroom problems seemingly restricted to the perspective of possessive individualism and developmental psychology, Nelson located students' difficulties in their 'deprived background.' This sort of pathologizing is quite consistent with the conventional analyses of many multicultural educators (Stone 1981), so would not necessarily be inconsistent with SUNTEP courses aimed at 'cross-cultural education.' Thus, the intern was willingly guided into analysis of student agency dependent upon the pathologization of the victim's family. Under these circumstances, 'modified materials' have conventionally contributed to illiteracy, not its alleviation (Carnoy and Levin 1985; Ortiz 1988; Shannon 1989).

Life for interns was embedded in a second relationship, that with the College of Education's Field Experience Office supervisor. It was the status and potential power of the College supervisor which caused anxiety, not so much the actual practices or personality. In general, the supervising teacher and the College supervisor formed a functional alliance. In Garry Valier's case, for example, '[my supervising teacher] would come out [after an observation session] with a totally, sometimes, a totally different idea of what [the College supervisor] would have. He'd have hardly anything written down at all, but he'd look at her [observation form] and he was influenced by it ... Somehow I think he felt that she was kind of the boss in a way' (personal communication, 17 December 1989; 26 April 1990).

Yet Valier's supervising teacher, Mike Deren, was primarily concerned that Valier become an effective classroom manager (Apple 1989; Ginsburg 1988) by the end of his internship: 'The thing he learned that he had to get under control was [the] respect the kids have to have of the teacher and basically the control ... management end of it, classroom control ... by the time he had completed his internship, he seemed to have those under control' (personal communication, 9 March 1990).

There is a third set of social relations in the classroom – that between children and classroom authority figures. For those interns who were invited into and accepted a relatively democratic mentoring relationship with their supervising teachers, child-adult relations constituted part of the bond between them. Garry Valier, for example, 'share[d] a lot of the same ideals and goals' with his supervising teacher, Mike Deren, whose philosophy of education began with the notion that 'you have to realize you're teaching human beings ... to do the best [you] can for the students' (personal communication, 17 December 1989; 9 March 1990). On the other hand, the internship complicated the views some students had of children after their introduction to child-centred education and critical inquiry in SUNTEP. Carole Trottier, for example, had forgotten that students might prefer to go along with conventional classroom routines: 'The first big surprise was how kids are comfortable with the way the system is or they're comfortable with the power situation, the teacher being in control ... They can play around, right? They can be the delinquent if they want. Or they can be an achiever and just rise right to the top. I mean, it was hard for them. They didn't like the power of the choice' (personal communication, 21 August 1990).

In her efforts to test a redefinition of the relations between students and teachers, Trottier encountered at least two student strategies: (1) those alienated by the hegemonic curriculum had learned that the principal and rational means of deriving pleasure from everyday life within school was 'being the delinquent'; (2) those who would benefit from the meritocracy, who at least in relative terms would 'rise right to the top,' had found that cooperation with the existing school regime and opposition to Trottier's innovations was in their interest. The existing curriculum structures and teaching practices served to include them while marginalizing those against whom they would compete. They might have little interest in reconstructing the norm.

In conclusion, a 'clash of strategies' (Connell 1985, 108) between an intern and a supervising teacher can lead to an attack on the developing identity of a Métis preservice teacher who resists conventional state practice as it operates in the classroom (Heald 1990). Thus, classroom practice likely to exclude Métis children can have the double effect of excluding Métis preservice teachers. More collegial and democratic strategies for intern supervision more effectively reproduce the hegemonic curriculum. Furthmore, the intern must learn to deal with other limitations deriving from the cultural construction of the extended practicum – limitations established as much by ideology as by social relations of power. To these I now turn.

The 'Boundaries'

As shown above, opportunities for SUNTEP interns to develop their conceptions of teacher's work are structured within intersecting sets of social relations. To some extent, the content of these relations is mediated by the underlying ideology of the supervising teacher with reference to her role as supervisor. These social relations and the general ideology of management/education form only two components in a field of contextualizing boundaries within which interns must survive and struggle to implement their already-formed conceptions of justified teacher's work. As Sharon Delorme argues, 'Interning is a really plastic environment. You don't necessarily always end up doing what you would like to do yourself, simply because there's all kinds of boundaries and you're there for one specific purpose, and that's to make it through the internship' (personal communication, 26 April 1990).

This section will identify the 'kinds of human-made boundaries' the intern is subject to. These boundaries help legitimate and in turn are legitimated by the social relations of the internship. That is, when the 'boundaries' constructed by the Tyler rationale, the hegemonic curriculum, and common sense racism are unquestioned or accepted, the power of supervisors is entrenched. Conversely, the power of the supervisors and the institutions of state schooling to impose these 'boundaries' helps legitimate them.

The internship is an introduction to the material limitations of conventional schooling for committed teaching intellectuals. In other words, interns soon experience the pressures of attempting to 'cover' a chosen curriculum within a finite number of weeks and days and 35-minute class periods as determined by the Tyler rationale. As R.W. Connell observes, 'the ... [class] period becomes a frame governing all technique' (1985, 76). If cuts are made, it is more likely to be the potentially transformative or counter-hegemonic content which is cut, simply because the production of knowledge of the Lubicon or of Oka, for example, must occur within a meaningful context for which there has been little prior development. Thus the intern who is aiming to teach for change is quickly introduced to hegemonic school routines and both the necessity and frustration of working against them.

Time constraints imposed by the Tyler rationale, then, can inhibit transformative teaching as much as the official curriculum content and internal structure. This is not, however, to ignore the power of the canon as a second boundary. Three of the key informants felt significantly restrained by the supervising teachers' expectations that they would teach with direct reference to the provincial curriculum. For example, if Sharon Delorme had a weakness, according to her supervising teacher Myrna Leggett, it was her penchant for 'spending too much time covering a topic ... It was great for the children but ... There's just so many things ... according to your curriculum' (personal communication, 25 April 1990). None of the supervisors saw curriculum content as problematic.

Racism constitutes both a boundary to intern practice and, to some extent, an exclusionary practice forcing interns out of the internship and the teaching work force. The boundary is partially constructed through commonplace racist discourse in some school staffrooms (S. Delorme, personal communication, 14 August 1990). In the context of the province's history of racism, this boundary can turn the internship into an intensely punishing condition and exclusionary practice. For the Aboriginal intern isolated among a group representing a dominant population, the prospect and experience of internship can be immensely intimidating or worse. Prior to the commencement of her internship, Dominique Chartier's 'biggest fear' was that she would be placed in a school staffed by 'mostly non-Natives.' She 'was terrified' until she received her posting to a school where she felt comfortable (personal communication, 9 January 1990). Darlene Bird was not so lucky, and her description deserves full reproduction:

I had requested that I be placed in a band-controlled school because I knew I'd have trouble functioning in a White school ... In a band-controlled school there'd be Indian teachers and I knew I'd feel comfortable – same people, same background, same experiences ... I got stuck in a White school and didn't feel part of the staff. I felt isolated ... They were talking about their new car, and fur coats ... that I couldn't relate to. So it affected the way I was teaching. On the [intern] evaluation [form] it showed – professional attributes, lesson presenting, and reacting behaviour [were criticized] ... that's where my uncomfortableness showed. There's a strong emphasis on the intern mixing with the staff on a professional basis [in the internship evaluation criteria]. And I couldn't relate to them on a professional basis because I felt inferior ... I felt like I had nothing in common with them ... [The College supervisor] dinged [marked down] me for not mixing with the staff.

I tried to fit in there for the first month. Then at a staff meeting there was a remark made ... After we went through the agenda, this one teacher commented about this boy, said that he was 'spitting.' I didn't know he was an Indian boy. But then this teacher said, 'Oh! Indians *always* spit all over the place! [original emphasis]. Then this other teacher said, 'Well, it's a characteristic of Indian people to spit.'

I was kind of dazed. I said to my cooperating teacher, 'I'm an Indian and I don't spit.' She grabbed my arm and said, 'Stand up and say that.' But I'm kind of shy, so I left. After that I didn't even bother. I started having my psychological problems. I was on nerve pills and seeing a psychiatrist. I couldn't handle it anymore at the school I was at, so my [College] supervisor said I could go over to the [Indian] Student Residence the last two weeks. The areas I was weak in at the school I was at, I was able to do then at the Residence. I was able to respond to the kids in a natural way. (Personal communication, 9 January 1990)

Significantly, phenomena experienced by Bird as 'racial' signifiers – 'their new car, and fur coats' – can also be recognized as markers of social class. Other incidents of prejudice against students' cultural backgrounds, in particular strict enforcement of codes for the usage of standard English (personal communications, 9 January 1990), represent both class and 'racial' bias. The response of the interns to incidents of racism and class prejudice was typically one of terror or isolation, which could result in pragmatic acceptance. This effect is also demonstrated in the experience of Brian Lepine:

I was sitting in the staffroom one morning. I had this movie, 'Daughters of the Country' [a four-part series depicting the history of Métis women] come in to show ... This teacher asked what they were about. So I told her. I went back to my table to work, and they got into this conversation about Indians. I wasn't in the conversation. She just flatly came out and said, 'I hate Indians.' They argued about it, but nobody did anything about it. I wasn't going to do anything about it because I was too scared myself. So I just let it go. (Personal communication, 9 January 1990)

Additionally, the account below suggests that a history of subordination to and pragmatic acceptance of state power and hegemonic ideology (Abercrombie, Hill, and Turner 1980) can preclude SUNTEP graduates from confronting racism in their schools. At the same time, the account below reveals the potential of 'epistemic privilege,' of SUNTEP graduates to be more 'sensitive' to Aboriginal children and to identify racist practices:

There wasn't any outward [racist] statements or anything. The school I was in was pretty progressive, because there was a lot of SUNTEP grads that worked there – four or five of them. The Native population was really high in that school, eh! But you could still see a lot of favouritism in the classroom ... Like they have these appointed kids like class monitors ...

The blond-haired, blue-eyed kids always had those jobs. We had to do an Assembly and two kids had to speak. The girl was a blond-haired, blue-eyed girl and the ... little boy was the same. (Larocque, personal communication, 9 January 1990)

Racism permeates decision-making about what counts as legimitate curriculum content as well. For example, when a SUNTEP intern noticed that the text she was teaching used colonial names for Aboriginal groups, she approached her supervising teacher with the suggestion that the names should 'maybe not be used.' The supervisor responded that the names should be used unchanged 'because if we didn't use them we were changing history' (personal communication, 9 January 1990). The implementation of hegemony through the power of friendly classroom supervisors to 'guide you' has been noted in the previous section. With reference to College supervisors, in a unit on racism, Garry Valier 'was told that I focused too much on Natives ... Not that they come out and tell you in so many words, but they guide you, politely ... And you sort of followed what they say ... You don't want to rock the boat, I mean, your future depends on that four months' (personal communication, 26 April 1990).

The implicitly racist assumption that SUNTEP students constitute an essentially unitary mass contributes to the denigration of the interns. Thus, the sense that they bear responsibility for the legacy and future of all SUNTEP students, rather than simply working as individual preservice teachers, operates as still another punishing condition for SUNTEP interns (Trottier, personal communication, 21 August 1990).

In sum, the Tyler rationale, the hegemonic curriculum or canon, and racism partially determine the specific realization of a set of social relations in which interns are largely powerless. Each of these boundaries is socially constructed and must be understood relationally. A hegemonic common sense permeates a school culture into which individual SUNTEP interns are inserted. Committed to a sharing culture and, for some, a counter-hegemonic teaching ideology, the students are forced to survive their internship without the cooperative cultural apparatus they have developed in SUNTEP. Conditions are worsened and, for some, made unbearable by the racism which permeates elementary and secondary schools (Young 1987) and teacher education itself.

To this point, however, only the context of the internship has been described. The three major boundaries/ideologies identified here – the Tyler rationale, Eurocentric adherence to the canon, and straightforward racism – are not isolated from each other, but operate integrally. Nor do they exhaust the list of boundary constructions/ideological impositions.

The following two sections document the specific structure and ideological content of the College of Education's extended practicum, that is, its curriculum, to show the ways in which the SUNTEP intern is further constrained in preparing for the teaching labour market.

Structure and Management of Internship

Particular administrative practices aim to ensure that SUNTEP interns do not enter the teaching pool without a Eurocentric subjectivity. Because the administrative practices are essentially coercive they are resisted. This section will briefly review those Field Experience Office administrative practices which transmit its ideology and transform interns' subjectivity so as to identify the key components of internship as a mechanism of social reproduction and illustrate SUNTEP students' resistance to these instruments. The guiding ideology for supervising interns during the extended practicum is known as 'developmental supervision' (Johnston et. al. 1989, 2). A detailed examination of the texts produced by the Field Experience Office reveals that its supervision model derives from the 'ideology of human relations' which is possessed by people who 'work to create a feeling of satisfaction among teachers by showing an interest in them as people. It is believed that a satisfied staff works harder and is easier to work with, to lead, and to control' (Sergiovanni 1982, 109).

Regardless of the good intentions of and commitment to 'humanistic supervision' made by the supervising teacher, the relationship is structured unequally and produces intern anxiety. As intern Dominique Chartier observed, 'No matter how good a relationship you have with a co-operating teacher, it's going to have some effect when she's sittin' there [observing the intern work], whether she's [officially] evaluating you or not ... I never had ... problems, but it was always there, even though she always treated me as an equal' (personal communication, 9 January 1990).

The stress of being subjected to observation is particularly evident during visits by the College supervisor. The supervision model used throughout the internship adheres to the stages of clinical supervision – planning, preconference, observation, and postconference – without question. R.W. Connell suggests that the principal problem with clinical supervision may be that it individualizes conceptions of the teaching process (personal communication, 24 November 1988). If implementation of the model disrupts cultural life for school teachers generally, it is even more disruptive for SUNTEP students. Solidarity can develop between interns who meet for the first time at the school they share (Delorme, personal communication, 14 August 1990). At least some SUNTEP interns maintain their cooperative survival and learning strategy by telephone during their practicums (Valier, personal communication, 26 April 1990). Still, SUN-TEP interns often feel isolated, as two of the strongest features of the SUN-TEP program – the strength of 'the community' and the progressive ideology – lead to an unexpected outcome:

> You need to bounce your ideas off people but you can't just bounce them off of anybody because they don't understand what you understand. I mean, you build a sense of philosophy ... within SUNTEP, and I find ... even still I have an observation about school and I have a sense that it isn't right ... that it should be done differently. But I can't just ask anybody, I can't just bounce that idea off of anybody because it doesn't really count ... I have to go back to SUNTEP, or some SUNTEP student. (Trottier, personal communication, 21 August 1990)

Although FEO is officially critical of 'the trivial concerns of rigid procedures' (Johnston et al. 1989, 9), this was not evident to either interns or supervising teachers. 'She was like a hawk back there,' Garry Valier recalls of his College supervisor. 'She would see one student who was off-task for, oh, just a matter of seconds, [and she] would be marked down as off-task' (personal communication, 17 December 1989). If daily contact and classroom-sharing can lead to bonding and accommodation by the intern to the supervising teacher's practices, a reciprocal movement is also detectable. Three of the four supervising teachers interviewed called for a more contextualized system of evaluation in which assessment of the intern's performance in the developing culture of the classroom is emphasized. Classroom supervisor Terry Altman's view is representative: 'Perhaps we shouldn't be encouraged as cooperating teachers to be watching for specific *little* things all the time' (personal communication, 9 March 1990). Still, supervising teachers resist the perceived *excesses* of the content and process of supervision and evaluation. In the final analysis, the principles of 'effective teaching' are accepted as common sense. Furthermore, the criteria on the final evaluation form, the supervising teacher's obligation to collect 'data' between the College supervisor's visits, and the framing of the intern's periodic seminars means that supervising teachers feel bound to meet the demands of the College of Education and its supervisors. There was little risk, then, in FEO's delegation of greater responsibility for final intern evaluation to supervising teachers.

One principal effect of the internship process is to foreclose the possibility of developing critical forms of teaching through practice in the classroom. Again, the official ideology of FEO proposes that 'the intern is given freedom to experiment and to develop a personal teaching style'

(Johnston et al. 1989, 37). Yet in marked contrast to her experience at SUNTEP, where 'we were strongly encouraged to be creative and try different approaches to teaching,' Sharon Delorme argued that 'many interns might be reluctant to experiment and risk failure when so much emphasis is placed on evaluation' (personal communication, 14 August 1990). Data from transcripts indicate that four key fourth-year informants did feel constrained because they 'wanted things to go well with the university ... so [they would] follow the university guidelines' (Valier, personal communication, 17 December 1989). This sense of constraint was consistently contrasted with their experience in SUNTEP, where they felt noticeably freer to develop a personal teaching ideology under supervision which, for them, was genuinely developmental.

Students' experience of the SUNTEP culture contrasted with their experiences under supervision in the internship. Their impulse to resist was thereby legitimized. An ethos of freedom to practice was contrasted with an ethos of control. At the same time, 'follow[ing] ... guidelines' so that 'things ... go well' can become habitual in a future working context never entirely free from supervision. What is clear here is that the management psychology of humanistic supervision is demystified by students' direct experiences under close supervision. This repressive system produces elements of the interns' good sense. However, there is little evidence that interns understand supervision either relationally or politically. Rather, their dominant reaction is cynicism and the development of survival strategies and tactics. If the internship structure, management ideology, and evaluative authority are the principal means by which the state sanctions SUNTEP graduates' incorporation into hegemonic teaching practice, the content of that sanctioned teaching practice must be examined more closely. The following section explores the specific content of FEO teaching ideology which supports and legitimizes that practice.

FEO Teaching Ideology

FEO proclaims that 'interns ... are expected to accept the role of teacher and strive to adapt to the school' (Johnston et al. 1989, 3). This functionalist ruling would approve of SUNTEP interns who uncritically reproduce teaching practices which have historically led to the departure and exclusion of Aboriginal children from schools. This section examines the teaching ideology of FEO through a further analysis of its textbook. It argues that teaching practice based on the theoretical underpinnings of FEO, on the one hand, and teaching practice aiming to produce conditions where Aboriginal and working-class children could obtain equal results in classrooms, on the other, are fundamentally incompatible. Furthermore, the strictures of FEO limit SUNTEP interns' freedom to develop personal teaching ideologies. In this sense, FEO ideology is again shown to be internally inconsistent and contradictory.

SUNTEP interns, along with all other interns registered in the University of Saskatchewan's College of Education, are subject to evaluation against a specific set of criteria encoded in *The Internship*, commonly known as the 'bible' (Delorme 9 December 1989; Valier 17 December 1989). The confinement engendered in many SUNTEP students by 'the bible' is clearly expressed by Bev Nolin: 'After our first [seminar, the College supervisor] says, "Now, ... this isn't the cookbook ... There's things in here you should follow, but don't think that ... you have to follow everything step for step." And I thought, Oh! Right on! She doesn't think like the university – that we have to do everything that's said in the manual. It turned out you did.' (personal communication, 17 December 1989). Three of four supervising teachers interviewed made direct and exclusive reference to 'the bible' when asked what criteria were used to focus their observations throughout the term.

Interns are evaluated against eight major criteria. The first is 'effective professional teaching attributes' (Johnston et al. 1989, 27). The ideology of professionalism is problematic (Densmore 1987; Ginsburg 1988; Larson 1977) but space constraints prevent the issue from being discussed here (see Hesch 1992b for an elaboration of the problem in the context of Aboriginal teacher education). The balance of the evaluation criteria are based on the ideology of 'the most current research in teacher effectiveness' (R. Hermanson, personal communication, 30 April 1990). Thus, the internship manual adheres to positivist, behaviourist prescriptions for teachers' practice, following the current virtual hegemony of 'effective teaching' magnates (Zeichner 1983; Beyer and Zeichner 1987).

There are a number of limitations to 'effective teaching' ideology, only some of which will be dealt with here. One is that 'effective teaching' prescriptions subscribe to the Tyler rationale. The view of the teacher upheld by the 'research on teaching' advocates posits the teacher as controller (Grundy 1987; McNeil 1982). The principle of control is quite explicit in *The Internship*. For example, the first justificatory statement is that 'to be a successful and effective teacher you must plan' (Johnston et al. 1989, 38) because 'lack of planning results in many difficulties, such as classroom management' (p. 38). *The Internship* claims that the scientific approach to planning educational practice is achieved 'by identifying an effective and logical sequence through which specific objectives ... can be met' (p. 39) and that 'the conceptualization of the subject matter to be taught means being able to organize the content into its teachable components' (p. 40). More (1987), however, cites research which shows that the sequential, segmented method of presenting a lesson runs contrary to the ways of knowing of some Aboriginal children. Chambers Erasmus (1989) argues that deductive 'discourse styles' favoured in conventional classroom activities are inconsistent with the discourse styles of at least some northern Aboriginal Canadians. Such classroom activities as 'critical thinking' can disrupt the cultural practices of some Aboriginal students.

An analysis of three interns' logs and collected records revealed ways in which these dictates are effected in the classroom. Interns' logs are records of their lesson and unit plans. Supervising teachers often write statements on the plans after or during supervisory observations of the interns. The binders which include the plans also hold copies of formal observation sheets from the College supervisor and the mid-term evaluation. Together, the documents provide an excellent insight into the ways in which the supervising teachers are 'implicated in the activities of class rule' through the 'documentary mode of management' (Ng, Muller, and Walker 1990, 316). For example, one criterion interns are expected to meet is to have 'presented the lesson in an effective sequence and time frame' (Johnston et al. 1989, 61). Sharon Delorme initially had some difficulty meeting this criterion, as her supervising teacher was moved to comment that 'the constant interruptions by many students interfered with your pacing, therefore you were unable to complete your lesson' (f/n 3 October 1989). On the other hand, interns are also expected to have 'maintained classroom control by using firm consistent management statements' (p. 88). Delorme satisfied her supervising teacher with her 'excellent voice. You use your voice to control and motivate students' (f/n 2 October 1989). A major theme of both FEO and classroom supervisors is whether interns have 'kept students on-task' (p. 86). One intern's supervising teacher was pleased that when 'Willie tried to change the subject you handled the situation beautifully' (f/n 2 October 1989). Interns are expected to demonstrate 'maturity and calmness in reacting to unexpected student behaviour' (p. 93). Her everyday supervisor 'liked the way you ignored Samuel G. when he blurted out an answer' (f/n 13 September 1989). A version of Taylorist time-motion study is conducted by supervising teachers to determine interns' capacity to work in an effective 'time frame.' Thus, Bev Nolin's observation sheets include this: '10:35 – off-task, Bobby, James; 10:45: Children on-task and keeping up; 11:00: off-task, Jane' (f/n 19 September 1989).

A second limitation of the 'effective teaching' ideology is its general failure to problematize curricular knowledge, and thus its implicit upholding of the canon. Ruth Hermanson claims that 'the co-operating [supervising] teacher is the subject specialist,' so that on questions of content, the 'College supervisor really needs to rely on the cooperating teacher' (personal communication, 30 April 1990). Yet the analysis of three interns' log-books shows that attention to content by the supervising teacher was minimal, and then only assessed its instrumental value, with comments such as 'very interesting' and 'not only attractive ... but purposeful.' On the other hand, this chapter has shown that curricular knowledge *is* problematic – when it challenges the security of the canon.

The Internship's precepts also subscribe to possessive individualism and meritocracy. The 'bible' proclaims that 'there is a need for greater individualization of content, assignments, and evaluation to meet the needs of the students' (Johnston et al. 1989, 41). Differences in behaviour between students in a classroom are interpreted by FEO as, for example, the tendency 'for a few of the brighter students to do all of the interacting' (Johnston et al. 1989, 143).

In sum, we should remember that the practices which derive from the empiricism and positivism upon which most teacher education depends, including 'effective teaching,' are nothing more than 'a historically locatable set of practices' (Rabinow 1986, 239). That is, empiricist and deductive rationality have been cited historically as the single legitimate form of reasoning, justified by the universality of Eurocentrism (Amin 1989). FEO requires Métis interns to reproduce a Eurocentric ideology through daily classroom tests supervised by others. SUNTEP students will not teach unless they satisfy agents of the state that they can reproduce the practices which excluded many of them and continue to exclude members of their original social category. That is, Métis, and at least some other Aboriginal people, are excluded from school through the operation of ideological and cultural practices rooted in a set of dominant schooling ideologies. The College of Education's Field Experience Office has constructed a problematic which SUNTEP students must negotiate in order to become certified teachers. That problematic comprises both active propagation of particular dominant schooling ideologies and the inhibition or preclusion of the construction of alternatives. Empiricism and behaviourism underlie the 'effective teaching' credo of FEO, so that the Tyler rationale, possessive individualism, meritocracy, and an unquestioning stance on the canon are taken as immutable, law-like truths. They are not viewed relationally. The propagation and inhibition/preclusion are enforced through the power of the state to evaluate and pronounce upon the ability of the intern to reproduce these dominant ideologies. These ideologies are precisely the same as those which either: (a) excluded the students themselves through the culturally reproductive practice of exit; or (b) forced students to reluctantly accommodate to them in order to graduate from Grade 12. It is to the contradiction between the interns' lives as they are immersed in their work and the shackles constructed by both FEO and common sense that this chapter now turns.

Praxis of the SUNTEP Intern

This section examines the accounts of four interns of their negotiation, more or less, between their existing conceptions of educational practice and the practices imposed by the internship model and 'bible.' The data suggest that the difficulties some interns face are little more than the trials of preparing to enter the labour market as new teaching recruits. The interns are not fundamentally opposed to the principles of 'effective teaching' and are suspicious of SUNTEP alternatives. To some extent, this is because of the self-interest of those SUNTEP students who are scrambling for niches in the established teaching profession by absorbing whatever passes as legitimate knowledge. Furthermore, not all entrants to SUN-TEP have had bad schooling experiences, so they would have only new knowledge shared by their SUNTEP peers and the 'official' SUNTEP pedagogy to convince them that schools, more than children's lives, are problematic. As well, respect for teachers and standard constructions of knowledge are elements of a contradictory response by both working-class and minority cultures to formal schooling (Connell 1985; Delpit 1988; Hogan 1982).

However, many SUNTEP students have a quite critical view of schooling as they know it, and are committed to changing those conditions. The balance of this section focuses on the activities of the three students who have been key informants and participants in the study: Sharon Delorme, Carole Trottier, and Garry Valier. These three are not taken as representative of the SUNTEP student population as a whole. Both Delorme and Trottier were asked to join this study *because* they could offer unique insights into the operation of SUNTEP and provide the most informed answers to the following question: Given all of the constraints of internship, in what ways do potentially transformative intellectuals pass the internship criteria *and* develop some competency as reskilled and critical teachers? Valier is a student who *did* undergo transformation during his SUNTEP years. Given that no surveys were employed during data collection, it is impossible to determine the extent to which these three are representative.

Sharon Delorme spoke of the difficulty of satisfying the specific criteria of *The Internship* while at the same time implementing her commitment to children: 'All of those things you may not feel comfortable doing, but you try to work around that the best possible way you can in order to give the kids an experience – not to damage them' (personal communication, 14 August 1990).

Delorme has outlined critical interns' basic strategy for negotiating their way successfully through the internship. This is not to say that all their classroom practices were incorporated into a carefully designed curriculum plan. Spontaneous resistance could arise in 'flashes' in the classroom. For example, when the College supervisor visited Carole Trottier:

> He said, 'There were three times [when] you didn't keep up your three seconds, so I'll put here [on the observation form, that] your direct questioning is good, but let's just say you need to work on your consistency in your questioning.' I said, 'You're making so many assumptions about your questioning. You're assuming that in that five seconds after I've asked the question, kids are pondering over it ... If fourteen people are sitting there with their hands up, I have to wait five seconds?' He said, 'Research shows ...' (Personal communication, 21 August 1990)

More typically, the interns would shrug their shoulders and accept being 'dinged' with some resignation. Acceptance does not imply incorporation of the 'effective teaching' view, however. Carole Trottier, for example, recalled how:

> The other thing ... [was] you weren't supposed to let anybody speak out ... to acknowledge that they spoke. As a classroom management technique you don't let kids just start hollering out answers ... You could lose control, maybe. You might even start a debate! ... I let [students] speak out of turn. He brought that up ... But he was locked and ... had no context for what he was looking for, so I wrote it off. But unfortunately it's on my observation sheet. (Personal communication, 21 August 1990)

Earlier, I have shown how first-year students used negative examples from their early life experience as a reference point for the formation of their teaching ideologies. Some SUNTEP interns have more immediate examples:

> I learned a lot from my cooperating teacher in terms of what I don't ever want to do ... to become. [For example] I don't want to teach from prepared unit plans that come from the department [of Education] ... or the Saskatchewan Teachers' Federation ... I used to think, 'Gosh, she's pretty

good,' watching her teach this Science unit on the future ... It was all laid out ... and she could just whip the kids through and they seemed to enjoy it ... She was their favourite teacher by far ... But afterwards, I'd think, 'What did she teach them really?' ... There is something to be said for having the kids enjoy it ... But there was something missing ... Maybe the context ... Like I tried to think ... of [when] the kids would ever ... think about that stuff again. (Trottier, personal communication, 21 August 1990)

Despite all its limitations, the internship provided some opportunities to test the developed strategic ideas and plans interns took out of the SUNTEP classrooms with them, to reinforce them if they proved valuable, to learn from seeing them implemented by a supervising teacher if possible, as well as from that teacher's negative examples. Sharon Delorme, for instance,

learned how to organize a classroom, different ways of presenting a novel study. I learned that attempting to control students by embarrassing or humiliating them was not only inappropriate but also ineffective. I learned that children will try to learn no matter what situation you present them with. I learned that I want to teach in ways that allow the children to have input into their learning. I learned that I do not want to stand up in front of them and lecture (the keeper of all knowledge). I learned that children really love books and poetry. (Personal communication, 14 August 1990)

Garry Valier, encouraged by his supervising teacher and others, found himself becoming 'less lenient ... It's like we took babysitting and teaching [in College]' (personal communication, 26 April 1990). Carole Trottier, on the other hand, inverted the discourse of FEO and turned the problem of classroom management into a 'teachable subject' – for herself: 'When I approached activities or tried to set up lessons and they didn't go well, sometimes I didn't care ... because it was a bridge to something else, or it was a learning experience for me to see what they're weakest in. Or which of my activities are more interesting to me than to them. And when I'd gone off on a crusade without them' (personal communication, 21 August 1990).

Trottier's deliberate distortion of FEO's premise that 'classroom management' is a 'teachable subject' whereby teachers can 'teach' students to behave, mirrors Tony Bennett's argument that 'oppositional cultures may at times use elements of the dominant culture against [it] ... by turning [the dominant culture] back upon itself, to create a space within and against it in which contradictory values can echo, reverberate and be heard' (quoted in Apple and Christian-Smith 1991, 10-11). Trottier 'wanted to give ... a medal' to a student who had been consistently 'off-task' during my observation of Trottier's classroom work. Trottier 'loved her spirit. I loved the fact that despite everybody's efforts to shut her up or to make her studious, she fought them ... She fought them really well' (personal communication, 21 August 1990).

At least three of the interns also attempted, quite unsuccessfully, to implement the SUNTEP principle and cultural practice of cooperative learning. They did not do this without risk. Their supervising teachers would defend their avoidance of the strategy in their classrooms through gentle reference to the inherent limitations of either the method or the students. For example, while Delorme's supervising teacher attributed the limited success of the strategy to the problem of working with 'a class of different levels' (M. Leggett, personal communication, 25 April 1990), Delorme located the problem in its lack of prior use. The differing perspectives may not be unrelated to the differing subject positions of the two adults, for the supervising teacher had an investment in the legitimacy of her own practice.

For teachers of difference, however, their own life histories *can* serve as a source of legitimacy to counter the authority of the supervisor. Carole Trottier, for example, used her past as a resource to resist the implied message from her supervising teacher. When she attempted to use group work, the students

> resisted it a lot ... I remember my co-operating teacher [asking] 'How do you feel about this group work stuff? I ... think there's a place for it, but it just isn't working that well.' I went home and I thought about that and ... thought, 'No, I'm right! They *have* to learn how to work in groups.' Always ... teachers didn't see that as a necessary skill ... If you could work on your own that was really good. Your ability to work in a group [would] probably cause problems because kids were talking ... If kids misbehaved a lot ... [teachers] didn't see that as something you're supposed to learn [about] at school. That was just a deficit. (Personal communication, 21 August 1990)

Delorme's resistance to the notion of the teacher as the 'keeper of all knowledge' was shared by the interns and meant that they could encourage open and challenging questioning by students, in part by displaying this behaviour. The democratization of classroom social relations informed the interns' cultural construction of classroom knowledge in another way as well. Garry Valier found he was frequently 'going off on a tangent' as he 'followed' the directions students went after he had introduced a theme of current student interest in his 'motivational set.' The experience taught him that 'sometimes they can be a guide to what you should be teaching ... It's almost like punishing them in a way [to teach textbook knowledge].' Valier proceeded to organize a unit around students' interests in earthquakes following the 1989 San Francisco tragedy, incorporating concepts he had only recently learned at university. 'They picked up on it and they knew that better than whatever else I was teaching in social studies' (personal communication, 27 October 1989). Valier's reluctance to 'punish' his students by focusing on the textbook resulted in his own punishment, however. When he 'got off on a tangent' with the students under College supervision he was disciplined because his 'motivational set ... was too long ... It was ten minutes' (personal communication, 27 October 1989).

If both FEO and the supervising teachers rarely problematized curriculum content, this was hardly true of the critical interns. In another articulation of her strategy, Sharon Delorme found that 'you survive by doing what you can ... to satisfy what's in that manual, but by stretching it too. Like sneaking in what you can almost so that other people don't even notice that that's what you've done' (personal communication, 14 August 1990).

For example, Delorme's assignment to teach a unit on Canadian pioneers was 'stretched' so that Aboriginal migration to the continent served as the case of the first 'pioneers.' She 'snuck in' a novel study whose hero was a modern Indian who helps save a rural American family from farm repossession. Questions in specific lessons asked if 'there [can] ever be a time when it is *okay* [original emphasis] to disobey rules or someone's orders?' (f/n 19 September 1989) and 'Is it fair to take away someone's house if they have not paid their taxes or their rent? Why?' (f/n 14 November 1989). Carole Trottier developed a series of lessons on child abuse at a time when it had become a local political issue. Garry Valier developed a unit on racism and taught about the Brazilian rain forests: 'The idea of ... certain companies getting people in Brazil to cut down part of the rain forest to raise cattle so they get cheaper beef for their hamburgers here in North America' (personal communication, 27 October 1989).

Strictly speaking, it is unfair to accuse mainstream teachers and FEO of taking the selection of curriculum content for granted. I have already shown that the legitimacy of the canon tends to be assumed, but that selection of innovative or critical content by interns is subject to review by supervisors. Although Sharon Delorme's responses to lessons with her provocative material read 'Motivation – excellent' (f/n 19 September 1989) and 'good variety of questions' (f/n 14 November 1989), it is more truthful to claim that school and university officials do not find curriculum knowledge problematic as long as it does not challenge the security of the canon. Despite these many boundaries, impositions, demands, and restrictions, the internship provided sufficient flexibility for principled and committed interns to maintain a sense of integrity in their work.

In our concluding set of interviews, I asked each of four key informants to articulate their ideal views of themselves as future teachers, to articulate a strategy for realizing their vision, and to explain the reasons for Aboriginal students exiting from and 'failure' in schools. In an intensive interview of fixed length aimed primarily at understanding their experience of internship and their negotiations with power, there was limited time to explore the intricacies of their answers, which were relatively brief. There were only four common denominators. Each spoke, both in their vision and in their strategy, of the need for personal freedom and empowerment for students. Each also expressed a primary commitment to process. Personal freedom, then, meant giving students power to determine what is to be learned, 'bringing their issues into the classroom' (Delorme, personal communication, 14 August 1990). None of the four advocated testing knowledge through written exams or assignments, and the most popular response was that students should be allowed to demonstrate their intellectual development through their interest in quests for knowledge. Each respondent focused on the practices of the school rather than the student in explaining Aboriginal exit and 'failure,' agreeing that the education system is designed to serve and match the interests of the white middle class. Only one related this problem to structural arrangements within society, however. While not common denominators, the themes of individual membership in a community, building bridges from students' immediate interests to critical awareness of the social order, and empowering students to act not only in determining the content of the curriculum but also in society at large were each mentioned more than once.

Conclusion

There is a polar opposition between the uniform call of the SUNTEP interns for a cultural construction which democratizes classroom relations in the interests of the students and the interests of FEO in controlling and homogenizing students and classroom life. FEO serves as a powerful mechanism for reproducing Eurocentric schooling. In contrast, the interns' teaching ideologies were built upon their own life histories and in the sharing and egalitarian culture of SUNTEP and, for some, perhaps, inherited Métis cultural forms. In the face of common-sense possessive individualism, the interns attempted to initiate cooperative learning strategies. An interest in equalizing educational opportunity was demonstrated in one intern's inventive strategy for ensuring that selected students were fed. The commitment to an anti-canonical curriculum was reinforced by examples of teachers' work being rooted not only in students' immediate experience but also in the need to confront racism and imperialism through alternative curriculum content. Resistance to the Tyler rationale was expressed not only in opposition to its constraints on the interns' labour but in defence of students' interests as well. Perhaps most importantly, the active resistance to or subversion of the requirements of the internship and the advice of their supervising teachers when so much was at risk offers promise for the long-term work of these teachers.

Notes

1 All names used in this chapter are pseudonyms.
2 The Gabriel Dumont Institute of Native Studies and Applied Research is an organization providing academic educational courses, services, research, and publication for Métis throughout the province of Saskatchewan.
3 Ross may be right in arguing that a different 'mentor's' guidance on discipline, guidance from a supervising teacher with whom she could identify, would have enabled her to control the class. Different teachers use different strategies to equally satisfactory effect (Connell 1985). 'Discipline' is not a thing or a bundle of techniques but a socially constructed 'state of play in a very complex set of relationships between schools and their clienteles, teachers and students, administrators and students' (Connell 1985, 109). Her resistance would have made it more difficult for her supervisor to conduct her own work as usual (Connell 1985). It also contributed to her own exclusion from the teaching work force.

References

Abercrombie, N., S. Hill, and B.S. Turner, 1980. *The dominant ideology thesis.* Boston: Allen and Unwin

Amin, S. 1989. *Eurocentrism.* New York: Monthly Review Press

Apple, M. 1985. *Education and power.* Boston: Ark Paperbacks

–. 1989. *Teachers and texts: A political economy of class and gender relations in education.* New York: Routledge, Chapman, and Hall

Apple, M., and L.K. Christian-Smith. 1991. The politics of the textbook. In

M. Apple and L.K. Christian-Smith, eds., *The politics of the textbook*, 1-21. London: Routledge

Beyer, L., and K. Zeichner. 1987. Teacher education in cultural context: Beyond reproduction. In T.S. Popkewitz, ed., *Critical studies in teacher education: Its folklore, theory, and practices*, 298-334. London, New York, and Philadelphia: Falmer Press

Britzman, D. 1991. *Practice makes practice: A critical study of learning to teach*. Albany: State University of New York Press

Carnoy, M., and H.M. Levin. 1985. *Schooling and work in the democratic state*. Stanford, CA: Stanford University Press

Chambers, Erasmus, C. 1989. Ways with stories: Listening to the stories Aboriginal people tell. *Language Arts* 66 (3):26-34

Connell, R.W. 1985. *Teacher's work*. Sydney: Allen and Unwin

-. et al. 1982. *Making the difference: Schools, families, and social division*. Boston: Allen and Unwin

Delpit, L.D. 1988. The silenced dialogue: Power and pedagogy in educating other people's children. *Harvard Educational Review* 58 (3):280-98

Densmore, K. 1987. Professionalism, proletarianization, and teacher work. In T.S. Popkewitz, ed., *Critical studies in teacher education: Its folklore, theory, and practice*, 130-60. London, New York, and Philadelphia: Falmer Press

Ginsburg, M. 1988. *Contradictions in teacher education and society: A critical analysis*. New York: Falmer Press

Giroux, H.A. 1988. *Teachers as intellectuals: Toward a critical pedgogy of learning*. Granby, MA: Bergin and Garvey

Giroux, H.A., and R.I. Simon. 1989. *Popular culture, schooling, and everyday life*. Granby, MA: Bergin and Garvey

Grundy, S. 1987. *Curriculum: Product or praxis*. London: Falmer Press

Heald, S. 1990. Making democracy practicable: Voluntarism and job creation. In R. Ng, G. Walker, and J. Muller, eds., *Community organization and the Canadian state*, 147-64. Toronto: Garamond Press

Hesch, R. 1992a. Aboriginal life experience and the fracturing of multiculturalist ideology. In V. Satzewich, ed., *Deconstructing a nation: Immigration, multiculturalism and racism in '90s Canada*, 423-68. Halifax: Fernwood

-. 1992b. Teachers on the borderlands: The ideological and cultural formation of aboriginal preservice teachers. Ph.D. dissertation, University of Toronto

Hogan, D. 1982. Education and class formation: The peculiarities of the Americans. In M.W. Apple, ed., *Cultural and economic reproduction in education*. London: Routledge and Kegan Paul

Jarolimek, J. and C.D. Foster. 1989. *Teaching and learning in the elementary school*, 4th ed. New York: Macmillan

Johnston, J.M. et al. 1989. *The internship and supervision for effective teaching*. Saskatoon: College of Education, University of Saskatchewan

Larson, M. 1977. *The rise of professionalism: A sociological analysis*. Berkeley and Los Angeles: University of California Press

Liston, D.P. 1988. *Capitalist schools*. New York and London: Routledge

McNeil, J.D. 1982. A scientific approach to supervision. In T.J. Sergiovanni, ed., *Supervision of Teaching*, 18-34. Alexandria, VA: ASCD

Ng, R., J. Muller, and G. Walker. 1990. Community, class struggles, and state formation. In R. Ng, G. Walker, and J. Muller, eds., *Community organization and the Canadian state*, 309-19. Toronto: Garamond Press

Ortiz, F.I. 1988. Hispanic-American children's experiences in classrooms: A comparison between Hispanic and non-Hispanic children. In L. Weis, ed., *Class, race, and gender in American education*, 63-86. Albany: State University of New York Press

Rabinow, P. 1986. Representations are social facts: Modernity and postmodernity in anthropology. In J. Clifford and G.E. Marcus, eds. *Writing culture*. Berkeley: University of California Press

Sergiovanni, T.J. 1982. The context for supervision. In T.J. Sergiovanni, ed., *Supervision of Teaching*, 108-18. Alexandria, VA: ASCD

Shannon, P. 1989. *Broken promises*. Granby, MA: Bergin and Garvey

Stone, M. 1981. *The education of the black child in Britain*. Glasgow: Fontana

Young, J. 1987. The cultural significance of male children's playground activities. In J. Young, ed., *Breaking the mosaic*, 190-210. Toronto: Garamond Press

Zeichner, K.M. 1983. Alternative paradigms of teacher education. *Journal of Teacher Education* 34 (3):3-9

10
The Challenge for Universities
Agnes Grant

Special Native teacher education programs (TEPs) have been in existence in Canada for over twenty years, so it is now possible to analyze and evaluate their impact on Native education. When the programs first started there were very high hopes for educational change.

Understandably, graduates of the programs can, at times, be quite despondent over the lack of progress. There are still schools run by very autocratic principals from various cultural groups and there are still teaching materials that should have been banned years ago. Of greater harm to children are inappropriate teaching methods which are still commonly practised. Native parents may still accept disciplinary methods which were used when they went to school because they believe that this is the way schools should be, and they cannot visualize that they can be different. A particular area of concern is integrated schools, often located in core areas of cities, where few Native teachers or administrators are found and where few changes have taken place.

Graduates of TEPs 'burn out' because they are mostly on the 'front line' of educational issues; they see successes and failures daily and often the failures overshadow the successes. In locally controlled schools they may be hampered by a struggling, perhaps poorly trained, administration, which comes from within their own community, thus increasing the stresses of the job.

On the other hand, what has happened in Native education since TEPs started in the early 1970s is nothing short of a renaissance. The practice of plane-loads of southerners flocking north to perform some service or other for Native people and then going back home as quickly as possible has largely ceased. To measure and appreciate the degree of progress we need only to reread *Wahbung: Our Tomorrows* (1971, 118-23) by the Indian Tribes of Manitoba, a very powerful document in its day. Some of the

recommendations were so basic that we take them for granted today. For example, it stated:
- that there must be a transfer of educational control to the local responsibility centre (reserve)
- that there be parental participation
- that local school boards be responsible for:
  - direct participation in curriculum development
  - administration of the physical education plant
  - coordination of educational programs, both internally and externally
- that teachers of Indian origin be hired to teach whenever possible
- that Native people be employed as teacher assistants
- that schools all be made non-denominational.

And so on.

Indian Control of Indian Education (1972) by the National Indian Brotherhood was a blueprint for local control of education. When local control first started it was newsworthy that some schools were *not* experiencing difficulties; today local control is so commonplace that it is accepted as the norm. The miracle of local control is that after the total domination of the Department of Indian Affairs for all those years, locally controlled schools evolved so rapidly and so successfully.

The success of TEPs can be viewed with satisfaction but other strategies for the future need to be planned. It is evident that what was done in the 1970s is not what needs to be done now. The early TEPs did a good job but should be evaluated in the context of the times in which they operated. Most crucial at that time was getting Native teachers into classrooms. To secure a stable teaching staff was imperative and it was recognized that non-Native teachers would never provide this stability. Teaching models from within the culture were also of great importance but the need for teachers who would stay for more than one year was even more crucial to any kind of educational success for the children.

TEPs train people who are disadvantaged financially, educationally, and socially (that is, isolated students who have not had the same opportunities or experiences as people in the south). It has always been realized, however, that TEP students possess unique advantages as well, even if these advantages are not recognized by mainline institutions.

A second part of the TEP mandate was influencing and changing the institution of higher learning, that is, the university. TEPs have had a profound effect on universities, though this is not always recognized by those who are closest to the system. For example, in 1972, there was one identified Indian graduate from Brandon University's Faculty of Education.

There still are very few Native students who graduate from the on-campus program but that is largely because most choose to train through TEPs. Those that do go through the regular program are now welcomed by many faculty members for their unique knowledge, and their particular expertise is nurtured. University campuses are still not the friendliest places for many Native students but they are not the actively unfriendly places that they were several decades ago. TEPs have played a large role in this change of mood.

One reason why there was not more rapid and more dramatic change at the institutional level was because many other issues needed attention. TEPs students were largely non-traditional students; that is, in the early years few had completed Grade 12. The universities already had mature-entry programs, which meant that a completed high school education was not necessary. The practical operation of this policy had to be ironed out. Ways had to be found of keeping the students in the programs, and that sometimes meant bending the rules. At that time, universities were much more structured than they are now so things taken for granted today were unheard of then.

The primary task of TEPs was to get teachers into the classrooms as fast as possible so unnecessarily antagonizing the institution was avoided. Any kind of institutional change was made very, very carefully. Examples of changes that occurred were allowing extra time to finish courses, or extra time to write exams for those who needed to translate into a Native language to think through an answer and then translate back into English. 'Incompletes' were granted for a wider variety of reasons, and more time was allowed between writing exams and submitting the marks because of the isolation of many students. Much energy went into building trust between university and TEPs staff because TEPs were viewed with great suspicion. There was real concern that TEPs 'watered down' university standards, and this is understandable because university standards have to be maintained and early TEPs students were non-traditional learners. The bigger issues of course content or courses within a program were not dealt with for many years; many still have not been addressed.

The result of attempting to meet university criteria as responsibly as possible was that early TEPs students were trained as though they were white middle-class trainees going into mainline schools. In the early years, there were staff members who believed that this approach was right and proper because of the prevailing assimilationist philosophy. This still continues to a large extent. The advantage of this approach is that graduates feel that they have 'made it' on the same terms as anyone else, and this is useful where employers use this as a hiring criterion. The disadvantage is that Native teachers are not being trained as effectively as they ought to be.

TEPs are not very different from on-campus education programs in this respect. All teacher trainees have to conform to a set of predetermined expectations which are not necessarily congruent with their past experiences or their future professional situations. Faculties of education are not known for adapting to their clientele; rather, the clientele is expected to conform to the ideas expounded by the professor. Children have always been expected to conform to the expectations of the teachers. If they don't, they are considered misfits and fail. John Holt, in *How Children Fail* (1964), closely examined this phenomenon and showed how the classroom is often the battlefield on which child and teacher try to gain advantage over each other instead of being a mutually supportive learning environment.

Some of the early teacher trainees never did conform and their success was in jeopardy. Some early TEP students had been teaching for years as permit teachers at the nursery/kindergarten/Grade 1 level. It is almost funny, in retrospect, to think that the university earnestly believed it had great truths to teach them. However, the Department of Indian Affairs had decreed that teachers be 'properly' qualified and no one argued with the concept, especially since it meant a sizeable pay increase. Early TEP students acquiesced in the training both because it was required of them and because they ardently desired to learn to be better teachers. An example was a woman, 'Mary,' who did want to learn more about teaching but would not compromise her high principles. She would not change her teaching style because what she was being taught was often inappropriate to the children. Also, Mary would not do things that she considered useless and a waste of her time (like written lesson plans). University expectations were intrusive for her and her classroom. How can the university respectfully set expectations for people like 'Mary' and how can they be evaluated? It is important that the most gifted people in the communities be encouraged to become teachers; often these are the non-traditional learners.

Many other graduates, not as experienced as 'Mary,' *have* to rely on the teaching of university professors. Whether in mainline education systems or locally controlled schools, the first few years are usually a matter of survival for new teachers. Consequently, they are happy to do what they were taught by supervisors and professors. As they gain experience and confidence, they start to question these teachings because they are often irrelevant to the situations in which they find themselves. They then begin to modify and adapt both materials and practices.

As more and more local education authorities develop education philosophies, culturally relevant schooling is introduced. Much of what happens in locally controlled schools is very different from what is taught at universities. This can present real problems for the universities. Often the school is run in a way that is acceptable to the community but may not meet university criteria for good classroom management. How can students undergoing field experience in a culturally different school be evaluated? They may perform well in a culturally comfortable way but this way may not be accepted by the faculty supervisor. It may not meet the criteria of the supervisor, or the supervisor may lack the knowledge of Native culture to understand the significance of what is happening in the classroom.

A rapidly increasing feature of locally controlled schools is that children receive some of their education in traditional fashion. This may be so foreign to university faculty that they have no basis on which to evaluate student teacher participation. Local people are often anxious to incorporate traditional education into the training of their teachers. Universities may pay lip service to this kind of education and the involvement of elders, but in truth they often are threatened by elders – threatened because they are losing control over something which was once their exclusive preserve. There is no doubt that universities must maintain standards of training, but they also must change and learn about new things if their present practices do not meet their clients' needs. Faculties of education show remarkably little interest in learning about educational approaches that are not validated by the literature of their own narrow cultural and socioeconomic group.

In some community-based TEPs, students have the opportunity to receive at least part of their training in traditional settings. What becomes important then, is how mainline institutions adapt to this aspect of First Nations self-determination while retaining university standards and expectations.

The way in which institutions validate knowledge, recognize socialization within divergent cultures, regard first language influences, and accept different spiritual beliefs and world-views are a few of the issues that need to be examined but they fall outside the scope of this chapter. This discussion is limited largely to how success is measured. How can university evaluation procedures and grades or credits be adapted to become more congruent with traditional Native education?

Elder wisdom is at the core of Native education, although some contemporary Native educators have not experienced elder instruction because of historical and social circumstances. A dichotomy exists because white middle-class society devalues the elderly. Knowledge that is respected by formal institutions comes only from within their own ranks. Obviously, a great gap separates mainline societies from traditional societies in attitudes towards elders. This presents a great challenge to the university.

But this gap can be overcome. The following is an example of a project which has resolved some of the difficulties.

Bear Lake/Stevenson Island Project

The Bear Lake/Stevenson Island Project at Island Lake, Manitoba, has been running since 1989. Victor Harper, the director of the project, is himself a graduate of a TEP. The philosophy of this program is that traditional education is all too often seen as an extra. The Island Lake people believe that traditional experiences ought to form the basis on which contemporary education builds. The Island Lake Tribal Council has developed its own 'Island Lake Education Mission Statement' which states, in part, that education must be 'holistic and realistic in that it relates not only to academic development but to our spiritual, emotional, psychological and physical growth.'

In describing the Stevenson River Project, Victor Harper explains:

The concepts of the traditional education system have been dormant for too long. The task ahead of the people ... in order to pursue SUCCESS in education and in life is to develop an alternative education program. The program has to include a marriage between the contemporary education system and the traditional education system.

In the past Native people have been told that academic schooling and traditional learning are mutually exclusive. It is the premise of this project that this is not the case, that by using traditional learning as a base, Island Lake children can maximize their performance and their quality of life. The main purpose of the project was to learn from seasonal trapping, hunting, and fishing experiences; to observe, participate and consider the experiences of children and adults, the ways by which they learn, how time is used, what resources for learning are presented by these experiences, the environment and the knowledge of elders. Central to this we wished to consider the role and responsibilities of parents and elders in educating their children and grandchildren.

From this experience we hoped to make some observations and recommendations for ways in which the learning concepts of traditional education can also become central to the school system and to make this information available to parents, elders, and school committees planning for the local control of education. (Harper 1989, 3)

Whole families go to these camps and the children's regular education continues, but with a difference. Victor Harper continues:

> Throughout the camp each person from young to old experienced both the role of teacher and learner. The educator participated in camp activities in order to learn. Parents and grandparents came into the school tent to participate and to see what children were doing. Children shared learning activities, helped each other and worked with younger children. Reading, writing, listening and game playing was done individually and in groups without direct adult supervision. Motivation was not a problem and 'academic' learning was happening. Often the whole family might be reading in the evening. (Harper 1989, 14)

In this situation learning is, indeed, holistic, and collaborative learning is the norm. Thinking about and working through the experiences gained in this fashion forms a bridge to the vicarious experiences which will later occur in the classroom.

When a new TEP was opened in the Island Lake area, community members were anxious to know whether the student teachers would be allowed to participate in the Bear Lake/Stevenson River Project and whether they would receive university credit for their experiences

Initially it was arranged that some students would gain part of their field experience with their elders. The first block of field experience was non-credit and so the issue of evaluation was not crucial. It soon became evident, however, that the criteria normally used by the university to give these students feedback were totally inappropriate. It was evident that since the elders were the instructors, only they could assess whether the students had performed satisfactorily and what their weaknesses and strengths were. The elders were willing to do this but did not wish to make the individual university-type evaluations. Camp life and work was a group endeavour and individual evaluations were felt to be culturally inappropriate.

Martin Wood, the elder 'in charge,' compiled a report for the university in which he made the following generalizations:

- The men seemed to be more comfortable with traditional activities than the women but the women asked many questions and three women were particularly curious about traditional food preparation.
- There was significant learning and excellent progress by all students.
- The women's language skills in Island Lake Cree were significantly higher than the men's.
- Aspiring professional educators must learn land-based skills in order to be truly prepared to teach the children.

The university expected students to keep a daily log as part of the field experience folder. They would write a report for Martin Wood (the elder) about what they had learned and they would submit one lesson plan based on an activity which happened in camp.

Keeping the log was difficult for many students. The wilderness experience was a family activity and many of the students had their children with them. The cooperating teacher pointed out that female students had to spend too much time looking after their children and thus did not have the time for their own personal development. A lesson to be drawn from this is that it is very difficult for two types of expectations to work simultaneously.

In general, the consensus was that the experience had been a good one and that more opportunity should be provided for this type of teacher training. Consequently, it was decided to offer a complete course to the teachers-in-training at Stevenson River. Connie Singleterry, a resident of Island Lake, a retired teacher, and an M.Ed. graduate, was asked to 'teach' the course. She works part-time with Victor Harper so has been involved in every phase of the project's development. It was understood that Victor would play as important a role as Connie in planning and implementing the course, but that ultimately, the course would be taught by the elders. The university calendar indicated that all the course requirements of 05.368 'Outdoor Education' could be met during this experience so that was the course for which the students registered.

Since this was a formal course for which students would receive three credit hours, evaluation became more important. Connie Singleterry, as the instructor, had to take ultimate responsibility for the grades assigned. Throughout the planning for the course, evaluation was discussed by planners and students. Some participants expressed concern about the evaluation criteria and grading system to be used. That this is an area of concern for students must be recognized. Grade point averages weigh very heavily with students. One recommendation was that in a future experience of this kind the possibility of awarding a 'pass' or 'fail' grade could be discussed with the department.

Elders also explained that criteria for measuring success would have to be individualized. Students arrived with various degrees of competency and those already proficient in the requisite skills were expected to show far more concern for the common good and to demonstrate appropriate leadership. If a highly proficient person did not show leadership that person would be rated lower even though all the requirements had been met.

The Stevenson River Project is one example where the usual university grading system does not further the objectives of the experience. Many other examples will emerge as TEP programs across Canada incorporate some form of traditional experience for their teacher trainees. There also are alternative schools like the Children of the Earth School in Winnipeg where high school students learn traditional as well as contemporary teachings. How can universities train teachers for such schools? A great deal of communication is needed to ensure that potentially stressful situations and misunderstandings are avoided. Situations could develop where the institution has one set of expectations, students another, and elders a third.

It becomes imperative that university evaluation be reexamined to identify ways in which student teachers can be evaluated in conformity with university standards while also allowing acceptable community and elder involvement. Oral narrative in data gathering is acceptable in other disciplines and elder wisdom in education can be recorded using the same tools and techniques. Women's studies programs are using more flexible methods of evaluation. Women's studies scholars, like Native educators, have felt that much of their knowledge has never been validated by the institution – the conventional evaluation methods do not work for them either. Journal-keeping is used in many women's studies courses and is also found in some education courses. Much can be learned from examining the techniques of other disciplines and adapting them to education.

Self-Initiation and Self-Analysis

Another method of 'evaluation' has been described and used very successfully by Professor Jake Redekopp from the University of Manitoba. He was with the faculty of education and has supervised many student teachers over the years. Eventually he became the director of student teaching. He was troubled by several aspects of student teaching: 'My experience is that almost all cooperating teachers and faculty supervisors put more time and energy into their tasks than is expected of them. However, many disparities exist in the quality of the efforts of this large group of committed professionals because of unclear expectations, role definitions and the varying degrees of supervisory skills' (Redekopp 1989, iv).

Though Professor Redekopp refers specifically to student teaching in his book, his system has great potential for any university course. His basic philosophy will not do violence to Native cultural practices.

Professor Redekopp's core theory is:

The elements of the supervisory philosophy are self-initiation and self-analysis. One without the other would seriously weaken the process. As well, the process cannot be expected to work to potential unless it is practised in a non-judgemental environment in which feedback about the supervisee's performance is based on observational data ...

The ideal supervisory process relies on interpersonal relationship skills that promote a willingness to make decisions for self and accept responsibility for the results of the decisions. For this to happen, a relationship between all parties involved must be based on a non-judgemental mind-set.

The non-judgemental mind-set seeks to understand in order to offer feedback in the most efficient way possible. When this happens, the supervisee is free to make decisions based on observed data. These decisions are personal property and responsibility. Therefore, a supervisee can make decisions based on outcomes whenever necessary without having to wait for someone else to make the decisions.

If we take the position that it is desirable for children to mature into self-sufficiency, then it seems wise to expose them to teachers who will provide the role model. To that end, it is recommended that the aspiring teacher, the supervisee, be allowed to practise in an environment in which it is safe to make decisions. The supervisee will then develop into a role model for self-sufficiency.

The supervisor must accept the responsibility for establishing the climate in which the supervisee can take responsibility for self. (Redekopp 1989, 11)

Integral to Professor Redekopp's theory is the fact that self-initiation is a process rather than a product. The capacity to make decisions increases with practice, so that it is important that one exercises the right to make decisions for self as often as possible. 'If, however, someone else has made the decisions, the probability exists that the individual will either be in a state of inertia waiting for another decision to be made or will escape from responsibility by blaming the bad results on someone else' (Redekopp 1989, 12).

It is the supervisee's responsibility to initiate a meeting with the supervisor and to ask for feedback based on observed data. Judgmental statements from observers, good or bad, negate the whole concept of developing an analytical mind-set. It is only after the supervisee has had ample opportunity to analyze the lesson and respond to the observed data that discussion of strengths and weaknesses and exploration of possibilities for future growth are appropriate. If necessary, evaluative statements can be made at this stage, but in all likelihood the supervisee will have analyzed the lesson appropriately. If, after ample time is provided, supervisees do not self-analyze convincingly, it must be concluded that they are probably not suited to teaching. The supervisee may be disappointed but will experience greater feelings of failure in the future if he or she continues in the profession.

It is the supervisee who should determine the degree of readiness for any given task, as well as prepare for self-analysis. Asking for information, and receiving it from the supervisor or other reliable sources, should be viewed as a privilege by the supervisee.

The supervisor who responds with evaluations, good or bad, without first listening to the self-analysis is establishing a hierarchial relationship. In such relationships, the chief task is to please the 'boss.' This has short-term benefits at best. A major disadvantage is that the relationship between supervisor and supervisee often becomes clouded with suspicion, mistrust, and fear (p. 15). Not only is this harmful to the learner, but a person judged by other people will be likely to sit in judgment on others as well.

Redekopp explains that where students self-initiate and self-analyze,

the supervisee will feel free to develop talents and skills most suited to the self. This places creativity at the core of the developmental process. After all, the creative minds of philosophers, inventors, and artists functioned most effectively whenever they freed themselves from expectations of other people. This does not imply disrespect for other people. As a matter of fact, respect for self, as well as others, is the foundation on which this entire discussion rests. (p. 15)

The learners need to practise positive self-assertiveness, which is the ability to direct personal actions and communications responsibly. It is free of negatives like stubbornness, obstinacy, or defiance. Self-initiation cannot thrive in an environment where power-plays are the norm.

Redekopp cautions:

Careful preparation is necessary if performance is to be analyzed success-fully. The preparation requires that the decisions made will lead to the establishment of reasonable objectives. A precise plan of action must be formulated in order to successfully achieve the objectives.

Since it is humanly impossible to establish reasonable objectives at all times, the careful preparation will make it possible to change an objective found inappropriate during the application, and substitute a more appro-priate one. Since the decision to change objectives is based on careful preparation, the process of self-analysis will remain in place. In most cases it will result in more positive self-analysis. (pp. 57, 58)

What makes this process of self-initiation and self-analysis so valuable is its inherent fairness. No amount of writing, philosophizing, or arguing will ever be as convincing as successful modelling. The proper application of the concept will convince the supervisees. A positive life-force will develop and people observing the process will be drawn to it.

Redekopp concludes:

> There is no global, simple way in which individuals will feel safe to make decisions for themselves. What seems probable is that an accepting environment will remove much of the fear of rejection. The feeling of acceptance will develop in a setting in which 'others' model respect, caring, listening, and taking responsibility for self. The ideal relationship finds its strengths in a setting which frees the self and the others to be what they were meant to be. (p. 77)

Self-Initiation and Self-Analysis and Native Educational Values Compared

This brief overview of the salient points of Professor Redekopp's theory of evaluation indicates many similarities between it and Native educational philosophy and cultural values. (Italicized statements are derived from Redekopp 1989.)

Non-judgmental environment. The ethic of non-interference as a way of thinking and acting sets Native cultures apart from the formal societal expectations and prescriptions of Euro-Canadian society. Every discussion on differences in culture and cultural values mentions this ethic as a crucial part of a world-view which Europeans cannot understand or accept. It was antithetical to the missionary view of converting others to what then was a very narrow interpretation of Christianity (Sealey and Kirkness 1973; Sealey 1980; Johnston 1976; Manuel and Posluns 1974).

Feedback based on observational data. Too often evaluation in our present educational systems is based on punishment. For example, poor attendance in class is overlooked because exam results will weed out those who have not acquired the requisite information, or marks are deducted from a paper because it is handed in late. Our acceptance of 50 per cent as the magic passing figure shows that our achievement standards are very artificial and very low. Observed data will point out whether the trainee teacher is ready to be trusted with other people's children. No-one would want to live by traditional ways if it were acceptable to upset a canoe 50 per cent of the time. Nor should it be acceptable if a teacher performs a task adequately only 50 per cent of the time.

A willingness to make decisions for self and accept the responsibility for the results of the decisions. Elders, for example, will not interfere with the way a person sets up a tent, but will advise and help if requested. If they observe someone setting up a tent carelessly they will not interfere and say 'You will be sorry!' If the occupants get wet, they have to accept that and cope with the consequences. In comparison, there are very few consequences when a student achieves a C grade rather than an A. The major consequence in our highly competitive education system is that the C person will be devalued and made to feel inadequate because all the rewards go to the A person.

Supervisors must be non-judgmental but must understand the trainees in order to offer feedback in the most efficient way possible. Elders will continue to teach and search for ways to teach until learners acquire the required tasks. It is generally believed in many Native cultures that teaching must be presented in four different ways to ensure that learners have experienced the lesson in a manner that will help each learner to remember. This thorough learning was essential in traditional societies so as to safeguard the welfare of the group.

Supervisee is free to make decisions based on observed data. Elders do not coerce people into learning but demonstrate and wait for learners to attempt tasks when they feel ready. The learners' decisions are not criticized but the learner must take responsibility for the outcome, for example, leaky tents. So a learner can make decisions based on outcome without having to wait for someone else to make decisions. Elders do not tell learners to fix tents; if learners do not learn from their mistakes they will merely get wet again the next time it rains.

Indecision results when a dependency relationship is fostered. In areas that potentially affect the common good of the group, elders do make decisions. Within the prescribed parameters, however, independent action is expected and fostered.

It is recommended that the aspiring teacher be allowed to practise in an environment in which it is safe to make decisions. Elders encourage and support; they do not hover and give advice or criticize. A learner is given ample time to work on skills without supervision or evaluation. Even wrong decisions, and the person's right to make them, are respected.

The supervisor must accept the responsibility for establishing the climate in which the supervisee can take responsibility for self. Elders use comparatively few words when they instruct. They model continuously, remaining as unobtrusive as possible in order to give the learner maximum freedom to learn in the most productive personal way.

Self-initiation is a process, not a product. Everything a trainee does is part of the learning process in Native culture and therefore a final exam or evaluation is not necessary.

Each self has to find its own best way of coping with daily challenges. This is basic to the non-interference ethic.

Because the capacity to make decisions increases with practice, it is important that one exercise the right to make decisions for self as often as possible. Again, the non-interference ethic allows independent decision-making constantly.

If someone else has made the decision, the individual will escape from responsibility by blaming the bad results on someone else. It is difficult to blame the elders because their teaching techniques are so loving, so non-directive, and so non-coercive!

The supervisee must initiate the post-learning conference. Elders wait to be approached; they rarely initiate structured teaching.

Judgment statements from observers, good or bad, negate the whole concept of developing an analytical mind-set. Elders do not make encouraging noises like, 'Good try!' or 'Well done!' Rather, it is expected that observed data will inform the learner of how productive performance has been.

When the supervisee has had ample opportunity to analyze the lesson and respond to the observed data, then, and only then, is it appropriate to talk about strengths and considerations. Elders are always willing to talk and instruct when a learner approaches them to learn something.

Some supervisees will not use self-analysis convincingly. When this does not improve with time, it must be concluded that they are not suited to the task of teaching. Anyone lacking the requisite skills will not be affirmed in their undertaking by the elders.

The perceptions of the supervisee are the key factor in the degree of readiness for a given task. The supervisee's state of readiness for self-analysis is also important. Elders do not push learners into learning, but wait to instruct the learner when the learner signifies readiness.

Asking for information, and receiving it, becomes a privilege. Young Native people, even those who have been raised in cities, understand that being instructed by elders is a rare privilege, denied them since Euro-Canadian education began to dominate the Canadian educational scene. The custom of taking a gift of tobacco is tangible evidence that Native people recognize the privilege of being instructed.

In a hierarchial relationship, the significant task is to please the 'boss.' The relationship often becomes clouded with suspicion, mistrust, and fear. In contrast, relationships with elders are characterized by love, trust, and acceptance.

Respect for self, as well as others, is the foundation on which this entire discussion rests. Respect characterizes all elder teaching. This is a two-way process – the learners respect the elders and the elders respect the learners.

Self-initiation and self-analysis requires that others will desist from making decisions for someone else. Elders do not generally make decisions for others.

Positive self-assertiveness is defined as the ability to direct personal actions responsibly and it is free of stubbornness, obstinacy, and defiance. These negative emotions are not aroused when elders teach since their non-interference ethic makes them non-judgmental and non-coercive.

Power-plays. Struggles over power are the most destructive aspect of our educational systems today; they have no place in the Native educational system.

Another requirement is to solicit feedback from reliable sources whenever possible. Elder feedback is constant, non-judgmental, and very generously given.

Careful preparation is necessary if performance is to be analyzed successfully. If objectives are found to be inappropriate, more appropriate ones can be substituted. Elders model careful preparation, informed flexibility, patience in adversity, and deliberate, carefully pondered plans which have been discussed with participants.

What makes the process particularly valuable is its inherent fairness. Because there is no power-play, no competition, elder instruction is intrinsically fair. There is no attempt to force inadequate people 'out' in Native communities; rather the concern is to help them develop their abilities.

While supervisees experience personal disappointment, it certainly does not compare with feelings of failure. The concept of failure, as manifested in Euro-Canadian education, does not exist in elder instruction. A person may 'fail' one task but be highly successful in other tasks or other areas of life, and there is generally no deadline by which a task has to be mastered.

No amount of writing, philosophizing, or arguing will ever be as convincing as successful modelling. People observing the process as it is being applied will sense the positive life-force and will be drawn to it. Elders model every aspect of their teachings. Native young people need the opportunity to move from an alienating education system back to the system where there are ideal relationships, and they can find strength in a setting which frees the self and others to be what they were meant to be. The importance of involving elders in the development of young Natives today is being recognized and is incorporated in many educational programs.

Conclusion

Following Professor Redekopp's model of evaluation or a variant thereof, or even adopting some of its principles, could dramatically reform university education as it exists today. But that is an ambitious undertaking, so perhaps it is more realistic to consider its use specifically where an attempt is being made to bring elder wisdom and university wisdom together.

At the Canadian Indian Teacher Education Programs (CITEP) conference at McGill University in June 1992, the possibility of using traditional education methods to train contemporary teachers was a recurring theme. In her concluding evaluation of the conference, Judy Cote, from the TEP at Nipissing University College, pointed out that finding ways to bring the wisdom of the elders and the wisdom of the university together is, indeed, the challenge for the 1990s.

References

Harper, Victor. 1989. Learning from the land to the school: The Bear Lake, Stevenson River Project. *Networks* 2 (2)

Holt, John. 1964. *How children fail*. New York: Dell

Indian Tribes of Manitoba. 1971. *Wahbung: Our tomorrows*. Winnipeg: Manitoba Indian Brotherhood

Johnston, Basil. 1976. *Ojibway heritage*. Toronto: McClelland and Stewart

Manuel, George, and Michael Posluns. 1974. *The fourth world: An Indian reality*. New York: Free Press

National Indian Brotherhood. 1972. *Indian control of Indian education*. National Indian Brotherhood

Redekopp, J.P. 1989. *Supervision based on self-initiation and self-analysis*. Winnipeg: Redekopp Consulting, and Edmonton: Life-Role Development Group

Sealey, D.B. 1980. *The education of Native peoples in Manitoba*. Winnipeg: University of Manitoba Press

Sealey, D.B., and Verna Kirkness. 1973. *Indians without tipis*. Agincourt: Book Society of Canada

11
Non-Native Teachers Teaching in Native Communities
John Taylor

Presently in Canada hundreds, perhaps thousands, of non-Native teachers work on reserves. Each year, due to the high turnover of non-Native teachers, many more are hired and begin teaching in Native communities. Ninety per cent of Native children in this country will, at one time or another, be taught by a non-Native teacher, and many of these children will receive most of their education from non-Native teachers. The Native student's self-image, perception of Native/non-Native interaction, and chance of graduating will all be influenced by their non-Native teachers. The school itself will be affected; its atmosphere, vitality, and community support will be influenced by the non-Natives working there. The effect that the non-Native teacher has on a school and its students is obviously not beyond control. However, to direct that influence the educational authorities, school administrators, and teachers themselves must all be aware of the non-Native teacher's role in the school and community.

This chapter is based on my personal experiences while teaching at two band-operated schools in western Canada. During the first three years of my teaching, I gathered information not only from the two schools at which I taught but also from numerous other band-operated schools which I visited. In the course of these visits and several conferences and workshops, I verified my belief that my experiences were not isolated occurrences.

After a short period as a teacher, I realized that virtually no support or direction was available to new non-Native teachers on culturally appropriate teaching methods or materials. Furthermore, the school administration gave little thought to the role it wanted non-Native teachers to play in its school. It became readily apparent that the majority of teachers were unsure of their role both in and out of school. Non-Native teachers begin their job with little support or previous training, and the role they play is never directly discussed with the people for whom they work.

Teacher Motivation and Predisposition to Change

Non-Native teachers entering a reserve school should not simply begin teaching and let their role in the school be shaped by circumstance. The relationship they develop with students, other teachers, parents, and the community will greatly influence how they are perceived, and this will alter their effectiveness as teachers. Many, perhaps most, non-Native teachers accept teaching positions on reserves with the intention of completing a couple of years before landing the job they really want. Often non-Native teachers envision their time at a reserve school as an 'interesting, learning experience.' Non-Native teachers sometimes believe that if they can survive this experience, they can survive anything. They hope that these two or three years will equip them to gain employment in a community (usually a non-Native southern community) where they plan to settle permanently. This prelude to their career may also enable them to pay off a student loan or accumulate the down payment for a house. Still other non-Native teachers see teaching on a reserve as an adventure that they can relate to their children and grandchildren.

The above scenarios have one preconceived notion in common – the reserve school is a temporary station to achieve or begin to achieve personal goals. Of course, this is not as selfish as it sounds. As teachers fresh to the profession, these non-Native people may feel strongly committed to their pupils and will quite often invest a lot of themselves in their work. The difficulty does not lie in commitment but in the teachers' perception of their role as teachers.

It is fair to say that non-Native teachers generally perceive themselves as dedicated professionals. If I do my job well that is sufficient; I have satisfied my employer and myself and I have given the child good, caring instruction. A young single teacher began work in a band-run school on the prairies after completing a Master's degree. For three years this teacher gave excellent instruction to her students. She worked tirelessly, regularly working from six a.m. to six p.m. and half-days on Saturdays and Sundays. While she found the students difficult to teach, her dedication to their learning was questioned by none. This teacher lived in a teacherage right beside the school. She had no car and walked to school daily. Other than that she rarely left her apartment. She did not interact with the community and only visited one or two other non-Native teachers occasionally. She completely isolated herself from the community, even though it was very active socially.

The reason for her seclusion was risk avoidance. She once indicated that she did not feel safe going onto the reserve. She also stated that she did not want to do anything or be seen in places that the school board might regard as inappropriate. Perhaps she might have risked community involvement if this was to be her permanent community. However, this teacher, like so many others, simply saw reserve teaching as a prelude to *her* career in *her* chosen community. Risks can come in the form of friendships and ties. Why should she become part of a community she was probably going to leave forever?

This type of risk-taking became very real for me when I lost a close friend who lived on the reserve. He had died a tragic death from exposure and I remember thinking at his funeral how the other non-Native teacher, who chose to avoid risks, could not feel the pain I felt that day.

This particular teacher left the band school after three years. She returned home where a new car awaited her. My point is not to condemn the teacher – far from it, for she was an excellent teacher in many ways. My point is that her preconception of her role as a teacher at a band-run school limited what she could do while she was there.

Interaction between non-Native teacher and community is important because it helps define how that community and its students perceive the teacher. Although few students express the thought openly, they are concerned about what their non-Native teacher thinks and feels about their reserve. They want their teacher to like and respect the community. Obvious isolation is interpreted by students as rejection of the community and, indirectly, of themselves. One student questioned this teacher's unwillingness to participate in the community and simply concluded that she did not like the place. A student needs to feel respected in order to give respect. Non-Native teachers will benefit by seeing the community in which they teach as their community; that is, the community in which they live. Participation in community daily life as well as major community events may cause the non-Native teacher to want to be part of reserve life and will, therefore, assist in establishing mutual respect between teacher and community.

However, if the initial involvement by the non-Native teacher is unpleasant, the teacher may withdraw and become negative. The reality is that the non-Native person may be met with hostility when attempting to enter the reserve's social milieu. On one occasion, a teacher went to a local bar whose clientele was largely Native. He became the focus of a Native customer's attention and abuse and was eventually attacked by him. He had to defend himself and leave the establishment.

Such incidents may lead non-Native teachers to view social interaction with the reserve as undesirable. Such stories often build up over the years and are passed down from year to year by non-Native staff members. These stories serve to deter socialization outside the circle of non-Native teachers. However, negative social experience does not have to result in avoidance of further community involvement. If it is understood that cross-cultural situations can and most likely will produce uncomfortable initial circumstances, the discomfort will not be as great. In this case the non-Native teacher will be more willing to attempt community participation a second time.

Most communities have several points of entry. The teacher needs to consider other, perhaps more suitable, avenues. Teachers' involvement will benefit their work and most likely their day-to-day lives. Each teacher is different and each should find a different way to participate in a community. The point is that the students and the community must know that you respect them and want to support them. In turn you may receive community support.

Culture Shock

For many non-Native teachers these simple suggestions are very hard to accept. The majority of non-Native teachers experience varying degrees of culture shock upon arriving at their jobs, and this shock may never leave them. Awareness of the concept of culture shock can make the adjustment easier. Culture shock is a state of mind. It occurs when a person is faced with an unfamiliar environment. The person no longer has the usual set of social stimuli to encourage appropriate behaviour. The result is often poor communication and strained relations.

One of my colleagues from eastern Canada was unhappy with life on the reserve. I asked her if she wanted to go home and her answer was 'No, just anywhere else.' This surprised and confused me. I told my friend from the community who was the Native Studies teacher, and he simply commented that it was culture shock. For this woman from eastern Canada, the reserve was frustratingly different from what she had experienced before. She had just left university and a very active life. As an outgoing and energetic person she was probably used to a great deal of socializing activity. She probably felt her social life had almost stopped and blamed this circumstance on the reserve. By saying 'anywhere else,' she expressed the perception that her discontent was not her fault. This is a very common reaction. To acknowledge that the fault might lie in her inability or unwillingness to adjust would have been difficult.

A similar example involved a non-Native couple who had been living on reserve for many years and continually found fault in the community around them. They would often verbalize their complaints to other non-Native teachers, expecting, and usually receiving, affirmation that certain things in the community were inadequate. These complaint sessions are what Berger and Luckman, in *The Social Construction Of Reality*, describe as 'Legitimation or Universe-maintenance.'[1] Legitimation is a process by which people justify their reality or their concepts of 'the way things should be.' Simply put, it is a method by which individuals convince themselves that their way is the right way. This process is necessary for people to protect their symbolic universe, which is a socially produced set of realities within which a group of people exist.

For five years this couple continued to plant flower beds around their house and find fault in others for not doing so. They simply could not accept that the particular community did not plant flower beds and that this was not a matter of right or wrong. Admission that the absence of flower beds was acceptable would threaten their reality, which had always included flower beds.

The male partner ran a student organization and was receiving very little parental support or involvement. Native parents generally hesitate, for obvious historical reasons, to become involved with schools. Adding to his difficulties was his failure to involve himself in the community and to get to know people and parents. Faced with minimal support from parents, the teacher was unable to refrain from passing judgment. He lashed out at the students in an assembly, asking, 'What is wrong with your parents?' The result of his not understanding his role as a non-Native teacher and of not nurturing his position in the community was painfully clear. This teacher's expression of frustration offended Native staff members and struck a blow at the students' self-image. It is an established educational principle that developing a positive self-image in students is important. In a Native community it is even more so. Many of these students are struggling with their identity and that identity should be a positive one. Students have to contend with prejudice, stereotypes, and lower standards of living, which affect their self-image. A non-Native teacher can either affirm or help to offset many of these negative influences.

The role of a teacher is complex and multilayered. The role of a non-Native teacher in a Native community is even more complex given the unique situation on reserves. The reserve presents the non-Native teacher with a different culture and different sets of cultural values and behaviour. The non-Native teacher's role is also more complex because the Native student faces more complex difficulties. The Native student must deal with such challenges as lack of parental involvement, multiple social problems, an unstable teaching population, and a general lack of resources. Acceptance of and interest in the student's community and way of life should provide the non-Native teacher with a better understanding of the student's difficulties.

The following example illustrates the need for non-Native teachers to be involved in and understand the community where they teach. The school concerned has well over 500 students and approximately forty-five staff, including roughly fifteen non-Native teachers. The remaining Native staff are largely from the community. A group of new non-Native teachers started together at this band-run school on the prairies. Several of them had known each other at university and most of them were from eastern Canada. It did not take long for these teachers to become close and slowly they began to form a community within a community. They started a supper club where they had weekly meals together, each taking turns as host. These social gatherings originated in past shared experiences but eventually became a 'defence' against what they perceived as a different and confusing community. At these meals they had a chance to maintain their universe – they could reminisce about home and the way things 'should be.' This was also their chance to complain about the community and the people and to discuss how strange things were. These meetings were necessary to remind them that although many things were different around them, they could continue to do things as they always had and be sure that they were right and correct. Before these teachers arrived, other non-Native teachers had met and shared similar attitudes, a common phenomenon on reserves across Canada.

A band, as a graduation present, was sending all of the graduating students on a week-long trip to attend an 'All Chiefs' conference in Alberta. All their expenses were paid and the students were given spending money. Several of the non-Native teachers found this arrangement amazing, outlandish, and alien. At the next staff meeting a few were heard to say that 'the students are spoiled and given everything and they don't have to work for anything.' Many of the Native teachers were angry and felt that the non-Native teachers had no business to comment. The Native teachers did not confront the people who had commented but the incident was discussed in several private conversations. The non-Native teachers were uncomfortable with a public gift which would have been inappropriate and unacceptable in their communities, even though they may have been given large gifts by their parents and perhaps been supported while in university. They failed to acknowledge the differences between the communities and accept the differences in cultural values. Many of the Native parents were unemployed and could not provide their children with something like this trip. The non-Native teachers could not see that in this different society the band often provided for everybody in the knowledge that many students could not be rewarded by their families.

The non-Native teachers wanted things to conform to their past experiences. They could not understand a different society and culture. This is a manifestation of culture shock. This is why they stuck together and did not enter their new community. To enter the community would be to accept it and to accept it would be to reject their own quite different pasts. Instead, the non-Native teacher simply tries to survive for two or three years in this 'crazy place.'

One non-Native teacher was speaking about a non-Native colleague who had been in the community two years longer than her and who was planning to leave. The first teacher said, 'I don't blame her for wanting to leave, she must want to get on with her life. It must be hard for her being alone here. I would have gone crazy by now if my husband wasn't here. Well maybe not, because Pat and Sarah and Becky are here.' This teacher regarded herself as isolated within the community. She also saw the other teacher as alone even though there were 1,000 people living around her. She felt her sanity was intact only because her husband and other non-Native teachers were there to support her or, as Berger and Luckman would say, to help her maintain her universe.[2]

To be successful, non-Native teachers entering Native communities must do so with an open mind, aware that life will be different and that different and new ways do not have to be threatening. With this acceptance, involvement in the life of the community becomes possible.

Reactions to Culture Shock

The examples above demonstrate non-Native teachers' ways of coping with culture shock, ways of maintaining their reality.

> Seeking to defend his senses against the shock waves of an alien world, he reaches for, or tries to construct, a culture shock absorber.[3]

> In order to retain some sanity, the visitor responds to Culture shock in one or all of the following four ways: escape, confrontation, encapsulation, integration.[4]

The most common method of dealing with culture shock for non-Native teachers is escape. Non-Native teachers simply avoid as much contact with the local Native community as possible. Teachers will spend free time in isolation doing what is familiar from 'home.' Perhaps they will spend their leisure time with other non-Native teachers, thus avoiding the shock of trying to communicate with and involve themselves in the different culture. The young woman from eastern Canada who spent most of her time at home and in her class working vigorously is a good example of this coping mechanism. Quite often, non-Native teachers visit friends or relatives in the closest city whenever possible. This 'family in the city' provides a further and more efficient escape route for non-Native teachers. The authors of *Culture Shock* describe the reasoning behind escaping: the visitors feel their stay 'is temporary; it is not worth trying to overcome the problems because in one or two years we will be leaving.'[5]

The second absorber of culture shock is confrontation. This is described by Berger and Luckman as the reality maintenance necessary to confirm the non-Native teacher's subjective reality. Subjective reality is personal understanding of and confidence in the reality of one's life and way of living. If the non-Native teacher's subjective reality is to remain intact, he/she must challenge the opposing culture which by its very existence calls into question the original reality. Confrontation is achieved largely through conversation and complaining. Robert and Nanthapa Cooper describe confrontation in Thailand:

> Some visitors are always complaining mostly to other visitors who feel the same way, but sometimes to Thais. Stated or implied in their criticisms of Thai values and behaviour is an assumption that things are better where they came from. Not-too-deep-down-inside they enjoy feeling superior to the world around them. They make sense; the Thai world 'doesn't make sense.' For these visitors Thai culture is there to fight against and to succeed in spite of.[6]

The Coopers here cite a similar sentiment to that of some non-Native teachers who live on reserve. Confrontation may take the form of 'complaint sessions' in the evening at non-Native teachers' homes or may be directed openly at the community such as that by the teacher who asked the students 'What is wrong with your parents?' Whether conversational confrontation is direct or indirect, it is the non-Native teachers' main method of protecting their reality. As Berger and Luckman point out, 'the most important vehicle of reality-maintenance is conversation.'[7]

One disturbing aspect of confrontation, particularity in teachers, is the fact that some non-Native teachers enjoy feeling superior to the world around them. This is not uncommon. In fact, for some non-Native teachers it is reason enough to remain in a particular community for a considerable time. On one occasion, two non-Native teachers were in direct verbal (and almost physical) confrontation with some community members after a hockey game. When the confrontation was over, one non-Native teacher remarked to the other, 'Don't worry about it, they're not going to

Hawaii for vacation.' This need to feel superior was part of their coping with culture shock.

Encapsulation is the practice of creating a 'culture bubble' in which to exist.[8] This could be a sports night, a supper club, or even a movie night. The purpose of these events is to give non-Native teachers on reserve the chance to simulate life 'back home,' to talk about similar interests or indulge similar emotions. Often these gatherings provide like-minded people an opportunity to find fault with the community and its different culture. If a non-Native teacher defends the local culture, he or she meets opposition. The non-Native group of teachers does not invite dissent and its dissatisfaction is made clear. Quite often, first-year non-Native teachers are more optimistic about and more tolerant towards their new community, but the veterans are quick to inform them that their optimism will fade into the so-called 'reality' of reserve life.

Encapsulation is desirable to non-Native teachers for one major reason: it saves mental energy. It does not require the ongoing effort to exist and operate in a different culture. Learning what to do and say in the new Native culture can often be stressful for the teacher. Socializing with new people always requires great effort. When this meeting occurs in a new culture, the social considerations are multiplied. Furthermore, it is not unusual for Native community members to test non-Natives by subjecting them to social discomfort. In one of my first social encounters a Native man put me through a range of experiences from awkward questions to racial remarks. His attack was so extreme that other Natives expressed anger at his behaviour. This same man eventually became a good friend and now displays far greater sensitivity towards me. Whatever the cause of the discomfort, the non-Native teacher will usually find it easier to avoid the situation.

The final coping mechanism is integration. The authors of *Culture Shock* use the term to mean 'to fit together.' They point out that 'integration is not assimilation' and that both parties retain their cultural identities.[9] Integration means making an effort to become part of the community, but it does not mean trying to become an Indian. Perhaps the non-Native teacher can go out and meet people and become involved in community events. This may simply mean joining in the local cribbage tournament or going to pow-wows or attending square dancing competitions. As mentioned earlier, this involvement may not be welcomed by all members of the community. Perhaps involvement may even be discouraged by the school administration. On one reserve school, the superintendent informed me privately that I was getting far too involved in the community and openly questioned certain of my friendships with individuals and families. Integration can be difficult and requires an effort. It is also necessary to avoid relying exclusively on other non-Native teachers as a source of reality maintenance.

The major difference between escape, confrontation, encapsulation, and integration is that the first three are largely naturally occurring sub-conscious actions. Integration is a conscious attempt to avoid the adverse consequences of culture shock. It is important for non-Native teachers to consciously attempt community involvement because their culture shock will be felt as much by students as by the teachers themselves.

Communication Difficulties between High- and Low-Context Cultures

The difficulties of adjusting to a new culture will vary depending on the two cultures involved. They become more obvious in light of Edward T. Hall's concepts of high- and low-context cultures in *Beyond Culture*. 'A high context (HC) communication or message is one in which most of the information is either in the physical context or internalized in the person, while very little is in the coded, explicit, transmitted part of the message. A low context (LC) communication is just the opposite; i.e., the mass of the information is vested in the explicit code.'[10] High-context culture tends to rely less on the spoken word and more on the context or on existing, non-verbal information. A great deal is left unsaid and situational factors deliver the greater part of an intended meaning. Low-context culture is highly verbal, most messages being sent by conversation. It will belabour explanation rather than risk unsuccessful communication.

Traditional Native Canadian culture is a high-context culture while Euro-Canadian society relies on low-context communication. The extent of culture shock is greatly increased when one culture is high context and the other is low context.

Non-Native teachers often experience frustration when they first communicate with the Native community around them. They often wish their Native colleagues would explain themselves more clearly and fully. Or perhaps the non-Native teacher receives only a single-line answer from a student. The teacher expects more and rehearses all the things that could be said, sometimes speaking the unspoken words or asking further questions to elicit further verbal explanations. Native colleagues or students grow puzzled and annoyed that their explanations are not adequate. They assume that the context or non-verbal information is obvious. Hall points out that 'it is often necessary in an intercultural situation for the LC person to have to go into much more detail than he is used to when he is dealing with HC people.'[11]

Not only is the context of communication between high- and low-context cultures different but so is the style. In my first month of teaching, a couple of my students wrote in their journals that I spoke too quickly and too loudly. Soon I learned to adjust and my students were more comfortable with my new style. I returned home for a visit. The first evening, my parents held an open house for friends and the usual debate about politics and religion raged. I soon experienced discomfort, because everyone was speaking very loudly, even yelling. Furthermore, speakers showed little regard for each other and often cut others off in mid-sentence. The discomfort was temporary and in a day or two I was back to my old conversational style.

A good example of the meeting of low- and high-context cultures is the staff meeting at reserve schools. The usual scenario in these meetings is that non-Native staff dominate the dialogue and often attempt to impose their standards and plans on the school. For Native staff members, dialogue is often unnecessary because they know from the context the direction or even the eventual outcome of a given issue. The drawback of this lack of communication is that non-Native and even Native administrators are often won over by the impressive and extensive dialogue of non-Native teachers. An example is a discussion on the eventual passing or failing of a student. The Native teacher's opinion was solicited and he simply stated briefly that the child should pass. Two non-Native teachers gave what they considered multiple reasons for the obvious failure of this student and the student did subsequently fail.

Lack of awareness of different styles of dialogue between the two cultures is a problem for both cultures. In my experience, Native teachers and administrators fall into the same trap as non-Native teachers and administrators. The faulty assumption is often shared by everyone that lengthy and strongly asserted opinions by non-Native teachers must be more valid than concise and often plainly stated opinions of Native colleagues.

While this low-context style can be effective, it usually causes great trouble for the non-Native teacher in a Native community. A low-context person often requires, and as a result provides, full explanations. In short, the low-context non-Native teacher can rarely keep his/her thoughts to him/herself, as witness the example of the non-Native teachers who opposed the trip for graduating students. They felt it necessary to express their disapproval at a staff meeting and angered many of the Native staff. As Hall states, 'If the LC person interacting with a high context culture does not really think things through and try to foresee all contingencies, he's headed for trouble.'[12] The 'trouble' results from conflicting realities.

The non-Native teachers had no experience of such gifts (which in part represented a cultural norm of expressed generosity), while the Native teacher had experienced them personally. Everything was satisfactory until non-Native teachers felt impelled to verbalize their disapproval of this novel experience.

Student Views of the Non-Native Teacher's Role

As discussed earlier, it is important for students to see that the teacher accepts and takes part in their community. This is particularly true of the junior/senior high school student. Primary/elementary school students are not sufficiently aware of the world to gauge their teacher's acceptance of and involvement in their community. However, they are still affected by their teacher's feelings and beliefs about the community. Lack of acceptance by the non-Native teacher of the student's community will very likely impair the effectiveness of learning.

Part of the difficulty lies in incompatible perceptions of the teacher's role. Non-Native teachers often come from large communities to teach on a reserve and do not see community involvement as part of their role as teachers. This role they see as school-centred, so that involvement in activities outside the classroom is not an issue for them. For many non-Native teachers their personal experience as students would have included little or no social contact with their teachers. The Native student perceives the role of the teacher more holistically. On one occasion, I told a student of my plans to travel to the neighbouring province for the weekend. He surprised me by asking if he could come along. For him the request was not at all unusual and demonstrated his view of what my role as a teacher entailed. For non-Native teachers this request might seem aggressive and the idea of such a joint trip inappropriate.

If a non-Native teacher harbours negative or, at best, neutral feelings towards the community, it is difficult for the teacher to keep them from students. The students either consciously or subconsciously detect the teacher's unwillingness to participate in reserve life. Many non-Native teachers on reserves who dislike the communities they work with continue to work there for various reasons. The students are less likely to respond to this type of teacher. There is little basis for trust between teacher and student and therefore a weak basis for teaching. Students rarely explain the reasons for the lack of trust; instead they simply refuse to work with the teacher. The excuse given by the student may be something as simple as 'she's/he's a jerk.' Often students will not say more because they may simply not understand why they dislike the teacher.

Even if a teacher has carefully planned a lesson, the student may not be receptive to learning if the student-teacher relationship is weak. By contrast, if there is a solid relationship as a basis for learning, the teacher has a foundation for demanding more from the student. 'After establishing positive interpersonal relationships at the beginning of the year, these teachers became demanding, as an aspect of their personal concern in a reciprocal obligation to further learning.'[13]

It is common for non-Native teachers to find one or more of their students reaching out and trying to establish friendships. In many cases the student's home or social life is such that he/she longs for friends, a 'big brother or sister' to look to for advice and companionship. As explained earlier, any involvement in the community carries elements of risk, and someone may become jealous or upset at this friendship. However, a student who reaches out should never be denied. This is an opportunity to help a student and build a relationship in which the teacher as a friend can ask the student to achieve and excel. Obviously life is not always so simple and straightforward, but this is an effective approach which, while it may not ensure success, will enhance the chances of it.

Native Curriculum Content

The use of Native content in the curriculum is another way for non-Native teachers to develop a positive relationship with students. While it is fully recognized that Native content is not only desirable but also necessary for effective teaching and learning in reserve schools, this goal has not been fully achieved. Many non-Native teachers feel that time spent on Native content materials is time spent poorly because they are prevented from achieving their goals for the year and students are prevented from accumulating the required academic knowledge by year's end. Some non-Native teachers do include Native content but give it only a small amount of time in their anxiety to move on to the 'important' material.

Part of the reason for excluding or glossing over Native content is because many non-Native teachers are uncomfortable with the material. They find it difficult to understand or relate to materials dealing with Native people and therefore avoid the discomfort. Also the non-Native teacher does not see the value in the material because it was never part of their own training. Once non-Native teachers recognize the worth of the material they will be more likely to take on the challenge of presenting it.

Native content is usually foreign to the non-Native teacher. First, teachers must locate and familiarize themselves with the material. Second, they must decide on an appropriate, effective way to present it. It is hard for the non-Native teacher to know what is appropriate and what is not. The real challenge, however, comes in presenting the material.

The non-Native teacher will receive varying levels of acceptance from students and parents. Quite often the students' immediate reaction to the presentation of Native material by non-Natives is discomfort and withdrawal. Their faces seem to say: 'Why is this white person talking to us about Indians?' With time, some students relax and begin to participate but others continue to display displeasure. It is important to let students teach you what they know about the topic. Teachers may be more knowledgeable about a topic they have researched, but the student is dealing in life experiences and knows things that non-Native persons do not know. For example, I was discussing the high number of Native inmates in federal prisons with a class and presented several 'textbook reasons' for this situation. One student told of a crime and the subsequent incarceration of a relative. The student was making his learning relevant to himself. Students must be allowed to discover their own levels of comfort in dealing with a topic which is essentially about themselves.

Many complications may arise in dealing with Native curriculum content, and these will vary from community to community. Non-Native teachers must be aware of the type of content appropriate to the community they are in. In one community school, discussion of anything to do with Native culture was known by everyone to be unacceptable. Pictures of eagles and teepees were considered appropriate but anything more was discouraged. Discussions of the sweat lodge or medicine wheel or sweet grass did not occur in that school. In fact the school was once closed down because of a confrontation between traditional and Christian people on the reserve. Today, Easter services are held in the gym and square dancing is encouraged in the cafeteria, but no drumming and sweet grass is allowed. Non-Native teachers may believe that more cultural teachings would benefit students but what they believe is irrelevant: their responsibility is to include Native content which is acceptable to the community. However, no community is homogeneous. Therefore, even appropriate Native content may still be met with resistance from some students and parents. Perhaps they wonder why more Native content is not being taught or why it is being taught at all. Providing satisfactory answers can be difficult.

In one instance I used a book in the classroom which presented some grim realities about Native life. The book was *In Search of April Raintree*.[14] It not only looked at some less attractive aspects of life for some Natives but also demonstrated the perseverance and determination of a person and a people. This book was a good vehicle for discussing how larger society had contributed to the emergence of some unappealing realities and what was being done to improve the situation.

One parent felt that this book should not be in the classroom because it made Native people look bad instead of presenting students with more positive examples. As well, some students were clearly uncomfortable with the topic and chuckled at certain parts of the book. I still felt that the book was worthwhile, in that it caused some students and perhaps parents to think about and attend to topics with which they were not comfortable. Finding Native content which is appropriate to a particular community and presenting it in an appealing way to students and parents is a difficult but necessary component of education in a reserve school.

Students may question and be uncomfortable with the Native content but in my experience the majority will eventually become interested and involved. They will respect the non-Native teacher for attempting to make their learning more appropriate and the student-teacher relationship will be strengthened.

Alcohol

Alcohol abuse is one of the most prominent issues on many reserves and may become a major issue for the non-Native teacher working on the reserve. Every teacher will need to make a decision about alcohol. Many non-Native teachers working on reserves are casual drinkers and are used to social drinking. While some non-Native teachers will have a relative or a friend with a drinking problem, few will come from a town which must deal with a community-wide alcohol problem. Many reserves do have such problems or the legacy of such problems. The superintendent of one band-run school told me that every family in the community 'had felt the negative effects of alcohol.'

The teacher will see first hand the difficulties that alcohol creates. At the primary/elementary level, behaviour problems manifest themselves as a result of parents who are abusers. At the senior high level the teacher will encounter sporadic attendance patterns and even students who already have a serious alcohol problem. For the non-Native teacher, accepting the seriousness of the alcohol issue within the community is important. It is also important to develop a well considered approach to the problem. For instance, what is the response to a senior student with a drinking problem? Will the non-Native teacher regard the problem as not his or hers but a community problem requiring a community solution? Teachers choosing to confront the issue of alcohol will do so in individual ways. Some may start youth groups which provide alcohol and drug education, others will simply attempt to advise and counsel receptive students. A common approach is to integrate related themes into the existing curriculum.

Although much can be done, many argue that the true test on alcohol for non-Native teachers is whether or not they themselves drink. It is probably true that most non-Native teachers working on reserves do drink alcohol. However, it is probably equally true that they do not drink in public where community members and students might see them. Their reason for this is that they are role models and should not display behaviour which they would not want their students to display. So these teachers often confine their drinking to small house parties or to trips home or to the city. Some non-Native teachers do not drink at all, usually for personal reasons, and it is often these who are most involved in attempts to combat the alcohol problem at the schools where they work.

Other non-Native teachers frequent local bars and attend parties on reserve. For these teachers, alcohol becomes a complex and sometimes overwhelming issue. They had previously visited bars and attended the odd party and had enjoyed this recreation without major controversy. Now they live in a small community where alcohol consumption never goes unnoticed. For the community, the teacher who 'goes out' will often become the focus of conversation, and will be asked numerous questions by students. For community members and students alike, most people they know who drink have drinking problems. Therefore, by association, the teacher who drinks has a drinking problem.

Suddenly, the teacher who is used to drinking without giving it much thought is persistently confronted by the issue of alcohol. The teacher will become acutely aware that his/her social drinking is noticed. A student who sees a teacher drinking will immediately assume that he/she is drunk. Some teachers resent having to adjust their lifestyles by either not drinking or drinking in private only.

A major concern of many school administrations is how to reduce and eliminate drinking among students. Many approaches to this problem are adopted, the most common being 'just say no.' While this is a sometimes successful approach it is not without its drawbacks. I do feel that other approaches should be considered. I have observed several alcohol education workshops for students. Often these involve various explanations of why a person should not drink. On one occasion two former alcoholics aggressively asserted that students who had begun to drink should quit. They spoke for an hour and it was apparent at the end that they had not made a connection with the students and had probably achieved very little. It was after this presentation that I began to think that 'just say no' was, perhaps, not the only valid approach. The reality is that the vast majority of students will begin, and continue, to drink so why do educators continue to push a message that is not going to be followed? When we realized that students were having sex, we took practical measures to educate them in that area. Why, then, do we not educate students about disciplined drinking? We could instruct them on appropriate reasons for drinking, times to drink, and amounts to drink. This is where a teacher who does drink could discuss and model appropriate social drinking. Students might relate to this educator and type of education more effectively. In band-run schools where alcohol abuse is a major issue, this is another approach for teachers to consider.

Because alcohol is such a major issue it engenders many strong opinions. Most Native communities have a number of reformed alcoholics. One such person strongly expressed his feeling that alcohol abuse was a big problem for the community and that anyone who drank, even socially, was part of the problem. A non-Native teacher may feel that alcohol is not a personal problem but still must answer to the view that even casual consumption contributes to a community-wide problem.

Every non-Native teacher fits somewhere into the community issue of alcohol abuse and must take a position with which they feel comfortable. It is a complex and difficult issue but it is important that the non-Native teacher is fully informed of it. Then the teacher must decide on their own about personal alcohol consumption and their approach to alcohol education.

Conclusion

I was asked by the superintendent of a band-run school what I thought my role in his community was. I had been giving that exact question a lot of thought. It was then that I realized that he had been giving it a lot of thought as well. I knew that our concepts of my role would not be the same. In fact, other teachers, Native and non-Native, had ideas on where I fitted into the community. Administrators, parents, and students also had their own perception of what non-Native teachers were to the community and where they fitted in. Everyone's beliefs varied and everyone's reasons for those beliefs varied.

In the end, I had to decide what role I would play in that community. That decision was mine but it was not a decision taken in isolation. It is important that each non-Native teacher takes time to consider the role he or she will play in the Native community where he or she teaches. The multilayered dynamics require a great deal of ongoing consideration. Constant analysis and redefinition is required.

It is also essential that non-Native teachers are aware of the community and the culture where they teach and live. The more aware teachers are, the more effective they can be in their jobs. Increased awareness of community will lead to culturally appropriate teaching styles and materials.

Non-Native teachers should be responsible for educating themselves about the community, culturally appropriate content, and culturally appropriate teaching methods. However, more effective non-Native teaching on reserves could be more easily achieved through organized teacher education in cross-cultural teaching specific to Native people. Candidates would no doubt be difficult to obtain in large numbers. Part of the answer is training workshops for working non-Native teachers (and perhaps Native teachers) which aim at increasing their awareness of their roles and effective teaching styles.

One important area which has not been addressed is hiring. The people responsible for hiring need to give greater consideration to hiring people who are suitable for cross-cultural teaching. This is an important issue for each reserve school board.

Most Native children will be taught by non-Native teachers. There have been many attempts to improve education for Canada's Native people. Yet little attention has been paid to improving training for the large non-Native teaching force which will continue to exist for a long time. When this issue is addressed by teacher education faculties, band school administrations, and by the teachers themselves the results should benefit Native students immensely.

Notes

1 Peter L. Berger and Thomas Luckman, *The Social Construction of Reality* (New York: Doubleday 1966), 92.
2 Ibid.
3 Robert and Nanthapa Cooper, *Culture Shock* (Singapore: Times Books 1982), 163.
4 Ibid., 164.
5 Ibid.
6 Ibid.
7 Berger and Luckman, *Social Construction of Reality*, 152.
8 Cooper, *Culture Shock*, 164.
9 Ibid., 165.
10 Edward T. Hall, *Beyond Culture* (New York: Doubleday 1976), 91.
11 Ibid., 127.
12 Ibid.
13 Jean Barman, Yvonne Hébert, and Don McCaskill, eds., *Indian Education in Canada*. Vol. 2, *The Challenge* (Vancouver: UBC Press 1987), 13.
14 Beatrice Culleton, *In Search of April Raintree* (Winnipeg: Pemmican 1984).

References
Barman, Jean, Yvonne Hébert, and Don McCaskill, eds. 1987. *Indian education in Canada*. Vol. 2, *The challenge*. Vancouver: UBC Press
Berger, Peter, and Thomas Luckman. 1966. *The social contruction of reality*. New York: Doubleday
Cooper, Robert, and Nanthapa Cooper. 1982. *Culture shock*. Singapore: Times Books
Culleton, Beatrice. 1984. *In search of April Raintree*. Winnipeg: Pemmican
Hall, Edward T. 1976. *Beyond culture*. New York: Doubleday

Northern Door:
Transforming First Nations Education

12

Treaties and Indian Education

James [sákéj] Youngblood Henderson

The federal government has continually said that education is a privilege, not a right. This barbaric idea derives from English law, which argues that education is a matter of financial ability, parental desire, and individual talent. When this rhetoric is applied to Indians, it creates an intolerable wrong. The First Nations treaties with the imperial Crown created an educational right in the Aboriginal families and a corresponding duty or obligation on the Crown to finance educational facilities and opportunities. In the legal history of colonial Canada, Crown obligations have been ignored by federal and provincial governments. Since 1982, however, these rights have been firmly entrenched in the constitution of Canada. The implications of constitutionalizing these rights are still unfolding.

The contemporary constitutional order of Canada embodies three related treaty provisions for the education of Indian children and an unresolved fiduciary obligation for past violations of treaty provisions for education. Together, these legal factors create a comprehensive justification for educational rights for First Nations as well as a curriculum to remedy colonialism.

The new constitutional order of Canada affirms and recognizes three models of an independent Aboriginal right – the right of treaty Indians to choose an appropriate educational system for their children. I will call this 'Aboriginal choice.' Some treaties transform the customary Aboriginal choice into a prerogative right and obligation. Other treaties allow federal discretion in implementing 'appropriate education' for treaty Indians. In exercising federal discretion against Aboriginal choice, a fiduciary duty is created by operation of law. In this chapter, I examine the issue of the Crown's obligations towards Indian education in the treaty order and discuss what the Crown must do to discharge this obligation in post-colonial Canada.

Treaty Order

The First Nation treaties with the imperial Crown created Canada. The conclusion and ratification of treaties are exclusively a matter for the Crown, as part of the royal prerogative.[1] The treaties were part of the foreign affairs of the British kingdom and the international treaty order, and were not subject to domestic Canadian law. The significance of these prerogative treaties lies in the fact that, in the absence of agreements, there are no compulsory binding rules between the Crown and First Nations in either international or domestic law. The prerogative treaties were consensual arrangements between nations for sharing territory and creating a new order.[2] These treaties were entered into before the provinces were created.

The prerogative treaties are sacred documents to First Nations because they empower the older values of Aboriginal society, and because they are a sacred vision of the future of the first people among multicultural immigrants. The intent of Aboriginal people to preserve Aboriginal rights, and their voice in administering their reserved authority and delegated treaty rights, cannot merely vanish into English words in treaties, constitutions, and laws. In 1982, the court in *Taylor* v. *Williams* established that in treaties 'the honour of the Crown is always involved and no appearance of "sharp dealing" should be sanctioned.'[3] Thus the courts hold the Crown to its constitutional treaty obligations. Moreover, the prerogative treaties which give rise to the educational right cannot be interpreted in a technical manner in English, but rather the words must be interpreted in the way in which they would naturally have been understood by the Indians.[4] The Aboriginal understanding of the right can be interpreted in the modern context.[5] The task of the courts and educators is hearing what has already been said by the Aboriginal signatories and guaranteed by the Crown, and translating it in the modern context.

Aboriginal Choice

Aboriginal control of education under Aboriginal culture and practice was a lifelong right and obligation. It was the original educational system in a family-based context. This extended family-based education system is an existing Aboriginal right under section 35(1) of the Constitution Act, 1982, and the reasoning of the *Sparrow* case discussed below.

Aboriginal control of education has always been a customary right. Education was not a separate function but a comprehensive experience in all families. Often, the unified educational experience is referred to as 'culture.' Aboriginal control of those experiences called education in modern society has always been an integral and inherent part of First Nations culture and has always been essential to the physical survival of First

Nations. Education has always been a family obligation.[6] Traditionally our elders and parents taught children our way of managing and prospering in harmony with the environment. Our communities were our classrooms, our families and our sacred order provided the methodology. Customary teaching and learning existed beyond the reach of the European schools imposed by either the provinces or federal government. The linguistic world-view and values were passed from generation to generation; they continue to shape Indian educational aspirations.

When European immigrants arrived, they brought different educational ideas based on an aristocratic society and an elitist view of how society should function. They wanted to apply their concepts to the Aboriginal peoples, but in the treaty process the Aboriginal peoples rejected external foreign control of their children and European concepts of civilization. Instead they chose to have education remain in the extended families. Aboriginal educational customs or laws were never expressly given or signed away in any treaty.

In the treaties between the British sovereign and First Nations in Atlantic Canada, for example, it is evident that Aboriginal families did not transfer any part of the Aboriginal choice on education to the Crown. They maintained education as a traditional right and duty of parents. They did not agree to send their children to non-Indian schools. The First Nations never delegated to the Crown any role in educating their people.

In these treaties with King George, Aboriginal choice concerning education was reserved to Aboriginal laws and customs. In this situation, the sovereign could not delegate this authority to either the Canadian federal government or the provincial governments, since no such rights had been delegated to the king. Without the clear and express wording of a delegation of Aboriginal authority from Aboriginal nations to the king, neither the king nor the state nor the colonists could interfere with Aboriginal education. If either the federal government or a provincial government interfered with this customary right, it would be liable for the damage and hardship created. This fact creates the modern obligation for post-secondary education as a restorative act.

The prerogative treaties have been held by the Supreme Court of Canada to be legally binding.[7] In these cases, the Aboriginal educational system remained in customary law and, since it was never delegated to the Crown in the treaties, was a protected Aboriginal right. Aboriginal choice continues as a constitutional obligation which has never been extinguished, although it has been regulated by different governments.

Under the Georgian treaties, the Grand Council's constitutional position to provide relevant educational opportunities to First Nations is similar to that of Roman Catholic schools under section 93(4) of the Constitution [British North America] Act, 1867. First Nations education is a separate right distinct from federal or provincial government interests in educating immigrants. Neither government was constitutionally competent to prejudice the First Nations right to establish and maintain reserve schools. Treaties preserved First Nations society from provincial society.

At Confederation, both Indians and lands reserved for Indians were exclusive matters of federal responsibility under sections 91(24) and 132 of the Constitution Act, 1867. These matters were outside provincial jurisdiction. Under this scheme, the federal government created 'Indians' as an exclusive constitutional class of people in the provinces which confederated, and 'Indians and lands for Indians' were transferred to federal jurisdiction, separate from provincial authority.

The lack of authority to impose on Aboriginal choice is witnessed in the first federal acts. In an 1868 law concerning Indians, parliament provided that the governor general in council was authorized to use moneys arising from the sale of Indian lands for 'contribution to schools frequented by such Indians.'[8] In effect, Indian lands financed Indian education. The following year, 1869, another federal act confirmed the Aboriginal choice model: it provided that traditional chiefs or chiefs in council could frame rules and regulations on the construction and maintenance of school houses.[9]

Treaty Choice and Crown Obligations

Her Majesty agrees to maintain a school in each reserve hereby made whenever the Indians of the reserve should desire it.[10]

Her Majesty agrees to maintain schools for instruction of such reserves hereby made as to Her Government of Her Dominion of Canada may seem advisable whenever the Indians of the reserve shall desire it.[11]

Her Majesty agrees to maintain a school in the reserve allotted to each Band as soon as they settle on said reserves and are prepared for a teacher.[12]

In 1870, the federal government created the North-West Territories as a federal territory[13] out of the country reserved to Indians by the Royal Proclamation of 1763.[14] Beginning in 1871, the First Nation treaties with the imperial Crown eventually created the western provinces of Canada.

In the treaties, the Crown agreed that First Nations were full partners in the administration of education, with the treaties defining First Nations duties. The English version of these nation-to-nation agreements purport that the First Nations ceded Aboriginal land to the imperial Crown in exchange for broad, conceptual obligations on the part of the Crown, in particular towards schooling or education. This is similar to the original idea that Indian lands would finance Indian education. These treaties created the unique constitutional duties of the First Nations in the shared territory.

Beginning in 1871, in treaties made during Queen Victoria's reign, the imperial Crown affirmed Aboriginal choice in education as a prerogative right. The central and common article of the Victorian treaties concerning legal jurisdiction provides, 'And further, Her Majesty agrees to maintain a school on each reserve hereby made *whenever* the Indians of the reserve should desire it.'[15]

Aboriginal consent is required before Her Majesty can create or maintain a school among First Nations. Provision of education rests on the choice of the community, which thus defines the nature of the schools. No authority to establish the content of the education system was delegated to the imperial Crown or to the dominion of Canada. Aboriginal choice also informs the nature and scope of the educational system. The Aboriginal choice model in the treaties establishes the constitutional relationship between parties and the nature of the duties. The continuing Aboriginal right to choose the type of school or education for Aboriginal children means that the Crown agreed to respect First Nations control of education.[16] This article imposed an automatic obligation on the Crown and governments in British North America.

In implementing the treaty obligation to provide schools on reserves, the federal parliament enacted the Indian Act in 1876. Existing laws were continued under sections 11 and 63(6). Consistent with the treaties' respect for Aboriginal choice, there was no federal legislation on the establishment of schools, the employment of teachers, curricula, or indeed any of the other numerous matters relating to educational programs. Yet, the act also enfranchised any Indian who had a profession or university degree.[17]

Aboriginal Choice and 'Advisable' Education

Her Majesty agrees to pay the salary of such teachers to instruct the children of said Indians as to Her Government of Canada may seem advisable, when said Indians are settled on their Reserve and shall desire teachers.[18]

Her Majesty agrees to pay the salary of such teachers to instruct the children of said Indians as Her Government of Canada may deem advisable.[19]

His Majesty agrees to pay such salaries of teachers to instruct the children of said Indians, and also to provide such school building and education equipment as may seem advisable to His Majesty's Government of Canada.[20]

His Majesty agrees to make such provisions as may from time to time be deemed advisable for the education of Indian children.[21]

His Majesty agrees to pay the salaries of teachers to instruct the children of said Indians in such manner as His Majesty's government may deem advisable.[22]

Beginning in 1873, these treaty provisions illustrate a subtle transition from Aboriginal choice to Crown obligation. While the language is based on the Aboriginal choice model, these treaties gave the federal government limited discretion in implementing Indian education. The significance of these clauses is that they created a legal obligation on the federal government. When the federal government began to exercise discretion in educational programs, there was a legal obligation not to harm the children in school and to pay adequate salaries to teachers. The location of the schools or the instruction is limited to the reserves. None of these treaties directly limits Aboriginal choice. In fact, the entire structure of the treaties illustrates the function of tribal choice.

'Advisable' education was still based on Aboriginal choice and desires. Both First Nations and the Crown agreed that educational services were necessary. The reserve community still had to desire education or be prepared to have a teacher. By 1899, the Crown and the First Nations had agreed to educational programs. Documents report Indians who desired and demanded teachers and education. The commissioners reported in Treaty 8 that the Indians 'seemed desirous of securing educational advantage for their children.'[23] As to education, the Indians were assured that there was no need for any special stipulation in the treaty, as it was the policy of the government to provide for the education of Indian children in every part of the country, as far as circumstances permitted.[24] Furthermore, the commissioners stated that the policy 'was as strong as a Treaty.' Because of this imperative, the treaty drafters dispensed with provision for Aboriginal choice in those treaties which read 'whenever the Indians of the reserve shall desire it.' Read in isolation, the new provision in Treaty 8 appeared to accept total federal choice in the education of Indians. In retrospect, this reading was a drastic problem – it appeared that federal discretion was total.

Implementation of Treaty Obligations

In these treaties, the chiefs and headmen promised the Crown to observe the treaties strictly. They are part of the Aboriginal constitutions as well as of the British kingdom, which includes Canada. These treaties recognize the treaty areas as protected states in the British kingdom that are governed exclusively by the specific terms of the treaties. Under British law, these terms do not transfer inherent Aboriginal sovereignty to the Crown, only Aboriginal allegiance as an autonomous political order. The spirit and wording of the article requiring strict interpretation of the treaties establishes them as binding law. This inviolate law of the treaties has special meaning for First Nations. First Nations only recognized law that resulted from consensual agreements that established rules to instruct people about the right way to live.[25] They had no idea of oppressive laws or laws based on force or terrorism.

In the language of the treaties, there is no broad delegation of civil or criminal authority or law over Aboriginal peoples to Her Majesty or any legislative body. In the absence of consensual delegation in the treaties, no independent, compulsory binding rule or law exists. Lacking clear and specific delegation from the First Nations, the Crown could not grant parliamentary supremacy to the federal government over Aboriginal people. In the United Kingdom, the role of law is to guarantee and protect treaty obligations and order. According to constitutional obligations, public laws placed limits on the pursuit of private ends for scarce resources and reinforced the need for collaborative order. As will be discussed later, federal and provincial authority derive from the prerogative treaties. Their laws could not be inconsistent with the treaties.

Treaty delegation of educational authority to the Crown was broad.[26] The education articles show that First Nations knew how to delegate authority to the federal government. Lacking such affirmative language in treaties, no implied authority exists in the Crown. As the treaties illustrate, Crown authority over First Nations and the shared territory is not inherent but is derived from Aboriginal choice.

The British sovereign never expressly transferred the entire administration of Indians to the federal government of Canada. The treaties were forged with the unitary imperial Crown, not the federal government. The imperial Crown authorized the implementation of treaty obligations under section 132 and the division of authority under sections 91 and 92 of the Constitution Act, 1867.[27] Both federal and provincial authorities shared the Crown's obligations within their respective jurisdictions.

No parliamentary sanction is required to bring a treaty into legal existence.[28] Sovereignty or prerogative treaties are considered to be directly incorporated into domestic law.[29] Included in this category are peace treaties, treaties establishing boundaries, treaties ceding or acquiring territory.[30] First Nations treaties qualify as sovereignty or prerogative treaties. The Crown negotiated, signed, and ratified all treaties. They were valid and operative imperial acts that were then submitted to colonial governors for implementation in their colonies.[31]

Often parliamentary action is required to implement a prerogative treaty in federal law.[32] It is undetermined whether First Nations treaties required domestic implementation, since they granted the Crown new powers, jurisdiction, and wealth. Few constitutional provisions inform the performance of treaty obligations as Canadian law. Under section 132 of the Constitution [British North America] Act, 1867 the imperial parliament had already delegated the necessary and proper authority to effect the treaty obligations of the imperial government in Canada.[33] Further, section 91(24) had granted exclusive federal authority over 'Indians and lands reserved for Indians.' Finally, in the letters patent of 1947, the Crown delegated its prerogative powers to the governor general of Canada.[34]

In 1880, parliament implemented the new treaty obligations on advisable education. The Indian Act extended the power of chiefs and chiefs in council or school committees to make rules and regulations concerning the education of children, but there was no recognized family or parental right. The Indian Act, in accordance with numbered treaty obligations, provided for a separate school system for Indians on Indian reserves or agreements on their education [114(1)(a)].[35] In 1884, the federal parliament gave the chiefs and councils authority to make regulations on the school attendance of children between six and fifteen years old.[36] In 1891, the treaty articles in the Indian Act regime created day schools. The minister of the interior and former Indian commissioner, Edgar Dewdney, told the House of Commons that:

I have never had much opinion of these day schools, but we have had to establish them on the different reserves because we are bound to do so by treaty. The Indians say they have a sufficient number of children on the reserve to attend a day school, and we have to establish one: but where those children go to school for a few hours and then return to their wigwams or houses, there is not much chance to improve them ... The sooner we can close the day schools and send the children to the boarding schools, the sooner we will be able to do something with them.[37]

In 1894, parliament gave the governor in council the authority to make regulations regarding attendance and punishment of parents and guardians of truant children.[38] The act also gave the governor in council authority to establish industrial or boarding schools for Indians, and gave justices or Indian agents authority to decide on the sending of Indian children to school and to transfer the children's annuities and interest moneys to the schools. Aboriginal choice was disappearing and plenary federal authority appeared.

The 1906 revision of the Indian Act created a 'school' category. Existing categories were placed under these sections. In the 1914 amendments, the governor in council's authority was expanded to off-reserve schools.[39] The minister of Indian affairs could also take reserve land for school purposes.[40] In 1920, the governor in council's authority was expanded to establish day schools on any reserve, to provide for transporting Indian students to and from schools, and to make regulations 'prescribing a standard for the buildings, equipment, teaching and discipline of and in all schools, and for the inspection of such schools.'[41] An expanded truancy law was established.[42] The chief and council were also given the right to inspect such schools.[43]

These acts went far beyond any power delegated by First Nations in the treaties. The revisions of the Indian Act in 1927 and 1951 continued to strengthen federal authorities. By 1951, the federal government had replaced the missionaries' authority with a perceived unlimited power to demand integrated education. In the 1951 revisions, parliament unilaterally terminated the chief's and band council's authority to frame rules and regulations for education, leaving the minister of Indian affairs with the exclusive authority.[44] The act, however, continued the religious affiliation of Indian schools and attendance and truancy provisions. In addition, the minister of Indian affairs was authorized to enter into agreements with provincial and territorial governments for Indian education.[45] Under these agreements, the federal government paid local school boards for Indian tuition, but the agreements did not confer rights of supervision over the curriculum, administration of teaching personnel, or methods or materials of instruction or management. Without reserving any rights, the issue of Aboriginal control and advisable education was diminished.

The number of Indian students dramatically increased in provincial schools, and in the absence of any requirement to revise the curriculum, they quickly became a 'cash cow.' In 1952 less than 8.5 per cent of Indian students attended public schools; ten years later (1962) this figure had grown to just over 30 per cent;[46] and by 1972 it was over 60 per cent.[47] This delegation of federal authority appears to be constitutionally questionable.[48] *Attorney-General of Nova Scotia* v. *Attorney General of Canada* established that legislative jurisdiction could not be delegated from parliament to the province where the Constitution [British North America] Act, 1867, gave exclusive legislative jurisdiction to parliament.[49]

Thus, under the guise of 'advisable education,' the Department of Indian Affairs implemented several different education strategies. These went beyond the delegated scope of the treaties. They interfered with the customary educational system, took children away from families by placing them in federal boarding schools, denied them their cultural and language rights, and deliberately imposed a foreign culture, language, and values on them. This process failed, although it almost destroyed First Nations culture. It was a breach of the treaties, which placed education exclusively under First Nations customary jurisdiction.

Federal government regulations were not benign intrusions; they were deliberate psychological experiments which attempted to destroy First Nations consciousness. These regulations not only placed unbearable constraints on the intellectual development of First Nations but also sought to extinguish their cultural heritage and languages. They arrested or delayed the full development of the Aboriginal personality. These actions cannot be justified, since Indian Affairs has not discharged the fiduciary obligation of the Crown to the First Nations.

Recent federal-provincial agreements were designed to remedy the failings of the federal education system, which sought to create a Canadian identity among First Nations by systematic discouragement of Aboriginal knowledge and values. This was a transparent attempt to win student allegiance to the larger order through immersion in mainstream education. Physical integration in provincial schools may be justified as good for society, but it cannot be justified as good for Indian children and students. It was not a student-centred undertaking or First Nations choice. Moreover, purchasing provincial educational services was an indirect way of funding provincial governments. At best, it was a moral imperative fuelled by the failure of federal policies for educating Indians and by guilt. Aboriginal choice and the aspirations of Indian students were treated as objects, not as part of a cultural heritage to protect, enhance, and nourish.

These questionable educational experiments created cultural and economic stagnation on the reserves. Unilateral federal action marginalized First Nations from the mainstream Canadian economy. As a result of the infringement of Aboriginal and treaty rights to education, the federal educational system left the average First Nations student with only seven years of formal education. The extent of the failure has many indices: disproportionate recourse to social welfare, make-work projects, and unemployment benefits; personal and familial dysfunction; high rates of morbidity and mortality due to substance abuse; and disenchantment with life itself. Unemployment rates on reserves remain at 60-90 per cent, the average income of First Nations is less than one-half the national average, and the suicide rate is three times the national rate. This rate doubles for youths between the ages of fifteen and twenty-four.[50] First Nations children were misunderstood, ignored, and treated as unteachable. Few Aboriginal people graduated from secondary schools and fewer still went to post-secondary institutions. Until 1968, those who attended post-secondary institutions automatically lost their Indian status, and were forbidden to live with their families on reserves. They were exiled to provincial society and their right to associate culturally with their people was denied.

To begin to correct this situation, since the mid-1970s the federal government has reluctantly agreed to a First Nations-controlled education system, albeit with limited financial resources. The emerging success of this initiative with First Nations students, a return to Aboriginal choice, has created a crisis in post-secondary educational funding. The federal government asserts that it cannot fund such success, and has begun to advance the idea of post-secondary education as a privilege.

Conclusions

In law, it is commonplace for historical agreements to impose a burden upon succeeding generations. As a result, the successors of those who signed the original agreements face many dilemmas. In the past, the Canadian government has pretended that treaties belong to some obscure prehistory. These treaty obligations have been ignored or misunderstood by federal and provincial governments. It is clear from the treaties that Indians have a right to education in Canada. This right was incorporated into the constitution of Canada. The educational system, however, has not attempted to conform to the new constitutional order.

The Constitution Act, 1982, establishes the division between colonial law and post-colonial law in Canada. Section 35(1) of the act affirms and recognizes existing Aboriginal and treaty rights as constitutional rights. As part of the supreme law of Canada,[51] the new constitution specifically directs and mandates recognition and affirmation of existing Aboriginal and treaty rights at every level of Canadian society.

Two judgments of the Supreme Court of Canada have established a framework for post-colonial interpretation of Aboriginal and treaty rights under the Constitution Act, 1982. They create new contexts for interpreting governmental responsibility and treaty rights in Canada. The Supreme Court of Canada's judgment in *R.* v. *Sparrow*[52] establishes the boundaries in deciding the Aboriginal right to fish and the scope of federal law and provincial regulation. It stated:

> The context of 1982 is surely enough to tell us that this is not just a codification of the case law on Aboriginal rights that had accumulated by 1982. Section 35 calls for just settlement for Aboriginal peoples. *It renounces the old rules of the game* under which the Crown established courts of law and denied those courts the authority to question sovereign claims made by the Crown.[53]

The court also directed:

> The Government has the responsibility to act in a fiduciary capacity with respect to Aboriginal peoples. The relationship between the Government and Aboriginals is trust-like, rather than adversarial, and contemporary recognition and affirmation of Aboriginal rights must be defined in light of this historic relationship.[54]

The court also held that section 35 of the 1982 act did not constitutionalize the existing bureaucratic law of Canada or the provinces affecting Indians.[55] On the subject of the meaning of section 35(1), the court held:

> There is no explicit language in the provision that authorizes this court or any court to assess the legitimacy of any government legislation that restricts Aboriginal rights. Yet, we find that the words 'recognition and affirmation' incorporate the fiduciary relationship referred to earlier and so import some restraints on the exercise of sovereign power ... We would not wish to set out an exhaustive list of the factors to be considered in the assessment of justifications. Suffice it to say that recognition and affirmation requires sensitivity to and respect for the rights of Aboriginal peoples on behalf of the government, courts and indeed all Canadians.[56]

Similarly, in 1984 in *Simon* v. *Queen*,[57] an appeal examining the legal status of a 1752 treaty between the British Crown and the Míkmaq Nation, the Supreme Court of Canada clearly explained that Canadian law must evolve. The old colonial rule must be decolonized. It is no longer acceptable to be bound by the judicial biases and prejudices of another era, and 'treaties and statutes relating to Indians should be liberally construed and doubtful expressions resolved in favour of the Indians.'[58]

Educators and administrators must decolonize Canada's education and understand the treaty right to education as a manifestation of Aboriginal choice. Despite the clear wording of the treaties in creating First Nations as full partners in the administration of education, the traditionally hostile bias and prejudices towards Aboriginal choice continue. Both federal and provincial governments continue to view education as individual integration and view the treaties and their obligations as relics of the past that can be ignored with impunity. They continue to assume that federal statutes can override the treaties. They continue to ignore the constitutional treaty order in their search for solutions to the educational problem of Indians.

Under sections 35(1) and 52 of the 1982 act, to the extent that provincial education law is inconsistent with the cultural aspirations of the Aboriginal people under the treaties or that it prejudices the federal government's authority to implement Aboriginal choice, provincial education law is null and of no force. If the Crown attempts to lessen or release itself from its explicit treaty obligations by legislation, its actions will be subject to a strict construction. The honour of the Crown – its promise to respect and implement Aboriginal choice in providing education – requires the courts to prevent 'sharp dealing' by either federal or provincial administrators or laws.

In the minister's role as Crown official, he or she cannot ignore the modern Aboriginal choice as expressed by the elected representatives of the reserve people. This would be one of the rejected old rules of the game. He or she should not be allowed to ignore the particular Aboriginal and treaty rights which created the Indian Act provisions. The modern choice is a return to the Aboriginal right which the treaty signatories wanted to exercise through time in the reserves. Aboriginal rights have been constitutionalized. They are now considered a legal right.[59] Under the constitutional protection of section 35(1), federal legislation may infringe a little on these rights, but it is clear that provincial legislative power cannot.[60] Section 35(1) shields contemporary Aboriginal rights from federal and provincial law, thus reversing the historical extension of provincial jurisdiction to reserves, which undercuts Aboriginal or band authority. It restores control of education to First Nations and families.

The imposition of the European school system totally failed First Nations society. The federal government has implemented a policy of band-controlled schools which presumes to restore Aboriginal choice. The means of exercising Aboriginal rights have changed, however, as First Nations communities restore their culture to modern education. Restoring Aboriginal control over education and its entrenchment in federal Indian policy is the overriding goal of First Nations. Thus the Aboriginal right to choose Aboriginal children's educational experiences continues in modern form rather than in original form, and is protected by constitutional law.

The absence of clear federal and provincial initiatives in the post-colonial order to comply fully with the constitutional obligations under the treaties continues to fuel frustration, anger, and conflict. The educational challenge is for federal, provincial, and treaty orders to work together as partners. The constitutional restoration of the treaty order mandates harmonization among the three orders. The Indian Act regime seems to be both incoherent and fatally incomplete. It was conceived and used as an expression of Eurocentric values. The harmonization of Aboriginal educational choice protected by treaties and the constitutional right to education created by the treaties will lead to many quandaries, but these are unavoidable in the creation of a post-colonial Canada.

Notes

1 Peter Hogg, *Constitutional Law of Canada* (Toronto: Carswell 1985), 242.
2 The treaty process followed the requirements of the 1763 Proclamation.
3 (1982) 34 O.R. (2d) 360.
4 *R. v. Nowegijich* [1983] 1 S.C.R. 29, [1983] 2 C.N.L.R. 89 at 94; *Simon v. the Queen* [1985] 2 S.C.R. 387, [1986] 1 C.N.L.R. 153; *R. v. Sioui* [1990] 1 S.C.R. 1025, [1990] C.N.L.R. 127.
5 *Simon v. the Queen* [1985] 2 S.C.R. 387, [1986] 1 C.N.L.R. 153.
6 The family obligation is broader than either the common law idea of parental rights (i.e., the father's) to determine the manner in which the child will be educated or the United Nations Human Rights standards. This prima facie parental right has been abrogated by and made subordinate to the legislative power of the state through provincial and federal enactments. At best, the state-supported institutions are considered agents of the parents.
7 *Simon v. the Queen* [1985] 2 S.C.R. 387, [1986] 1 C.N.L.R. 153; *R. v. Sioui* [1990] 1 S.C.R. 1025, [1990] C.N.L.R. 127
8 Canada, 31 Victoria, c. 42, s. 11.
9 Canada, 32 Victoria, c. 6, s. 12(6).
10 Treaties 1 and 2.
11 Treaties 3, 5, 6. Treaty 5 also provided 'Her Majesty or Her Successors, may in Her good pleasure, see fit to grant to the Mission established at or near Beren's River by the Methodist Church of Canada, [land] for a church, schoolhouse, parsonage, burial ground and farm, or other mission purposes.' This treaty is the first to acknowledge the involvement of the church in the education of

Indian children and a commitment of Indian lands specifically to a church organization for the purposes of providing these services.

12 Treaty 4.

13 Under section 146 of the Constitution [B.N.A.] Act, 1867, the federal government admitted these reserved lands as a territory of Canada (Rupert's Land and North-Western Territory Order, 1870 [UK]).

14 The 1763 Proclamation of King George III reserved unceded Aboriginal land in the west as Indian country, and the Indian nations were protected by the imperial Crown. The 1763 Proclamation is one of the founding constitutional documents of Canada.

15 Treaties 1 and 2 (emphasis added).

16 Attempts by either the provincial or federal governments to limit the treaty phrases would give the impression of 'sharp dealing' and also substitute their thoughts for those of the First Nations. The Supreme Court of Canada has established the position that treaties and statutes relating to Indians are to be liberally construed, and ambiguous terms are to be decided as the Indians understood the terms (*R.* v. *Nowegijich* [1983] 1 S.C.R. 29, [1983] 2 C.N.L.R. 89 at 94; *Simon* v. *the Queen* [1985] 2 S.C.R. 387, [1986] 1 C.N.L.R. 153). These cases argued for Aboriginal-language definition, not English-language definition of schools.

17 Canada, 39 Victoria, c. 18, 86(1).

18 Treaty 7 (1877).

19 Treaty 8 (1899).

20 Treaty 9 (1905).

21 Treaty 10 (1906).

22 Treaty 11 (1921).

23 Canada, *Treaty No. 8 and Reports of Commission* (Ottawa: Queen's Printer 1899), 5. The same comment is made in the Treaty 10 report: Canada, *Treaty No. 10 and Reports of Commission* (Ottawa: Queen's Printer 1906), 6, 'There was evidence [of] a marked desire to secure educational privileges for their children.'

24 Alexander Morris, *The Treaties of Canada with the Indians of Manitoba and Northwest Territories* (Toronto: Willing and Williamson 1880), 49.

25 Manitoba, *Public Inquiry into the Aboriginal Justice Inquiry of Manitoba*, vol. 1, *The Justice System and Aboriginal People 1991* (Altona: D.W. Friesen and Son 1991), 17-46.

26 The education article is unlike the articles prohibiting intoxicating liquor or those referring to the 'Government of the ceded country' in harvesting natural resources in the treaty territory. On the reserves and in the North-West Territories, the chiefs and headmen in Treaties 2, 4, and 6b specifically agreed not to allow intoxicating liquor. They also agreed that all laws regarding intoxicating liquor enacted by the government of the dominion of Canada were valid within their customary legal system. Most of the chiefs and headmen agreed to allow partial regulation 'by the Government of the country,' acting under the authority of Her Majesty, of their prerogative rights of hunting, trapping, and fishing in the treaty territory.

27 Hogg, *Constitutional Law*.

28 Ibid, 244.
29 A. Jacomy-Millette, *Treaty Law in Canada* (Ottawa: University of Ottawa Press 1975), 207-8.
30 Ibid., 208-16.
31 Hogg, *Constitutional Law*, 249.
32 Ibid., 245.
33 It provides that '[t]he Parliament and government of Canada shall have all powers necessary or proper for performing the obligation of Canada or of any province thereof, as part of the British Empire, toward foreign countries, arising under treaties between the Empire and such foreign countries.'
34 R.S.C. 1985, Appendix II, No. 35. Clause 2 authorizes the governor general 'to exercise all power and authorities lawfully belonging to Us [the Crown] in respect of Canada.'
35 The act did not provide for off-reserve education or delegation of education to provincial governments [s. 4(3)]. This was seen as a provincial power.
36 Canada, 47 Victoria, c. 27, s. 8. The need for these regulations is reported by Superintendent R.H. Pidcock, 'The school I'm sorry to say is not so well attended as could be desired. The children are not adverse to learning, but their parents see in education the downfall of all of their most cherished customs.' Cited in John Malcolm MacLeod, 'Indian Education in Canada,' M.A. thesis, University of New Brunswick 1974, 14.
37 Canada. *Debates of the House of Commons for 1891*, 1741.
38 Canada, 37-8 Victoria, c. 32, s. 11.
39 Canada, 4-5 George, c. 35, s. 1.
40 Canada, 4-5 George, c. 35, s. 2.
41 Canada, 10-11 George V, s. 50, s. 1.
42 Canada, 10-11 George V, s. 50, s. 1.
43 Canada, 10-11 George V, s. 50, s. 1(5).
44 Canada, R.S., c. 149, s. 115.
45 Canada, R.S., c. 149, s. 114, 115. By order in council P.C. 1958-8/1578 the federal minister was authorized to enter into agreements with provincial and territorial school boards for the education of Indian children. Most provincial school acts had to be amended to give boards of trustees authority to enter into these agreements.
46 MacLeod, 'Indian Education in Canada,' 22. The actual figure for Indian schools in 1952 was 25,590 students, and public schools had 2,365. In 1962, Indian schools had 32,355 students and public schools had 15,241.
47 Leslie Gue, *Native Education in Canada* (Edmonton: OECD Educational Review Study, University of Alberta 1974), 2.
48 The official response was that the Indian Affairs Branch was merely paying in lieu of Indians' having to pay taxes for school purposes. However, under most funding formulae, land title taxes account for less than 10 per cent of the cost of public instruction.
49 [1951] S.C.R. 31.
50 Basic Department Data 1992, Indian and Northern Affairs Canada.
51 Section 52 of the Constitution Act, 1982.

52 [1990] 1 S.C.R. 1075, [1990] 3 C.N.L.R. 160.

53 Ibid. at 1106 (emphasis added).

54 Ibid. at 1108.

55 Ibid.

56 Ibid. at 1109, 1119.

57 [1985] 2 S.C.R. 387, [1986] 1 C.N.L.R. 153.

58 *R.* v. *Nowegijich* [1983] 1 S.C.R. 29, [1983] 2 C.N.L.R. 89 at 94; *Simon* v. *the Queen* [1985] 2 S.C.R 387, [1986] 1 C.N.L.R. 153; *R.* v. *Sioui* [1990] 1 S.C.R. 1025, [1990] C.N.L.R. 127.

59 *R.* v. *Sparrow* [1990] 1 S.C.R. 1075, [1990] 3 C.N.L.R. 160.

60 Ibid. at 22.

13
Taking Control: Contradiction and First Nations Adult Education

Celia Haig-Brown

> Nothing comes into being except through struggle; struggle is involved in the development of all things; and it is through struggle that things are negated and pass away. Conflict and contradiction are inevitable ... Struggle, and the negativity involved in it, are not merely destructive, but also productive. Struggle is a good thing, not a bad thing.
>
> – Sean Sayers (1980a, 23)

The dialectical contradiction to which Sayers refers guides part of the analysis in an ethnography investigating developing First Nations control in the Native Education Centre (NEC) in Vancouver, Canada. This conceptualization of contradiction informs several aspects of the Centre: relationships between First Nations and non-Native society; relationships between success, accompanying growth, and increasing bureaucracy; relationships among an urban diversity of First Nations; and the notion of 'cultural self-hatred.' Very importantly, it acknowledges that struggle is integral to development. Battiste points out that these issues of conflict are often misinterpreted among Native educators who tend to personalize their conflicts.[1] The fact that transformative work is often fraught with conflict must be recognized as a productive aspect of that work, not as a personal shortcoming.

This urban adult education centre began in 1968 with one teacher and about fifteen students in a program designed to help the latter prepare for employment or further education. By 1988-9, the year of the study, the Centre had grown to more than 350 students, fifty full- and part-time staff, and nine programs. The Centre is guided by a First Nations board of directors. All the students are Aboriginal, as is the majority of the staff.

The larger study (Haig-Brown 1995), of which this chapter forms part, focuses on the relationship between the understandings and practices of the people in the adult education centre and the 1972 document *Indian*

Control of Indian Education written by the national predecessor in Canada of the Assembly of First Nations. This chapter is almost an epilogue to that study. While the notion of contradiction emerged as the study progressed, it is separate and different from the other parts of the ethnography (which focus on the ways people in the Centre made sense of control). The major part of the study was organized around themes which emerged from research with the people in the Centre. Significantly, these overlapped with the major themes of the 1972 document – responsibility, programs, teachers, and facilities – with funding as an insistent subtext.

On the other hand, this chapter emphasizes an understanding which I, a non-Native researcher, saw emerging from the study. Although other study participants mentioned contradiction and the related notions of conflict, tension, and dilemma, they did not focus on them as central to understanding the process of taking control. Yet I became convinced that the notion of dialectical contradiction provides a useful analytical view for people who are seeking control in education. It allows for acceptance of conflict as a central aspect of development and, by implication, not as a personal weakness. The purpose of this chapter is to demonstrate the applicability and usefulness of contradiction.

As the study progressed I found myself thinking more and more about contradictions within the work and talk of the people, including myself, associated with the Centre. While we did not always name the tension which the Centre brought to our lives as contradiction, struggle was often a focus of our conversations about control and the Centre. This struggle frequently centred on the conflicting commitment to develop awareness and understanding of students' Aboriginal origins and to find improved opportunities for advanced education or employment in a society often indifferent to and at times actively destructive of First Nations cultures. When I finally articulated my understanding of the tensions which I repeatedly felt and heard as contradiction, the appropriateness of this notion became more and more important to a developing description and analysis of control in the Centre.

In keeping with my concern for praxis[2] (Freire 1970) and Lather's (1986) articulation of catalytic validity,[3] I hope that the analysis will have importance for people in the academic community and for people engaged in taking control. For the academic community, consideration of First Nations control is placed within the existing discourse on control and contradiction, two concepts which have historical and credible places there. For those involved in taking control, contradiction allows them to name the tension with which they live and acknowledge that the discomfort inherent in this kind of work is an essential aspect of it, not a personal deficiency. It gives a name to the awkward situation of walking with one foot in each of two worlds.

Dialectical Contradiction

I am not examining contradiction as it is defined in formal logic, i.e., a thing cannot both be and not be at the same time. My reflections on the narratives of people at NEC moved me to examine contradiction very carefully both in the ways people used it in conversation and in the ways that philosophers wrote about it. Consistent with contextualization, an important part of the ethnography on which this chapter is based and one consistent with many First Nations world-views, dialectics examines all phenomena as part of the world of interaction, motion, and change. It insists on seeing things as historical. Things are 'embedded in the world,' are related in interaction, and are changeable and transient, not stable or ultimate. Rest is conditional, temporary, transitory, and relative (Lenin in Sayers 1980a, 4). Societies and cultures (including First Nations and institutions such as NEC) are historical things which keep developing and changing.

The basis of dialectical understanding of the world is the statement of the Greek philosopher, Heraclitus (540-475 BC), that all is in flux. His famous example, that one can never step in the same river twice, is often referred to by those who work with dialectics. Dialectics stands opposed to positivism and its project, sometimes mistakenly seen as *the* project of European philosophy, of isolating things and examining and analyzing them (most often as static). Change and development are analytically arrested and the world becomes a collection of inactive things which are indifferent to one another. Positivism treats societies and institutions as static and ahistorical; they exist as they are. The positivistic 'outlook is succinctly summarized in Bishop Butler's saying, "Everything is what it is and not another thing"'(Sayers 1980a, 2). The dialectical view, by contrast, sees identity as trivial.

> Everything has self-identity ... but the matter does not end there; for nothing is *merely* self-identical and self-contained, except what is abstract, isolated, static and unchanging. All real, concrete things are part of the world of interaction, motion and change; and for them we must recognize that things are not merely self-subsistent, but exist essentially in relation to other things [original emphasis]. (Sayers 1980a, 3)

The things referred to may be ideas, propositions, cultures, social institutions, people, or objects. The quotation echoes Native American science educator Greg Cajete's (1986) claim that 'Native American epistemologies are in general highly "mutualistic" and oriented toward holistic and contextual processes.' He contrasts them to classical Western scientific logic, which he defines as 'hierarchical, uniformistic, classificational, quantitative and reflect[ing] ... only one direction in the relationship between cause and effect.' He sees mutualism, holism, and contextualization as involving logic 'which is symbiotic, relational, qualitative, interactionist, and reflect[ing] the notion of many possible directions in the relationship between cause and effect' (p. 130). Historical, physical, and social contextualization aid the articulation of the complex relations between the larger society and the Centre and its various parts. The Centre is a place of interaction, motion, and change.

At the heart of the dialectical outlook is the notion of contradiction. Mao Tse-tung[4] refers to contradiction as the 'essential and continuous principle in the development of all things' (1986, 266). He comments further:

> In order to understand the development of a thing we should study it internally and in its relations with other things; in other words, the development of things should be seen as their internal and necessary self-movement, while each thing in its movement is interrelated and interacts on the things around it ... Contradictoriness within a thing is the fundamental cause of its development, while its interrelations and interactions are secondary causes. (p. 271)

Because contradiction realizes that all is in flux, it allows one to look at the process of a thing's 'becoming,' i.e., there is recognition that even as a thing exists, it is changing, and change is essential to its existence. Contradiction is an attempt to acknowledge the fluidity of all things and to discuss things in their ever-changing contexts. In the Centre, taking control is a process, based on fluidity, changing with each day. The Centre is always becoming, always becoming something new, slip-sliding away from what it was at any previous moment. New staff, new students, new programs, new policies are merely the overt dimensions of its changing nature.

Contradiction, because it focuses on interrelations, also demands consideration of context. Seeing context as inseparable from the thing examined, Sayers, restating Hegel, posits that 'concrete things are not indifferent to one another, but rather in interaction and conflict with each other ... A thing is determinate and has its own identity only by maintaining itself distinct from other things, by opposing other things.' In clarifying the locus of this opposition, Sayers states that 'the concept of contradiction is required in order to stress that such concrete opposition is not external and accidental to things, but rather essential and necessary: it is internal to things and part of their nature ... The dialectical concept of contradiction is that of a concrete unity of opposites' (1980a, 8). The Native Education Centre exists in opposition to other educational institutions and other aspects of society around it. Without the majority society and its impact on First Nations people, there would be no need for or even possibility of such a place. While it exists in opposition to the social order which has excluded First Nations people from education and many lines of employment, it also depends on this social order for its raison d'etre. 'It is so with all opposites; in given conditions, on the one hand they are opposed to each other, and on the other they are interconnected, interpenetrating, interpermeating and interdependent, and this character is described as identity' (Mao 1986, 297).

Contradiction addresses development as the unity of opposites: the division of unity into mutually exclusive opposites and their reciprocal relationship. These relationships are rarely simple. The Centre is an educational institution within Canadian society. It is also an educational place for First Nations people, many of whom, in not completing their education successfully, may be said to be oppressed by members of the majority society. In its development, the Centre exists as a unity of these opposites.

The Principal Contradiction and What the People Said

This brings us to the principal contradiction of the Centre: 'If in any process, there are a number of contradictions, one of them must be the principal contradiction playing the leading and decisive role, while the rest occupy a secondary and subordinate position' (Mao 1986, 291). The Native Education Centre is an institution which simultaneously prepares First Nations people who want to participate in an exclusionary, majority non-Native society while attempting to enhance and develop their awareness and appreciation of their First Nations' cultures and heritage. While some students decide to work in First Nations organizations and communities, many move into jobs and further education in predominantly non-Native institutions.

In their conversations with me, which were a major source of material for my study, many people in the Centre referred to the tensions this contradiction creates. The examples below present the dilemmas based on this primary contradiction. They encompass funding issues, the place of traditional values in programs, attendance policies, and even the conduct of board meetings. A conflict of values was central as people articulated their thoughts. Over and over, people at the Centre spoke of commitment to

Native values in some form and their expression in the Centre's programs and process. When asked, people at the Centre talked about respect as central to Native values: respect for land, for elders, and for all life. They also spoke of spirituality, sharing, and the learning and use of Native languages.[5] The mostly non-Native funding agencies, prospective employers, educators, and others in control in society may know or understand little of these values or of First Nations histories, cultures, and concerns. Struggle between the world-views of students, staff, and board and of certifiers, employers, and funders is central to the everyday operation of the Centre. The words of the people there reveal their views of working within this contradiction.

For the First Nations administrator, John,[6] the principal contradiction emerges in his attempts to balance the conflicting goals of 'Indian values and beliefs' and continued or expanded funding and accreditation of programs:

> Instructional practices and administrative and counselling services reflect value and belief perspectives ... that are culturally consistent with what is perceived to be Indian values and beliefs. Not always can that be accomplished in the context of meeting external, non-Indian institutions, agencies, departments, whatever, that fund us or that make requirements of us because of their stated beliefs and values about what is in fact important in education.

Control of the Centre's programs through funding is an on-going concern. Unlike most colleges and universities, there is no core funding. Each year, hours are spent record-keeping and preparing grant applications to ensure the continuation of existing programs. The relationship between values and beliefs and administrative needs and procedures related to government accountability is a complex one which underlies at least some of the concerns in the comments that follow.

Bob, a non-Native instructor, identified the principal struggle in the Centre as that between meeting the needs of funders and being 'useful' to the Native community. The Centre makes every effort to provide training and education to enable students to participate in and contribute to First Nations communities or non-Native society. In light of funders' demands, these efforts also encompass the primary contradiction. Bob went on:

> From our understanding, there is a lot of confusion about where we are going. I think we are caught between reacting to government funding requirements, for example, this whole question of attendance and

placement rates and stuff like that, and also the courses we offer are market-driven in terms of what the government is prepared to fund and not necessarily what is useful to the Native community.

The non-Native coordinator of the Native Public Administration Program focused on the productive side of this same struggle, the students' place in it:

You're trying to be all things to all people and you're trying to balance the private sector versus the public sector and the non-profit sector, and you're trying to appeal to the Native and non-Native communities. It's a constant juggling act, but it makes it very exciting because then we have this breadth of experience that we can provide that gives them [the students] a really big picture of what the world is all about.

Lisa, a non-Native program coordinator, saw the contradictions that students face as part of being First Nations persons in this society:

I do see that because the Native Ed. Centre has to operate within the financial and social structure of all other training institutes and community colleges, that the conflict between Native values and the majority values create tension around things like attendance and how much academic versus how much practical, that kind of stuff and where the loyalties are. But that's something that I see as just part of the growth of the Native community. Most Native people that I have talked to say that we have to live in both worlds anyway, and you have to learn to work that out.

Looking at traditional lifestyle, Joanne,[7] Northern Tutchone, member of the Wolf Clan, and student in the science and health careers preparation program, also mentioned two worlds: 'People can't go back to the life of a long time ago; so we'll have to just put them together – put two worlds together ... You can't just leave the Western influence that we have. You can't just totally disregard that. We have to learn to live amongst you people.'

It is the prospect of living with the contradiction of two worlds, which is at the same time one world, which holds the promise of new knowledge and new forms of discourse.

Bringing in values, Loretta, a First Nations instructor, talked of actively discussing with students the contradictions they face as First Nations people:

What I told the students on the first day that I was with them downstairs, because of the society that we're living in today, in order for them to suc-ceed, they need to hold onto those traditional values ... At the same time, they'll be working or going to school within a white society. And because of those values, they would probably succeed [in their programs]. That's the first thing I did with them on the first day.

Students and program designers ponder the amalgamation of differing world-views in the future. It is of course possible to be a First Nations per-son and a business executive at the same time. But such coexistence may be fraught with tension. A Haida man at the Centre's biennial community think-tank talked about redefining the word corporation to include respect for future generations. Similarly, the coordinator of the Native Public Administration Program emphasized the benefits of articulating the conflict in the outlooks of various potential employers:

We look at those contradictions, then we look at underlying values that are present. So in the first course, when they start off, they do an intro-duction to economics. The way I handle it is, from an economic perspec-tive, in terms of looking at capitalism, and socialism, then the reality of a mixed economy, and the fact that both sectors exist side by side. Eventually they have to decide for themselves where their thinking lies ... for instance, say they start a fish plant and they generate revenue. Do they want to distribute those profits to the people who own the actual plant or do they want to reinvest those in the community?

Always there is awareness that the Centre is an education institution for First Nations peoples which exists within a dominant, historically oppres-sive, non-Native society. In order to attract students, it must meet their changing needs by acknowledging their histories, cultures, and current concerns in some way.

A few people cited evidence of students being required to meet expecta-tions not associated with Native values. In its statement in 1972 on Indian control, the National Indian Brotherhood cited self-reliance and respect for personal freedom as integral to First Nations cultures. One First Nations counsellor commented:

The values and things that are placed in the students, that they're sup-posed to live by while they are in this building, is not Native. There is not very much room for them to make decisions, personal decisions. Not when it comes to their attendance, their availability, their own personal circumstances. Not much of that is taken into consideration. There is a lot of non-Native values placed on them.

The attendance policies are a direct reflection of the principal contradiction of meeting conflicting expectations. For example, federal funding from the Canada Employment and Immigration Commission is directly related to daily attendance. As a result, major emphasis on attendance at times led to considerable distress among both staff and students. Many people felt that attendance should be the students' responsibility. They are adults. In other post-secondary institutions this is usually the case, although deductions are made in some upgrading programs for days missed. On the other hand, these institutions do not depend solely on individual students for funding as they have core funding.

At the Centre, there was also concern that enforcement of attendance policies took precedence over accommodation of the system to the needs and personal and community responsibilities of adult First Nations people. Childcare, family funerals, a domestic crisis in northern BC become situations which interfere with attendance rather than understandable responsibilities of adult life. In most First Nations communities, family commitments throughout the extended family remain paramount. A First Nations counsellor said: 'I think the attendance policy either has to be scrapped or put on the back burner. It's not the total school; it's not why the students are here. If they are away, it's going to be for a good reason. If they are away, it's their business. They're just going to have to catch up and take things into their own hands that way.' The policy that three days of unexcused absence can result in dismissal is regarded as inappropriate by some students and instructors. Like the counsellor above, they feel that asking a student to explain absences may be an undue invasion of privacy.

In like manner, time limits for assignments, courses, and programs are an issue for some. A non-Native instructor remarked that 'if you talk about this as a Native organization, we impose fairly strict time limits on how long it takes people to finish a program, and we monitor attendance. We run on a white schedule basically. People aren't allowed to hang out and explore things at their own speed.' While the speaker might be accused of stereotyping First Nations perceptions of time, he sees inflexible scheduling as antithetical to some First Nations students' approaches to learning. Again the contradiction exists between the demands of the institution, often dictated indirectly by outside forces, and the preferences of students who may want to approach education more slowly than the schedule allows. Although the Centre is more flexible than comparable non-Native adult education institutions and allows students leaves of absence for a variety of reasons, its structure cannot always accommodate those students who simply want to proceed at their own rate or pursue an unorthodox line of study. Differentiating between these students and those who 'just slack off,' always a difficult task, is often accentuated by the need for cross-cultural understanding.

Other aspects of the Centre's organization which reflect First Nations control also imply contradiction. The Centre remains a unity of opposites as it works to meet the requirements of First Nations and non-Native people. The administrator said that 'irrespective of the fact of having an Indian board of Directors, many Indian administrators and Indian teachers and so on, it doesn't necessarily translate into Indian control if the power for making decisions in many cases rests outside of the institution.' Paul, a non-Native instructor, directly mentioned conflict as central to the operations. 'I think one can come into real conflict with some of the other values of making sure that the outside world thinks we're legitimate and getting approval of King Ed [a mainstream provincial community college with which the Centre is affiliated] and those kinds of places.' Every year the very real possibility of rejection of a proposal and the resultant cancellation of a proposed or on-going program recurs. The loss of any one of the Centre's programs is the loss of having a possible program which reflects First Nations values. Teachers must operate within certain limits if the program and subsequent developments are to continue.

The Shuswap president of the board of directors also referred to conflicting values. He spoke of a debate about whether the board should use the talking stick – a traditional means of organizing gatherings where several people speak – Robert's Rules of Order, or consensus:

> I don't want to pretend that there has not been, there's not all kinds of basis for an adversarial relationship [with non-Native society]. But I think there's more to be gained by pursuing the traditional value of mutual coexistence ...

> For me it's a bit of a contradiction ... telling people we're going to go by consensus. And I'll tell you when you've reached the consensus.

This passage raises at least two contradictions. What is the possibility of relating to non-Native society while 'pursuing the traditional value of mutual coexistence?' Further, what is the significance of dictating the use of consensus?

The contradiction between the goals of successful further education or employment and enhancing and maintaining First Nations cultures is the principal one, but other contradictions exist within the Centre. While they arise out of the principal one and are related to it, they are also different from it and each other. These contradictions include growth as benefit and detriment, the diversity of nationalities within the Centre, and manifestations of 'cultural self-hatred.'

Success, Growth, and Bureaucracy

There is an irony in the contradiction that the success of the Centre's programs engenders increasing size which in turn threatens success unless other changes are made. The Centre started with several students and a teacher in 1968. Since then it has undergone three moves, several changes in administration, and the construction of a million-dollar facility. More importantly, it has grown from 30-40 students in a single program with one instructor to 361 students, nine programs, and over fifty full- and part-time staff in 1988-9.

With increasing size comes increasing bureaucracy. Compared to many other educational institutions, the Native Education Centre remains small and unbureaucratic. Nevertheless, the Centre's initial success was attributed to the very personal style of instruction. The first teacher, the late Ray Collins,[8] demonstrated concern for his students and focused on humanistic and 'personal' approaches to teaching. He had previous experience of working with First Nations people and many knew and respected him. Former students spoke highly of him. When he was laid off from his job with the Department of Indian Affairs in 1968, First Nations people marched to have him reinstated and thus enabled him to participate with them in starting the Centre. John, the next long-term administrator, also taught, advocated, and practised Paulo Freire's (1970) respectful approaches to teaching.

However, by 1988, the Native Education Centre was a very different place, primarily because of its success and growth. Glen, a First Nations board member, saw its growth as:

> Cost/benefit. The benefit is that there's more opportunity in terms of numbers of students and numbers of programs. Those are our benefits. The costs I suppose have increased. They [staff] have to be increasingly aware of effort that has to be exerted to maintain the personal contact, the individualization. When it was smaller, with fifteen students and a couple of teachers, personal contact was always there.

James, a non-Native administrator who had known the Centre in its earlier days, concurred:

Bigger is not necessarily better. There's so many good points to it. Like now, we're reaching a larger number of students ... The size of the building now is – one of the negative things about it is that it's very institutional ... There's more paper, more rules, more policies. That area is really, it's the price of success. Lots of times faculty will reminisce about the days when we didn't have all these problems ... The size of the staff, the hassles and problems we have working in conjunction with institutions like Douglas College, having to hire their instructors, follow their rules. They're not adaptable in many cases ... not having worked with Native people, understood the Centre and how it works and the reason behind it.

A non-Native teacher, Paul, who worked at the Centre during its latter period of growth talked of the changes:

In the early days of the Centre, everybody was involved. It was a very communal thing. But as it's grown bigger, people feel more and more left out of some of the events. For that reason, I think the Centre has probably reached a size where it should stop growing ... I think the bigger it gets the more rules you need somehow and the more room there is for people not being happy with the policy that becomes further and further away from you.

While the advantages of growth are clear, the costs in terms of decreased personal contact and increased regulation are seemingly inescapable.

During the year of the study, there was structural reorganization which reflected concerns about the effects of growth on administrative workload and organization. These had changed very little despite the tremendous growth of the Centre during John's tenure as administrator. He himself spoke of the changes. Initially, he had seen the Centre and its staff of three as committed to community-based education, serving and reaching out into the community. Later, he felt the need to protect that aspect of the Centre:

That's part of my oppressiveness with the staff here: that people feel that this is a college and it isn't. It's a community-based education centre. Big difference ... That's the philosophy, part of the philosophy of me and the Centre from the days that we started. That's not always the philosophy of the teaching staff and of course, that's not always the philosophy of the students now because students are here for an agenda that's maybe different.

The Centre's administrator also saw a need for change in the administrative structure. With increasing demands on his time for everything from funding, hiring, negotiating contracts, and evaluating staff to the daily and annual operations of the Centre, the job required more than a single person, no matter how committed, could give. 'I'd like to have a person, a sort of administrative assistant in charge of personnel ... They need more of a mediator-type person, like yourself. Someone who tries to acknowledge people's feelings, share. I'm not good at that.' Other people associated with the Centre also articulated a need for change. A non-Native instructor who worked well within the existing administrative structure said:

> There isn't a lot of involvement of staff. I think staff feel very alienated about that. They don't feel part of this vision. It's primarily the administrator's vision that's being implemented. I'm working within that framework and saying, 'Well, okay, that's his idea.' I think that's what most instructors do. What does that mean to me then and how do I make sure that my students get their needs met and also how do I maintain some integrity as an instructor?
>
> ... I have definitely no complaint in that area, personally, within my program. Like I said, that's why I'm saying what I'm saying to you now. It's a reflection of what I sense all around me. I have been given a lot of flexibility and a lot of support. I basically am not in confrontation with him, because I think basically his heart is in the right place. His head is not always. That's one of the difficulties ...
>
> Basically the management style has got to change. It's got to be more democratic. People have got to have more say; they've got to have more access to decision-making.

In what the president called 'a strategic planning exercise,' in March 1989, board members worked hard with selected staff to examine future directions for the Centre. One outcome of the meeting was that the administrator's job was divided into two positions, one for funding and general administration, the other with responsibility for programs and associated personnel.

During the year of the study, the administrator had to encounter his own contradictions. He saw his own teaching as reflecting Paulo Freire's adult education approaches, which emphasize critical consciousness of the world and emancipation. Yet, primarily because of time limitations, he felt forced to be authoritarian on many issues in the day-to-day operation of the Centre.

The administrator's strong desire for community-based education revealed another contradiction. Students who seek competence in a particular area such as tourism or word processing may feel that concerns of the larger First Nations community are secondary. Responding to the concerns of students, the immediate 'community' may, and many would argue should, take precedence over interests of the First Nations community outside the Centre. Student pressure for change sometimes accentuates the contradiction between First Nations and majority educational values. The students themselves want education that will prepare them for participation in majority society. They are less concerned with education reflecting or promoting tradition. John, who has been associated with the Centre for about ten years, remarked:

> At the beginning, when I first got here, the academic component was far less important because it was far less important to the students ... As we developed many skills training programs, the kinds of students we get in many cases – not all the time for sure, but in many cases – have come to grips with the cultural and personal problems and have a greater need for academic competency so that they can continue on employment or further training.

This focus by students on the Centre's principal contradiction (between enhancing First Nations culture and providing employment and educational opportunities for students) required improved articulation with mainstream institutions. This allows for ease of transfer, but reduces emphasis on a First Nations community presence. For the upgrading students, the group most like the initial group in the Centre, cultural and life skills activities remained part of educational development. Each afternoon from Tuesday to Friday was dedicated to them, an example of a contradiction not resolved, but transformed.

Hiring became another major conflict area associated with increased size and the need for more staff. The difficulty of finding committed staff for a Centre which seemed unable to demonstrate much commitment to them was paramount. No job security, the unspoken fear that unionization would lead to wage and working demands that would jeopardize programs because they could not be adequately funded with available resources, and the myriad problems associated with annual grant funding all compound this contradiction. The administrator's burning ambition to ensure the Centre's continuance and growth, and his insistence that staff share his ardour, augmented the difficulties. His comments about people seeking job security are especially noteworthy:

People have this belief they have to sign up for unions or long-term contracts and have salary scales and a variety of other infrastructural type
things and job security for the rest of their life ... I think [these] are all
things that make what is wrong with community colleges ... People have
to live on the edge in my opinion in order to be – they have to be hungry,
I guess is a better word – to be able to give as well as to receive ... So I
have that belief in hunger and risk, experimentation, and people working
real hard and burning themselves out and leaving and new people come
in and work real hard and burn themselves out and leaving.

The decision of some of the staff to leave the Centre to work elsewhere reflects the impact of this belief. Initially in the Centre, success through culturally sensitive and personalized approaches and programs led to growth.
With increasing size came increasing bureaucracy and the decreasing
possibility of serious responses to staff concerns which, of course, also
grew and diversified.

Urban First Nations

Another contradiction is that this is an urban education centre. This is
tied directly to the principal contradiction and in some ways results from
it. The Vancouver area is traditionally the land of the Musqueam and the
Squamish. Now, as a major urban centre, it attracts First Nations people
from across the country.

In the Native Education Centre, these diverse First Nations people con-
verge. Because there are many groups and relatively few individuals from
each group at the Centre, there is no practical alternative. Given the many
common issues and concerns, however, this may be a strengthening
move. Within this consolidation, there is room for celebrating diversity.

Pan-Indianism refers to the increasing influence of some First Nations
cultures as various cultures meet and interact in new environments. In
itself, it is a site of conflict. In a recent article, R. Carlos Nakai, a Navajo-
Ute belonging to the Naashteezhi Dinee Taachiinii clan, opposes Pan-
Indianism as destructive and confusing to original cultures:

We need to realize that we don't think homogeneously either ... The philosophy from a band or a family is from individuals thinking together,
comparing notes with each other. The onslaught now, with the New Age
idea of Indians, is that all Native people are supposed to think one way
about one thing or another ... We don't work that way, we are not products of an externalized system of theosophy. (1989, 38)

He focuses on pow-wows as a site of confusion:

> It started up in 1932. We took all the society dances and turned it into
> one big thing and called it pow-wow. Their original intent was to get the
> tourists off the train and into Pawnee Oklahoma to buy the stuff that we
> made by hand ... Well, a lot of those songs have words. The words talk
> about how we are. But they've been changed so that now the focus is
> somewhere else. What we're doing is allowing the American people to let
> us confuse ourselves. (1989, 38)

Helen Carr, a non-Native theorist, takes a different view of pan-Indianism:

> When the National Indian Council was founded in 1961, one of its aims
> was to 'recognize the inherent strength of the American Indian heritage'
> ... Since then, emphasis on Pan-Indianism and on a common heritage has
> grown among Native American political groups ... Liberal whites have of
> course decried the earlier colonialist attitude that saw all Native American
> groups as one amorphous and brutish other. To emphasize the difference
> between Sioux and Iroquois, Zuni and Pima, has rightly seemed of funda-
> mental importance to any growth of understanding between Euro-
> americans and Native Americans. However this segmented view of the
> different groups of Indians has helped to perpetuate a sense that their cul-
> ture consists of limited, simple units, and has obscured the existence of
> traditions and forms of knowledge shared in much the same way as, for
> example, cultural traditions in Europe and Western Asia. What is needed
> is not the occasional sentimental generalization about Indians as ecolo-
> gists or mystics, but a serious consideration of their cosmologies, philoso-
> phies and arts in a way that acknowledges the long history of complex
> interrelations and borrowings. (1986, 1)

Discussing the sweet grass ceremony used daily in one class, Lisa, a non-
Native coordinator, commented, 'One of the things that the class has
been really strong on, and they struggle with sometimes, is there is no
such thing as one right way.' She went on to describe something she
called 'unifying culture':

> I think it's one of the things that's been a by-product of the government
> policy to exterminate Native people. That, in an attempt to break the cul-
> ture, in fact what they've done is help unify the culture ... Also I would
> guess that the other thing that's happened is that the culture has been

under attack for so long that people are more willing to be eclectic and say, basically it's all good stuff and we'll go with it ... I've heard several Native people say that, that for all the bad things the residential school did, it got Native people to know one another from various parts of the country and it created a Native nation.

On the other hand, the concept of a 'unifying culture' does at some point minimize differences which people like Nakai are wont to reemphasize.

The contradiction is also evident in the culture classes at the Centre. Meeting the challenge to find resource people in the community, the classes, almost all given by First Nations instructors, have included beading, leatherwork, drumming and singing, drum-making, and North West Coast art. In some ways, these are part of a developing understanding of what constitutes material 'Indian' culture. Students participating in the classes may be from communities which did not and do not include such activities in their daily lives. Yet the value of such classes in unifying diverse First Nations people is clear. Decrying complaints about prairie culture, one student said, 'Pow-wow music is universal. Everybody can dance to that.' Not wanting to be confined to his own cultural understandings, another student said of the Centre, 'Actually what really interests me is all the Native people that are from all different areas and their traditions and their customs and their habits. That's what really makes it interesting.'

Languages are a related site of contradiction. Partly because students come from diverse language backgrounds, no one has decided which language should be taught. Sam, a counsellor, observed:

There was a discussion not too long ago ... Some of the students had approached one of the instructors ... and said they would like to see the language being spoken. It was brought back that if we do one language, we have to do them all ... The end of the discussion was that if they were going to teach some language, it would be Cree because the Cree language is apparently spoken from Alberta to Ontario. So it's basically the national Native language.

While it seems ironic to offer a language which is peripheral in British Columbia, the person interviewed felt that it was a good place to start, and that most importantly some language should be taught. Although the course in Cree was offered at night before my study began, no language courses were offered in the year of this study.

There were interesting efforts to transform the contradiction between unity and diversity. A First Nations science instructor illustrated changes in states of matter by whipping the juice of soapberries into a delectable substance known in English as Indian ice cream. This substance is familiar to most of BC's twenty-six First Nations. In class she introduced the word for this substance in her language and had the students give it in their languages as well. By this naming, contradiction is transformed from unspoken tension into acknowledgment of difference. As well as learning the conventional, Western scientific name, students also have a common term, learn diverse First Nations names, and, coincidentally, reinforce the existence and names of the cultures from which these names spring, cultures which simultaneously unite and divide the people of the Centre.

Controversy about the Centre within the Native community, which Lisa defined as 'Native people in British Columbia,' was seen as healthy. 'I do think the Native Ed. Centre works for change. I know that some of the controversy in the community is around whether it does it the right way or the way other people would like to see it done, all that kind of stuff. But that kind of controversy is healthy. You have to work those things out.' One of the main emphases of Indian control of Indian education, as expressed in the National Indian Brotherhood document, is that First Nations people must determine their own best education. Outside experts cannot legislate or decide upon it. First Nations people must be in control. Change must come not from outside forces which have failed to make the necessary changes to First Nations education in the province, but from within the First Nations cultures in all their diversity.

'Cultural Self-Hatred'

'Cultural self-hatred,' a term used by Jane Middleton-Moz in her workshop with the students in Native Family Violence and Community Service Training, refers to learned self-helplessness, a socialized belief that no matter what you do, as a member of a particular cultural group you cannot make a difference. While members of mainstream society, operating from positions of privilege, may just as negatively internalize dominance (Sawyer 1989, 5), many First Nations people grow up hearing and believing negative stereotypes about their personal and cultural backgrounds.

This internalized contradiction is evident at the Centre as people question their decisions to participate in a program and a Centre which proudly identifies itself as First Nations. By their participation, they tacitly accept their origins.

While acknowledging the importance of the existence of First Nations teachers to First Nations control, a First Nations teacher provided an example of the conflict she encounters when she teaches in the Centre:

One thing I've noticed ever since I've been working with adults is that, because the students are also exposed to non-Native instructors, is that sometimes just because I'm Indian they think I'm not competent as an instructor ... I guess they're so conditioned to thinking that white instructors know the curriculum. But just because you're Native they feel that maybe she doesn't know this, and they might hesitate sometimes to ask ... like sometimes they might go ask a non-Native instructor something, some particular question that they might have had, rather than asking me ... Sometimes. Not all of them, but there's a few.

A staff member spoke of students' concerns with the programs: 'They don't think they're getting as good an education because they're only doing Native stuff ... They've been conditioned to think that Native stuff isn't as good as ... That's something they bring with them.' When working with admissions she tried to convey this to students, but 'they're so nervous and anxious to get in that they don't really hear what you say at that point.' Later, some seem to think that if the program let them in, it cannot be any good. A student mentioned that she would attend a non-Native broadcasting program rather than the First Nations one available in another institution because 'it has a higher credibility and higher chance of employment in the mainstream, at CBC [Canadian Broadcasting Corporation].' As this is probably an accurate perception, it is a disturbing reflection of persisting racism. It exemplifies an attitude which occasionally surfaces in relation to various other First Nations programs. Further study of its pervasiveness throughout First Nations programs across the country could be enlightening.

Another student criticized the negative stereotypes she had heard in the Centre. In particular, she referred to the derogatory comments about 'welfare Wednesday,' the day when some students receive their school living allowances, and about cafeteria food as 'Indian food.' 'That bothers me. I grew up on a reserve that taught me respect and to eat whatever people prepare without complaining.' A staff member spoke of her on-going discomfort with her First Nations origins. 'I still don't consider myself Native, not to the same degree they [the students] are ... I don't have a good opinion of Native people.' She pointed out that she wanted to disconnect herself from her memories of her alcoholic father. 'I'm not one of those drunken Indians.'

Another student mentioned that her 'granny told all her kids to marry white if they could get away with it.' She herself had a non-Native father and a First Nations mother, and she worked to transform the contradiction she felt: 'For a long time I was bitter and unhappy. I didn't know what I was. Like really terrible identity crisis. But sometimes I close my eyes and I see this vision. I see myself and I can see a white person and an Indian person on each side of me holding my hand.'

Students and First Nations instructors specified residential schools as prime sites for developing cultural self-hatred. Janice, a First Nations instructor, commented: 'By the time I went through the residential school system, I had a very negative attitude towards my parents and towards my friends ... I started seeing some of my brothers and sisters as ugly looking because they were Indian ... When I got to Grade 8, I was so ashamed to be Indian ... If my friends ever tried to talk about Indians, I'd just change the subject.' She began to change her attitude as a young adult, when she attended a meeting at her non-Native foster mother's insistence. Both her parents had died when Janice was a young child.

> There were mostly white people there, which I was quite shocked at. I thought why would a white person be interested in Native people? ... The women I saw in the film reminded me so much of my mom, how I remember her during the salmon season and berry-picking season, with her gum boots and baggy dress, kerchief on her head ... I felt really good. Then I saw them dancing. Like whenever I heard Native people sing or dance on TV or videos or whatever, I was supremely embarrassed. But this time when I watched I saw the beauty in their brown skin and wide faces and high cheekbones ... So when we were driving home ... I said, 'You know what? This is the first time in my life I've ever seen Indian people as beautiful people' ... So, it was a slow growing process from there.

Janice describes in this passage the transformation of a contradiction with which she lives. For her, this gathering served to transform cultural self-hatred into growing appreciation of the beauty of her family and First Nations people generally.

Formal education itself is a contradictory proposition for some. One of the board members talked of her attendance at university in the 1970s and the response of some of the community members:

> I think a lot of people ... really felt that [First Nations] people who went to school and got degrees and became, in their eyes, professionals or whatever, were just copping out and just turning their backs ... It doesn't

have to happen that way. I think that if we do have a really effective education system where we're aware that we don't have to give up our values and our identity, then it can be even more successful ... To me, values in terms of education means there is more than one way of learning.

Sam, a counsellor, talked of a related dilemma he feels about his band and the best place to use his education:

My education coordinator is always on my case about going back to the reserve and teaching because I owe them, because they paid for my education. Whereas I don't believe that ... You might probably have more impact on non-Native people. When they look at you and they say, 'Oh my gosh. This is a Native person.' All Natives aren't this or that or whatever idea they have about being Native. The impact is greater than running back to the reserve and teaching and applying your skills there. Mind you, you do provide a really good role model for the younger students or people on reserve which is valid.

Contradiction Transformed

A final consideration of contradictions centres on what becomes of them. Are they resolved? Do they wither and disappear? How does contradiction relate to the process of development?

Sayers says that 'the outcome of a concrete contradiction, the outcome of a real clashing of opposites is a result, something determinate, a new thing, which is equally contradictory and hence equally subject to change and eventual dissolution' (1980a, 12). Norman gives us a slightly different view:

In Hegel's terminology contradictions, when they are resolved, do not cease to be contradictions. The opposition between the two sides does not simply disappear; rather, the contradiction is resolved by showing how the opposites can co-exist within a unity. But the fact that this unity is still a unity of opposites is the reason for calling it a 'contradiction.' (1980b, 55)

If one returned to study the Centre today, one would find that some of the contradictions raised in this chapter still exist and others have been transformed. But, as long as the Centre continues to exist, it will be, like all human institutions, the site of struggle, conflict, and contradiction. This understanding is not new to First Nations people. One First Nations person, a former board member, commented in these terms on the concept of contradiction as useful in considering First Nations education: 'Unity in diversity has been a concept dealt with by First Nations since time immemorial.' Contradiction as the 'essential and continuous principle in the development of all things' still exists in whatever the original contradiction or thing becomes. This First Nations observer went on to emphasize that in this process traditional First Nations values and beliefs are reexamined and either kept or altered. Her experience of developing a curriculum based on Sto:lo culture with the guidance of elders has given her much practical experience of altering and adapting traditional educational values and understandings of curriculum for use in elementary and secondary classrooms. The values and beliefs exist in a non-Native social context and must be constantly reexamined, kept, or adapted in practice. Rather than seeking final resolution or reconciliation of contradiction, as the comments in this chapter show, one may seek transformation, acknowledging the inevitability of conflict and of continuing tension. Resolution is temporary. It leads only to another contradiction in another thing.

In academic study, 'this dialectical world outlook teaches us primarily how to observe and analyze the movement of opposites in different things and, on the basis of such analysis, to indicate the methods for [temporarily] resolving contradictions ... By assiduous study, ignorance can be transformed into knowledge, scanty knowledge into substantial knowledge' (Mao 1986, 293, 294). The possibility of this transformation has influenced my work. There is no final resolution, no end to struggle in sight. There are possibilities that observing, analyzing, and naming – tasks which this chapter has attempted – will transform ignorance into knowledge of First Nations struggles to take control of education. Naming contradiction may also lead to the recognition that personal blame for conflict is almost always inappropriate. Struggle is central to development.

In 1972, the National Indian Brotherhood called for curricula which would 'reinforce Indian identity' and 'provide training necessary for making a good living in modern society' (1972, 3). While many First Nations people have managed to work successfully with the various contradictions that they encounter, other people continue to find the tensions treacherous and demanding. Through their work in education, students in the Native Education Centre encounter and transform contradictions daily.

The notion of contradiction is significant to those who work with members of traditionally oppressed groups that seek fuller participation in society. It can play an important role in shaping the work of people involved in First Nations education. Acknowledging flux, it allows their focus to shift from individuals as 'problems' to the relations of power within which people work. By naming the tensions, people can begin to address them as issues. Contradiction is one possible name.

By acknowledging opposition, by allowing and encouraging the articulation of students' personal and cultural struggles in the classroom, teachers, administrators, and curriculum developers allow for legitimation of these experiences. As Loretta discusses with students the reality of their position as First Nations students in 'a white society,' she allows their experience into the classroom. Following a Freirian model which respects learners, teachers in the Native Adult Basic Education (NABE) program in the Centre start with students' life experiences. No longer are the expressed contradictions limited to those which the teacher might anticipate. A typical day begins with the symbolic talking circle and a prayer. In a continuing effort to facilitate dialogue, or what Ellsworth (1989) more realistically renames 'talking across differences,' open discussion of the contradictions with which students live daily serves as a focus. In recognizing education as development, and contradiction as essential to the development of all things, teachers see the opposites with which students work and can build their work together by articulating these contradictions. In the NABE class, students use their developing reading, writing, and organizational skills to hold an elders day for the Centre. Each guest receives a copy of the book they have prepared, entitled *The Teachings of the Elders*. Students honour the elders with a quilt which they have made together, each square representing one student's connection to First Nations.[9]

Contradictory opposites are not binary, symmetrical opposites. The unity of contradiction also acknowledges that 'a thing is determinate and has its own identity only by maintaining itself distinct from other things, by opposing other things' (Sayers 1980a, 8). Recognizing the complexity of power relations in the Native Education Centre, First Nations people submit to learning about the majority society in order to struggle against the existing repressive order. In the Centre they form new knowledge, their own regime of truth,[10] which challenges those regimes which previously excluded them. In an introductory history class, the linear timeline, a non-Native concept, includes First Nations discovery of a lost and nameless European in 1492 and the date of the Royal Proclamation, a significant document in land claims struggles in British Columbia. A First Nations reader of a draft of this chapter added that 'First Nations are also asserting our own ways – our own form of discourse – so important and beneficial for non-Native societies.'

One need only stop by the Centre during an open house to get a sense of this form of discourse. Speakers begin with a prayer; they include their first languages in their addresses; there is a special brand of humour, some of it bitter-sweet. Above all, there is a current of respect running through the talk. Although topics may be either harsh or celebratory, the words which reveal the essence of First Nations discourse are those which arise from respect for life, for interrelationships among all things, for spiritual understanding, and for an acceptance of the inexplicable. One need only spend time with a student in a science class to gain a strong sense of First Nations discourse. 'My people believe that the rocks have souls,' a student comments to the non-Native teacher who has just finished a talk on the characteristics of living things. The sensitive teacher, one who under-stands the contradictory nature of her work, can use this comment for on-going discussion of the relationship between Western science and First Nations articulations of their understanding of the world.

The personal contradiction with which I began this study persists: I am a non-Native person focusing on First Nations control of education, hop-ing in some way to contribute to the discourse. I hope that the study and this chapter help in the struggle to transform the oppressive relationships, particularly in education, which have existed between non-Native and First Nations peoples on this continent. I leave you with a final image of one contradiction transformed. George Longfish, of the University of California and originally of the Six Nations Reserve in Ontario, writes:

> Stand on the back of the Turtle, our mother, and look at the land and wonder what it would have been like if Columbus would have been suc-cessful in his pursuit of India and avoided the eastern shore of this conti-nent. Wipe your Indian hands on your Levi jeans, get into your Toyota pick-up. Throw in a tape of Mozart, Led Zepplin [sic] or ceremonial Sioux songs: then throw back your head and laugh – you are a survivor of a col-onized people. (1989, 22)

Notes

This chapter is an adaptation of Chapter 9 of Celia Haig-Brown, *Taking Control: Power and Contradiction in First Nations Adult Education* (Vancouver: UBC Press 1995).

1 Marie Battiste, personal communication, 11 March 1992.
2 To paraphrase Freire, I see praxis as on-going action and reflection upon the world in order to transform it. Very simply put, Freire writes of education as a political act and suggests that it may be used to promote the status quo or to promote change in the form of praxis.

3 Lather writes of catalytic validity as related to 'the emancipatory intent of praxis-oriented research.' It represents, she says, 'the degree to which the research process re-orients, focuses and energizes participants toward knowing reality in order to transform it' (1991, 68).

4 While Mao's role in the bloody Cultural Revolution may throw his theoretical work into question, I continue to find his essay on contradiction particularly incisive. The inconclusive controversy over using the theoretical works of people who have engaged in heinous political and personal activities is one we must continue to address – another tension, another contradiction. As another controversial theorist once said, 'Let [s]he who is without sin throw the first stone.'

5 For a more detailed presentation and analysis of perceptions of people at the Centre on First Nations values, see Haig-Brown 1995.

6 All names used in this chapter, unless otherwise indicated, are pseudonyms.

7 Joanne asked that I use her given name and the name of her band.

8 Ray Collins read drafts of this work and asked that his name be used.

9 For more examples of the way the Centre deals with contradictions in policy and programs, see Haig-Brown 1995.

10 Foucault states: '"Truth" is to be understood as a system of ordered procedures for the production, regulation, distribution, circulation and operation of statements. "Truth" is linked in a circular relation with systems of power which produce and sustain it, and to effects of power which it induces and which extend it. A "regime" of truth' (1980, 133).

References

Cajete, Gregory A. 1986. Science: A Native American perspective. Ph.D. dissertation, International College, Los Angeles

Carr, Helen. 1986. The hero twins. *New Scholar* 10 (1 and 2):1-17

Ellsworth, Elizabeth. 1989. Why doesn't this feel empowering? Working through the repressive myths of critical pedagogy. *Harvard Educational Review* 59:297-324

Foucault, Michel. 1980. Edited by Colin Gordon. *Power/knowledge: Selected interviews and other writings 1972-1977*. New York: Pantheon

Freire, Paulo. 1970. *Pedagogy of the oppressed*. New York: Seaberry

Haig-Brown, Celia. 1995. *Taking control: Power and contradiction in First Nations adult education*. Vancouver: UBC Press

Lather, Patti. 1986. Issues of validity in openly ideological research: Between a rock and a soft place. *Interchange* 17 (4):63-84

–. 1991. *Getting smart: Feminist research and pedagogy with/in the postmodern*. New York: Routledge

Longfish, George, and Joan Randall. Contradictions in Indian Territory. Quoted in Kay Walkingstick. 1989. Like a longfish out of water. *Northeast Indian Quarterly* 6 (3):16-23

McCarthy, Cameron. 1988. 'Rethinking liberal and radical perspectives on racial inequality in schooling: Making the case for nonsynchrony.' *Harvard Educational Review* 58 (3)

Mao Tse-Tung. 1986. On contradiction. In David McLellan, ed., *The essential left: Five classic texts on the principles of socialism.* London: Unwin Paperbacks

Nakai, R. Carlos. 1989. Living in two worlds. *Northeast Indian Quarterly* 6 (3)

National Indian Brotherhood. 1972. *Indian control of Indian education.* Ottawa: National Indian Brotherhood

Norman, Richard. 1980a. On the Hegelian origins. In R. Norman and S. Sayers, eds., *Hegel, Marx and the Dialectic: A debate.* Sussex: Harvester Press

–. 1980b. The problem of contradiction. In R. Norman and S. Sayers, eds., *Hegel, Marx and the Dialectic: A debate.* Sussex: Harvester Press

Norman, Richard, and Sean Sayers. 1980. *Hegel, Marx and dialectic: A debate.* Sussex: Harvester Press

Sawyer, Janet. 1989. Internalized dominance. *Angles* (January):4-5

Sayers, Sean. 1980a. On the Marxist dialectic. In R. Norman and S. Sayers, eds., *Hegel, Marx and the Dialectic: A debate.* Sussex: Harvester Press

–. 1980b. Dualism, materialism and dialectics. In R. Norman and S. Sayers, eds., *Hegel, Marx and the Dialectic: A debate.* Sussex: Harvester Press

14

Locally Developed Native Studies Curriculum: An Historical and Philosophical Rationale

Jo-ann Archibald

Many First Nations' communities, school districts, and publishing companies in British Columbia are involved in developing Native Studies curricula.[1] In First Nations schools, one objective is to incorporate relevant cultural curricula. Provincial social studies curricula revisions have prescribed First Nations content for some grade levels. The Ministry of Education, through the director of First Nations education, has made funding available for programs which focus on meeting the special needs of First Nations students. The development of First Nations curricula also responds to the perceived historical failure of mainstream education systems to help First Nations students.

Much has been said and written about the general phases of First Nations education, especially the residential and public school systems. Topics have chiefly included the type of education offered, the types of teachers, and personal reactions to both. Very little documentation exists on the goals or aims of school curricula in relation to cultural differences, or the influential curricula decisionmakers, or First Nations reactions to the curricula of various educational systems. This chapter examines these three topics by tracing the historical experience of First Nations education in British Columbia, with specific reference to the Sto:lo people of the Fraser Valley area.[2]

Historical phases of First Nations education are categorized in relation to the decision-making bodies that influenced major curriculum goals and objectives. These influential groups include traditional Sto:lo people, religious organizations, governments (federal and provincial), and contemporary First Nations people. The particular methods of addressing cultural differences and of studying First Nations culture are outlined in each phase. The dominant goal of assimilation in the curricula of mainstream education systems will be pointed out. First Nations resistance to this will be explained and some resulting problems discussed. It will be argued that a customary solution to problems associated with cultural differences has been curriculum change. It will also be argued that First Nations resistance to assimilation has hastened the involvement of First Nations people in curriculum development at school district or local levels.

An example of one of these curriculum solutions, Sto:lo Sitel, is presented as a case study. Curriculum development and implementation experiences will be outlined. This locally developed Native Studies curriculum is currently used in public and band-controlled schools in the Fraser Valley. While the writer was working with the Sto:lo Sitel project, pertinent philosophical considerations kept emerging. They continue to influence development and implementation and are highlighted in this chapter.

Phases of First Nations Education

Traditional Sto:lo Education

A romantic view of traditional First Nations education has young people seated on the ground listening attentively to elders telling stories imbued with moral principles that are woven into explanations of 'mother nature.' The lack of an 'institutionalized' school system together with this romantic notion have led many educators to believe that First Nations people had no education system with a credible depth of knowledge, understanding, and viable educational principles.

First Nations people traditionally adopted a holistic approach to education. Principles of spiritual, physical, and emotional growth, as well as economic and physical survival skills, were developed in each individual to ensure eventual family and village survival. Certain learning specialities in these areas were emphasized, including independence, self-reliance, observation, discovery, empirical practicality, and respect for nature.

The Sto:lo people of the Upper Fraser Valley adhered to the following educational principles before contact with Europeans. Each day, extended family members taught survival and interacting skills to the children. Oral instruction was minimal, the emphasis being on observation and experience. Such activities were sequentially organized. Young children were given toys and tasks which resembled adult tools and jobs. In time, these tools and tasks became more complex.

The elders were the most respected teachers. Important teachings on values and higher knowledge of history and environment were imparted through their stories and private talks with children. The elders also had a major responsibility in preparing the younger generation for specialized roles.

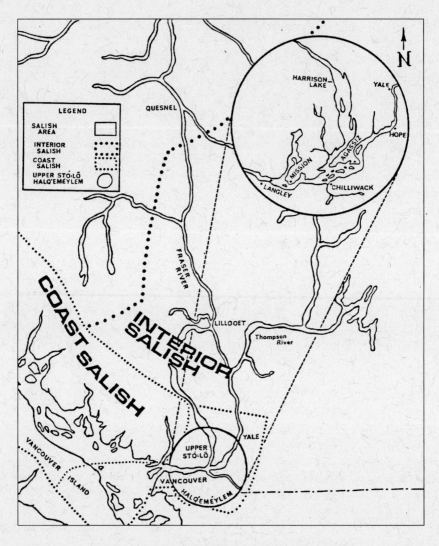

Map 14.1 An outline of the Sto:lo geographical area

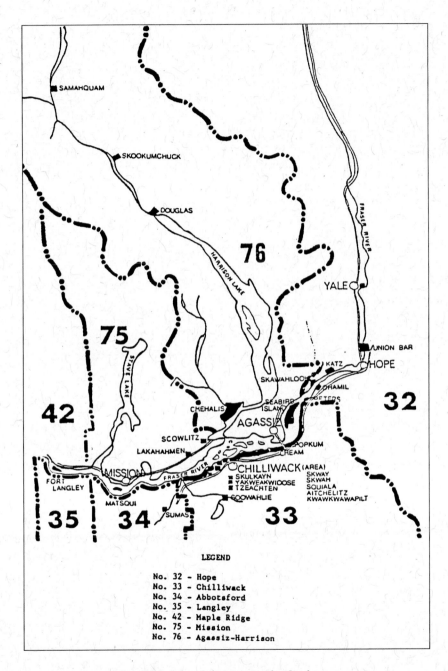

Map 14.2 School districts in the Sto:lo area

Generally, educational expectations and the roles of all villagers were clearly defined and structured. Goals reflected the values of sharing, cooperation, and respect for the environment, oneself, and others. The curriculum content included training in cultural, historical, environmental, and physical (body) knowledge. Community members and the environment became teaching resources. Individual involvement in and responsibility for education created a lifelong learning process.

The success of this system depended on the strength and wisdom of parents and elders. To ensure social and physical survival, training was strictly adhered to. Young people who were disobedient or lazy were either shunned, ignored, or spoken to privately by adults. Discipline was not physical. The educational process was not static; it allowed for adaptation to environmental change and outside cultural influences. These changes were controlled and directed by the Sto:lo people until the arrival of the missionaries.

Influence of Religion

The Christian religious period began in the Sto:lo area in 1841 with the visit of the Roman Catholic Oblate missionary, Father Demers. For the next hundred years, the Roman Catholics and Methodists exerted a powerful influence on the education of Sto:lo children. Despite differences in religious doctrine and organizational philosophy and practice, both shared the common goal of 'Christianizing and civilizing' First Nations children. Christianizing and other efforts at 'civilizing' were initially rebuffed by many Sto:lo people who did not want to lose their language, values, and traditions. Education at this time came to be associated with a formal building where a single non-Native teacher gave religious and English language instruction. Anything associated with First Nations culture was disregarded or forbidden in the missionary system.

Initially, Roman Catholic Oblate missionaries incorporated Sto:lo values and customs into their conversion methods to gain cooperation and support. Support for missionaries increased when Sto:lo culture was harmed by disease and alcohol. Missionaries were the only people to help the Sto:lo overcome alcohol abuse. Periodically they were local spokespeople for Sto:lo land concerns to government officials. Nonetheless, some cultural practices incompatible with Catholic doctrine, such as First Nations spiritualism, continued among many Sto:lo families and were taught to the young.

Separating the young from the elders was advocated by most missionaries as the only effective method of Christianizing and civilizing the Sto:lo.

In 1914, Thomas Crosby expressed the commonly held rationale for establishing schools which separated children from their families: 'The missionary finds among a people that are so constantly moving about that if he is to expect real, good work it must be done by gathering a number of the children together in Home or Boarding school or Industrial Institution where they can be kept constantly and regularly at school and away from the evil influences of heathen life' (Crosby 1914, 84).

To reciprocate the help given by the Oblate missionaries, some parents consented to send their children to the first missionary-industrial school at St Mary's, Mission. This consent was all the involvement that First Nations people were allowed in the education of their children. Religious educational aims focused on conversion and gradual civilization. The 'knowledge of most worth' was considered to be Catholicism, English, and later, the general subjects of grammar, spelling, and arithmetic, in that order. Industrial pursuits such as farming, stock-raising, and 'housewifery' were taught, and were practised to keep the school running.

The goal of the Oblate missionaries was to force and direct the acculturation of Sto:lo children. First Nations children were neither to mix with non-First Nations peoples nor to remain in their villages. However, separate 'reduction' villages created by the Jesuits and other religious groups did not arise, because Sto:lo parents took their children out of school for seasonal work activities. Elders and parents were beginning to see inimical attitudes being instilled in their children. Their First Nations language was forbidden in school and their strong cultural beliefs were dismissed as mere superstition. Sto:lo people disagreed with the Oblates' harsh discipline and alien values on work, time, health habits, and spiritualism.

The churches and federal government united forces to counteract First Nations resistance. The government increased financial assistance to the churches to improve the industrial trade courses and standards of academic subjects. Criteria for content, teaching resources, and administrative control were left to the church. Half-day plans in which children studied for half of each day and worked for the other half continued in the newer 'industrial' schools. Even though First Nations parents legally lost the ability to say 'no' to their child's school attendance, absenteeism continued as a form of resistance.

Had these costly industrial schools succeeded in their objectives, First Nations children would have lost their cultural identity by being assimilated into white communities. The aim of the government was to teach industrial skills so that students could obtain jobs in the white community and live away from reserves. However, the majority of First Nations students could not obtain jobs in their trades upon leaving school and returned to the reserves, where they remained.

Influence of Governments

Federal Government

The early twentieth century witnessed greater government control of First Nations education. After 1910, curricula guidelines became the responsibility of the federal government. However, the religious denominations still provided administrative and teaching staff. Religion, basic English, and mathematics skills, along with manual trades and homemaking, constituted the schools' curricula. Assimilation, that is, 'Christianizing' and civilizing,' was still a goal of the curriculum. Suppression of First Nations culture was advocated through policies of forbidding the speaking of Native languages and of continuing family separation. Children lived away from families during the school year, and were usually separated from brothers and sisters who were attending the same school.

During the summer vacation, children would still participate with their families in traditional food-gathering expeditions and work activities. No doubt the extended periods of separation changed family interactions and cultural lifestyles. Despite this, many elders and parents continued to practise cultural traditions and beliefs. At functions such as funerals and important meetings, they made speeches in the Halq'emeylem language about the need to uphold the traditions associated with the function being held.

Finally, many parents and band chiefs refused to send their children to residential schools because of the rampant spread of tuberculosis. Another common reason for this decision was that the schools were full or overcrowded. Parents began to request that schools be built on reserves so that children could live with their families.

Reserve day schools were eventually resisted in the same way by First Nations people because of the quality of education being offered in them. Teacher qualifications and skills and curriculum materials were of questionable quality. At an elders' meeting, a member from Chehalis reserve received support when she said, 'Our parents would send us to school [on the reserve] when there was nothing better to do' (personal communication).

Provincial Government

In the 1950s, the goal of assimilation was fused with that of integration when the British Columbia provincial government took responsibility for educating First Nations children. Again, Sto:lo children were expected to conform to the expectations of a government school system. Public schools emphasized the need for First Nations parents to send their children to school in order to develop school-valued skills and knowledge in an integrated setting. Once again, little attention was paid to the cultural differences of First Nations children. Initially, public schools assumed that First Nations children had to adapt to the provincial system. Preservice training for most teachers did not prepare them to understand or accommodate the First Nations child's cultural values and experiences. When asked about the treatment of First Nations children in the classroom, a typical teacher might respond, 'I treat all the children the same; we don't make distinctions according to race.'

Cultural differences were later seen as the cause of education problems among First Nations children. Culturally deprived students were helped through remedial or readiness programs which actually separated First Nations children from regular classroom experiences. This created additional social and self-concept barriers for them. Evidently, the child's cultural background was not considered relevant to understanding the motivation for learning.

Studies which examined the results of the early experience of integration (Parminter 1959; Peterson 1959; Hawthorn 1967) all made recommendations about recognizing the First Nations child's cultural differences. Improvements to curricula, teacher in-service training, and increased communication between home and school were prime examples of these recommendations, and they later engendered significant changes in the public school system.

The 1970s witnessed increased interest in local Native Studies curriculum development projects. This stemmed from Canadian surveys and studies which found that existing curricula lacked relevant content and appropriate teaching methodology (McDiarmid and Pratt 1971; Manitoba Indian Brotherhood 1974; Werner, Connors, Aoki, Dahlie 1977). Frequently, the study of First Nations culture was superficial. First Nations involvement was encouraged in all curriculum development phases to provide sufficient depth and accuracy of content, assist teachers to develop cultural knowledge, and provide role models in the classroom.

Influence of Contemporary First Nations People

The sudden increase in First Nations involvement signalled a shift in the goal of education from assimilation to non-assimilation. With the acceptance of the education policy *Indian Control of Indian Education* by First Nations people across Canada, the federal government and even some provincial educational administrators opened the way for major changes to educational systems in British Columbia. First Nations education groups at provincial and local levels became stronger politically and more assertive in their relations with federal and provincial education authorities. They demanded more administrative control over their educational programs. Curriculum development became a priority for many groups.

Provincial school districts began to work with local First Nations groups to establish new First Nations-oriented programs with more First Nations support staff. Some bands gained administrative control over education and established their own schools on reserve. These band-controlled schools differed greatly from the old reserve day schools. Provincial core curricula were adapted to include more First Nations content. First Nations people participated as teachers, teacher aides, and administrators. Once again, the use of extended family teachers and the reinforcement of cultural values and traditions featured prominently in First Nations education. Other sources of impetus behind the increase in locally developed Native Studies included the creation of a provincial First Nations education branch,[3] a supportive provincial First Nations education policy, availability of funds, and revisions to the provincial social studies curriculum which advocated the use of locally developed materials.

A survey conducted by More, Purcell, and Mirehouse (1981) outlined First Nations education projects in British Columbia schools. Two main classifications emerged from the study. One was curriculum oriented and the other was oriented towards support services. The following are the main types of projects surveyed:

Curriculum oriented:
• Crafts
• First Nations culture – traditional
• First Nations culture – contemporary
• First Nations language
• First Nations studies
• Language arts

Support-service oriented:
• Academic skills development (e.g., learning assistance, tutorials)
• Alternative classes and schools
• Support workers (e.g., home-school coordinators, teacher aides)

Other trends included more subject areas with Native-oriented curricula, a variety of teaching resources, and more First Nations para-professionals in schools.

The influence of First Nations people on educational curricula over the last two decades has contributed to the quality and quantity of locally developed Native Studies curricula. Perhaps students now have an opportunity to learn about First Nations cultures, past and present, in a relevant, meaningful way. After all, this was one of the main purposes of First Nations involvement in curriculum development. A logical question then emerges: Will the implementation of Native Studies curricula developed by First Nations people really achieve the desired results?

Since 1974, many Sto:lo people have been involved in a locally developed Native Studies curriculum. The curriculum model and the Sto:lo people's approaches to its implementation reflect their involvement and intended goals. The following case study describes the curriculum processes and the Sto:lo philosophical stance. Pertinent considerations which have emerged since the program began are also summarized.

Sto:lo Sitel: A Case Study of a Locally Developed Native Studies Curriculum

The Beginning

The elders living in the Sto:lo area began meeting formally in 1968 to work on a cultural heritage project. Their main purpose was to document the Halq'emeylem First Nations language, traditions, and stories. Another purpose was to socialize with one another. For many, meetings were their only opportunity to see friends. The Coqualeetza Education Training Centre began to offer cultural programs in 1970. The elders' project was fused with the cultural centre and became known as the Coqualeetza Elders' Group. Communication with First Nations educators in the Fraser Valley was initiated through the elders' weekly meetings. The two groups set cultural documentation and the development of a cultural curriculum as shared projects.

The elders realized that in order for Sto:lo culture to continue, their knowledge had to be recorded. Oral transmission of knowledge could no longer be relied upon to serve this purpose. The experience of the First Nations educators led them to associate First Nations students' school problems with lack of strong self-identity and insufficient knowledge of cultural differences. They also felt that previous First Nations education programs operated on a crisis or problem-oriented basis, such as the support services given to students after they had got into trouble or had problems. It was recommended that this project be preventive by developing First Nations students' pride in their cultural heritage and increasing mainstream awareness of cultural differences. What began was a sequenced elementary social studies curriculum, the Sto:lo Sitel.

Many teachers had requested teaching resources on local First Nations culture, and the elders agreed that non-First Nations children would also benefit from learning about Sto:lo lifestyles. Social studies seemed the most appropriate area of the curriculum in which to place this subject matter. Added to this was the fact that most local First Nations children attended public schools.

A year was spent on securing adequate funding, developing a support-group system, and establishing communication with the twenty-four First Nations bands of the Sto:lo Nation. The support group represented First Nations education workers, parents, and others with essential Sto:lo knowledge and skills in curriculum development. Their function was to provide direction and support to the curriculum staff. Involvement of First Nations band members was encouraged. Many meetings were held to inform parents of the project and to encourage their participation.

Sto:lo Sitel Units

Because the Sto:lo Sitel curriculum was to be used mainly in the public schools, the provincial social studies guidelines were followed. The major concepts and skills were taught through Sto:lo cultural content and examples. The following list outlines and describes the units designed for each grade level. Each unit contains a comparison between traditional and contemporary lifestyles. A variety of multimedia teaching resources were developed for each unit:

Grade 1 – Upper Sto:lo Families. Special traditions, kinship patterns, examples of lifestyles, and beliefs important to traditional and contemporary Sto:lo families are included. Elders' teachings about family love and strength are exemplified in two stories.

Grade 2 – Upper Sto:lo Communities. Roles of Sto:lo community members are depicted. The concept of a reserve as a community is developed and examined through the example of Seabird Island reserve. Services provided by reserve communities are also compared to non-First Nations communities.

Grade 3 – Upper Sto:lo Interaction. Interaction between Sto:lo people and their environment is emphasized. Chehalis reserve is used to exemplify the relationship between people and their environmental resources. Interaction between First Nations and non-First Nations communities is also included.

Grade 4 – Upper Sto:lo Food.
Part I – Fishing
Part II – Plant Gathering
Part III – Hunting

Techniques of food acquisition and preparation, hunters' skill development, men's and women's roles, and pertinent traditions are covered. Changes are examined.

Grade 5 – Upper Sto:lo Nation. The strength of Sto:lo culture is exemplified in the precontact and fur trade eras. The relationship between the Sto:lo people and federal/provincial governments is also studied.

Grade 6 – Upper Sto:lo Art, Music, and Games. The function of these practices in Sto:lo lifestyles is emphasized. Relevant beliefs connected to each are studied.

Grade 7 – Upper Sto:lo Cultural Stages. The major historical events experienced by Sto:lo people from precontact time to contemporary times are studied. How the First Nations people adapted to cultural change, and how they have maintained an ethnic identity, is emphasized. Stereotyping is also examined. Historical data are introduced.

Timeline
The Sto:lo Sitel curriculum has undergone three general phases: planning, development, and implementation. Figures 14.1, 14.2, and 14.3 outline the major activities of each phase.

The Sto:lo Sitel Curriculum Development Process
The Sto:lo Sitel curriculum development process consists of five main components: (1) situational analysis; (2) objectives; (3) active research; (4) learning experiences; and (5) evaluation. In *situational analysis* a variety of methods were used to gather information to aid curriculum development. Peoples' viewpoints and research surveys were primary sources of information. The fundamental *objectives* provided guidelines for developing grade level and unit objectives. The term 'active' was used to describe the type of *research* conducted because researchers were actively involved in interviewing Sto:lo elders and collecting data from various institutions. *Learning experiences* combined contemporary teaching methodologies and learning resources with traditional Sto:lo principles of education. *Evaluation* measured student learning of content and compared attitudes before and after each unit was covered. These curriculum components were also evaluated by First Nations educators, teachers, and parents.

Situational Analysis
As previously stated, the structure of the Sto:lo Sitel emerged from continuing discussions between elders and First Nations educators. Results from surveys and interviews were used as additional proof of the need for improved curricula. The educational situation of First Nations students

Figure 14.1

Planning, 1974-6

Establishing organizational structure
- location of office and work space within Coqualeetza Education Training Centre
- establishment of office procedures, use of equipment
- hiring of curriculum coordinator

Establishing liaison with
- advisory committee
- Coqualeetza Elders' Group
- participating First Nations communities (chiefs, parents, education committees)
- school district personnel (superintendents, supervisors, teachers)
- resource persons, technical and curriculum consultants

Acquiring funding
- mainly government grants

Completing situational analysis
- needs assessment

Establishing Sto:lo Sitel curriculum model
- philosophy to follow *Indian Control of Indian Education* policy
- objectives
- content topics selected in accordance with Ministry of Education guidelines for social studies
- integrative inquiry teaching model specified

Investigating
- audiovisual and production techniques
- copyright procedures

Completing approval process
- with the seven school districts in the Sto:lo nation. School boards to sanction local curricula utilized in their schools

Researching other First Nations curriculum programs

---

was analyzed by those most affected, family members and staff. As the project continued, more people were asked to participate. Because this project has been operating officially for over two decades, many changes have occurred. In order to meet the changing needs, situational analysis became an ongoing process. The support groups have supplied information from their interactions with First Nations community members and school staff members. Regular scheduled meetings have become a forum for discussing issues and for planning new directions.

Figure 14.2

___

Development, 1976-82

Gathering research data
- oral and written

Developing draft copy of grade-level units
- first one completed was Grade 4, *Upper Sto:lo Food*. A unit consists of:
  - lessons (teachers' guidebook)
  - audiovisual teaching aids (picture study cards, filmstrips, cassette tapes, storybooks, and games)
  - evaluation questionnaire

Completing pilot testing
- with volunteer teachers

Completing unit revisions
- based on pilot testing results through classroom observation, discussion with teachers and First Nations education coordinators, and written evaluation questionnaires

Continuing verification
- of content and teaching materials with the elders, for draft and revised copies

Increasing field testing of units
- as more copies are made available. Minimum of one year of field testing required before units are published

___

Objectives

These three objectives are in the *Sto:lo Sitel Curriculum Development Guide*:
(1) to help First Nations students develop a more positive self-image
(2) to help non-First Nations students develop an increased awareness of and a more positive attitude towards Upper Sto:lo people
(3) to provide students with the opportunity to make a running comparison of traditional and contemporary Upper Sto:lo culture, focusing on culture change, social organization, technology, child-rearing, language, and world-view.

These objectives were further refined for each unit and were matched to the grade level objectives, skills, and concepts prescribed by the Ministry of Education. Teachers could then justify teaching Sto:lo Sitel units at an elementary grade level because students would be learning the necessary concepts and skills through the use of First Nations-related content.

The objectives have basically remained unchanged since the units were first drafted. The guiding function of the objectives has allowed the project developers to keep the fundamental purposes of the curriculum in sight.

Figure 14.3

Implementation, 1978-82

Publishing sufficient units
- for school districts to purchase
- additional copies of reference books, storybooks, and games published for public sale

Negotiating implementation process
- with each school district

Providing teacher in-service training
- introducing the curriculum units
- developing the teachers' cultural awareness
- providing support services to teachers utilizing the units
- arranging for resource speakers, assisting with lesson planning, or assisting teachers, were examples

Training liaison workers
- to serve as intermediaries between the curriculum project and schools

Publishing reference booklets
- to provide teachers with background information about the Sto:lo Sitel curriculum and about Sto:lo culture

Active Research

When the Sto:lo Sitel curriculum development project began, written information on Sto:lo history and culture was scarce. Because the Sto:lo are classified within the anthropological boundaries of the Coast Salish, many people were not aware that a distinction existed. The curriculum staff did not realize the extent of work involved in documentation. The prime source of knowledge was the elders' memories. The elders said that many of their teachings had been put to 'sleep' for so long that it would take awhile to recall them. For years they had not assumed a leadership role, and they had begun to believe that their knowledge was no longer useful to the younger generations. Those who had contributed information to early anthropologists were suspicious of anyone wanting to write books based on their knowledge because of the limited responses they had had from the earlier writers and researchers. Preliminary work on building trust between curriculum staff and elders was vital.

Various methods were used to obtain information. The elders' weekly meetings provided a regular forum for asking questions and verifying written information. Interviews with individuals and small groups took place. Archival data were collected and verified. The First Nations language and history programs at Coqualeetza also shared written information with the Sto:lo Sitel staff.

The information acquired provided a base of knowledge upon which to build a curriculum. Data-gathering continues actively. Documentation and verification processes increase as more elders participate in these tasks.

Learning Experiences
Both the teaching methodology and the structure of audiovisual learning materials were greatly influenced by the philosophy of the *Indian Control of Indian Education* policy. For curriculum, the *Sto:lo Sitel Curriculum Development Guide* states these guiding principles thus:

> Education must encompass our traditional patterns of teaching and learning in which children learn best by doing and experiencing, as opposed to using only written materials. These patterns encompass:
> - independence
> - self-reliance
> - observation
> - discovery
> - practical experience
> - respect for nature

The integrative inquiry process was selected as the teaching model for two main reasons. First, it was assumed that teachers would be familiar with the inquiry technique because it is a common approach to teaching social studies. Second, the integrative inquiry model resembled the holistic approach to traditional Sto:lo education. The relationship between cultural components could be emphasized, rather than isolating and analyzing the components separately. The former method of learning would enable a more complete view of the culture being studied to emerge. Earlier First Nations-oriented curricula tended to isolate and analyze. The integrative inquiry process, as used by the Sto:lo Sitel, is exemplified in the unit *Upper Sto:lo Families*. In this Grade 1 unit, the students learn about:
- the extended family function, roles, and closeness
- traditional name-giving ceremony, which is one way of recording and perpetuating history
- the function of house structure, past and present
- family rules and methods of learning them
- values ascribed to interacting with family members.

Throughout the unit the relationship between these cultural phenomena was developed. The teaching materials consisted of picture study cards, filmstrips, cassette tapes with stories, and storybooks. They were designed and developed in a lesson plan to encourage active student participation. Participation involved the use of the students' senses in structured learning activities, such as role-playing, problem-solving, simulation games, and group discussion. Learning by doing was reinforced through follow-up activities where students could work individually or cooperatively. Where possible, Sto:lo principles of learning and teaching were incorporated into the lessons and learning resources. Experiential learning was a prime example. Others included respecting people and their property, and sharing and cooperating with others.

Defining these principles proved lengthy. The elders gave examples of teachings handed down from previous generations, which many regarded as fundamental to our existence. These teachings encompassed values and beliefs for individual, family, and group survival. The methods for learning were described and integrated into either teaching methodology or learning resources. The following example will illustrate this process.

One unit of the Grade 4 program, *Upper Sto:lo Hunting*, focused on hunting methods, skill development for hunters, animals hunted, food preparation and other uses of animals, and values with respect to nature and resources. Skilled hunters were responsible for teaching young boys. Their training began when they 'came to their senses,' which would occur at the age of eight or nine. A training schedule was established which included developing physical strength and endurance, plus learning how to use various types of hunting equipment. The boys accompanied the older hunters on their journey mainly to observe and learn about the environment. Each boy continued his supervised training until he killed his first deer. This event marked a passage into manhood. As a display of generosity and thankfulness, the deer was cooked at a feast and distributed among village members.

The lesson format of the inquiry process emphasized the importance of skill development through training. Activities where students had to draw and then construct small models of hunting tools aimed at developing appreciation of these skills and reinforcing the knowledge acquired. A student information booklet included a section in story form in which two young Sto:lo boys were trained to become hunters. Students could imagine themselves in the same situation because they could identify with the thoughts and feelings of the boys. These experiences would allow them to further identify with Sto:lo culture.

Throughout the curriculum development process Sto:lo principles for teaching and learning have become more defined. Those working directly in development or liaison roles have been kept informed of this information. Because the development of learning experiences has involved so many Sto:lo adults and teachers, knowledge of Sto:lo culture has proportionately increased in scope and depth.

Evaluation

Various continuous evaluation measures have been used, including assessment of student learning and field testing by teachers. Sto:lo parents and community groups' opinions were the main components of evaluation. With each unit, student pre- and post-tests were designed to measure cognitive learning and to monitor prevalent attitudes. Teachers completed a questionnaire after teaching each unit. The effectiveness and quality of the teaching materials and their suggested application were measured. Meetings were held with parents and interest groups to examine the content and general learning approach. A formative evaluation was also contracted to a professional educational institution.

The dynamic nature of the Sto:lo Sitel curriculum has influenced the consistency and purpose of evaluation. Evaluation was more intense when units were first drafted and pilot tested. When the publication stage was complete, and implementation was in process, evaluation assumed a monitoring role. Future needs will require intensive evaluation to see if implementing a locally developed Native Studies curriculum has had any relevant impact on student attitudes towards First Nations cultures.

Sto:lo Sitel Implementation

By 1979, draft units for Grade 4 were ready for pilot testing in public schools. This expanded into field testing after revisions were completed and ten sets of unit materials were produced. These copies were loaned to volunteer teachers. Field testing of the Grade 4 materials provides a chronological outline of public school implementation of the curriculum. Figure 14.4 outlines the process of public school implementation.

There are two band-controlled schools in the Sto:lo area, Chehalis Community School and Seabird Island School. Chehalis school had 138 students from kindergarten to Grade 11 during the 1982-3 school year. It had operated as a federally run elementary reserve day school between 1914 and 1971, and administrative control was transferred to the band in 1972. Secondary students attended the local public high school in Agassiz until 1982. Seabird Island's school is smaller with 62 students from kindergarten to Grade 6. It had been an elementary reserve day school until 1969. When the day school closed, the children attended either public schools in Agassiz or a parochial school in Chilliwack. In 1978 the band decided to take over educational administration and reopened the

Figure 14.4

Public school implementation

(1) Establishing implementation conditions (1976-7)
   Key Points
   - school district administration was cooperative
   - liaison worker appointed by one school district (First Nations education coordinator)
   - involvement of the Sto:lo people was crucial

   Major activities of project staff
   - conducted orientation workshops for liaison worker and volunteer teachers (curriculum and culture)
   - sponsored special cultural program to accompany units used in schools
   - acquired funding

(2) Expanding implementation (1978-82)
   Key Points
   - school districts authorized or prescribed Sto:lo Sitel curriculum
   - Sto:lo Nation maintained copyright and editorial rights (*Indian Control of Indian Education* policy followed)
   - multiple copies of units published
   - more liaison workers hired for other school districts

   Major activities of project staff
   - conducted lengthy orientation sessions for new liaison workers and teachers
   - expanded Sto:lo Sitel Advisory Committee to include liaison workers (meeting once a month). Staff sponsored this committee

(3) Maintaining implementation (1982-)
   Key Points
   - Sto:lo Sitel Advisory Committee continued to function as support system to liaison workers
   - initial emphasis on support for classroom teachers and students by providing cultural reinforcement programs
   - later, emphasis changed to teachers' cultural awareness. The need for Sto:lo resource teachers continued

   Major activities of project staff
   - conducted orientation for Sto:lo resource teachers
   - assisted with special in-school cultural programs
   - sponsored special cultural awareness sessions for teachers and school administrators

---

old school building. Parents in both bands can now choose to send their children to either the band-operated or the public school. Children from other bands are also accepted at these two schools. Both schools follow the provincial guidelines and core curricula, but also emphasize curricula with First Nations content and programs. Figure 14.5 provides a chronological outline of implementation.

Figure 14.5

Band-controlled school implementation

(1) Establishing implementation conditions (1976-8)
   Key Points
   - developed a working relationship with school board and teaching staff
   - had to prove similarity of Sto:lo Sitel curriculum concepts and skills to provincial social studies concepts and skills to gain acceptance as credible learning institution

   Major activities of project staff
   - participated in the bands' cultural awareness sessions for school staff
   - conducted curriculum orientation sessions for band members, school board members, and teaching staff
   - conducted special cultural in-school programs

(2) Expanding implementation (1978-82)
   Key Points
   - Sto:lo Sitel accepted as part of the schools' core curricula
   - curriculum materials were readily available for school use (complimentary copy given to each school)
   - liaison workers were appointed from each band
   - teachers were receptive

(3) Maintaining implementation (1982-)
   Key Points
   - as more responsibility for implementation was taken over by liaison workers, there was less direct contact between project staff and school staff
   - cultural programs of each school expanded so that Sto:lo Sitel was one component of their cultural curricula

   Major activities of project staff
   - continued to give support to liaison workers

Findings

The case study of the Sto:lo Sitel project demonstrates the process of First Nations involvement, the curriculum model, the development process, and implementation in public and band-controlled schools. From the examination of the Sto:lo Sitel project the following general findings emerge:

- Increased structure for scope/sequence required more development time. Teacher evaluations showed that teachers preferred units complete with lesson plans and teaching resources. Implementation was facilitated when learning outcomes and skills correlated with those prescribed by the provincial Ministry of Education.
- Gaining approval for authorized and prescribed use of Sto:lo Sitel in public and band-controlled schools took much time and effort. The latter have prescribed usage, while the public school districts have authorized the use of the Sto:lo Sitel units. Reaching the prescribed stage has depended on availability of materials. The decision to publish sufficient copies was based on this need. The time required to publish materials has been prolonged because of funding and resource limitations. The main consideration still is that availability increases prospects for prescription and usage.
- Constant support services to teachers have eased problems associated with teaching new curricula. A variety of methods for increasing teachers' cultural awareness were also introduced. Liaison workers have played a key role in this process. More teachers have utilized the units and provided support to teachers in their school who are new to Sto:lo Sitel. Teachers in the two band-controlled schools have been very receptive to Sto:lo Sitel. Their genuine interest plus the direction provided by the local school authorities were contributing factors.
- Many people were involved throughout the curriculum development and implementation processes. The following factors necessitated this degree of involvement:
  - servicing the seven school districts and two band-controlled schools within the Sto:lo geographical area. This included working with teachers, administrators, and liaison workers
  - following the *Indian Control of Indian Education* policy, which initiated community involvement
  - working with elders and other Sto:lo people to ensure accuracy of content and to gain approval of the teaching model.
  Various types of orientation programs were sponsored to familiarize curriculum stakeholders with the Sto:lo project. Initially only a core staff existed. They often worked cooperatively with staff from other bands that had short-term employment programs in order to complete the immense workload. The most useful method of acquiring and retaining help was to have bands or school districts assign someone to work with the Sto:lo Sitel project as part of his/her job responsibilities.
- New directions for the Sto:lo Sitel project have emerged because of the varied and increased community and school involvement. Core staff

occasionally had to discontinue work on unit development in order to meet these requests. For example, a secondary level Sto:lo Studies curriculum was developed to meet the needs of First Nations students in alternative classes and to meet requests from high school teachers for resource materials. This program was also revised for use in adult upgrading classes. The project staff have continued to assist liaison workers trying to initiate new cultural programs for their areas. They have helped with lesson planning and the design and acquisition of teaching materials.

• Numerous meetings and workshops have been held about curriculum business, project promotion, and information sharing with other curriculum developers. The latter have occurred because the Sto:lo Sitel was also developed as a curriculum model. The premise was that other Native Studies projects could follow the curriculum design but use their own cultural content. Some projects used the Sto:lo Sitel curriculum model, while others adopted some of the ideas.

These six major factors have shown how the Sto:lo Sitel's longevity has increased from the projected three years to the present. What will be the future for the Sto:lo Sitel curriculum? How can it retain a place in school curricula? These questions will influence the future considerations of the Sto:lo Sitel staff.

Future Considerations

The dynamic nature of locally developed Native Studies curricula must be recognized and planned for in order to be used effectively. The section on implementation illustrated the time and effort required before Sto:lo Sitel could be used in public and band-controlled schools. Developers must examine the educational situation where their curriculum is to be used and analyze the benefits and limitations of implementation. This project has demonstrated two distinct approaches to using locally developed Native Studies curricula.

Between 1976 and 1982, public school teachers received a generous amount of implementation support from the Sto:lo curriculum stakeholders. These activities have gradually reached saturation level. Ongoing implementation will require two major forces. One force is continuous support and help from the Sto:lo Sitel staff and liaison workers. A second is the cooperation and support between public school teachers and administrators and the Sto:lo group. To date, most of the effort for developing and implementing the Sto:lo Sitel has come from the Sto:lo people. Teachers and administrators have played a secondary role. Their active involvement would be beneficial in the following ways:

- to update the project staff on teachers' needs and suggestions
- to plan appropriate future implementation strategies
- to keep implementation active
- to encourage and help fellow teachers use the Sto:lo Sitel unit effectively.

I believe that locally developed Native Studies curricula are accepted more readily and used more meaningfully in band-controlled schools than in the public school system. Chehalis and Seabird Island schools have displayed the necessary flexibility and commitment to implement Native-oriented curricula. They have also provided additional support staff and services. In this situation, the Sto:lo Sitel as presently developed should provide a basic framework for learning Sto:lo history and culture. To obtain maximum benefits, more teaching resources and cultural activities are required. The Sto:lo Sitel staff must continue to work closely with Chehalis and Seabird Island educational staff to ensure relevant use of the curriculum units.

Today, many First Nations people adopt a strongly non-assimilationist stance through the development of First Nations-oriented curricula. This approach has been greatly influenced by past educational experiences. Historical examination of First Nations education reveals First Nations resistance to education systems that opposed cultural teaching and learning patterns. The fruits of this resistance have been the new First Nations education systems and the improved Native-oriented curricula for public schools. Each of these developments has facilitated the practice of First Nations cultural teaching and learning patterns by encouraging First Nations involvement in curriculum development. First Nations people who are involved in this type of curriculum work must continually reexamine their efforts to ensure both quality and the eventual attainment of their fundamental objectives.

Notes

An earlier version of this chapter appeared in Harvey McCue, ed., *Selected Papers from the 1984/86 Mokakit Conference* (Vancouver: Mokakit Education Research Association 1986).

1 'First Nations' is used inclusively to mean all people of Aboriginal ancestry. 'Native' is used interchangeably with 'First Nations.'
2 Maps 14.1 and 14.2 illustrate the geographical boundaries of the Upper Sto:lo people. The term *Sto:lo* will be used in this chapter. Map 14.1 shows the relationship between the Sto:lo cultural area and the larger Coast Salish boundaries. Map 14.2 highlights the School Districts in the Sto:lo area.
3 In 1992, it was renamed the Aboriginal Education Branch.

References

Aoki, T. 1973. Towards devolution in the control of education on a Native reserve in Alberta: The Hobbema curriculum story. *Council of Anthropology and Education Newsletter* 4 (2)

Archibald, Jo-ann. 1977. *Sto:lo Sitel curriculum development guide*, 4th ed. Sardis: Coqualeetza Education Training Centre

Ashworth, Mary. 1979. *The forces which shaped them. A history of the education of minority group children in BC.* Vancouver: New Star Books

Bowd, Alan. 1977. Ten years after the Hawthorn Report: Changing psychological implications for the education of Canadian Native people. *Canadian Psychological Review* 16 (4):332-45

–, Daniel McDougall, and Carolyn Yewchuck. 1982. Psychological perspectives on Native education. In Alan Bowd, Daniel McDougall, and Carolyn Yewchuk, eds., *Educational psychology: A Canadian perspective*, 276-95. Toronto: Gage

British Columbia Ministry of Education. 1982. *Social Studies curriculum guide. Grade K-11.* Victoria: Curriculum Development Branch

Canada, Department of Indian Affairs and Northern Development. 1932-6. *Central registry system, school files.* Vol. 6387, file 806-1 (part 1)

Canada, Royal Commission on Indian Affairs. 1916. *Report of the Royal Commission on Indian Affairs for the province of British Columbia.* 4 vols. Victoria: Acme Press

Coqualeetza Education Training Centre. 1975. *Education needs of Native Indians: A consultancy report to Fraser Valley College.* Sardis: Coqualeetza Education Training Centre

–. 1979-82. *Sto:lo Sitel report*, 3rd ed. Sardis: Coqualeetza Education Training Centre

Crosby, Thomas. 1914. *Up and down the North Pacific coast by canoe and mission ship.* Toronto: Missionary Society of the Methodist Church

Duff, Wilson. 1964. *Indian history of British Columbia.* Victoria: BC Provincial Museum

–. 1952. *The Upper Stalo Indians of the Fraser Valley, British Columbia. Anthropology in British Columbia.* Memoir 1. Victoria: BC Provincial Museum

Edmeston, H. 1956. *The Coqualeetza story 1886-1956.* Sardis: n.p.

Hawthorn, H. 1967. *A survey of contemporary Indians in Canada.* Vol. 2. Ottawa: Queen's Printer

Kennedy, Jacqueline. 1969. Roman Catholic missionary effort and Indian acculturation in the Fraser Valley 1860-1900. B.A. essay, Department of History, University of British Columbia

Klesner, Peg. 1982. *Language arts for Native Indian students.* Victoria: Curriculum Branch, BC Ministry of Education

Knight, Rolf. 1978. *Indians at work.* Vancouver: New Star Books

La Roque, Emma. 1975. *Defeathering the Indian.* Agincourt: Book Society of Canada

Manitoba Indian Brotherhood. 1974. *The shocking truth about Indians in textbooks: Textbook evaluation*. Winnipeg: Manitoba Indian Brotherhood

McDiarmid, Garett, and David Pratt. 1971. *Teaching prejudice*. Toronto: Ontario Institute for Studies in Education

More, Arthur J., Susan Purcell, and Grace Mirehouse. 1981. *Indian education projects in BC schools*. Vancouver: University of British Columbia

National Indian Brotherhood. 1972. *Indian control of Indian education*. Ottawa: National Indian Brotherhood

Parminter, Alfred. 1959. The development of integrated schooling for British Columbia Indian children. M.A. thesis, University of British Columbia

Peterson, Lester Ray. 1959. Indian education in British Columbia. M.A. thesis, University of British Columbia

Sealy, D. Bruce, and Verna J. Kirkness (eds.) 1973. *Indians without tipis. A resource book by Indians and Métis*. Winnipeg: William Clare

Union of BC Indian Chiefs. 1975. *Understanding the Master Tuition Agreement*. Vancouver: Union of BC Indian Chiefs

Vallery, H.J. 1942. A history of Indian education in Canada. M.A. thesis, Queen's University

Werner, Walter, Bryan Connors, Ted Aoki, and Jorgen Dahlie. 1977. *Whose culture? Whose heritage? Ethnicity within Canadian social studies curricula*. Vancouver: Centre for the Study of Curriculum and Instruction, University of British Columbia

15

The Sacred Circle:
An Aboriginal Approach to Healing
Education at an Urban High School
Robert Regnier

The Joe Duquette High School parents' council in Saskatoon identified its high school as 'a healing place.' The school uses the Sacred Circle as a spiritual foundation for the social and cultural dimensions of healing education in upgrading and academic programs for Aboriginal youths between fourteen and twenty-one years old. This chapter examines the school's work as an expression of an Aboriginal spirituality/metaphysics in which teaching as healing comprises 'transition toward meaning, wholeness, connectedness, and balance' (Katz and St. Denis 1991, 24). The school integrates its academic program with Aboriginal spirituality to help those students who suffer from 'chemical dependency, alienation, racism, denial, self-mutilation and other forms of violation and abuse.'

The failure of Saskatchewan schools to meet the educational needs of Aboriginal students has been evident in extremely high dropout rates. The Aboriginal high school dropout rate in inner city schools in Saskatchewan was 90.5 per cent in 1981 (Saskatchewan Education 1985, 2). In response to this phenomenon and the associated social and cultural problems for urban Aboriginal youth, the parent council and faculty eventually adopted the Sacred Circle as the basis for an educational milieu. Within this milieu, staff and council designed program and pedagogical approaches to assist students to cope with the taxing emotional and social challenges in their lives. The staff and council held that teaching the mind alone did not constitute education, and that students could not be educated without addressing their emotional and spiritual beings. For this more holistic education, they turned to the Sacred Circle.

The Sacred Circle is a symbolic circle which incorporates the spiritual beliefs of many Indian tribes of North America (Sanderson 1991, 45-6). 'Put simply, the Amerindian genius, acknowledging as it does the universal interdependence of all beings, physical and spiritual, tries by every means available to establish intellectual and emotional contact between them, so as to guarantee them – for they are all "relatives" – abundance, equality, and therefore, peace. This is the sacred circle of life' (Sioui 1992, xxi).

By selecting the Sacred Circle within Cree cosmology as a foundation for educational practice, the Joe Duquette High School demonstrates how a non-Eurocentric framework for emancipatory education in an urban context can offer insights for other First Nations. Many other First Nations share Sacred Circle ideals, although not within the same grounded culture as the Plains Cree. Cree cosmology sees human beings and nature as connected and unified, views time as cyclical rather than linear, and allows for a sense of ultimate meaning and purpose within a heritage open to cross-cultural possibilities.

The Joe Duquette High School

Mission Statement. The Joe Duquette High School is a healing place which nurtures the mind, body and soul of its students. The school offers a program of studies which affirms the contemporary worldview of Indian people. The school supports the uniqueness and creativity of the individual and fosters self-actualization in a cooperative environment.

This school, located in Saskatoon, a city of about 200,000 in Saskatchewan, began in 1980 as the Saskatoon Native Survival School. It had fifty students and three classrooms. The school was established through a unique three-party agreement between the Saskatoon Native Survival School's parents' council, the Saskatoon Catholic Board of Education, and the Saskatchewan Department of Education. In this agreement, the school undertook to provide an alternative experience that responds directly to the educational needs of urban Native youth. The general objective is to provide courses on First Nations culture in an environment that supports the development of academic skills and self-esteem. In 1988, the school changed its name, and by 1993, 150 students were enrolled and fourteen faculty were employed, including a cook, janitor, social worker, counsellor, elder, principal, vice-principal, and ten teachers.

The healing approach at Joe Duquette emerged with the development of First Nations education in Canada. In the last two decades, First Nations have succeeded in participating in constitutional negotiations, having many land claims recognized, attaining increased local governance, and in operating cultural and social institutions. Concomitantly, the Indian Control of Indian Education movement achieved band control of schools on Indian reserves, Native survival schools were established in urban areas, and 'Native Way' schools promoted culturally grounded education throughout the country. Educational developments were rooted in notions of survival, self-determination, self-sufficiency, and cultural revival and moved beyond multicultural, assimilationist, and integrationist ideologies which disregard cultural alienation, poverty, powerlessness, and a distinct world-view.

Joe Duquette faculty adopted a healing approach and drew upon Sacred Circle teachings to direct their work. To address the social issues in students' lives directly, the school uses several approaches. Peer self-help groups, drug and alcohol treatment centres, workshops, events (e.g., Drug and Alcohol Awareness Week), survival skills in the curriculum, and work-contact groups such as Alcoholics Anonymous had been only relatively successful before 1990. The council and staff adopted a more comprehensive and substantive approach to healing education by implementing a one-year project, the Natotowin Healing Project. This project began in summer 1990 when school staff participated in a one-week in-service healing education session with Lee Brown from Round Lake, British Columbia, and Phil Lane of the Four Worlds Development Project in Lethbridge. It extended throughout the year as staff met regularly to assess and advance the school's development. This change came about after students and staff encountered and studied the Sacred Circle approaches to alcoholism and sexual abuse adopted by Aboriginal drug and alcohol treatment centres in Saskatchewan and some Aboriginal communities in Canada. The Sacred Circle offered a healing approach to education based on a holistic spiritual perspective on students and their place in the world.

The school's spiritual perspective is sustained by daily sweet grass ceremonies, feasts on special occasions, special ceremonies, and sweat lodges. Teachers conduct talking/healing circles to build communities of trust so that students can speak about their feelings and lives. They also teach survival skills in which the Sacred Circle helps students think critically about health and development. As well, they use storytelling circles and collective improvisation through which students dramatize their learning. Drumming and dancing circles introduce students to aesthetic dimensions of culture that unify psyches and social relations through celebration. Support circles for students generate peer backing in dealing with abuse. To support and expand its work, the school has established a theatre as well as day care and young offender programs.

Joe Duquette is thus a school that offers imaginative educational practices for advancing First Nations urban culture. The healing and Sacred Circle foundations provide for movement towards the 'good,' towards positive human growth and development, and towards creative responses to many challenges faced by urban First Nations youth in their quest for a good life. By recognizing the existential immediacy of students' lives and the urgent historic need to create and revitalize cultural frameworks for education, schools can address the spiritual crisis created by cultural genocide and structural racism. Many First Nations youths look for immediate responses to their urgent needs. The school offers programs, processes, and structures to take up this urgency.

Education and the Sacred Circle

Joe Duquette High School uses the Sacred Circle as a broad perspective for understanding and developing its educational offerings. Sacred Circle accounts are passed from generation to generation through ceremonies, legends, and storytelling. Sacred Circle symbolism is enacted in meetings, sun dances, sweat lodges, sweet grass ceremonies, pipe ceremonies, and feasts where participants confer, celebrate, and pray. This symbolism represents unity, interdependence, and harmony among all beings in the universe, and time as the continual recurrence of natural patterns. These cyclical patterns and recurrences constitute the reality in which humans can understand purpose and meaning.

The cyclical movement in these patterns is the process of attaining wholeness, interdependence, and balance in four phases. The symbolic Sacred Circle is divided into four directions (north, south, east, and west) representing the four races (white, black, red, and yellow), the four aspects of humanness (emotional, physical, mental, and spiritual), the four cycles of life (birth, childhood, adulthood, and death), the four elements (fire, water, wind, and earth), and the four seasons (spring, summer, fall, and winter). Wholeness in the cycle of the year requires movement through all the seasons; wholeness in life requires movement through the phases of human life; and wholeness in human growth requires the development of all aspects of humanity. The year, life, and human growth can attain completion through this natural movement to wholeness. From this perspective, education for human development reflects the special responsibility that human beings have for all things. This responsibility is mirrored in language which presents them as relatives: Mother Earth, Father Sun, Grandmother Moon, Brother Animals, and Sister Plants, for example, characterize humanity's close relationships with all things. Education through the Sacred Circle allows people to see harmony and balance in their interconnectedness with all things.

The concept of the sacred circle or way of life is supported by an underlying belief that the Creator created the world in balance and harmony and gave a purpose and power to all living things. All powers are eventually traced back to the Creator. It becomes the responsibility of mankind for keeping the world in order and following the sacred laws and way of life that was given to them by the Creator. Mankind was responsible to maintain this balance and harmony, defined in the Cree language as 'Wanuskewin,' by correctly carrying out the obligations that went with it. These obligations are passed on, and are reinforced through stories 'acimowina' that told of events of long ago in which individuals restored harmony and balance to this world. (Fiddler and Sanderson 1991, 10)

The Circle is used to inform research, construct educational models, develop curricula, and interpret learning theory. In 'Toward a Redefinition of American Indian/Alaska Education,' Eber Hampton uses the six dimensions of the Sacred Circle to analyze data from interviews addressing 'What is Indian about Indian Education' (Hampton 1993, 280). In her 'reflexive examination of the underlying premises about authority in anthropological discourse in the broader context of respect' (Te Hennepe, 1993, 193), Sheila Te Hennepe uses metaphorical concentric circles based upon the Sacred Circle to understand discourse in a specific context. Pepper and Henry model self-esteem through the medicine wheel (Pepper and Henry 1991).

Important curriculum development has been based upon the Sacred Circle. Members of the Four Worlds Project in Lethbridge, Alberta, consulted with elders and cultural leaders from forty tribes in North America in 1982 'to address the root causes of Native alcohol and drug abuse' (Bopp et al. 1988b). In 1987, elders and cultural leaders reviewed 'philosophy, guiding principles, activities and strategies for human and community development' (Bopp et al. 1988b) which have been implemented by the Four Worlds Development Project in producing curriculum materials. *The Sacred Tree* and *The Sacred Tree: Curriculum Guide* (Bopp et al. 1988a and b) are designed to be an 'effective drug and alcohol abuse prevention curriculum' (Bopp et al. 1988b, 13). They are intended to 'set into motion a kind of personal reflection that will touch the very core of their personal existence.' This curriculum offers students ideals, ethical reflection, and a way to envision the good through a healing 'journey' from the medicine wheel perspective. It exemplifies the resources produced by this centre to assist youth to grow, change, and develop out of destructive drug and alcohol abuse.

Lee Brown of the Round Lake treatment centre has interpreted Sacred Circle insights through the Anisa model of learning. 'The primary aim of the Anisa model is to learn how to learn' (Brown n.d., 1). The model presents learning as a process of differentiating experience into contrasting elements and integrating these elements into a pattern applicable to new situations (Brown n.d., 2). To guide learning through the circular movement that occurs throughout life, the model offers learners notions of body-awareness, self-image, self-concept, self-esteem, and self-determination to help students construct a 'learning identity.' Lee interprets these notions within Sacred Circle quadrants to offer students many possibilities for developing learning strategies (Brown n.d., 10-12).

The Sacred Circle and Healing

The Sacred Circle is also called the medicine wheel in Plains Indian cultures. Health, part of the same metaphysic as reality itself, means having a meaningful vision of one's wholeness, connectedness, and balance. Shared visions of well-being are renewed and celebrated in rituals and ceremonies that restore person, community, and nation. Illness is loss of meaningful vision, purpose, or direction which results in fragmentation, isolation, and imbalance or distortion in one's life. Aboriginal healing which includes adherence to the medicine wheel approach has assumed significant proportions in Canada in the last decade. This growth is evident in the fourth Women and Wellness Conference held in Saskatoon in October 1993. Here 1,700 First Nations women, primarily from western Canada, heard presentations on acceptance of AIDS victims, alcoholism and parenthood, suicide awareness, co-dependency, sexual abuse and healing circles, and recovery from addiction. Attendance at this annual conference, one of many on these issues, has grown significantly since the first one in 1990. The healing movement is also evident in healing approaches to community development. Community healing circles attempt to address longstanding and deeply ingrained practices in communities. Furthermore, this movement is applied to developing human justice that builds upon the restoration of harmony and balance in the lives of victims and offenders. Sentencing circles which involve the community, draw on elders to mediate, and provide rehabilitation rather than punishment characterize some medicine wheel-based approaches.

Simultaneously, North American First Nations have tackled the monumental task of constructing and reconstructing educational institutions and practices in order to address the crisis of meaning for indigenous youth. Healing education attempts to transcend neo-colonial teaching which assumes inherited educational goals, curricula, and frameworks without addressing the immediate reality of students. The practice of teaching as healing offers many possibilities for Aboriginal students. In 'Teacher as Healer,' Katz and St. Denis present a model of 'teaching as healing' based on their study of elders and medicine people in Cree and Fijian cultures: 'The "teacher as healer" is one who, infused with spiritual understanding, seeks to make things whole ... seeks to respect and foster interconnections – between herself, her students, and the subject matter; between the school, the community, and the universe at large – while respecting each part of these interconnected webs' (Katz and St. Denis 1991, 24).

In this model the teacher is responsible not only for envisioning the whole and understanding wholeness but also for allowing learning which strives for wholeness. This requires that teachers move beyond personal needs to serve the sacredness or goodness of the whole family, community, or nation. Envisioning the purpose of school from this perspective means not only considering the wholeness of individuals. It also means providing for the learning of all students, not just those who suit current educational approaches. It also means restoring learning or schooling to those who have been marginalized, denied, or rejected. This restoration may require teachers to courageously adopt learning approaches and structures that promote holistic learning by the marginalized rather than the interests of the privileged.

Breaking the Sacred Circle

When Western governments attacked Aboriginal cultures through schooling and other policies, they targeted Aboriginal world-views. Schooling practices distanced people from their Aboriginal identity and placed them beyond the influence of the Sacred Circle. Identities were reconstructed in isolation from Aboriginal world-views through residential schools. These practised Western metaphysics and religion, which individualized and isolated students. By removing them from family and community, schools socially and politically reoriented Aboriginal youth away from the natural cyclical process involving rituals, ceremonies, and gatherings. The denial and purging of Aboriginal metaphysics was the foundation of much social and cultural disorganization and many destructive lifestyles.

Aboriginal people have suffered the most severe social, economic, and educational problems in Canada. Many communities, for example, have chronically high alcoholism rates. Schools in these communities were not seen as having anything to do with alcoholism. However, people began to ask 'What is the point of graduating a drunk or drug addict?' If the purpose of education is to make a better life possible, then school must address the real lives of students. For school to make learning possible, it must help students address the root determinants of learning in their lives. An academic program that ignores alcohol- or drug-related learning problems fails to understand that confronting abuse can be the beginning of one's education. Abuse cannot simply be tolerated as an inevitable condition separate from whatever form of academic education occurs. In the medical metaphor, abuse is the symptom of an illness, the cause of which must be diagnosed. Acknowledging abuse and searching for its roots makes healing possible. Healing education committed to restoring wholeness in each student takes up the extremes of abuse as a central determinant of educational possibility.

By 1976, a sixteen-year-old boy in Saskatchewan had a 70 per cent chance of being imprisoned by the age of twenty-five (York 1989, 146). In Prince Albert, Saskatchewan, 50 per cent of the federal penitentiary population is Aboriginal, whereas Aboriginals account for less than 5 per cent of the national population. While the Saskatchewan population is 15 to 20 per cent Aboriginal, 75 per cent of the provincial correctional centre population is Aboriginal, and 85 per cent of the women's correctional centre is Aboriginal. In Manitoba in 1989, Aboriginals comprised 52 per cent of the inmates in federal and provincial jails, although Aboriginals comprise only 4.5 per cent of the province's population (Lajeunesse 1990, 2). York's comment that 'prison has become for young native people the contemporary equivalent of what the Indian residential school represented for their parents' (York 1989, 147) is a poignant reminder that institutional change has not necessarily improved life for Aboriginal youths. The disproportionately high number of Aboriginal youths who have had early encounters with the law is related to poverty and racism. Arrest, youth detention centres, court appearances, lawyers, social service agencies, incarceration, and the stigma of a criminal record are all part of a social process that criminalizes very many Aboriginal youths. Education to liberate individuals from ostracism, isolation, and guilt from criminalization must include them in the circle of life. Instead of punishment and blame through exclusion, education for justice must restore Aboriginal youths to self-worth and community.

The annual suicide of about 5,000 Canadian Indians under twenty-five years of age is a rate six times higher than that for non-Indians. Some researchers believe the true rate is twelve times higher than the Canadian average. A University of Lethbridge sociologist who specializes in suicide has not found another racial group with suicide rates nearly as high as that among Canadian Indians, not even in the worst US ghettos (York 1989). In a wellness survey conducted at the Joe Duquette High School of 110 students in the fall of 1993, '51 per cent of the students indicated they have often (10 per cent) or sometimes (40.1 per cent) thought of committing suicide, but half of these (25.5 per cent) have attempted to commit suicide at least once' (Wellness Survey 1993, 3). At the heart of education is the desire and will to live. School programs that fail to acknowledge and celebrate the sacredness and goodness of life fail to reinforce students' desire and will to live life to the fullest. Education based on the Sacred Circle is intended to reinforce that desire and will.

In founding its healing education program in the Sacred Circle, Joe Duquette High School deals with the social needs of youth. Although many First Nations youth issues in Saskatoon are addressed by various social service, justice, education, youth service, and recreational organizations, the overall approach of these agencies is ineffective, and vulnerable First Nations youth are not well served. The 1993 Community Response to Street Youth and Runaways in Saskatoon, a study by the Centre for Applied Population Studies at Carleton University, confirms the limited success of these agencies. It shows that 'a majority of the runaways and street youth in Saskatoon are aboriginal' (Caputo, Weiler, and Kelly 1993, p. 5). While not all vulnerable youths are street youths or runaways, the study provides clear insight into the limitations of agency services. It reports that the community's current response to the at-risk group 'is not effective' (p. 19). The authors conclude that 'most agree that the present system is not effective in dealing with the needs of Saskatoon's street youth ... despite high costs, often well intentioned service providers and numerous programs which in themselves are considered relevant and effective' (p. 19). Present service approaches are not community-based. Moreover, workers are generally unaware of or lack support to promote services centred in First Nations communities and are unfamiliar with culturally based addiction prevention and healing programs for First Nations youth and young adults. The Carleton study acknowledges that 'the system is primarily focused upon individuals' (p. 37) and calls for change 'to address the need for community development' (p. 37).

Joe Duquette School Practice

In an effort to improve the school's offerings to students, over the last thirteen years various programs and initiatives have been experimented with by the school faculty and parent council. The academic program has been altered and adjusted to incorporate First Nations perspectives, cultural development and revitalization have become central components, several social supports for students have been developed, and First Nations spirituality has become a central foundation. I describe below ways in which the school has institutionalized ceremonies and rituals, social support practices, cultural activities, classroom approaches, and healing education programs.

Ceremonies and Rituals

The school conducts feasts, sweat lodges, and sweet grass ceremonies in which students are invited to participate. Participation is viewed as central to the students' cultural and spiritual learning. On these occasions, students are affirmed as valuable and important members of the community and universe and are helped to meet personal, social, and academic challenges. Feasts are special events which include a ceremonial meal where food is served according to specific protocols. There is a pipe ceremony during which an elder says a ritual prayer with those present. Sweat lodges are prayer rituals conducted by elders outside the city in canvas-covered willow lodges. These lodges are conducted when students or faculty approach elders through the appropriate protocol to undertake a sweat that will help them resolve challenges such as addiction.

Students and staff meet weekly in the gymnasium for a sweet grass ceremony. Sweet grass is a prairie grass picked for ceremonial uses. When burned, it gives off an aromatic smoke which symbolizes spiritual purification and prayer. Participants in the ceremony sit in a circle. As a braid of smouldering sweet grass is carried clockwise, each participant 'smudges' by wafting the smoke towards his or her body. The smoke reflects the unity of participants with one another, the larger community, the Creator, the grandfathers and grandmothers, and creation. A teacher offers a prayer of good intentions, makes announcements, and introduces guests. In this ritual affirmation, everyone is welcomed into community with the others. This ceremony affirms unity and reconciliation with others. It anticipates that students and teachers will break this unity, but that they will remain in ultimate harmony with one another. 'The ceremony ritually overcomes the separateness of history, culture, custom, and geography of students from any of the seventy First Nations in Saskatchewan, northern and rural communities, and other parts of Canada' (Regnier 1994). Through it, teachers, principal, janitor, students, vice-principal, cook, secretary, and social worker, Native and non-Native, female and male, join in community. It can be the 'first step to overcoming isolation, self denial, exclusion, disenfranchisement, alienation and loss of identity' (Regnier 1994). Students come to trust that revealing their pain will not result in isolation or rejection but rather in a response that will move them to conciliation and harmony.

Social Support Practices

Joe Duquette High School offers breakfast and lunch for all students. All teachers are available to students for counselling, an availability highlighted by the absence of a separate faculty lounge. Instead, students and staff meet daily in shared dining facilities where interaction continues. Students are assisted by a school social worker and a school counsellor who appear with them in court, help them resolve social assistance matters, find accommodation in group homes that the parents' council has established (in apartments, or with designated guardians), and arrange drug and alcohol treatment in Native-run rehabilitation centres. To assist students to develop mutual support, the staff instituted a weekly support circle, and a men's support and a women's support circle after school. The weekly support circle, which has met since 1986 after class, helps students suffering from abuse and negative lifestyles assist one another with a culturally and spiritually based approach. In gender circles, counsellors help students reflect upon and support one another in addressing gender-specific issues.

Cultural Programs

Reestablishing and recreating Aboriginal cultural self-understanding in the urban context has been of central importance in the school. To effect this, the staff and parent council have undertaken several projects. Elders are available for counselling, consulting, and continuing participation in school and classroom functions throughout the year. Each spring the school offers a cultural camp outside the city where students can learn and celebrate in a natural environment. In a partnership program between the school and the Wanuskewin National Park, students participate in park programs and projects that focus on local First Nations history. Students participate as dancers and drummers at local pow-wows where they also operate a concession, and the school organizes pow-wows to which they invite the community and other participants. Cultural interest in provincial and international Aboriginal peoples is reflected in the selection of course materials and participation in local cultural events.

Teachers and an elder offer a drumming circle and a dancing circle. The school elder teaches a group of boys to play the drum, sing honour and flag songs, and look after the drum. The drum group plays at special events, at conferences, in ceremonies, and in jail. Because drumming is sacred and a community responsibility, drummers must be drug- and alcohol-free, reliable, and willing to play at events when called upon to do so. Drumming is a way of recognizing the sacred. On one occasion, for example, the drum group performed an honour song to recognize the courage of a person who spoke publicly about his struggle with AIDS (Bell 1993). In the dance circle, students learn traditional and fancy cultural dances and perform in the community. These presentations bring honour and respect to those who are being affirmed and recognized. The many hours of practice demonstrate to students the capacity of the culture to celebrate life.

Classroom Approaches

While offering upgrading and academic programs that conform to provincial requirements, the school incorporates elements of the Sacred Circle and medicine wheel into its classroom teaching. Native literature is incorporated into English courses, and First Nations-related events, culture, and society are a focus in social studies, for example. In addition, the program offers modern survival skills courses where students learn about the medicine wheel and how to interpret it explicitly in their lives. To engage students in creative and critical reflection on their lives, teachers use talking/healing circles and storytelling and collective improvisation to assist English language development in a culturally relevant and socially imaginative manner.

Classroom Talking/Healing Circles

The purpose of talking circles is to create a safe environment for people to share their views with others. This process helps people gain trust in each other. They believe that what they say will be heard and accepted without criticism.

Community healing at Joe Duquette High School is based on mutual support that is made possible by the empathy of students towards each other which has been fostered in classroom healing circles. Each day, each classroom teacher supervises a healing circle in which students learn to listen to what other students say about their lives. In contrast with regular lessons, which focus away from self, the healing circles focus on self. Students are encouraged to view one another from a perspective of 'sacredness' or the 'good' as reflected in medicine wheel teachings. As students discuss and interpret their experiences and feelings, the teacher guides the movement to harmony.

Rupert Ross's understanding of the movement to harmony in the culture of the Oji-Cree in northern Ontario reflects the general direction of the healing circle. Ross sees movement to harmony based on the attitude of elders who 'do their best to convince people that they are one step away from heaven instead of one step away from hell' (Ross 1992, 169). Using the elders' example, he emphasizes how important it is to build self-esteem, but self-esteem is not merely a tactic of positive reinforcement.

I believe instead that it is a necessary manifestation of a core conviction: the conviction that each person is derived from the Creator, is defined by the Creator's goodness, and can aspire to a spiritual sanctity that approximates at least in kind, that possessed by the Creator. When a person misbehaves and causes harm, it does not prove that he is a malevolent creature, only that he is in need of assistance to bring himself back to himself again. Furthermore, within this belief system, each person, each community is under the Creator's duty to offer assistance when it is needed. (Ross 1992, 174)

Within this framework, healing circles are intended to be places where students can grow in the practice of recognizing their own sanctity, the sanctity of others, and the sanctity of the community. By learning to respect what each has to say, students soon develop confidence and self-esteem and are increasingly willing to share experiences and feelings with others. Students learn to reflect on and share their pain with others in a circle in which their personal integrity is maintained and recreated. Students learn to affirm one another and interact supportively. Because adolescents significantly influence one another as peers, the educational task is to help them learn to listen, be compassionate, and act in solidarity by creating conditions for this learning.

The healing circle begins with the ritual of smudging and the teacher's broad comments on the value of dialogue and the class's potential as a healing community. Each day the class may address issues or have a particular focus. Students are invited to speak about what they feel or think. As a talking stone or other object is passed from person to person in the circle, students talk about their lives. Some don't talk. 'When they speak, others listen, help them express themselves, empathize with their predicament, reflect upon their circumstance, suggest how they might improve their situation, and offer assistance. The community takes the personal reality of the student as curriculum. Teachers help students learn to be compassionate, to be accepting and to share. Students move from silence to dialogue, isolation to connectedness and interdependence' (Regnier 1994).

Story Circle and Collective Improvisation Pedagogy

In one teaching approach used at the school for more than a decade, story circle and improvisational theatre techniques are used to have students produce dramatic performances. The core of the teaching method is the story circle, made up of students and teachers. The group sits on the floor in a circle: announcements are made; information shared; the plan for the session is introduced. The 'story circle' emerges as a daily ritual. It always follows the same structure: one person initiates a story with a phrase or sentence; the next repeats the phrase or sentence; then another adds to the story, and so on around the circle until every one has contributed (Murphy and Smillie 1988, 35). By improvising these stories, and with the variations and extensions to this clockwise speaking movement, students learn to listen, speak, share, and care with and for one another. 'What seems so extraordinary about experiences at the Saskatchewan Native Survival School [now Joe Duquette] is not the quality of acting because making actors is not the highest priority – but the quality of the group experiences' (Murphy and Smillie 1988, 40).

This approach reaches back to the oratorical practices of Plains Cree storytelling and ceremony. Its liberating and empowering dynamic is founded in Paulo Freire's *Pedagogy of the Oppressed* and Constance Stanislovsky's emphasis on spontaneity. Through this approach, students are encouraged to reflect critically and act upon their experiences, feelings, and aspirations. Within the circle – made sacred through the teacher's guidance, developing student sensibility, and ancestral myths – 'student lives become curriculum as students improvise and construct imaginative responses to the conditions and situations depicted by them' (Regnier 1994). By reenacting and replaying the stories, students learn to identify patterns and processes that are meaningful in their lives.

School Programs

As Joe Duquette developed, three programs were devised to expand and support the school's work. The Saskatoon Native Theatre has taken up the storytelling and collective improvisation work, the E-Tankanawasot Day Care provides community care with student mothers and families, and the Meyo-Macetawin program works with young offenders. The theatre experience deepens students' self-esteem, develops a positive public image, exercises students' social imagination, and improves their academic performance. The day care and the young offenders programs extend the school to students who might otherwise be excluded from supportive relationships and learning opportunities.

Saskatoon Native Theatre

With the success of story circles and collective improvisation, the school incorporated the Saskatoon Native Theatre in 1985, which operates through the school with the parents' council acting as the board of directors. The theatre solicits funding and produces public performances by students using versions of storytelling and improvisational theatre approaches. Students have produced several plays which present the voice of urban Native youth in its quest for identity, meaning, and purpose based on imaginative reflection on their experience, interests, and aspirations. The theatre has produced *Indians 'R' Us* (1988), *Troubled Spirits* (1987), *Family Violators Will Be Towed Away* (1986), and *Street Zone* (1985). These plays show student quests for security, identity, family, and education against the backdrop of struggles with racism, alcoholism, and self-confidence. Through these productions and performances, students build friendships, make public presentations, travel to festivals, meet students in other centres, as well as benefit from the cultural, social, and academic skills needed for such an undertaking.

E-Tankanawasot (holding an infant) Day Care

The E-Tankanawasot Day Care Centre Corporation provides a nurturing and stimulating program at Joe Duquette High School for infants under eighteen months. The program was started in 1992 and serves about ten students at the school. It builds an environment for infants, families, caregivers, and the school as community, and is intended to build life-affirming support and relationships. In a society that hides, ostracizes, and isolates students with children from their peers, family, and community, this program recognizes the importance of supporting student families and mothers, of building a community with them. Prospective mothers prepare for their children by visiting the centre, where they receive support from the accepting spirit of the Sacred Circle. The milieu of appreciation and encouragement brings students back to school as soon as possible after the birth of their children. Here they and the staff can care for the children as they complete their schooling.

Meyo-Macetawin

This program, which started in 1993, challenges youth to examine 'their attitudes, values and beliefs' and to replace 'feelings of self-hate, boredom, anger and hopelessness with meaningful educational, therapeutic and structured activities' (Meyo-Macetawin n.d.). The program targets youth referred by young offenders case workers through the Department of Social Services. These youths are not a threat to the community but have criminal convictions, previous custodial sentences, systems-generated charges (failure to comply, breaches), family services involvement indicating dysfunctional families and protection, some substance abuse, and school attendance or work problems. This project is undertaken by the school in partnership with the Federation of Saskatchewan Indian Nations. It focuses directly on keeping young offenders within the circle of community and spiritual renewal at the school.

Conclusion

The Sacred Circle offers a perspective which allows healing education structures and programs to be created for Aboriginal youth. This perspective has been studied by several theorists who offer many possibilities for its continued development as a means of advancing Aboriginal education. It has been an important perspective for promoting the healing movement. Work at the Joe Duquette High School demonstrates the use of the medicine wheel perspective to shape healing education in response to the circumstances of many urban Aboriginal youths. The school has become a centre for spiritual practice, social support, cultural activity, and pedagogical development designed to assist students. Although grounded in Plains Cree and broad Plains First Nations culture, many of the practices are transferable to other First Nations who wish to use the Sacred Circle for developing school programs.

Note

This paper is a revision of an unpublished paper written in consultation with Emil Bell in 1993, 'The Sacred Circle: A First Nations Approach to Healing Education at an Urban High School.' Emil Bell is the chairperson of the Joe Duquette High School parents' council.

1 For a review of survival schools see R.H. Regnier, 'Survival Schools as Emancipatory Education,' *Canadian Journal of Native Education* 14, 2 (1987):42-54; and D. McCaskill, 'The Revitalisation of Indian Culture: Indian Cultural Survival Schools,' in J. Barman, Y. Hébert, and D. McCaskill, eds. *Indian Education in Canada*. Vol. 2, *The Challenge* (Vancouver: University of British Columbia Press 1987), 153-79.

References

Access Network. n.d. *The sacred circle*. Edmonton: University of Alberta. Video

Alkali Lake Indian Band. 1985. *In honour of all*. Alkali Lake, British Columbia. Video

Bell, Emil. 1993. Personal communication

Bopp J. et al. 1988a. *The sacred tree*. Lethbridge: Four Worlds Development Project

–. *The sacred tree: Curriculum guide*. 1988b. Lethbridge: Four Worlds Development Project

Brown, L. n.d. Learning: A study of the values, identity, culture and learning in the classroom. Unpublished paper, Round Lake, British Columbia

Caputo, T., R. Weiler, and K. Kelly. 1993. The community response to street youth and runaways in Saskatoon. Unpublished paper, Centre for Applied Population Studies, Carleton University, Ottawa

Earth Ambassadors. n.d. *Issaquah*. Washington: Phil Lucas Productions. Video

Fiddler, S., and J. Sanderson. 1991. Medicine wheel concept: From the world-view of the Plains and Cree culture. Unpublished paper, Saskatchewan Indian Federated College, Regina

Four Worlds Development Project. 1990. Guidelines for talking circles. *Four Worlds Exchange* 1, 4 (11-12 March): 2-3

Hampton, E. 1993. Toward a redefinition of American Indian/Alaska Native education. *Canadian Journal of Native Education* 20 (2):261-309

Hunt, N.B. 1981. *Indians of the Great Plains*. Bedfordbury, UK: Orbis

Katz, R., and V. St. Denis. 1991. Teacher as healer. *Journal of Indigenous Studies* 2 (2):24-36

King C. 1991. Indian world view and time. In E.J. McCullough and R.L. Calder, eds., *Time as a human resource*, 182-7. Calgary: University of Calgary Press

Lajeunesse, T. 1990. Cross cultural issues in the justice system: The case of Aboriginal people in Canada. Unpublished manuscript

Lucas, P. 1989. *Circle of healing*, pt. 1 and 2. In *Man alive*. Toronto: CBC Video

Meyo-Macetawin. n.d. Pamphlet, Saskatoon: Meyo-Macetawin Project

Murphy, K., and R. Smillie. 1988. Story circles: A method of acting and taking care of people. *Our Schools, Our Selves* 1 (1):33-41

Pepper, F.C., and S.L. Henry. 1991. An Indian perspective of self-esteem. *Canadian Journal of Native Education* 18 (2):145-60

Poilieve, A. 1992. Sacred circle teaching, at the Joe Duquette High School. Interview with Robert Regnier, Saskatoon

Regnier R.H. 1994. The sacred circle: A process pedagogy of healing. *Interchange* 25 (2):129-44

–. 1987. Survival schools as emancipatory education. *Canadian Journal of Native Education* 14 (2):42-54

–. 1988. Acting and taking care of one another. *Our Schools/ Our Selves* 1 (1):22-32

Ross, R. 1992. *Dancing with a ghost: Exploring Indian reality*. Markham, ON: Octopus Publishing

Sanderson J.L. 1991. Aboriginal pedagogy: An adult education paradigm. M.A. project, Department of Communication, Continuing and Vocational Education, University of Saskatchewan

Saskatchewan Education. 1985. *Inner city dropout study*. Regina: Government of Saskatchewan

Sioui, G. 1992. *For an Amerindian autohistory: An essay on the foundations of a social ethic*. Kingston: McGill-Queen's University Press

Te Hennepe, Sheila. 1993. Issues of respect: Reflections on First Nations student experience in post-secondary anthropology classrooms. *Canadian Native Journal of Education* 20 (2)

Wellness Survey, Joe Duquette High School, September 1993, p. 7

Whitehead, A.N. [1929] 1957. *The aims of education*. New York: Free Press

York, G. 1989. *The dispossessed: Life and death in Native Canada*. Toronto: Lester and Orpen Dennys

Bibliography of First Nations Pedagogy

Kathy Vermette

Learning Styles

Anderson, Starla. Discourse performance of Native Indian students: A case study with implications for academic instruction. Ph.D. dissertation, University of British Columbia, 1987

Atleo, Richard. *An examination of Native education in British Columbia: Kindergarten readiness and self-image and academic achievement.* Vancouver: Native Brotherhood of British Columbia 1993

Boseker, Barbara J., and Sandra L. Gordon. What Native Americans have taught us as teacher educators. *Journal of American Indian Education* 22, 3 (1983):20-4

Browne, Dauna Bell. Learning styles and Native Americans. *Canadian Journal of Native Education* 17, 1 (1990):23-35

Chrisjohn, R.D., and M. Peters. The right-brained Indian: Fact or fiction? *Journal of American Indian Education* 25, 2 (1986):1-7

Clifton, Rodney A., and Lance W. Roberts. Social psychological dispositions and academic achievement of Inuit and non-Inuit students. *Alberta Journal of Educational Research* 34, 4 (1988):332-43

Dunn, R., J. Beaudry, and A. Klavas. Survey of research on learning styles. *Educational Leadership* 46, 6 (1989):50-8

Garrett, J. Understanding Indian children from Indian elders. *Children Today* 22, 4 (1993-4):18-21

Goller, Claudine. Teaching Native students in an urban setting. *Multiculturalism* 7, 3 (1984):17-20

Hartley, Elizabeth Ann. Through Navajo eyes: Examining differences in gifted-ness. *Journal of American Indian Education* 31, 1 (1991):53-64

Heit, M. *Possible differences in communication styles between Indian/Métis and non-Native peoples.* Regina: Department of Education 1986

Hurlburt, Graham, Eldon Gade, and John McLaughlin. Teaching attitudes and study attitudes of Indian education students. *Journal of American Indian Education* 29, 3 (1990):12-18

Hvitfeldt, Christina. Traditional culture, perceptual style, and learning: The classroom behavior of adults. *Adult Education Quarterly* 36, 2

(1986):65-77

Kaulback, Brent. Styles of learning among Native children: A review of the research. *Canadian Journal of Native Education* 11, 3 (1984):27-37

Kleinfeld, J. *Effective teachers of Indian and Eskimo high school students.* Fairbanks: University of Alaska Institute of Social, Economic, and Government Research 1972

–, and Patricia Nelson. *Adapting instruction to Native Americans 'learning styles': An iconoclastic view.* Fairbanks: University of Alaska 1988

Marashio, P. Enlighten my mind: Examining the learning process through Native Americans' ways. *Journal of American Indian Education* 21, 2 (1982):2-9

Marshall, Carol. The power of the learning styles philosophy. *Educational Leadership* 48, 2 (1990):62

More, A. Native Indian learning styles: A review for researchers and teachers. *Journal of American Indian Education* 27, 1 (1987):17-29

–. Native Indian students and their learning styles: Research results and classroom applications. *BC Journal of Special Education* 11, 1 (1987):23-7

Pepper, F.C., and S.L. Henry. Social and cultural effects on Indian learning style: Classroom implications. *Canadian Journal of Native Education* 13, 1 (1986):54-61

Preston, Jo-Anne Nowell. Ethnography of communication and its implications for teachers of Native Indian students. M.A. thesis, University of British Columbia, 1986

Rhodes, Robert W. Measurements of Navajo and Hopi Brain Dominance and Learning Styles. *Journal of American Indian Education* 29, 3 (1991):29-40

Saskatchewan Education. *Preparing for the year 2000.* Regina, SK: Saskatchewan Departmant of Education 1987

–. *Instructional approaches: A framework for professional practice.* Regina, SK: Saskatchewan Department of Education 1991

Sawyer, Don. Native learning styles: Shorthand for instructional adaptations? *Canadian Journal of Native Education* 18, 1 (1991):99-105

Shutiva, Charmaine L. Creativity differences between reservation and urban American Indians. *Journal of American Indian Education* 31, 1 (1991):33-52

Swisher, Karen, and Donna Deyhle. The styles of learning are different, but the teaching is just the same: Suggestions for teachers of American Indian youth. *Journal of American Indian Education*, Special Issue (1989):1-14

Wauters, Joan, Joan Bruce, David Black, and Phillip Hocker. Learning styles: A study of Alaska Native and non-Native students. *Journal of American Indian Education*, Special Issue (1989):53-62

Williams, David George. Simultaneous and sequential processing, reading, and neurological maturation of Native Indian (Tsimshian) children. Ph.D. dissertation, University of British Columbia, 1986

Teaching Styles

Adams, D. A case study – self-determination and Indian education. *Journal of American Indian Education* (January 1974):21-7

Arbess, S. *New strategies in Indian education.* Victoria, BC: Ministry of

Education 1981

Brown, A.D. The cross-over effect: A legitimate issue in Indian education. *Multicultural Education and the American Indian* (1979):93-107

Burnaby, B. *Languages and their roles in Native education.* Toronto: Ontario Institute for Studies in Education 1982

Campbell, Mary Ellen. *The 5 B's of success for teaching Aboriginal students.* Saskatoon: University of Saskatchewan, College of Education 1991

Cazden, C. *Classroom discourse: The language of teaching and learning.* Portsmouth, NH: Heinemann Educational 1988

Collier, John Jr. *Alaskan Eskimo education: A film analysis of cultural confrontation in the schools.* New York: Holt, Rinehart and Winston 1973

Cooley, R.E., and R. Ballenger. Culture retention programs and their impact on Native American cultures. In R.N. St. Clair and W.L. Leap, eds., *Language renewal among American Indian tribes: Issues, problems and prospects.* Arlington, VA: National Clearinghouse for Bilingual Education 1982

Cummins, J. *Heritage language education.* Toronto: Ministry of Education 1983

Dreikurs, R., R. Grunwald, and F.C. Pepper. *Maintaining sanity in the classroom,* 2nd ed. New York: Harper and Row 1982

Dumont, R.V. Jr. Learning English and how to be silent: Studies in Sioux and Cherokee classrooms. In C.B. Cazden, V.P. John, and D. Hymes, eds., *Functions of language in the classroom.* New York: Teachers College Press 1972

Erickson, Frederick. *Timing and context in everyday discourse: Implication for the study of referential and social meaning.* Sociolinguistic Working Paper No. 67. Austin, TX: Southwest Educational Development Laboratory 1980

Foerster, L.M., and D. Little Soldier. Classroom communication and the Indian child. *Language Arts* 57, 1 (1980):45-9

Freark, E.S., and M.M. LeBrasseur. Touch a child – they are my people: Ways to teach American Indian children. *Journal of American Indian Education* 21, 3 (1982):6-12

Goodenough, W.P. Multi-culturalism as the normal human experience. *Anthropology and Education Quarterly* 7, 4 (1976):7-18

Harrison, B.G. Informal learning among Yupik Eskimos: An ethnographic study of one Alaskan village. Ph.D. dissertation, University of Oregon 1981

Jobidon, O., ed. *Successes in Indian education: A sharing. A conference to assess the state of the art.* Victoria: BC Ministry of Education 1984

Kleinfeld, J. Effects of nonverbally communicated personal warmth on the intelligence test performance of Indian and Eskimo adolescents. *Journal of Social Psychology* 91 (1973):149-50

–. *Eskimo school on the Andreafsky: A study of effective bicultural education.* New York: Praeger 1979

–, G.W. McDiarmid, S. Grubis, and W. Parrett. Doing research on effective cross-cultural teaching; the teacher tale. *Peabody Journal of Education* 61 (1983):87-8

Lee, D.D. A socio-anthropological view of independent learning. In G.T. Gleason, ed., *The theory and nature of independent learning.* Scranton, PA: International Textbook 1967

Lee, R. Classroom strategies for Native students. *Canadian Journal of Native Education* 9, 4 (1982):25-6

Leith, S., and K. Slentz. Successful teaching strategies in selected northern Manitoba schools. *Canadian Journal of Native Education* 12 (1980):24-30

Longstreet, W.S. Learning and diversity: The ethnic factor. *Educational Research Quarterly* 2, 4 (1978):60-73

Macias, J. The hidden curriculum of Papago teachers: American Indian strategies for mitigating cultural discontinuity in early schooling. In G. Spindler and L. Spindler, eds., *Interpretive ethnography of education at home and abroad.* Toronto: Copp Clark Pitman 1987

Modiano, N. Using Native instructional patterns for teacher training: A Chiapas experiment. In R. Troike and N. Modiano, eds., *Proceedings of the first Inter-American Conference on Bilingual Education.* Arlington, VA: Center for Applied Linguistics 1975

Morey, S.M., and O.L. Gilliam. *Respect for life: The traditional upbringing of American Indian children.* Garden City, NY: Waldorf Press 1974

Nakonechny, Carole. Classroom communication: A case study of Native Indian adolescents. M.A. thesis, University of British Columbia, 1986

Paine, R., ed. *The white Arctic: Anthropological essays on tutelage and ethnicity.* St John's: Memorial University 1977

Pepper, Floy C. *Effective practices in Indian education: A teachers monograph.* Portland, OR: Northwest Regional Educational Laboratory 1985

Philips, S. *The invisible culture: Communication in classroom and community on the Warm Springs Indian Reservation.* New York: Longman 1983

Resnick, L.B. Learning in school and out. *Educational Researcher* 16, 9 (1987):13-20

Scollon, R. *Tempo, density, and silence: Rhythms in ordinary folk.* Fairbanks: Center for Cross-Cultural Studies, University of Alaska 1981

Scollon, R., and S. Scollon. *Narrative, literacy and face in interethnic communication.* Norwood, NJ: Ablex 1981

Shearwood, P. Literacy among the Aboriginal peoples of the Northwest Territories. *Canadian Modern Language Review* 43, 4 (1987):630-42

Silliman, E., and L.C. Wilkinson, *Communicating for learning: Classroom observation and collaboration.* Gaithersberg, MD: Aspen 1991

Sindell, P. Some discontinuities in the enculturation of Mistassini Cree children. In G.D. Spindler, ed., *Education and cultural process: Anthropological approaches.* Prospect Heights, IL: Waveland 1987

Smith, J.C. When is a disadvantage a handicap? *Journal of American Indian Education* 19, 2 (1980):13-18

Stairs, A. Beyond cultural inclusion: An Inuit example of indigenous educational development. In T. Skutnabb-Kangas and J. Cummins, eds., *Minority education: From shame to struggle.* Clevedon, UK: Multilingual Matters 1988a

–. Native models for learning: A reply to Lauren Resnick. *Educational Researcher* 17, 6 (1988b):4, 6

–. The professional development of Native educators: Context, culture, and language. *TESL Canada Journal* 5, 2 (1988c)

Streeter, Sandra Kay. Parents: The Indian child's first teacher. In Jon Reyhner, ed., *Teaching the Indian child: A bilingual/multicultural approach,* 2nd ed. Billings: Eastern Montana College 1988

Swisher, Karen. Cooperative learning and the education of American Indian/Alaskan Native Students: A review of the literature and suggestions for implementation. *Journal of American Indian Education* 29, 2 (1990): 37-9

Trueba, H. Culturally based explanations of minority students' academic achievement. *Anthropology and Education Quarterly* 19, 3 (1988):270-87

Whyte, Kenneth, Strategies for teaching Indian and Métis students. *Canadian Journal of Native Education* 3, 13 (1986):1-20

Wolcott, H. The anthropology of learning. *Anthropology and Education Quarterly* 13, 2 (1982):83-108

Wyatt, J. Native involvement in curriculum development: The Native teacher as culture broker. *Interchange* 8, 1 (1978-9):17-28

Teacher/Community Relationships

Ada, A.F. The Pajaro Valley experience working with Spanish-speaking parents to develop children's reading and writing skills through the use of children's literature. In T. Skutnabb-Kangas and J. Cummins, eds., *Minority education: From shame to struggle.* Clevedon GB: Multilingual Matters 1988

Becker, H.J., and J.L. Epstein. Parent involvement: A survey of teacher practices. *Elementary School Journal* 83, 2 (1982):85-102

Bernstein, B. Elaborated and restricted codes: Their social origins and some consequences. *American Anthropologist* 66, 6 (1964):55-69

Bing, E. Effect of child rearing practices on development of differential cognitive abilities. *Child Development* 34 (1963):631-48

Coller, Albert A. A study of the attitudes of Slavey Indian parents toward education in Hay River. M.A. thesis, University of Saskatchewan 1976

Cotton, W.E. Alaska's 'Molly Hootch Case': High schools and the village voice. *Educational Research Quarterly* 8, 4 (1984):30-43

Crean, Fioca. The perceptions of Native parents and professionals regarding the education of urban Native children. M.A. thesis, University of Toronto 1979

Cummins, Bryan. Indian control of Indian education: A Burkian interpretation. *Canadian Journal of Native Education* 12, 3 (1985):15-20

Cummins, Jim. *Bilingualism and special education: Issues in assessment and pedagogy.* San Diego: College Hill 1984

–. Empowering minority students: A framework for intervention. *Harvard Educational Review* 56 (1986):18-36

–. Empowering Indian students: What teachers and parents can do. In Jon Reyhner, ed., *Teaching the Indian child: A bilingual/multicultural approach.* Billings, MT: Eastern Montana College 1988

Davis, Sydney. The participation of Indian and Métis parents in the school system. *Canadian Journal of Native Education* 13, 2 (1986):32-9

Featherly, B. The relation between the oral language proficiency and reading achievement of First Grade Crow Indian Children. Ph.D. dissertation, Montana State University 1985

Hakuta, K., and R.M. Diaz. The relationship between degree of bilingualism and cognitive ability: A critical discussion and some new longitudinal data. In K.E. Nelson, ed., *Children's Language*. Hillsdale, NJ: Erlbaum 1985

Howes, G.R., H.G. Weiss, and M.S. Weiss. *How to raise your child to be a winner*. New York: Rawson, Wade 1980

Kincheloe, J.L., T.S. Kincheloe, and G.H. Staley, eds. Introduction. *Journal of Thought* 19, 3 (1984):5-10

Lambert, W.E. Culture and language as factors in learning and education. In A. Wolfgang, ed., *Education of immigrant students*. Toronto: Ontario Institute for Studies in Education 1975

Levine, R.A. Parental goals: A cross-cultural review. In J.J. Lerchter, ed., *The family as educator*. New York: Teachers College Press 1974

Little Bear, Dick. Teachers and parents: Working together. In Jon Reyhner, ed., *Teaching the Indian child: A bilingual/multicultural approach*, 2nd ed. Billings: Eastern Montana College 1988

Litvak, E., and H.J. Meyer. *School, family and neighborhood: The theory and practice of school community relations*. New York: Columbia University Press 1974

Lucas, B., C. Lusthaus, and H. Gibbs. Parent advisory committees in Quebec: An experiment in mandated parental participation. *Interchange* 10, 1 (1979)

Maestas, J.R., ed. *Contemporary Native American address*. Provo, UT: Brigham Young University 1976

Michel, George J. School community relations and resources in effective schools. *Canadian Journal of Native Education* 12, 3 (1985)

Ogbu, J.U. *Minority education and caste*. New York: Academic Press 1978

Richardson, D. Theophilus, and Zena A.C. Richardson. Changes and parental involvement in Indian education. *Canadian Journal of Native Education* 13, 3 (1986):21-5

Sattes, B.D. Parent involvement: A review of the literature. Occasional paper 21. Charleston, WV: Appalachia Educational Laboratory 1985

Saxe, R.W. *School community relations in transition*. Berkeley, CA: McCutchan 1984

Tizard, J., W.N. Schofield, and J. Hewison. Collaboration between teachers and parents in assisting children's reading. *British Journal of Educational Psychology* 52 (1982):1-15

Watson, R., M. Brown, and K.H.J. Swick. The relationship of parents' support to children's school achievement. *Child Welfare* 62, 2 (1983):175-80

Language and Culture

Anderson, B., and J. Barnitz. Cross-cultural schemata and reading comprehension instruction. *Journal of Reading* 28, 2 (1984):102-8

Battiste, Marie Ann. An historical investigation of the social and cultural consequences of Micmac literacy. Ed.D. dissertation, Stanford University 1984

–. Micmac literacy and cognitive assimilation. In *Indian education in Canada*. Vol. 1, *The legacy*. ed. J. Barman, Y. Hébert, and D. McCaskill. Vancouver: UBC Press 1986

–. Mi'kmaq linguistic integrity: A case study of Mi'kmawey School. In *Indian education in Canada*. Vol. 2, *The challenge*, ed. J. Barman, Y. Hébert, and D. McCaskill. Vancouver: UBC Press 1987

Berger, Beverley Ann. Implementation of an art programme designed to develop cultural awareness among Indians in an urban Native Indian alternative class: A case study. M.A. thesis, University of British Columbia, 1983

Berry, J.W. Temne and Eskimo perceptual skills. *International Journal of Psychology* 1 (1966):207-29

–. Independence and conformity in subsistence level societies. *Journal of Personality and Social Psychology* 7, 4 (1967):415-18

–. *Human ecology and cognitive style: Comparative studies in cultural and psychological adaptation*. New York: Sage-Halstead 1976

Brant, C. Native ethics and rules of behaviour. *Canadian Journal of Psychiatry* 35, 6 (1990):534-9

Cajete, Gregory. *Look to the mountain: An ecology of Indigenous education*. Durango, CO: Kivaki Press 1994

Chrisjohn, R., S. Towson, and M. Peters. Indian achievement in schools: Adaptation to hostile environments. In J.W. Berry, S. Irvine, and E.B. Hunt, eds., *Indigenous cognition: Functioning in cultural context*. Dordrecht, Netherlands: Nijhoff 1988

Clifton, Rodney A., and Lance W. Roberts. Exploring the value orientations of Inuit and White students: An empirical inquiry. *Canadian Journal of Native Education* 16, 1 (1989):12-23

Corson, David. *Language, minority education, and gender: Linking social justice and power*. Toronto: OISE 1993

Crago, M.B. Cultural context in communicative interaction of young Inuit children. Ph.D. dissertation, McGill University 1988

Darnell, R. Reflections on Cree interactional etiquette: educational implications. Working papers in sociolinguistics, no. 57. Austin, TX: Southwestern Educational Developmental Laboratory 1979

DeFaveri, I. Contemporary ecology and traditional native thought. *Canadian Journal of Native Education* 12, 1 (1984):1-9

Dorais, L.J. *Language and education in Arctic Canada: Some background data. Proceedings of the Conference on Language and Educational Policy in the North*. Berkeley: University of California 1992

Dyal, J.A. Cross-cultural research with the locus of control construct. In H.M. Lefcourt, ed., *Research with the locus of control construct 3*. San Francisco: Academic Press 1984

Erickson, F. Talking down: Some cultural sources of miscommunication in interactional interviews. In A. Wolfgang, ed., *Nonverbal behavior: Applications and cultural implications*. New York: Academic Press 1979

–. Transformation and school success: The politics and culture of educational achievement. *Anthropology and Educational Quarterly* 18 (1987):335-57

–, and G. Mohatt. Cultural organization of participation structures in two classrooms of Indian students. In G. Spindler, ed., *Doing the ethnography of schooling: Educational anthropology in action*. Toronto: Holt, Rinehart and Winston 1982

Eriks-Brophy, A. The transformation of classroom discourse: An Inuit example. M.A. thesis, McGill University 1992

Falgout, S., and P. Levin. Introduction: Transforming knowledge: Western schooling in the Pacific. *Anthropology and Education Quarterly* 23, 1 (1992): 3-9

Goniwiecha, Mark C. Native language dictionaries and grammars of Alaska, northern Canada, and Greenland. *RSR Reference Services Review* 16, 1,2 (1988):121-34

Gump, P. Education as an environmental enterprise. In R. Weinberg and F. Wood, eds., *Observation of Pupils and Teachers in Mainstream and Special Education*. Reston, VA: Council for Exceptional Children 1975

Hampton, Eber. 'Toward a redefinition of American Indian/Alaska Native education.' *Canadian Journal of Native Education* 20, 2 (1994):261-310

Heath, S.B. *Ways with words: Language, life and work in communities and classrooms*. Cambridge: Cambridge University Press 1983

Hosgood, Kathleen Marie. Study of the language development of five-year-old children attending the Chilcotin Indian Day School and the Redstone Indian Day School. M.A. thesis, University of Victoria, 1983

Kawagley, Angayuqaq Oscar. A Yupiaq world view: Implications for cultural, educational and technological adaptation in a contemporary world. Ph.D. dissertation, University of British Columbia, 1993

Kirkness, Verna J. Aboriginal languages in Canada: From confusion to certainty. *Journal of Indigenous Studies* 1, 2 (1989):97-103

Lipka, J. Toward a culturally based pedagogy: A case study of one Yup'ik Eskimo teacher. *Anthropology and Education Quarterly* 22 (1991):203-23

MacWhinney, B., and C. Snow. The child language data exchange system: An update. *Journal of Child Language* 17 (1990):457-72

McPhie, Judith Lynn. Attitude change through cultural immersion: A grade four enrichment curriculum in pre-contact Squamish longhouse life. M.A. thesis, Simon Fraser University, 1987

McShane, D., and J.W. Berry. Native North Americans: Indian and Inuit abilities. In S.H. Irvine and J.W. Berry, eds., *Human abilities in cultural context*. Cambridge: Cambridge University Press 1988

Mehan, H. *Learning lessons*. Cambridge, MA: Harvard University Press 1979

Morris, Sonia, Keith McLeod, and Marcel Danesi. *Aboriginal languages and education: The Canadian experience*. Oakville, ON: Mosaic Press 1993

Oakes, Jill. Culture: From the igloo to the classroom. *Canadian Journal of Native Education* 15, 2 (1988):41-8

Ogbu, J.U. Research currents: Cultural-ecological influences on minority school learning. *Language Arts* 67, 8 (1985):60-9

Ovando, C.J. School and community attitudes in an Athapaskan bush village. *Educational Research Quarterly* 8, 4 (1984):12-29

Pfeiffer, B.A. Designing a bilingual curriculum. In R. Troike and N. Modiano, eds., *Proceedings of the First Inter-American Conference on Bilingual Education*. Arlington, VA: Center for Applied Linguistics 1975

Philips, S.U. Participant structures and communicative competence: Warm Springs children, community and classroom. In C.B. Cazden, V. John, and D. Hymes, eds., *Functions of language in the classroom*. New York: Teachers College Press 1972

–. *The invisible culture: Communication in classroom and community on the Warm Springs Indian Reservation*. New York: Longman 1983

Platero, D. Bilingual education in the Navajo Nation. In R. Troike and N. Modiano, eds., *Proceedings of the First Inter-American Conference on Bilingual Education*. Arlington, VA: Center for Applied Linguistics 1975

Regnier, Robert. Survival schools as emancipatory education. *Canadian Journal of Native Education* 14, 2 (1987):12-23

Roberts, L., R. Clifton, and J. Wiseman. Exploring the value of orientations of Inuit and white students: An empirical inquiry. *Canadian Journal of Native Education* 16, 1 (1989):12-23

Spolsky, B., ed. *The language education of minority children*. Rowly, MA: Newbury House 1972

Vernon, P.E. Educational and intellectual development among Canadian Indians and Eskimos. *Educational Review* 18 (1966):79-91

Volterra, V., and T. Taeschner. The acquisition and development of language by bilingual children. *Journal of Child Language* 5 (1978):311-26

Warnika, E.J. Report of Lethbridge Native Education Task Force to Boards of Lethbridge School District No. 51 and Lethbridge Catholic Separate School District No. 9. *Canadian Journal of Native Education* 13, 3 (1986):37-41

Williamson, Karla Jessen. Consequence of schooling: Cultural discontinuity amongst the Inuit. *Canadian Journal of Education* 14, 2 (1987):60-9

Wilman, D. The natural language of Inuit children: A key to Inuktitut literacy. Ph.D. dissertation, University of New Mexico 1985

Curriculum and Content

Abrahamson, Sherry Cheryl Gail. Relationship between parental support for literacy, school attendance and the reading behaviors of Musequeam children. M.A. thesis, University of British Columbia, 1987

Ahenakew, F. Text-based grammars in Cree language education. In S. Weryackwe, ed., *Proceedings: Selected papers and biographics*. Choctaw, OK: Sixth Annual International Native American Language Issues Institute 1986

Allen, J. *Assiniboine reading primers*. Hays, MT: Hays-Lodge Pole Public Schools 1987

BC Global Education Project. Teaching our common future. *Teacher* 4, 7 (1992):92-4

BC Indian Education Study. *Native literacy and life skills curriculum guidelines: A resource book for adult basic education*. Victoria, BC: Ministry of Advanced Education n.d.

Bryant, Harriet Willis. Investigation into the effectiveness of two strategy training approaches on the reading achievement of grade one Indian children. Ph.D. dissertation, University of British Columbia, 1986

Calahasen, Pearl. An analysis of the mutualistic process of developing learning resources for and about Native people. *Multiculturalism Magazine* 12, 3 (1989):15-20

Cheek, H. A suggested research map for Native American mathematics education. *Journal of American Indian Education* 23, 2 (1984):1-9

Dulce Public Schools. *Stories about us.* Dulce, NM: Dulce Public Schools (Jicarilla Apache Reservation) 1977

Elofson, Warren. Improving Native education in the province of Alberta. *Canadian Journal of Native Education* 15, 1 (1988):31-8

Freire, Paulo. *Pedagogy of the oppressed.* New York: Continuum Publishing 1970

–. *Education for critical consciousness.* New York: Continuum Publishing 1973

–. *Pedagogy in process: The letters to Guinea-Bissau.* New York: Continuum Publishing 1983

Grundy, Shirley. *Curriculum: Product or praxis.* New York: Falmer Press 1987

Kroeber, Karl. *Traditional literatures of the American Indian: Texts and interpretations.* Lincoln: University of Nebraska Press 1981

Krupat, Arnold. *The voice in the margin: Native American literature and the canon.* Berkeley: University of California Press 1989

Lipka, Jerry. A cautionary tale of curriculum development in Yup'ik Eskimo communities. *Anthropology and Education Quarterly* 20, 3 (1989):216-31

–. Culturally negotiated schooling: Toward a Yup'ik mathematics. *Journal of American Indian Education* (1994):15-30

–. Integrating cultural form and content in one Yup'ik Eskimo classroom: A case study. *Canadian Journal of Native Education* 17, 2 (1990):18-32

Maristuen-Rodakowski, Julie. The Turtle Mountain reservation in North Dakota: Its history as depicted in Louise Erdrich's 'Love Medicine' and 'Beet Queen.' *American Indian Culture and Research Journal* 12, 3 (1988):33-48

Northwest Territories, Legislative Assembly. Special Committee on Education. *Learning: Tradition and change in the Northwest Territories.* Yellowknife, NT: Government of the Northwest Territories 1982

Reyhner, Jon, ed. *Teaching the Indian child: A bilingual/multicultural approach.* Billings: Eastern Montana College 1988

Sasse, Mary Hawley. Teaching Native American literature in the high school: Theory and practice. M.A. thesis, Southern Illinois University 1979

Sherzer, Joel, and Anthony C. Woodbury. *Native American discourse: Poetics and rhetoric.* New York: Cambridge University Press 1987

Shor, Ira. *Freire for the classroom.* Portsmouth, NH: Boynton and Cook 1987

–, and Paulo Freire. *A pedagogy for liberation: Dialogues on transforming education.* South Hadley, MS: Bergin and Garvey 1987

Smith, M. Astronomy in the native-oriented classroom. *Journal of American Indian Education* 23, 2 (1984):16-73

Spindler, G.D. Why have minority groups in North America been disadvantaged in their schools. In G. Spindler, ed., *Education and Cultural Process*, 2nd ed. Prospect Heights, IL: Waveland 1987

Stiles, J. Mark. *Communications and information technologies and the education of Canada's Native peoples*. New Technology in Canadian Education Series, 6. Toronto: TV Ontario 1984

Torres, Carlos A. Paulo Freire's *Pedagogy of the Oppressed*: Twenty years after. *Aurora* 13, 3 (1990):12-14

University of British Columbia, Summer Science Program for First Nations Youth. House of Learning offers an awesome summer. *Kahtou* 6, 16 (1988):11-13

Weiler, Kathleen. *Women teaching for change*. South Hadley, MS: Bergin and Garvey 1988

Contributors

Jo-ann Archibald is a member of the Sto:lo Nation. The director of the First Nations House of Learning at the University of British Columbia and president of the Mokakit Educational Research Association, she is completing her Ph.D. dissertation at Simon Fraser University on First Nations storywork.

Jean Barman is senior editor of *Indian Education in Canada,* vol. 1, *The Legacy* and vol. 2, *The Challenge,* published by UBC Press in 1986-7. Author of *The West beyond the West: A History of British Columbia,* she is a professor in the Department of Educational Studies at the University of British Columbia.

Marie Battiste, a member of the Mi'kmaq Nation, is an associate professor at the University of Saskatchewan in the Indian and Northern Education Department. She received her doctorate from Stanford University and has worked as teacher, principal, education director, and curriculum developer with Mi'kmaq Nation band-operated schools.

Sharilyn Calliou, a member of the Michel Band of Alberta, was born in Edmonton in 1953. She has enjoyed a variety of jobs from seismic camp cook to dishwasher to file clerk. From 1979 to 1989 she taught in an inner-city community school with the Calgary Board of Education. Currently, she is a lecturer with the Faculty of Education at the University of British Columbia in the Native Indian Teacher Education Program.

Willie Ermine is Cree and a member of the Sturgeon Lake First Nation. He is program coordinator and lecturer at the Saskatchewan Indian Federated College and a graduate student at the University of Saskatchewan. He is also an artist working towards *mamtowisowin.*

Agnes Grant has worked in the Native teacher-training program at Brandon University in Manitoba since 1972, and she is currently a travelling professor teaching Native studies and educational courses. An expert on Native literature, she is editor of *Our Bit of Truth: An Anthology of Canadian Native Literature,* author of *James McKay: A Métis Builder of Canada,* and co-author of *Joining the Circle: A Practitioner's Guide to Responsive Education for Native Students.*

Celia Haig-Brown is an associate professor at Simon Fraser University in British Columbia. Author of the prize-winning *Resistance and Renewal: Surviving the Indian Residential School,* she has just published *Taking Control: Power and Contradiction in First Nations Adult Education* with UBC Press.

Eber Hampton, a member of the Chickasaw Nation, is president of Saskatchewan Indian Federated College in Regina. An Ed.D. from Harvard University, he has directed the American Indian Program at the Harvard Graduate School of Education and has been associate dean of the College of Rural Education at the University of Alaska, Fairbanks.

James [sákéj] Youngblood Henderson is a member of the Chickasaw Nation. A Doctor in Jurisprudence from Harvard Law School, he is research director at the Native Law Centre, College of Law, at the University of Saskatchewan. He is co-author of *The Road: Indian Tribes and Political Liberty, Continuing Poundmaker and Riel's Quest,* and other writings on Aboriginal constitutional and treaty law.

Rick Hesch is an assistant professor in the Faculty of Education at the University of Lethbridge, specializing in teacher education and critical pedagogy. His recent publications concern teacher education for Aboriginal people.

Robert Leavitt is a professor in the Faculty of Education at the University of New Brunswick, where he is director of the Micmac-Maliseet Institute. He is author of *Maliseet and Micmac: First Nations of the Maritimes,* a textbook for a Grade 12 Native Studies course now being piloted in New Brunswick schools. He is currently editing and translating historical Maliseet-Passamaquoddy texts and developing a dictionary in the language.

Madeleine MacIvor is a Métis woman who works for the First Nations House of Learning at the University of British Columbia. She is a board member of the Canadian Aboriginal Science and Engineering Society and the Mokakit Educational Research Association. Her interest in science education began when she was a student in the Native Indian Teacher Education Program at UBC and continued in her M.A. thesis, where she examined science education as a form of social control in a religious mission.

Ron Mackay is professor and chairman of the Department of Applied Linguistics at Concordia University in Montreal. Specializing in project design, management, and evaluation, he has worked extensively in education and land management in Canada and abroad.

Lawrence Myles, who has held teaching positions in Nigeria, Germany, and Canada, works as a senior research associate in educational program evaluation and testing. He is a Ph.D. candidate in educational evaluation at l'Univeristé de Montreal.

Robert Regnier teaches educational theory in the Department of Educational Foundations at the University of Saskatchewan. A former principal and long-time supporter of the Joe Duquette High School in Saskatoon, he is currently studying healing and education from a medicine wheel perspective, and he writes in the areas of critical and process pedagogy.

Arlene Stairs is a cultural psychologist researching and writing about education as cultural negotiation, cultural models of learning, and indigenous language literacies. She worked for over a decade in the eastern Canadian Arctic when Inuit teacher education was evolving there, and she is now an assistant professor in the Faculty of Education at Queen's University in Ontario.

Shirley Sterling, whose Nlakapamux name is Seepeetza, is a Nlakapamux or Thompson speaker and a member of the Interior Salish Nation. From the age of five and a half until high school graduation, she attended the Kamloops Indian Residential School, which was the impetus behind her prize-winning young people's novel, *My Name is Seepeetza*. She is a doctoral student in Curriculum Studies at the University of British Columbia, working on oral tradition in First Nations education.

John Taylor taught for four years in Native communities in western Canada before becoming a Master's student at Trent University in Ontario. Having spent his first year in the program in Thailand working with its indigenous peoples, John is currently undertaking a study of non-indigenous teachers in indigenous communities in Canada.

Kathy Vermette, a Métis graduate of the Saskatchewan Native Teacher Education Program, is a sessional lecturer at Saskatchewan Indian Federated College and the University of Saskatchewan. She is also a graduate student at the University of Saskatchewan.

Index

Set in Stone by Val Speidel

Printed and bound in Canada by Friesens

Copy-editor: Peter Colenbrander

Proofreader: Joanne Richardson

Indexer: Annette Lorek